Dawa T. Norbu was born in Tibet and educated at St. Stephens College, Delhi. He did his doctorate at the University of California (Berkeley). At the same time he taught at the University of San Francisco and San Francisco State University, California.

He has published over 26 scholarly papers in such international journals as *Asian Survey*, *China Quarterly*, *International Studies* and *Pacific Affairs*. His last book was *Culture and the Politics of Third World Nationalism* (Routledge, 1992). He is at present Professor of Central Asian Studies at Jawaharlal Nehru University, New Delhi and an Honorary Fellow of the University of Durham in the UK.

TIBET
The Road Ahead

Dawa T. Norbu

RIDER

LONDON · SYDNEY · AUCKLAND · JONANNESBURG

To the memory of
my beloved mother, Akyi (1915-1985).

To my brother, Kesang Tenzing Bhutia and
my daughter, Tara Lynne Hopkins.

1 3 5 7 9 10 8 6 4 2

Copyright © Dawa T. Norbu 1997

First published in 1997 by HarperCollins Publishers India Pvt Ltd,
7/16 Ansari Road, Daryaganj, New Delhi 110 002

Published in Great Britain in 1998 by Rider, an imprint of
Ebury Press
Random House UK Ltd
Random House
20 Vauxhall Bridge Road
London SW1V 2SA
www.randomhouse.co.uk
This edition published in 1999

Random House Australia (Pty) Ltd
20 Alfred Street
Milsons Point, Sydney
New South Wales 2016 Australia

Random House New Zealand Limited
18 Poland Road, Glenfield
Auckland 10 New Zealand

Random House South Africa (Pty) Limited
Endulini, 5A Jubilee Road
Parktown 2193, South Africa

Random House UK Limited Reg. No. 954009

Papers used by Rider Books are natural, recyclable products made from
wood grown in sustainable forests.

Printed and bound in Great Britain by
Cox & Wyman, Reading, Berks.

A CIP catalogue record for this book is available from the British Library

ISBN 0 7126 7063 7

Contents

PART II *(1960-95)*

Acknowledgements

I AM grateful to Robbie Barnett and his incomparable institution (Tibet Information Network) for providing me with the latest information on Tibet, which in many ways enabled me to update and enlarge this book; to the late Mr. Jampa for making those delightful drawings which illustrate this book; and to Christophe Besuchet for drawing the map of Tibet with skill and accuracy and to Professor Priyadarsi Mukherji for helping me with the transliteration of Chinese names into the Pinyin system, which is used throughout the text, except with Tibetan names.

A number of people have been kind and helpful in my career, especially in the early years of my life in exile. I am grateful to Dennis L. Bark, John Billington, Jill Buxton, the late Sir William Collins, Daisy Fowles, Peter and Patricia Kaim-Caudle, Judith Kendra, R.K. Mehra, Marlene Mitchell, the late Dr. James R. Minto, Chris Mullin, Professor Keith Pratt, Professor Leo Rose, Professor Robert Scalapino, Professors M.L. Sondhi and Parimal Kumar Das, Tenzin Geyche Tethong, Tsewang Norbu and Dick Wilson for their kindness and encouragement throughout my schooling.

I recall with love and affection my dear mother who died in Bodhgaya (1985) and my favourite sister Donkar who died in Darjeeling in 1981. My brothers and sisters continue to be a great source of moral support and strength: Kesang Tenzing Bhutia and his wife Chungla, Abu and his wife Tseten, my sisters Yanchung and Dawa Bhuti. I would also like to thank

Tara and Suzan Hopkins for their love and understanding which I can never forget.

I would also like to thank my publisher and his professional team of expert editors who have won my admiration and respect. Their skilful and sensitive editorial interventions made my transition from academic prose to literary narrative possible, especially in the last five chapters. I am truly indebted especially to Maya Mozoomdar, Ashwini Bhatia, Aradhana Bisht and Shamanthaka Subramanian.

Last but not least, I would like to express my grateful thanks to my wife Rinchen Lhamo for giving me the boon of time to do what I like – read, think and write – while she cheerfully looked after me and our son, Jamyang. Her simplicity and charm are my living links with the old world.

Finally, I hope this book will tell Tara and Jamyang something more about their father's early life and the land of his birth.

Most writers' ambition is to write books that can come out in paperback, which the average person can afford, and I am no exception. This is particularly true of authors whose intention is not only to make money and fame but more to promote understanding of a just cause. In this respect I am grateful to Judith Kendra and Rider Books for making this fair-priced edition possible. Judith Kendra's and Barbara Bagnall's characteristic combination of courtesy and efficiency has made working for this edition a pleasant experience.

DN

Preface

WRITERS, BOTH Tibetan and Western, have in the past projected an image of Tibet that is not only deceptive but also harmful to the Tibetan cause – the romantic and mystical image of Shangri-la, where lamas fly like birds, where everyone is religious and everyone is happy. While there is some truth in such a view, it does exaggerate one aspect of Tibet to the exclusion of other, disturbing elements. For example, Tibetans who have written books in the past have shown a masterly evasion of the feudal character of Tibet. Chinese propaganda has skilfully exploited this evasion, playing upon the universal ignorance of the true nature of the old 'feudalism'. People have been left with a one-sided picture.

I was not satisfied with either view. As I talked about Tibet with Naxalites (Indian Maoists who were at the peak of their 'revolutionary activities' when I first went to university in India), I found the conventional Tibetan explanations quite inadequate, and the Chinese views too one-sided. Under such circumstances I felt I should try to write a book that simply unfolded what really went on in Tibet. The fact that I was neither a lama nor an aristocrat helped such an attempt. The wisest course, I decided, would be to start the whole analysis afresh by journeying back to a possible beginning and find out for myself, first of all how our family lived under the Tibetan regime and, secondly, how we reacted to the Chinese 'liberation' from 1950 till the time we left Tibet.

Despite opposite viewpoints – the romantic and the feudal

– I have never had any preconceived notions to prove or dis-
prove either point of view; anyone looking for contradictions
will find plenty in the book. What I have done is to listen carefully and patiently to whatever our family members, my mother
in particular, had to say about the past, and draw my own conclusions based on my interpretation of the facts. In the case of
basic institutions, such as the legal system which our family
came up against, which had a universal application in Tibet, I
studied other cases from different parts of the country to verify
our experience. This was also my method over the important
Chinese initiatives in Tibet.

Obviously, since it was impossible to put everything about
the Tibetan society into one book, I have had to choose what to
include. The criteria for selection have been their political
importance and human interest. I have been exceptionally fortunate in having a family that had experienced almost all the
basic aspects of Tibetan life, including the more questionable
ones, and because of our ill-defined class position (by
Communist Chinese reckoning we were 'lower-middle peasant'), we were able to experience and observe many different
walks of life. Thanks to the Jack-of-all-trades nature of our
family, I only rarely had to go outside the limits of my family's
experiences.

Is it possible to come to any definite conclusion from our
limited experience of Communism? When in 1969 I joined the
St. Stephen's College (Delhi), to my surprise I found the very
people from whom we had escaped a decade ago right next
door. In fact my college proved to be the centre of the Naxalite
activities in Delhi. They used the same jargon, had the same
convictions, and they held identical views to the Chinese
Communists. One of their popular slogans was: 'China's way is
our way; and China's Chairman Mao our Chairman.'

As a lone Tibetan, I could not escape their notice. Soon they
crowded around, questioning and cross-questioning me. In our
closed-door debates and discussions, I became more frank but

the Naxalites did not move an inch from their positions. Not, at least, until May 1973, when one of my 'comrades' came to see me. He had been underground for nearly two years, and like his other comrades he was thoroughly disillusioned with Chinese ideological pretensions. His views on Tibet also had undergone a change.

I was able to understand the Chinese point of view better from the Naxalites than I could possibly have done from the Chinese themselves. The Naxalites naturally felt my reaction to the Chinese actions in Tibet was biased. That may have been true, because after all I am a Tibetan and was too close to all I had gone through for a clear perspective. But I discovered through our long discussions that nothing would convince the converted Maoist that there had not been 'exploitation and oppression' under the old system.

The Naxalites, nearly all of whom came from the most well-to-do Indian families, echoed China's claim that Tibet has always been a part of China. The truth, of course, is much more complicated than this; one can prove exactly the reverse from history. In fact, relations between the two countries are so complex that either side can always find several reasons to prove its point of view. I tried to meet the Maoists on their own ground, on their own ideological terms. Communist China's claims of 'suzerainty' or 'sovereignty' are feudal and imperialist; but these same claims became the justification for the 'liberation' of Tibet. This directly contradicts what Lenin said: 'If Finland, if Poland, if the Ukraine break away from Russia, there is nothing bad about that. Anyone who says there is, is a chauvinist. No nation can be free if it oppresses other nations.' Mao himself, in 1931, when Chairman of the first Chinese Soviet Republic, declared in its constitution: 'The Soviet Government of China recognizes the right of self-determination of the national minorities in China, their right to complete separation from China and to the formation of an independent State for each national minority. All Mongolians, Tibetans, Miao, Yao,

Koreans and others living on the territory of China shall enjoy the full right of self-determination, i.e., they may either join the Union of Chinese Soviets or secede from it and form their own State, as they may prefer.'

The Naxalites replied to this by saying that Tibetans were much better off now than they were before the 'liberation'. And they gave instances of the roads, schools, hospitals and so on built in Tibet to prove their point. I did not deny all these achievements – except the roads, which were built for strategic purposes. I tried to inform them, however, that we (our family and nearly 700 people from my hometown) had tasted Mao's version of Marxism-Leninism, while they only read about it in books. I asked them why, if the Chinese government believed Tibetans were happier now than before the 'liberation', it did not accept the Dalai Lama's challenge for a plebiscite to allow Tibet to determine her own future.

The Naxalites pointed out that our experience of Communism was too short to draw any definite conclusions. They further explained that the 'transition period' is always fraught with difficulties, and they quoted Chairman Mao's saying: 'Revolution is not a dinner party.' While it was true that actual Communist control was established only in 1959, the Tibetans had experienced the more insidious and deceptive forms of Chinese Communism ever since 1951. To the Tibetans, dependability is one of the greatest virtues; by 1959 the Chinese became the epitome of undependability. Therefore, as far as my mother and other relations were concerned, they felt justified in coming to a 'definite conclusion' by the end of 1959. I further believe that if the Tibetans in Tibet – who constitute the overwhelming majority – were given a fair chance to air their views on both the Tibetan and Chinese regimes, they would say they had come to a similar conclusion.

My narrative in the first person stops with our arrival in India in late 1959 (Chapter 16). But the tragedy in Tibet continues unabated. In fact with the internationalization of the

'Tibetan Question' since 1989, the basic questions that agitated me while writing the first part of this book, published under the title *Red Star Over Tibet* (Collins 1974), have once again come to the forefront. Was the traditional Tibetan society as cruel and feudal as the Chinese propaganda and their sympathizers paint? Was Tibet independent or autonomous before 1950? Are the Tibetans happy and contented under the Chinese rule now? What do they really want?

These are not purely academic questions; for the Dalai Lama has often declared that the ultimate power to decide Tibet's future rests with the Tibetan people alone, and nobody else. Similarly the Chinese Communists justify their 'liberation' of Tibet supposedly for the benefit of the 'Tibetan masses'. But the irony is that the Tibetan peasants and nomads are still voiceless and powerless. I do not claim to know their hearts and minds, even though I once shared the same social background. But, the reader is likely to find clues to some of the questions that might have troubled him regarding Tibet: the claims and counter-claims made concerning the Tibetan tragedy today. If it promotes a better understanding of the Tibetan Question or serves the nonpartisan cause of the Tibetan people, my labour would not have been in vain. Although I now have the status of an academic, at heart I strongly feel at one with the common people of Tibet.

After we left Sakya in late 1959, the most traumatic experience of the deeply religious Tibetans in Tibet was undoubtedly the Cultural Revolution (1966-69). The fanatical Red Guards, mostly Chinese, destroyed nearly 95 percent of Tibetan Buddhist monasteries, temples, religious institutions and even private chapels. It was a monumental loss to human civilization. But more than that, it was the incredibly intense human suffering that the soul-destroying 'revolution' entailed. The magnitude and intensity of that human suffering had to be experienced in order to believe it. As my aunt Dechen Tsomo told me in 1983, her guru died as a result of that shock and trauma. As the real embodiments of their highest ideals and values were destroyed right in front of their eyes, many Tibetans lost their sanity and committed suicide. The 'Great Proletarian Cultural Revolution' was a direct assault on Tibetan Buddhism, and therefore a deliberate attempt to destroy Tibetan identity. In doing so, many Chinese Red Guards saw in this an excellent opportunity to Sinicize the Tibetans.

After Mao's Cultural Revolution of the 1960s, Deng Xiaoping's liberalization of the Chinese economy and society since 1979 appeared to most Tibetans in rural areas as a blessing in disguise. More specifically, Deng's Tibet policy included a dialogue with the Dalai Lama (Chapter 20), and liberalization of the Tibetan economy and society (Chapter 18). It appears that Deng's intention was that the Dalai Lama could be enticed to return to 'the great motherland' and that the Tibetan people's loyalty to the Chinese could be bought with a liberal dose of economic reforms and a limited religious freedom. But as events were to prove, the Chinese leaders could neither persuade the Dalai Lama to return unconditionally nor could they purchase Tibetan loyalty to the Han state. In fact, instead of enjoying the economic benefits, the politically conscious sections of the Tibetan population revolted in the late 1980s. This revolt fits in with the general pattern of previous revolts: whenever Beijing relaxes its iron grip over Tibet, Tibetans tend to break out in revolt. This means that the Tibetan people are not yet reconciled to the Chinese takeover and subsequent domination. The fact is Beijing has ruled Tibet by sheer force. This state of affairs is neither good for Chinese credibility nor is it in the interest of Tibetan people. Obviously, a rule by force cannot go on forever, and it is in the Chinese interest to find a peaceful and durable solution to the conflict in Tibet.

Such a solution was conceived by Deng Xiaoping when he returned to power in late 1978. But the peace process was derailed by hardliners in the Chinese bureaucracy once Deng became politically inactive and after Hu Yaobang fell from power. These two leaders, who initiated the peace process and showed a singular interest in the Tibetan Question were crucial to any possible breakthrough in the Sino-Tibetan dialogue. But they are no longer on the Chinese political scene.

Still, there is some hope now. Some prominent Chinese dissidents and overseas Chinese intellectuals have recently drafted a liberal constitution for a 'federal' China whose specific articles have largely met the Dalai Lama's political demands made in Washington, D.C. (1987) and in Strasbourg (1988). It is possible that those who drafted this liberal constitution for a federal China may not themselves come to power in Beijing in the near future; but their pioneering and practical ideas, contained in the Constitution, might fall on fertile ground once the democratic upsurge in China gains ground. As the globalization of the Chinese economy gains greater momentum, the operation of the market forces will become a reality, which in turn will necessitate expansion of freedom in civil society. At any rate, the People's Republic of China cannot remain for too long an island of Maoist monolith. Change is a matter of time, if His Holiness the Dalai Lama continues to show more patience.

In this new edition I also give a portrait of the Panchen Lama (Chapter 19) about whose life and work the outside world knows so little. Even the sketchy information available to me at the moment suggests that the Xth Panchen Lama was the tragic hero of the Tibetans under Chinese occupation. He embodied their hopes and aspirations; he articulated their problems and grievances before Beijing; he fought for their civil rights within China; and sometimes he even risked his personal safety for the sake of Tibetans under Chinese captivity. Yet the world ignored him for the last 35 years, as if he was a Chinese stooge.

In short, this book represents my personal quest for the truth concerning the old and the new Tibet. As a Tibetan commoner who was fortunate enough to have received a decent modern education after experiencing the old and the new Tibet, I have often been confronted with the Tibetan Question as a moral and intellectual challenge. After all, the author along with his family had lived through what others argue and debate about Tibet today.

I focussed not on Lhasa (about which so many books have been written), nor on Sakya *per se* for that matter, but on *rural* Tibet. Sakya became for me a familiar terrain (in an amateur, anthropological sense), where I would observe Tibetan folk reactions to the old and the new society at the grass roots level.

The autobiographical framework and the family story it unfolds may also be seen as a reflection of the cross-section of Tibetan society, old and new. For instance, up to 1959 Tibet remained a purely pre-industrial and deeply religious society. And after the Dalai Lama's escape in March 1959, the Chinese Communists imposed highly centralized policies and programmes all over Outer Tibet (Tibet Autonomous Region today). Therefore, my family's experiences are fairly similar to those of other Tibetan commoners living in other parts of Tibet. All this may be considered a Sakya regional variation of the basic Tibetan pattern. This is in keeping with my personal quest I mentioned earlier: to let the untold story of Tibetan commoners in the 20th century unfold itself through the eyes and ears of one ordinary family.

JNU, New Delhi   DAWA T. NORBU
October, 1996

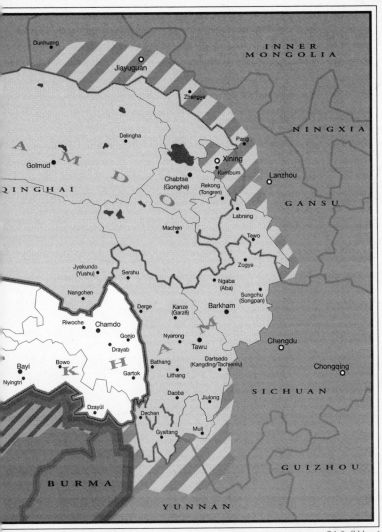

Dunhuang

INNER MONGOLIA

Jiayuguan

Zhangye

NINGXIA

Delingha

Pang

A M D O

Xining

Kumbum

Lanzhou

Golmud

Chabtsa (Gonghe)

Rekong (Tongren)

QINGHAI

GANSU

Labrang

Machen

Tewo

Jyekundo (Yushu)

Sershu

Zogye

Ngaba (Aba)

Sungchu (Songpan)

Nangchen

Derge

Kanze (Garzê)

Barkham

Riwoche

Chamdo

Gonjo

Nyarong

Tawu

Chengdu

Drayab

Bayi

Bowo

K

H

A

M

Bathang

Dartsedo (Kangding/Tachienlu)

Chongqing

Nyingtri

Gartok

Lithang

Daoba

Jiulong

SICHUAN

Dzayül

Dechen

Muli

Gyaltang

GUIZHOU

BURMA

YUNNAN

© Atelier Golok, 1996

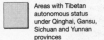

PART I
1950-59

ONE

The Life of a Missionary

MY FIRST memory is of a balmy late autumn evening in 1951, the year when the great floods occurred – the Year of the Iron Hare, as the Tibetans call it.[1] My father was sitting on the dirty, worn-out carpet, alternately drinking *chang* (home-brewed beer)[2] and blowing out clouds of snuff. When he had some drink inside him, he always took more notice of me. My mother was sitting by the oven, preparing the evening meal. Both my parents wanted me to come to them. My father smiled at me and said: 'If you are my son, come to me. Come, Dawa Norbu.' My mother smiled and made the same request. I can still remember the mental torture of having to make that choice between my parents.

We lived in a five-room, single-storey house in the village of Tashigang, five miles outside the town of Sakya, to which we were soon to move. The house was simple and strongly built, in marked contrast to the complex monastic architecture. It had a broad stone base, about three feet high, and above this six feet of walling made of mud bricks cemented by cow dung and straw. The main room had only three windows – snow and dust-storms made any more inadvisable. A small window looked out on our fields. There was a low chimney, and a massive door always open to both men and animals. The most expensive part of the house was the ceiling, made of wood

1   A special Tibetan Calendar and its European equivalent is given in Annexure II.
2   A glossary of Tibetan words used in this book appears in Annexure I.

transported from the foothills of the distant Himalayas. It consisted of a large log right across the house, supported by a central pillar. Across the log, beams were laid a foot apart, and above the beams were slats.

Our furniture was equally simple. Two oblong platforms, made of mud six inches thick, served as seats for the whole family during the day and as beds for our parents at night. A black, tea-stained table, covered with greasy wooden bowls, stood between the seats. In the left-hand corner of the room was our sooty, smoky stove, made of stone and clay and about three feet square. In front of the oven was a small container for dry fuel, which formed my mother's favourite seat. Behind it were two shelves filled with dust-covered earthenware pots of all shapes and sizes. The kitchen space was dominated by a huge copper vessel, holding about twenty gallons of water, brought from the river half a mile away. Ladles, pans and other kitchen utensils hung from the vessel's brim.

The other rooms consisted of a chapel furnished with images of the Buddha and *Bodhisattvas*, *thankas* (Buddhist painted scrolls) and three trunks containing our best clothes; a storeroom with an underground granary; and a big, bleak room, with a ceiling supported by pillars, where we children slept. The doors opened on to the courtyard where our donkeys and cows were kept.

Our lifestyle, then, was simple enough, although it was an accident that my parents had ever got married.

My father, Thubkye Choephal, was the youngest of four sons from a once-prosperous peasant family called Zongpa in Gang-shong, two days' journey on foot from Sakya. Being the youngest, he was sent to a little monastery called Chokhor Lhunpo (Abode of Religion), about five miles from Sakya, in the village where my mother lived. In those days the monasteries were run like feudal estates, possessing about a third of the country's land, and employing the lay population to farm and do other manual work. Thus they were closely involved with the laymen's world. The monks gave the laymen spiritual sustenance, and the laymen gave the monks material sustenance.

When the turn came for my mother's parents to carry out manual duties, my mother, Akyi, was often sent to fetch water for the monastic community. Father, a novice of about twenty – a testing age for his vows of celibacy – met her and fell in love. Apart from the shame of having to face his fellow monks again, he also felt a deep personal regret at his own spiritual debasement. He knew he had fallen from the spiritual heights of the monastery.

All monks were held in the greatest respect, because they were one of the constituents of the Buddhist Trinity (*Kunchok-Sum*) consisting of Buddha, *dharma* (the law) and *Sangha* (the Religious Community). Hence Father's self-secularization was no small tragedy.

A novice monk took four basic vows: to abstain from violence, from theft and from falsehood, and to practise celibacy. On breaking any of these vows he ceased to be a part of the Holy *Sangha*, and was stripped of his monkhood. Of the four, the vow of celibacy was the most serious, and the breaking of it gave the greatest sense of guilt. In typical Tibetan fashion, Father did not confess directly to having violated his vow of celibacy; such an admission would have appeared disrespectful, if not a direct act of defiance to the ecclesiastical authority. Frankness in bad habits was deprecated by Tibetans; it suggested a lack of fear and respect. A Tibetan teacher would rather have his pupil smoking secretly than in front of him. So Father lied and said that he had stoned a cat to death. Mother tells me that for about a week he hid himself in a friend's house while all the formalities were being completed by a lay friend.

First of all, a written petition was delivered to the Abbot, to the effect that Father's *karma* (sum of deeds) did not allow him to continue his monkhood; that he had broken a vow; and finally could he now, please, withdraw from the monastery? Father was not permitted to re-enter the monastery until he had received a white *song-du* (a ribbon-like strip of cloth worn around the neck, carrying blessings). This strip of cloth had a symbolic significance. Normally the monks wore a red *song-du* and laymen white. The secularized monk had to finance a 'morning tea', a kind of farewell party, and to distribute gifts of coins to the congregation of monks, whose fellowship he was soon to share no more. Finally five senior monks, in the monastery's holiest altar room, prayed for forgiveness for the vow-breaker. At last the formalities were over, and Father was free.

He had become accustomed to the monastic life of plenty and comfort, and was ill-equipped to stand on his own two feet. Naturally, he had some minor difficulties in his prescribed theological course, but these were delights compared with the harsh reality of life on the Roof of the World. Now he had to be prepared to weather the storm both literally and figuratively. Monks were forbidden to do any manual work. To touch an agricultural implement was an act of sin, for agriculture entailed the sin of killing insects. However, Father reluctantly

heeded the proverb: 'If your *karma* places you in the caste of a butcher, why should you hesitate to kill animals?' But having no experience of farming or rearing children he was not handy either at home or in the fields. He was profitably employed on a roving religious mission to Chang Thang, the northern plateau of Tibet.

I have always wondered if Father missed his benevolent monastery. I think he must have done. But I am glad that he was neither a parasite nor a hypocrite. Many of the monasteries had degenerated considerably since their pious beginnings. The monks' scholarship, assuming they had any, benefited hardly anyone except themselves; and barring rare exceptions, they were possessive and materialistic. On the whole, it was better for my father to earn his own living than to carry on under false pretences.

Thus Father was out in the complex world of the Tibetan family system. Both polygamy and polyandry were practised – for economic reasons. If each son were to choose his own partner, and go his own way, the property and land would be fragmented, causing disintegration of an ancient family, as happened with Father's family. Most families tried to remain united, and not only for economic advantage. My mother summed up the general attitude when I told her that I wanted to go abroad for further study. 'I am your mother and you are my son only for this short mortal life. Why must we separate when we are at liberty to live together?'

The ambition of every true-blooded Tibetan farmer was to have a large, peaceable, prosperous family. Usually daughters were given away in marriage, and sons inherited the family property and land. Where a family had a daughter but no son the daughter was married to an outsider who came to live with his new wife's family. Thus a new marriage did not always mean a new home. If a family did not have a child it usually adopted one to save its line from dying out. The formation of a new family was very rare indeed, and was treated with contempt or pity. My parents fell into this unfortunate category. Mother's defence was to say: 'I am a new householder. I have inherited no wealth or land.' Whenever she found I had spilt even a drop of *thukpa* she punished me.

Mother's parents were rich, and gave her cooking utensils, seven bags of barley, and a cow. But Father had nothing much to contribute towards the construction of a 'new kitchen' – the Tibetan metaphor for a new home. Luckily, Grandfather took Father as his personal bearer to the mission areas in Chang Thang. My maternal grandfather was a distant descendant of a famous tantric practitioner, and, as often happened in Tibet, had inherited his powers of yoga. As the head lama of a roving mission from the Sakya monastery he made his fortune in the land of the nomads.

The Sakya sect had reached its period of greatest influence in the thirteenth century, a time of remarkable intellectual and spiritual development in the history of Tibet. Religious expansion invariably culminated in the building of monasteries and temples, and Sakya prospered accordingly. These expensive monasteries were not simple shrines; they were complex works of art and unique architecture, the quintessence of our culture. They were the treasures of the Tibetan people, embodying most of the fruit of their toil and sweat. Every monastery I knew in Sakya was filled with gold, silver and bronze images. The statues were studded lavishly with precious stones, and in front of them were silver and gold butter lamps burning perpetually. The Tibetans believed that to give charity unstintingly was to store up provisions for 'the solitary journey'. To offer your earthly possessions to a lama was to ensure light in darkness after death, and to live for your faith was to reserve a ferry-boat that would carry you to eternal bliss. The main function of the roving religious missions, initiated in the thirteenth century and dispatched thereafter to the nomads of Chang Thang, was to collect donations; a minor purpose was to convert the barbarous nomads themselves.

During my father's time the Sakya Monastery sent eight such missions to different parts of Chang Thang. Each contingent consisted of a contractor, four servants and a tantric practitioner (in this case my grandfather). Father was a glorified servant. Getting such a contract was one of the surest ways of becoming rich, and consequently only the reputable *tralpa* families were granted the contracts. The lama of the mission was hired by the contractor and approved by the Sakya Lama. In recent years I have met my grandfather's treasurer in Kalimpong, India; he escaped from Tibet in 1964. As he nostalgically described the missions, he sighed every now and then with sincere repentance. He confessed that he had been a most sinful man because he took most of the donations from Chang Thang. As a sign of true repentance, he renounced the world and became a monk at the age of 68. Never too late!

The departures of these missions were unforgettable for their stately ceremonial. I recall one such occasion. It was the end of the Second Month (April), still cold and windy, a bleak and gloomy morning that gave a foretaste of the hardships the party would have to endure on the sky-touching mountain passes and unending desolate plateau of Chang Thang, 'the land of no man and no dog', as the Tibetans called it. I had gone with Mother to see Father off. The Tibetan farewell was deliberately performed to please the gods and goddesses, so that they would be guides, protectors and companions to the traveller. Mother was in her best dress and ceremonial jewellery, to please the capricious gods more than Father. She carried a kettle of *chang* in one hand, and in the other a bowl heaped with *tsampa* topped with a piece of butter. She offered Father three cups of *chang*, and made a ritual smear of *tsampa* on his left shoulder for good luck. Father in return made one on Mother's right shoulder. On the rim of the cup was a tiny strip of *tsampa* which stuck on the bridge of Father's nose when he completed the third cup. Then they both threw *tsampa* into the air, for the gods were everywhere. Finally Mother encircled his neck with a ceremonial scarf (*khadar*), while tears rolled down her cheeks. Personally, I did not make a fuss about his departure; I was more attached to Mother as most children are. Besides, he gave me two *sang* coins as a parting present.

The thirty yaks, laden with provisions, presents for the nomads and goods for barter, had been huddling together while the goodbye ceremony was performed, and now moved slowly off. Four high-spirited horses, saddled and bridled, followed the cautious yaks. The party proceeded on its way. Mother, in a voice strained with emotion, half-crying and half-shouting, called through the wind: 'Look after yourself!' Father waved his hand in acknowledgement. One by one the yaks crossed the rickety bridge and were soon out of sight. We returned home.

Chang Thang in Tibetan means 'the Northern Plains', and by our own Himalayan standard this bleak, barren plateau is indeed a plain. Dotted with low mountains about 14,000 feet high and scattered with salt and fresh lakes, Chang Thang forms about one-third of Tibet. Many square miles are whitened by a surface crust of alkali – the country's salt mine. Potash, soda and borax are found around the lakes in great abundance. There are few of the large snow-fed rivers that abound elsewhere in Tibet. Since Chang Thang is fairly flat and sparsely populated, many experts think that it is an ideal site for a nuclear power station. Recent refugees report that the Chinese have already installed a radar and missile complex near Rudok, and non-Tibetan sources think the missiles have ranges of 600 to 2000 miles. It is the least inhabited and the most inhospitable part of Tibet – a misanthrope's heaven. The four elements of snow, frost, wind and sun, in combination with the undulating desolate plains and the naked rocks and cliffs, create an austere grandeur and subtle beauty unique to Chang Thang.

Some of the scattered inhabitants of this desolate plateau visited our town in the Eleventh Month, when the Sakya Dochen, the biggest religious festival of the Sakya sect, was held. Their physical appearance and way of life made them seem like barbarians. They wore rough sheepskin garments and furry hats, and lived in thick black tents, woven from yaks' wool. But, judged according to their moral and ethical standards, these simple people were quite civilized. Beneath their primitive looks the natural virtues of man were concealed. Their generosity and hospitality, their cheerfulness and strength of character were legendary in Tibet.

Because of their isolation from the mainstream of Tibetan life, these nomads developed a culture of their own, based on Buddhism in its more mystic and tantric forms. Their picturesque dialect was full of allusions and metaphors derived from nature in the raw. The most leisurely folk among the Tibetan commoners, the nomadic herdsmen, were glib talkers and good story-tellers. The women did all the dairy work, cooking and weaving; the men attended to the animals and did the sewing. They were religious without being orthodox. Father would tell me, in a voice full of awe and admiration, how they could challenge Grandfather in religious dialectical discussion. Pacified by Buddhism, these herdsmen (Chang-Dokpa, we called them) were surprisingly law-abiding and kept to the even tenor of their obsolete ways. They lived and moved in small groups, each with its own elected leader, or *pon*. A number of groups within a large pastoral area formed a *garpa*.

The central government appointed an administrator from among the nomads, a post that tended to become hereditary as the years passed. This tribal organization solved most of the problems. A governor, invariably an aristocrat from Lhasa, administered (or maladministered) the vast province of Western Tibet, including Chang Thang. A monk was appointed as his colleague, of equal or even higher rank. One was expected to watch over the other, so that the dangers of autocracy and despotism were minimized. Apart from the political motive, this system of administration headed jointly by a lay aristocrat and a lama was in keeping with the concept of ideal Tibetan government.

The governor was there primarily to collect taxes of sheep, goats, yaks, salt and butter from the nomads. His biggest headache was cattle-raiding. (Although the nomads did not raid each other's cattle, there were professional gangsters who did.) Father would tell us proudly that he saw and met the governor at Rudok Dzong. On one occasion Father shocked us all by telling us that he had seen two men, completely white from head to foot, speaking a strange sonorous language. He met them at Gartok near the Kashmir border. I did not believe him then, for I had never heard of the world outside Tibet, and I was convinced that no other race apart from Tibetans existed! I have recently made a number of enquiries regarding the two white men, and it now appears that they were the Italians Tucci and Gherci. This is confirmed by their book *Secrets of Tibet*, in which they mention Sakya lamas collecting donations in Western Tibet.

I had always been fascinated by tales of Chang Thang. Whenever Father was in his pleasantest mood, he described his experiences there to the family circle. In his quiet, withdrawn moments, I would pester him for tales of Chang Thang, which seemed to be a Tibetan 'Garden of Eden'. The entire region was common ground. However, a particular group of herdsmen and their families normally moved to the summer or winter season. This in some cases tended to foster private ownership of land in the otherwise common ground of Chang Thang. They made two major moves in a year. In summer they ascended to the highlands, which made Father's journey more tedious and devious, and in winter they came down to the warm, lush valleys. Whenever I hear talk about this other Eden, I remember Father's description of a landscape of yaks, sheep and goats grazing on a vast expanse of pasture, tended by a singing shepherd. The summer camps on the highlands, where nature was more bounteous than anywhere else, demonstrated a perfect harmony between man and nature.

A couple of huge black tents, pitched on a level green plot of ground, formed the natural palace of the nomads. Like altars, the encircling mountains and their lofty peaks rose above and behind the camp. To the nomads their whiteness symbolized purity of mind, evident in their pastoral songs and ballads. Blue smoke, like incense from a censer, curled out through the door of the tent and flew upward with the morning breeze. This was the nomads' daily offering to the local gods and goddesses. The smoke and prayer-flags acted as guides to the roving mission. When there was no smoke visible, the prayer-flag of a conspicuous colour, usually the lucky colour of the father of the family whose tent it was, fluttered and signalled to the lonely travellers. A few yards away from the tent there was always a gigantic sheep dog, bigger than any sheep, furiously barking at the stranger. This vicious, angry barking would set off every other dog round about. Unchained dogs often attacked and ate the luckless traveller – so the popular story ran, and is generally believed. The dogs were the nomads' army, employed to guard their tents and chase away wolves.

On the surrounding stretches of green, herds of yaks, sheep and goats would be grazing happily, dots of black and white on the vast green background. The high-pitched, sleepy, slow notes of a herdsman's flute reverberated through the tranquil hills and valleys. When his herd scattered too much, he used his sling to bring them back. There was no other noise or sound, except the maids singing as they milked in the morning and evening.

In winter Chang Thang was very different. Once Father had a frightening ordeal while returning in the Tenth Month. The mission had had a particularly successful season that year, but when they were returning from Chang Thang it began to snow heavily. (Usually most snow fell in the Eleventh and Twelfth Months.) In the Tibetan phrase, 'the sky was broken' for two days. After the first day of continuous snowfall the herd of sheep and goats, numbering about two thousand, were covered with snow. The next morning the yaks, numbering about a hundred, were covered upto their horns. Father recalled sadly that when he looked through the tent-flaps there was not the slightest movement where the suffering sheep and goats

had been standing. A few yaks feebly moved their horns in utter helplessness and desperation under the white avalanche, and even they – the sons of snow – perished. When Nature lost her temper, even the tantric *mantras* were powerless. After the snowfall came the biting gales that swept across the snow-covered plateau. This was the cruel side of Chang Thang. The monastery had to have its statutory share of offerings, whether the mission was successful or not. Father's party had lost almost all they had collected, but they had somehow to get the same amount of donations for the monastery. Father had to make another short trip to Chang Thang in the latter part of the year.

While on his missions, my grandfather carried out his tantric religio-medical practices among the nomads. The most formidable foes in Chang Thang were not the mortal robbers, who could be controlled and punished if necessary; the enemies of these hardy herdsmen were the ungovernable forces of nature – snow, frost and disease – before which they were helpless. They needed someone more powerful and capable of combating them – a tantric lama, such as my grandfather. When the lives of men and beasts were threatened by snow and avalanche, he was their saviour. The remedy was to pour water over an iron basin, perforated like a sieve, which was covered by another, unperforated basin. The lama would concentrate hard, and make strange faces to show that he was invoking a deity to stop the snowfall. Father assured me that it often worked. To provide for times when Grandfather was absent, the nomads were given a time-hallowed concoction containing snow-dissipating *mantras* and blessed dirt and dust from the Sakya monastery. This mixture was burnt to produce smoke when too much snow fell.

Grandfather was also a doctor specializing in the treatment of skin diseases. Animals, sheep in particular, commonly suffered from foot-rot, a contagious disease, which sometimes killed off a whole flock. The herdsmen suffered from cold blisters and sores, as well as other blemishes. These skin diseases were attributed to the evil doings of the serpent-gods. Logically enough, the physician tried to cure the root of a particular disease by negotiating with the disease-givers through religious rites. I myself had experience of this. As a little boy I had sores all over my head, leaving deep, permanent scars. Rasha Lama-la, our local tantric practitioner, spat on the sore spots, silently saying healing *mantras* which gave esoteric power to his saliva.

Grandfather's similar religio-medical treatments were in great demand in Chang Thang.

Apart from their medical activities, the lamas were meant to serve as roving missionaries to the nomads. They executed all the rites relating to the deaths that had occurred in the previous year; and carried out the rituals of *kusang* and *tsewang*. *Kusang* was one of the reminders of *Bon*, the Shamanist cult of Tibet, which was periodically practised by the laity. The requirements for *kusang* were juniper leaves and pieces of sandalwood, which were burnt on a high vantage-point to produce clouds of smoke; barley grains and *tsampa*, which were offered in small heaps; and *chang*. While reading the sacred text, the ritual expert drummed and clashed his cymbals at intervals, to ensure good luck. Meanwhile the nomads whispered their prayers: 'O ye gods, give us success in whatever we do! In war, give us victory! In business, give us profits! On raids, give us booty.' *Tsewang* was performed in order to prolong one's life. The lama invoked the god of life, Tsepakme, for his blessing on those whose lives would otherwise be curtailed by climactic events. Grandfather discharged further mysterious duties in the wilderness of Chang Thang. When butter could not be churned and curd could not be formed, he was asked to exorcise the evil spirits haunting the churn.

The Tibetans believe that evil spirits can enter the bodies of human beings, who become mentally metamorphosed and physically stronger than usual. I have seen with my own eyes a tantric lama driving an evil spirit from the body of Namgyal, our next-door neighbour. She was in a fit, with staring eyes and foaming mouth, as she uttered the words: 'I am hurt. I have come to avenge myself on Namgyal.' The spirit refused to tell its name, although those who knew the woman deduced that it was the spirit of the mistress of Namgyal's husband, Acho Dawa. The lama arrived, invoked his deity, uttered tantric *mantras* and exorcised the haunted woman with his lamaist sceptre (*phurpa*). He struck her gently on the head several times with this, until she became perceptibly calmer. When at last the spirit was driven out, she began crying loudly: 'What happened to me?' Father used to tell me that Grandfather was most effective in exorcising spirits among the nomads, perhaps because of their strong faith. When a naïve nomad saw a life-saving miracle in the hours of distress and disaster, his faith was fortified and then his submission to the dictates of *dharma* becomes understandable. The nomads, like most Tibetans, believed more in the mysteries and superstitions of neo-Buddhism than in the rational teachings of the Buddha.

On one occasion a religious mission like my father's employed two lamas, one a tantric lama and the other professing *sutra* (the sayings of Buddha). A distressed nomad approached the *sutra* lama to exorcise an evil spirit that had invaded his wife's body. The monk replied: 'I do not possess yogic powers to chase spirits, but I can teach you *dharma*.' The nomad retorted in an epigram: 'If you have diligence you can know even the secret *dharma*. But mine is an emergency.' So he turned to the tantric lama, who restored the woman to her normal self. Since then tantric beliefs have had the upperhand in Chang Thang, so the story goes.

Tantric teachings were kept in great secrecy, not so much because the existing practitioners might lose their profession if more joined their guild, as because the teachings might be misused or misinterpreted consciously or unconsciously. They are like atomic energy, with equal destructive and constructive potential, and their road is a dangerous one. If you travel by a donkey you do not face any risk, but your journey will be long; on the other hand, if you fly, you take much greater risks but your journey will be shorter. If these esoteric teachings are pursued diligently and channelled in the right direction, the adept can attain Buddhahood in his lifetime, like the greatest Tibetan yogi, Milarepa. Theoretically, the tantric teacher scrutinizes the personality and character of his disciple for twelve years before transmitting any esoteric knowledge. However, in

the Tibetan countryside unscrupulous, capricious lamas misused their powers to bring down hailstones and directly caused
famine. Such people, according to Buddhism, are guaranteed
tickets to hell.

For seven months the mission party visited every corner of
the Chang Thang valleys and hills where smoke was to be seen.
Every year the same lama with the same servants toured the
same huge area; so the lama-disciple relationship also became
one of friendship. By his second trip Father had made a number
of friends among the nomads. He took hand-woven woollen
garments and barley as presents for them. Not a grain of barley
grew in Chang Thang. The inhabitants' staple diet was cheese
and meat, and as a result they were better built than most
Tibetans. Father profitably traded our barley for their salt,
sheep and butter.

In each camp the lama would make his old familiar speech,
which the attentive audience knew by heart. It went something
like this: 'Your last year's offerings and donations were safely
received by the brethren of Sakya Monastery. The rites were
performed and blessings were sought as you requested. It is
hoped that you will have the benefit of every blessing and
worship. For the sake of all sentient beings, the clarion call of the
Lord Buddha must be sounded perpetually throughout the
world. Therefore we have been directed by the Abbot to appeal
to the charitable and the generous for their support, so that we
may preserve and propagate the Sakya sect and the *dharma*.'

Although each offering was recorded, together with the
specific purpose for which it was offered, the monastery
received very little out of the total donations and offerings. This
was not the fault of the mission, because they paid the exact
amount decreed centuries earlier; rather, it was typical of the
decadent monastic authority, for whom even economic values
were absolute, like the Buddha's teachings. Tradition decreed
that the contractor, known honourably as treasurer, and the
lama should take the biggest share of the donations.

The richest nomads were described as the owners of 'a million whites (sheep) and a thousand blacks (yaks)'. Such men made the greatest contributions called 'a hundred offerings': a hundred sheep, about three yaks, and loads of butter and salt. The poorest possessed about a thousand sheep and eighty yaks. They offered about ten sheep and some butter. The actual amounts depended more on a person's generosity than on his wealth. When the mission had a good season, it brought back about seventy yaks, five thousand sheep, and fifteen horses. Most of the yaks would be loaded with butter well-packed in yak skins, salt, soda and wool. The stronger sheep also carried little bags of salt, day and night whether grazing or resting, for they were too numerous and so too much bother to load and unload. Over 70 per cent of the total collection in fact went to the treasurer. The monastery, whose mask the mission wore to obtain offerings, received only 635 sheep and goats (more of the latter because of less value), 670 silver coins called *tamka*, three yaks and seventeen *khels* of butter.

Bribery, which in due course became a national institution, must have been greatly encouraged by the traditions of Tibetan generosity. The impulsive and generous Tibetan would never see any friend or authority empty-handed. 'How can I see my friend (or lord) when I have nothing to present to him?' was the usual attitude. On their return from Chang Thang, the mission would make its first presentation to the Trichen (reigning lama) of Sakya and his holy family. The Trichen's dues were three hundred *khels* of butter, a hundred silver coins, and a *khadar*. The holy mother and her princesses received five coins and a *khadar* each. The second presentation was made to the governor: three *khels* of butter, fifty silver coins and a *khadar* of the second highest grade. These presents, like most levies in Tibet, were initially voluntary offerings but gradually they became statutory. The tantric lama received as his honorary salary three yaks and fifty sheep, salted butter, soda and wool. Father's share was rather disappointing: a yak, fifteen sheep, a *khel* of butter and two bags of salt. His profits from bartering were more satisfactory than his wages.

By early in the Eleventh Month Mother would be busy with her rosary, trying to find Father's arrival by means of an oracle. She closed her eyes in meditation, and prayed that her personal deity might tell through the symbolic number of beads what she most desired to know. Rubbing the rosary between her hands clasped in prayer, she suddenly slackened her concentration and began to blow exultantly over the rosary. Next she reverently lifted the rosary to her forehead and prayed even more earnestly. With her eyes still closed, to see the deities more clearly, she drew the rosary across her wrinkled face and haphazardly pinched the beads with the thumb and forefinger of each hand. Each hand eliminated three beads from either end simultaneously, until she had from one to four beads left. One bead suggested 'immediately'; two meant 'bad'; three, 'good luck'; and four a setback. The operation was repeated three times in order to confirm the divine revelation. As Mother indulged herself in these absurdities, I sat quietly beside her, praying earnestly that only one bead might be left in the end, for that was a happy result.

TWO

My Father's Death

IN TIBET there were three main ways for a commoner to climb the social ladder. First, if he became an abbot or a high lama, his lay followers would offer him gifts of all kinds in exchange for his blessings. Second, if he was a servant capable of combining fidelity and diplomacy, his master might promote him to the coveted post of treasurer. This was usually the highest promotion that a plebeian could gain. He would have free access to the coffers, and the executive power to run an estate would virtually rest in his hands. The third and the least dishonest way of becoming a respectable middle-class citizen was through trading, though it was considered spiritually the most mundane of the three avenues. Trading was hazardous, not so much because of commercial inflation and deflation as of the dangers of highwaymen. Hardships and hazards could not have held the Tibetans back, but most of them lacked the spirit of enterprise. In Sakya, out of a total of thirteen trading families, only three, of which our family was one, were Tibetan nationals. The majority were Nepali Buddhists and Kashmiri Muslims, who constituted the richest and most progressive section of our society.

During his roving stewardship to Grandfather, Father learned some of the elements of business. He found that trading provided a substantial supplementary income to tilling, and this appealed to him. His profits from Chang Thang amounted to 600 *sang*. With this small capital he made several trips to Shigatse to buy a donkey-load of essential consumer goods manufactured mostly in India. (Sakya, though historically important, was not well known to the few foreigners who caught a glimpse of Tibet, because it was off the trade route, which was from Sikkim via Yatung, Phari, Gyantse, Shigatse and Lhasa.) The biggest drawback of such a small-scale business in a small locality was that most of the goods had to be sold on credit. 'I will not run away with your debt. I can pay you the price of a matchbox in due time,' was the customer's usual response if a trader refused him credit. Mother had no doubts about her customers' honesty, and used to send us children to nag for money from door to door, before a seasonal trip to Shigatse. We often had embarrassing, even frightening, experiences. We would knock at a door, calling out 'Sorry' as we did so and out would come a drunkard. With children's innocence we would ask him to pay the price of a cup of tea leaves – or some such item – and he would chase us away, staggering after us with a knife in hand. Despite such episodes, our gross profit was about 200 per cent.

So far everything had gone well, and it seemed that our family was on a sound footing. Within five years our capital increased to 2,000 *sang*. We bought two more donkeys and a black mare. Like all Tibetans, my parents were extremely fond of jewellery. Tibetan scholars invariably compared our highest ideals and personages to jewels or gems; for instance, the Dalai Lama and the Buddhist Trinity were both described in this fashion. The rich preferred keeping jewellery to money, which in any case could not be invested. The marks of our prosperity were a gold earring weighing three *tolas* for Father, and a long necklace of turquoise and coral for Mother. I had a singularly happy childhood while Father was alive, flaunting sweets and pieces of dried biscuit before the other children.

The acreage we had under cultivation increased with our flourishing business. The farmers made a minimum use of money. They took essential goods on credit, and instead of paying in cash later, they often persuaded the seller (*tsongpa*) to take a few acres of land on lease for five or six years. So tilling and trading went hand in hand. Farming was an essential part of our self-sufficient economy. It provided animal fodder in winter, grain for home consumption, and agricultural training for our sisters. I remember how Mother half-rejoiced and half-feared when we had two successive bumper crops, with a yield of about 100 per cent. There was a popular Tibetan belief that every triumph must be followed by tragedy and every success by failure. So it happened to us.

On normal days Mother looked after our apronful of goods in the Sakya bazaar, situated on the right bank of the river. If you had visited this sleepy little bazaar in summer, you would have seen about eleven tents pitched round about. You would have heard no noise except of the river, and the voices of a few leisurely customers spinning thread and cracking jokes with the seller. They all sat comfortably around the goods from India spread out on the stone dais which served as a counter. And if anyone went away quickly, one of the regular customers would point towards the Hill of Cremation with the words: 'Your business will never be finished until your own smoke rises from that hill!' However, the bazaar became more lively during religious festivals and functions. Most Tibetan public entertainments were religious in nature; the only secular entertainments were the operas (*Ihamo*) sponsored by one of the important houses of Sakya. All shows were free, whether given by lamas or by laity. In Sakya there were twelve or thirteen lamaic ceremonies ('casting the *tormas*') every year.

Tormas were sacrificial cakes, made of *tsampa* and adorned with cones of coloured butter. They were the characteristic offerings of tantric Buddhism. Since they were gifts to appease the gods, they were of various designs and tints to suit the whims of the heavenly recipients. They were offered to gods, demigods, spirits and guardian deities to avert dangers to the citizens and to guard against epidemics, plagues, droughts and famine. In Tibet every god as well as every man had his price.

According to Tibetan Buddhism, these lesser gods did not have the spiritual power and knowledge to show the laity the path to *nirvana*, so we did not take refuge in them. They were believed to be capable of helping humans only in and for this world, and not beyond it. That is why practically every month there was a *torma* festival in Sakya.

With the passage of time, these festivals gained commercial and social importance. They were like village fairs, where the villagers from the nearby valleys and the nomads from the distant hills gathered enthusiastically to make new acquaintances and to renew the old ones. Here they could barter their agricultural and dairy products with Indian luxuries – tobacco, matchboxes, cotton shirts, and sweets. But commerce did not overshadow the original pious purpose of these festivals; they remained a tremendous demonstration of inborn faith. The farmer dusted, oiled, combed and replaited his tuft of hair. He dressed up in his best clothes – a black or white woollen *chuba*, or a cotton shirt, and a pair of new felt boots. The women dressed up more elaborately, in six prescribed articles of clothing, and wore jewellery, as tradition demanded. How enthralling it was to mingle with that happy, contented crowd, and to feel its pulse of inner peace and wild external excitement! These simple faithful people hardly missed any religious festival, braving numbing cold or dust storms of unimaginable force to get to Sakya.

Of all the thirteen festivals, the one celebrated in the Year of the Water Dragon (1952) remains clear in my memory. It was held at Phuntsog Phodrang, the house of the senior Sakya lama. For my parents these events were fundamentally big sale days. Large crowds would gather for all sorts of activities, both sacred and profane. Early one morning in the Second Month our whole family set out to Phuntsog Phodrang, about three miles from Sakya. Mother was in her ceremonial jewellery and best clothes; so was Father. We had all oiled our faces and hair liberally, for greasy faces meant prosperity. As we walked, I could see a few blades of new green grass in the sunny corners of the awakening fields. In the mud near the canal mules, donkeys and horses were digging with their forelegs for fresh grass roots. In some of the fields, still dark and frozen, boys and girls were delving hopefully for sweet pinkish potatoes, as small as tiny grass roots. It was the season of blizzards and dust storms, which usually blew in the afternoon. Everywhere you looked there were monstrous clouds of sand and dust sweeping across from west to east. Even able-bodied men with loads of manure were often blown off their feet by gales. It was commonly believed that the more stormy the *torma*-festival day was, the more angry were the gods, and the more eager to drive away diseases and dangers from Phuntsog Phodrang in particular and from Sakya in general. These solemn considerations were lost on me; the day meant nothing but sheer excitement and entertainment.

While my parents and sisters displayed our goods near the front gate of Phuntsog Phodrang, my brother Abu and I went to watch the lamas dancing. This annual casting of *tormas* was preceded by a week's recital of scriptures and performance of tantric rites. All the monks of the Sakya monastery were employed there. The junior monks read the teachings of the Buddha and commentaries on them, while the senior lamas prepared *tormas* and performed the relevant rituals. The festival culminated on the seventh day with the casting of *tormas* in the open air. However, before this dramatic climax, agile young lamas in gorgeous costumes and hideous masks danced through the day. These dances (*chams*) were performed to the accompaniment of the deafening music of drums, bells, conch shells, cymbals and other instruments. Every gesture of the hands and the dagger or spear held in them, and every foot movement, was a symbolic expression of the deity whose part that particular dancer played. I watched the whole day as each god appeared from the high stage and joined the line of gods and goddesses in the courtyard. The lamas danced, not with pleasure, but with wrath. The spectators were submissive and awestruck in the presence of these mighty, infuriated gods.

When the sun was about to set, the dancers, led by the lama musicians, moved in a long procession towards a nearby vantage point where the *tormas* were cast away. Immediately, the crowd dispersed in every direction. They were recharged with blessings, and felt relieved of all possible dangers and ills. There was a tremendous air of confidence as the crowd broke up. As friends parted, they would say: 'Now I have no worries. If I die, it will be because of the inviolable law of *karma*, and not by any mishap.' The strong gales that afternoon ensured the success of the festival, but it was misfortune for us. When Abu and I arrived at the bazaar, we saw Mother nervously taking grit from Father's eyes, and my sisters emptying out sand-filled aluminium utensils and dusting other saleable articles. The sudden gales had almost blinded Father, who had had trouble with his eyes before. From the number of currency notes and coins, the barley and wheat bags, and the amount of wool and butter, I knew that the sales had been good. The feverish excitement of the day was dampened by this nasty accident, and we hastened home.

The next morning Father's eyes were crimson and swollen. Though Mother had managed to take out most of the sand grains the previous evening, dusk had been falling fast, and we suspected that some sand was still left inside. Remembering Father's earlier troubles my parents took this trifling accident seriously.

When a person in Tibet was ill, he would not dream of consulting a physician before seeing his favourite lama. Our lama was called Zongchung Rinpoche, the most ascetic and aged lama I have ever seen. He lived in perpetual retreat in a small dilapidated monastery standing on Ponto Hill, away from the main Sakya Monastery. Even as a high-spirited little boy, I used to admire Zongchung Rinpoche and those like him. Now I would prostrate myself before such a lama, not so much for his mystic power as for his total absence of hypocrisy. He left practically no gap between Buddhist precept and *Sangha* practice. Whether his denunciation of earthly existence was right or wrong, his sincerity commanded my admiration and respect. Mother went to see him. According to Tibetan belief, disease has three root causes: lack of good luck (*lungta*), your *karma*, and disease-giving demons. Mother returned from her visit to the lama trying to conceal her concern. He had told her that Father's store of luck was running low, for which the remedy was to erect new prayer-flags and thus to appease our guardian deities. One of the deities of Phuntsog Phodrang was responsible for the accident. This she-deity was displeased with the festival, and had aimed her magic wand of diseases and mishaps at the participant who was most unfortunate. This was Father, whose horoscopic chart was black at the time. As directed by the lama, we invited three monks to execute the prescribed rituals, which were intended to flatter, please and bribe the goddess so that she would leave Father alone.

Unfortunately, the rites did not improve Father's eyes. The swelling of his eyelids slightly lessened, but dark red fleshy growths had formed in the corners of each eye. He was naturally upset, and his worries had a pernicious effect on his general health, which deteriorated each day. We were no less worried. Mother realized that it was high time she brought in a physician, but before doing so, she approached the same lama again to ask if medical treatment would be auspicious. Fortunately, the oracle was in favour of consulting a doctor.

The lama had more to tell us. The she-deity was appeased; but, alas, there was yet another deity haunting and hurting Father. This demon belonged to a wicked woman, who had let him loose on Father by means of devilish incantations. Prompted by hints from the lama, Mother was clever enough to piece together this mysterious jigsaw puzzle. She deduced that the invoker of the demon was a woman who had fought with my eldest sister, Donkar, while watering the fields, and who wanted revenge. Tibetans sadly lacked the virtues of forgiveness; those who could forgive and forget the past were considered inconsistent and infirm. If you believe in the power of good prayers, you must believe equally in that of evil prayers. Our lamas tell us that heartfelt prayers are concentrated and conse-

crated human thoughts, which are kinetic energy. When we are praying we are focussing our mental energy to help or harm some person. Prayer, like sunlight focussed through a powerful magnifying glass, can produce either harmful heat or helpful light. In Tibet some people used prayer sacrilegiously to pay off old scores. The remedy was seldom direct negotiation with the person concerned, but rather to perform mysterious rites. Mother made a miniature effigy of a woman out of *pak*, set it up on a piece of broken pottery, and with all due seriousness placed in front of it a cupful of the food which Father had left in his bowl, together with strips of an old garment of his which she put around its neck. Then Donkar placed it 'facing south at the junction of three paths', as directed by the oracle.

The arrival of the physician – an elderly gentleman of stern, sad countenance and cautious gait – relieved our mounting anxiety. He smelt strongly of an aromatic herbal concoction, the invisible badge of his profession. His young apprentice carried the medical bag with grovelling reverence, and was nervously carrying out his master's directions. No sooner were we relieved, however, than we were again scared by the doctor's prognosis. He warned Father quite frankly that unless he stopped worrying he might die, not because of his eyes but through a nervous breakdown. He then treated Father in a rough and ready fashion. With a small penknife he scraped off the fleshy growths from the fast-closing eyes, as crudely as a butcher dismembering a sheep. Father tried to conceal the agonizing pain, tightening his mouth and compressing his eyelids, but his expression revealed his suffering only too clearly. My whole body writhed in pain and sympathy. I can still hear Mother's expostulation loud and clear: 'O Kunchok-Sum! Why should he suffer so much? How I wish half his pain could be transferred to me! Have mercy on us, God of Infinite Compassion!'

Though Tibetan medical practice could not compare with Western techniques, we had a fairly advanced medical expertise of our own. Tibet had received most of her medical ideas from India, China, and even from Iran – ideas that formed the basis of numerous manuals and theses, written by Tibetan luminaries so that the assimilated knowledge became uniquely Tibetan.

Tibetan medicine attempts to cure the patient as a whole rather than curing a particular disease in isolation; for it recognizes the relationship between mind and body. As such its techniques include psychotherapy, astrology and essentially herbal medicines. These medicines react slowly but steadily and are particularly suited to curing some old diseases, while remaining almost ineffective in emergencies.

Historically, surgery in Tibet was widely practised before King Muni Tsenpo's reign (AD 799-804), but he banned it after a heart operation on the queen failed. Diagrams of various surgical tools used during those days are still in existence; I saw some recently at the Tibetan medical centre in Dharamsala. Despite the official ban, expert physicians continued to operate though on rare cases. As late as in 1956, a Lhasan physician operated successfully on a man's skull which was broken during a horseride. The man, who now has a partial sheep-skull, is still alive, and now lives in India.

There was always an acute shortage of physicians. In the entire country there was only one medical college, the Chakpori College in Lhasa. In our part of Tibet, medical training and knowledge were passed down from father to son. The doctor we invited was from a town two days' journey on foot from Sakya.

By now Father had been bedridden for three months. His general health was fluctuating, but his eyes were gradually getting worse. Still we had faith in the doctor. Each time he opened his oily medical bag, fitted with numerous pockets, he would take out some powdered medicine resembling spice, and brownish shiny pills, with the words: 'This medicine is very expensive. Its ingredients are mostly precious stones and herbs unobtainable in Tibet.' This was, as I understand now, an indication of the fee he expected; a physician's fee was not fixed.

Since Father was the pivot of our family, there was no end to Mother's gratitude. One day I heard her crying in despair:

'Doctor, please save his right eye at least. We'll offer you our horse.' (The mare was our single most valuable possession.) The get-well rites and the medical treatment bankrupted us. After the third operation, Father lost his left eye, and sight in his right eye was failing fast. This aggravated his mental agony. His hoarse groans of unbearable pain sank into the deepest recesses of my young heart. 'If I must lose both my eyes, I would rather die than live. But who will help my wife to bring up this house full of children? O Kunchok-Sum, open thy third eye and see us! I am the most sinful man living.' Turning to the physician he pleaded: 'Doctor, save my right eye. Surely you can do something? Please try ...' His voice failed and he fainted.

We were all stricken by the terrible knowledge that our beloved father was fast closing his eyes, to dwell in perpetual darkness and nevermore to see the wonders of creation, and above all the faces of his family. The disturbed state of his mind was threatening his very existence. I never saw any indication that he feared death, even after nearly four months of illness and mental suffering. However, there was ample evidence that he felt guilty and sorry at leaving behind seven children for his wife to bring up single-handed. Grief reduced him to a skeleton. There was nothing much that the doctor could do about his sight; nevertheless, he continued to feed Father with his powdered herbs. As a last resort, he cauterised Father's chest, but cauterisation had no appreciable healing effect. By then he had high blood pressure and had developed retention of urea, as my mother later told me.

During those dark days Mother suffered almost as much as Father. For the ninth time she hastened to Zongchung Rinpoche. He implied that Father's days were numbered because of the patient's precarious 'spiritual and physical imbalances'. His cosmic harmony was out of joint. To counteract the spiritual imbalance, we bought a sheep and thereby saved 'the life of a sheep about to be slaughtered'. This sheep, termed *tsethar* or rescued life, was allowed to live out its full term. And for the physical imbalance, we performed the rite of *lusgyur*, or bodily transformation. The lama re-christened Father and recommended a complete set of new red clothes, which made him symbolically a new man with a new body. Every other lama we consulted gave Father protective relics and ribbons to prolong his life, until his gaunt neck was heavily laden with them.

The Tibetans believed that those who visited the sick, especially those with telepathic gifts, would increase the patient's suffering. Usually a heavily smoking fire was lit near the gate as the accepted warning notice to visitors. Whenever Father writhed and rolled on the bed in pain, it was certain that a visitor was coming, making the invisible spirit pierce the stricken patient. Donkar usually performed the simple exorcising procedure. A little incense that had been blessed by the lama was burnt, and the patient was enveloped in smoke until he almost choked. Afterwards the burnt incense, believed to carry the pain, was cast away and Donkar spat after it. There was scarcely any life in Father, but he lingered on because of his anxiety about us. Eventually his *karma* got the upper hand, and he died on the eighth day of the Eighth Month in the year of the Water Dragon (1952). Just before the end Mother poured a few drops of *jinlap* into his mouth, which was open in a desperate attempt to utter his last thoughts. His bulging, pale grey eyeballs moved from left to right as he tried to see his wailing wife and weeping children for the last time. *Jinlap* was a solution in water of pills that had been blessed by a high lama; it supposedly had the power to immediately transport the dead person to the Western Paradise of Peace, if he had the requisite faith. At least it was a safeguard against his sinking into hell. As soon as father was dead, our uncle shrouded the corpse. Mother, wailing and struggling to cling to the body, was escorted from the death chamber, along with us children.

Immediately someone was sent to ask Zongchung Rinpoche to carry out the *pho-wa* service. *Pho-wa*, defined as the extraction of consciousness, was a mystic chant that commanded the spirit not to haunt its family and not to cling to the world of spirits, but to seek the 'white path' to the Western Paradise of Peace. In other words, it was meant to give the dead person the right start in his new life, enabling him to face reality. *Pho-wa* was always performed by the favourite and most venerated lama of the deceased. Zongchung Rimpoche did not come to our house, as he was in retreat, but carried out the hour-long service in his cell. He mentally concentrated upon the deceased, visualizing his body and calling my father's spirit to his presence.

In the same way as *pho-wa* was a guide to the deceased in other worlds, so the death horoscope was a directive to the survivors in this world. An astrologer was immediately consulted. The data he needed were the correct age, the approximate time of death (afternoon or evening) and the ages of every living member of the family. He chalked out on a slate geometric figures and calculated and re-calculated. After each calculation he consulted his book. The astrological results announced were incredible. Father had been a woman in his previous life, with 'six family members in a farm house, whose door faced north'. As a philanthropic woman, she had sowed adequate and appropriate seeds to reap the harvest of *karma* – which was to become a monk. But misfortune (*barched*) held up his journey to *nirvana:* that is, he fell from monkhood to laity.

Regarding his next rebirth, the astrologer added that if an image of Chenrezig, the Buddha of Compassion, were consecrated, he would be reborn as a male in a land where the teachings of the Buddha were heard. Otherwise he would be born again as an animal, and it would take aeons before he got a chance to enter a human womb. The astrologer told some incredible truths – tangible, stark facts. He described all the scars and moles Father had, and the direction he was facing while dying. He told us that Father's *sog* (life-force) had been exhausted on the fourth day of the Fourth Month, but that the

rites sustained him for nearly four months longer. Mother observed that from the beginning of the Fourth Month Father had
become pale and lifeless. She knew he was beyond redemption.

The Tibetans believe that there are many impediments
before the deceased can face reality. 'Reality' here means that
the deceased must not delude himself by haunting his family or
his relatives but must go where the lama leads. Almost everyone dies with his wishes unfulfilled, food unfinished, wealth
unused and relatives separated from him. When a person is
about to die, all these things come to his mind in a flash. Thus
his consciousness inclines him towards some of these aspirations and desires, though all are immaterial to him now.
Father's first impulse of consciousness was towards our family.
This was understandable enough, as all of us were weeping and
wailing around his deathbed when he was passing, and his
biggest grief was for our unfledged family. His second impulse
was towards his parental home. Since his consciousness or
spirit haunting us was detrimental to our well-being, certain
rites were recommended which were supposed to direct the
spirit to the 'white path'.

A new altar was improvised, where the corpse was placed
benevolently like a principal deity in a monastery. A galaxy of
votive butter lamps (*chomé*) were lit and stacks of incense burnt
before an effigy of the deceased, and near the head of the
shrouded corpse sat the lama, the custodian of Father's spirit,
chanting sad dirges. He and his assistant read and re-read the
Bardo Thodol (the book that guides the souls of the dead) in
relays day and night for three days until the corpse was disposed of. Thus the death chamber became a newly hallowed
chapel. We children and weeping and wailing relatives were
not permitted to enter this room, which acquired an odour of
sanctity during the three days. Silence was necessary for the
lama to transmit the message of *Bardo Thodol* to the spirit. The
occasional sounds of his hand-drum and deep brass bell were a
stimulus to sorrow. While fast asleep I would be suddenly

awakened by these sounds, and become sad again.

The astrologer announced that the corpse should leave at dawn on the third day. That was one of the saddest days of my childhood, and I wept and wailed more than ever before. Before the corpse was moved, everyone present, led by Mother, prostrated themselves. I prayed that Father might be born again into our family as a brother, little realizing that it would involve Mother's remarriage. Then the funeral organizer tied the corpse into the embryonic posture, which symbolized the birth into another life, and also made it easier to carry. All the doors of our neighbourhood, particularly those of our friends, were barred with a line of sand. It was believed that each grain of sand appeared as a hill to the spirit; hence it would be impossible for it to visit and later haunt its friends and relatives. Theoretically speaking, the corpse was by then nothing but the four elements – earth, water, fire and air – as the spirit was transferred to the effigy, which was taken to the lama. However, the neighbours were taking no risks.

After the corpse was disposed of, the life-size effigy, dressed in a complete set of Father's clothes, was carried to the lama. An inscription (*chang-ku*) was inserted in the front of the effigy's head, bearing the words:

> *I, the world-leaver, Thubkye Choephal, adore and take refuge in thee, my most venerated Lama, and all the deities peaceful and wrathful. May the Lord of Compassion, Phakpa Chenrezig, forgive my accumulated sins and impurities of former countless lives and show me the white path to the world of eternal bliss.*

The clothes became the lama's possession. Zongchung Rinpoche told us that he dreamed of Father the night before the effigy arrived. When the effigy arrived at the lama's place, the *chang-ku* was burnt. By the colour of the flame the lama could tell whether the deceased was on or off the white path. Unfortunately, the flame threw doubts about Father's solitary journey towards reality, as I learned much later.

When both the body and the spirit of Father had left our house, the place became empty. Sounds of the bell and drum ceased. The dirge-like *Bardo Thodol* was chanted no more. Mother stopped crying, she was too exhausted. The corpse had contaminated the atmosphere of our locality, and purification was essential to keep away the anger of the local deities. Sweeping was not enough; a lama came to restore the sanctity of our house, praying and sprinkling it with holy water.

While all this was taking place, I climbed the terrace and sunned myself there, as was my habit. That morning my swollen eyes were riveted on Rinchen Gang Hill, where the cremation was taking place. I watched the heavy black smoke rising. Soon vultures from all directions dipped and hovered over the town, as if locating the house that was giving them a feast, and then flew majestically towards the hill. Whenever anyone saw flocks of vultures flying towards the Cremation Hill, he would instinctively utter '*Om Mani Padme Hum*', for it was certain that someone had passed away. 'Cremation' is not quite accurate. The flesh was cut off and given to the vultures – the last act of Buddhist charity. The bones were cremated; some of the ashes were scattered in mountain streams, and some, mixed with clay, were moulded into tiny images of the Buddha.

Throughout that mournful day our friends and relatives came to condole with us. Hardly anyone sent messages. They all personally came to console and comfort Mother, giving the grief-stricken widow money, as was the custom, and serving her tea and *chang* which they had brought. Their solace was down-to-earth, as though saying. 'Akyi, please think deeply and reasonably. Every man has to die. We mortals cannot divert our *karma*, which flows like the Ganges. Your unceasing tears will poison your health. Think of your little children. If you die, what will happen to them? Your useless moaning will make the departed unwilling to follow the white path. There is nothing better than to perform the due rites, give charity to beggars and make generous offerings to the *Sangha*. If you pray, you will be reunited in your next life with the departed.'

Our father died on a Saturday, an astrologically inauspicious day both for the dead and the living. As was the tradition, we observed mourning rituals for 49 days. Every Saturday of the seven weeks, three or four monks came to the house to perform the death rituals, known as 'Forty-nine Offerings'. We believed that during these 49 days the deceased passed through different psychic experiences, all crucial before rebirth. Mother told us to say *'Om Mani Padme Hum'* as many times as we could, to kill no insects and to eat no meat. On the ritual days our doorsteps were crowded with beggars, all uttering *'Mani'* for the deceased. Abu was sent to replenish butter lamps in monasteries. In short, it was a seven-week-long period of accumulating merit, believed to be the only influential power capable of helping the deceased. Meritorious deeds were like water to the thirsty in a desert, like food to the starving in a famine-stricken land. In addition, we were required to keep up our spirits – a difficult if not impossible task. Our aunts (Mother had five sisters) repeatedly warned us that we should not weep during the 49 days, especially on the weekly ritual days. While undergoing after-death experiences and trials, the spirit would still visit its home occasionally. If the spirit saw its relatives weeping it would not be able to face reality, which was the only way to be born again. On the other hand, if a wife pretended to high spirits, she faced adverse criticism from the public, and was accused of being glad that her husband had died. Our hair we left uncombed and unoiled, looking like a yak's tail. Our grimy faces were covered in layers of dirt by streams of tears, and our dark, sober clothes were thrown on anyhow.

Hardly a fortnight had passed when death again stalked through our family. My youngest sister, only two years old, was carried away by chickenpox, and a week later my four-year-old brother Choephal followed her. After the third death, Mother was grief-stricken and on the verge of insanity; she had suffered three losses within a month. I cried more for Mother than for the three dead. As a child mourning the death of someone close, my grief evaporated soon after cremation; but Mother remained a living vessel of sorrow and grief. Fortunately, full death rituals were not usually done for children. The generally accepted explanation was not that children were worthless as human lives, but that they had had no time to commit fresh sins.

It was amazing that those successive waves of grief did not kill Mother. Whenever she did not seek refuge in *dharma*, she truly seemed to be going mad; we were terrified that we children would have to join the hordes of beggars in the streets and near the monastery gate. No modern medical treatment could have cured her, but her faith did so. After each solemn ritual she felt better. She believed beyond the shadow of a doubt that the prescribed rituals constructed bridges and boats for the deceased. Her simple but profound faith gave meaning to her otherwise empty life. She found comfort in rituals, the symbolic and demonstrative aspects of lamaism. Above all, there was always the prospect of a higher rebirth and the promise of *nirvana*, if rites were duly performed and life lived according to the laws of *dharma*. She believed that her husband would be reborn as the son of a nomad.

I wish I could find it possible to share this unquestioning belief of hers. But to start with, my infant faith was disturbed by the infiltration of Chinese communist ideology. Then, after our escape from Tibet, when we were drifting along the Himalayan foothills, I was awarded a scholarship in Kalimpong. My faith wavered still further, mainly due to a new psychological environment. I remember a particular incident which amply illustrates the shaky state of my beliefs. It was 1967. My class was doing *Twelfth Night*. The clown, disguised as a curate, asks Malvolio: 'What is the opinion of Pythagoras concerning wild fowl?' Malvolio from the dark house replies: 'That the soul of our grandam might haply inhabit a bird.' The whole class roared with laughter. I joined in half-heartedly. I was neither as negative as my class-mates, including the teacher, who thought that the theory of rebirth was a joke; nor was I as positive as my mother, who felt that rebirth was as certain as the certitude of death. Ever since then I have been seeking explanations.

I held many conversations with lamas of all types, from the most ignorant to the most scholarly. A typical discussion with a *geshé* (doctor of divinity) went something like this:

'What happens to the deceased immediately after death?' I asked him, plunging straightaway into the heart of the matter.

He replied: 'The uncertain period extending from the moment of death to the moment of rebirth is called *Bardo* in Tibetan. This indefinite time is like a railway station where the dead spirit, having left its earthly home, waits and struggles for a ticket. How fast you get your ticket, and what class it is, depend upon your pocket and power. Similarly your rebirth depends on your *karma* and death rituals. The ordinary layman experiences four crucial stages of *Bardo*. But a man of a certain degree of spiritual attainment escapes these. He will be reborn as a nobleman, or go to the Western Paradise of Peace – heaven.'

'Will you escape these stages?' I asked him.

'I don't think so,' he said, with humility. When I asked him further how he knew that religious adepts take short cuts in *Bardo*, he replied with true conviction: 'That which satisfies your conscience will satisfy the Precious Trinity. If you are confident through your yogic training that you can escape these terrors of *Bardo*, you will do so certainly. However, it takes rigorous mental training to achieve such conviction. Our great forefathers sacrificed their lives for the propagation, development and preservation of the holy *dharma*. We Tibetans have for centuries been exploring the human mind, while the so-called advanced nations have been exploring the world. Our world is eternal and infinite; theirs is external and finite.'

I was tempted to remind him that we Tibetans have been living on the spiritual greatness and reputation of our forefathers. From about the seventeenth century, the Tibetan lamas took a long rest until the Chinese invasion in 1950; there was no significant scriptural and intellectual progress. But I refrained from mentioning this.

'What does our consciousness feel when we are dead?' I asked him.

'The body, like a worn-out mechanical case for the soul, is left as an inert, tangible organism, while the mind seems to disappear. From the moment of physical annihilation, the sixth mind or the deepest human consciousness falls into a trance, that is to say, consciousness does not become conscious of the fact that it is dead. This swooning state is like a dream or temporary unconsciousness experienced after a nasty accident.

'After three or four days of mental rest, so to speak, your spirit discovers its separation from your body. As you can imagine, this phase is frightening. You are at once possessed with desires, fears and regrets. You desire more fervently than ever before to live with your family now left on a different planet altogether. You crave for and cling desperately to the wealth you have accumulated. You become conscious of the unfulfilled desires cherished through aeons of past existences. You are hopeless; you are helpless; you are in a panic.

'If you are a spiritually unapprenticed man you try to run away. But you cannot. Wherever you may try to escape to you will find horrors at your heels. Why? Because that which tries to escape is your consciousness, and also that which terrified you is your consciousness. The mind untrained in the ways of *dharma* is horrified by the apparitions in *Bardo*. Actually, these visions, pleasant or unpleasant, benevolent or diabolical, are nothing but hallucinations. Imagine after-death experiences as a film. Your consciousness transcending death is the projector, the film on the screen and the cinema-goer, all in one. Consciousness is pleased or terrified by its own mental shadows.'

He paused, and the graphic pictures of *Bardo* I had seen

depicted on the walls of every monastery in Sakya rushed to my mind. These conventional and standard diagrams of *Bardo* were so deeply implanted in the Tibetan head that every Tibetan must anticipate similar visions after death.

The *geshé* continued: 'The sublimest human sentiments are personified into benign deities with benevolent smiles. They appear to be friends in a hostile world. They are manifestations of the psychic heart of your consciousness. But soon rationality takes over. The psychic brain of your consciousness projects visions of the most terrifying and hideous-looking deities. They are the blood-curdlers of the dead. When the stream of peaceful deities projected by the psychic heart is finished, the deceased realizes its separation from the world. It naturally reacts violently. This reaction is prompted by reason. Truth hurts; hence the wrathful deities that appear before the frightened mind.

'The *Bardo Thodol* is read repeatedly, clearly and loudly before the corpse, in order to awaken the dreamer to reality. The *Book of the Dead* tells your consciousness that the visions are nightmares of *Bardo* and should not be mistaken for reality. This way of preparation for the art of dying is as good or bad as last-minute cramming for your examinations. The best way is to practise *dharma* throughout your life.'

'Might not *Bardo* experiences be nightmares, just before we die?' I interrupted.

'No,' he replied. 'When you die you become objective. The mind is stripped of all its pretences. That is why we stress the cultivation of wisdom and virtue. Only when *dharma* becomes part of your sixth mind are you armed to face anything – even death.'

'How can you prove that the doctrine of rebirth is true?' I asked.

The *geshé* answered: 'The so-called instincts inherent in every human being are inherited from previous lives. How else does an infant find its mother's breast? How else does a youngster know how to satisfy his sexual desires without being taught? Similarly, the so-called born geniuses have inherited intellects from their previous lives. When twins go to the same school, one may excel in mathematics, while the other fails in it, although they are taught by the same teacher in the same class.' He stopped with a triumphant note.

Seeing that I still looked doubtful, he continued: 'Have you not seen all the cases of rebirth reported in the papers? Don't you know how the Dalai Lama identified his own objects as a lad of three? He spotted the exact rosary and the walking-stick used in his previous life. He recognized some of the old lamas from Lhasa.'

'Why can't everybody remember his past lives? And why are rebirth cases observed only where the belief prevails?' I asked.

He answered sharply: 'If you have not sown seeds, why should you reap the fruit? Everybody does not strive for virtue. The ability to recall the past is not accidental; it has a definite cause. You can develop this power through correct and constant meditation. In Tibet many lamas were successful. As to your second question, if you close your eyes, how can you see anything? If a girl in China were to recall her past husband or friend, she would find herself in a mental hospital. Do you think that people would voluntarily recall their past lives under such circumstances?'

Human beings are victims of desires. So logically enough they crave for rebirth, and are repeatedly reborn until they achieve Buddhahood. One of the redeeming and rational features of Buddhism is that you are responsible for your present life, and you will be responsible for your own future also. This is the doctrine of *karma*, the sum total of an individual's deeds, speech and thoughts, which determines his future existence as it has always determined it in the past.

THREE

The Monks of Sakya

AS I write this chapter, a solemn, serene picture of our household altar room on a ritual day projects itself before my eyes. Around the small, neat altar, tiny butter votive lamps burnt their wicks down to the last centimetre. The final curls of incense smoke rolled and disappeared up to heaven. *Tormas*, conical sacrificial cakes, made of *tsampa* and ornamented with multi-coloured pieces of butter, along with other humble offerings, were arranged in neat rows before the altar. The dedicated day's offerings and scriptural readings were over. Four or five saffron-robed monks relaxed after the service was over before returning to their monastery, reciting their rosaries and murmuring prayers, intercepted by full-throated laughter over a mundane joke or so.

Most of the lay population was illiterate, and there were certain rites which even the educated layman could not perform. In our family Father and Abu could read, but Mother used to argue that it was far more spiritually effective to have the lamas reading the scriptures for us than to have any layman reading them. We had about eight monk friends who performed all the complicated rites in times of disaster, disease or rejoicing. I used to love such occasions for the special meals and the stories that went with them. When the ritual experts had completed their task – which to the eyes of childhood seemed mechanically executed – one of the lamas, usually the youngest, called Sherab-la, would tell me how great and ancient the Sakya sect was.

Sherab-la, occasionally prompted by the older lamas, would carry me back to the past spiritual greatness of Sakya. I felt elevated by these feasts of sectarian chauvinism, which made the room seem forlorn. In the intervals of silence I looked at the hazy, heatless rays of the sun shining through our wire-netted window, and as the dull red beams climbed higher and higher up the opposite wall, and as the evening breeze rose and sent gusts of air through the glassless window frames, I felt sad. For after Mother had offered them two silver coins each, the monks would leave for the monastery. Meanwhile the incredible tales of Sakya captured my youthful mind and lingered on.

In the year AD 1042 the Indian saint-scholar, Atisha, came from Bengal to reform Tibetan Buddhism, which had become decadent. Journeying through Tsang (Western Tibet), he came across a little village in the small State of Zangtu. (At the time Tibet had disintegrated into numerous petty states and principalities.) There a miracle happened. Atisha beheld a miraculously white, enormous disc, glowing with mystic symbols of the god Avalokitesvara and the god Manjusri, on the centre of Ponto Hill. The hill formed a natural canopied backdrop to this blessed village. Dismounting, Atisha prostrated himself before the sacred signs. Today, a few weatherworn, yellowish mud-brick *chortens* (pagodas) stand as living monuments to Atisha's mystic trance. This place is called Chak-tsal Gyap, the Pass of Prostration. At the place where the divine revelation took place is a conspicuous spot of white earth – Sakya is the Tibetan for 'white earth'.

If you stop at the Pass of Prostration and look at Sakya, once the capital of Tibet, you will see a brown hill about 18,000 feet high, looking like a majestic elephant and facing towards the east. More than a hundred red-painted monasteries are scattered like precious stones on the hill. At the hill's foot are about two hundred mud houses, painted blue and white, some of them standing among the monasteries; and on the four corners of each flat roof are coloured prayer-flags. As you approach you will see that a crystal-clear and fast-flowing river runs by the little town, eroding the banks on which the houses stand.

In Sakya, as everywhere else in Tibet, there were two types of temples, *lhakhang* and *gonkhang*. The former housed Buddhas, *Bodhisattvas* (saints) and scholar saints; the latter, tantric deities and guardian spirits. The two stood in sharp contrast, and two distinct atmospheres prevailed in them. Every month Mother used to send me to the tantric *gonkhangs* to offer *chang* and *chema* (*tsampa* and butter). The hideous-looking gods and goddesses, with their multiple heads and hands, petrified me. Their faces were curved in violent anger, and I always had the impression that they were not satisfied with our offering and wanted my liver as well. Their multiple hands were armed with spears, axes and daggers, and they wore necklaces of human skulls. These child-scaring images were supposed to provide appropriate objects for meditation. Some were guardian spirits – the spirits of the dead who by the law of their *karma* were forbidden further rebirth and were compelled to remain perpetually in this state. They were believed to be able to help us to achieve secular and materialistic ends in this world. Most of these *gonkhangs* were built on the hill, side by side with the *lhakhangs*.

Hanging on the walls of each *gonkhang* were stacks of swords and muskets used in the wars of conquest that had made Tibet the greatest military power in Central Asia during the seventh and eighth centuries before Buddhism killed the martial spirit of Tibetans. Perhaps no religion in the world has changed a people's way of life so dramatically as Buddhism did in Tibet. The Tibetans, who had been the most dreaded and fiercest warriors in Central Asia, literally 'put down their weapons at the lotus feet of lamas' and followed the 'white path of peace' pointed by the Buddha.

The whole family went to the *lhakhangs* to replenish the butter lamps on the tenth, thirteenth or fifteenth of every month; these dates were holy days, and charities and offerings made then would be more meritorious. Our favourite cathedral was

the most famous and largest *lhakhang* in Sakya, built on the valley floor. This calm place was utterly different from the
terrifying *gonkhangs*. The statues, images of Buddha,
Bodhisattvas and saintly scholars looked benevolent and beautiful. The interior decorations, all of a religious nature, held the
pilgrims spellbound. Many a time I got left behind, looking at
wall-paintings and frescoes which depicted the lives of saints or
of the Buddha, or which illustrated his teachings while Mother
and the rest had gone after their usual three prostrations and
prayers. The *lhakhang* contained four chapels, in which golden
chortens held relics of the departed Sakya Lamas, and accom-
modated about two hundred monks with separate quarters.
This was a *Sutra* institution, and its monks did not follow tantric
practices. However, in the Great Sakya Monastery, as in most
established monasteries in Tibet, both the *Sutra* and the tantric
aspects of Buddhism were considered necessary for the attainment of Buddhahood. The monks on the north of the river practised tantric Buddhism, and those on the south followed the
Sutra. Such a division of religious practice and specialization
indicates the extent to which Buddhism became institutional-
ized in Tibet.

The Sakya river had its source in a high mountain called
Taktsenma, overlooking the holy city on the east. Halfway up
this snow-clad mountain, among the rock and shale, a number
of caves were carved out for hermits – monks who had
renounced the monastic life of ease and plenty, and laymen
who had permanently left their families, herds of yaks and
fields of barley behind. Below Mount Taktsenma, the lower
slopes undulate gently down to the valley. The two palaces of
the Sakya Lamas, Phuntsog Phodrang and Dolma Phodrang,
stood among willows and elms on the western bank of a tributary of the river.

My family naturally belonged to the Sakya sect, though I
must admit that I am now a vague Buddhist, having no inner
urge to follow any sect in particular. However, unlike the

various Christian denominations, the lay Tibetans are not rigid about their sectarian faith and practice. My mother declared herself nonsectarian and worshipped all incarnate lamas, regardless of their sects. Nor is it theologically necessary for the laity, whose average ambition may be simply to lead a decent Buddhist life, to follow a particular sect. Only the lamas, who by their theoretical renunciation of the world, are supposed to choose the most suitable means – and so a particular sect – and then concentrate on attaining *nirvana*.

The formation of the four major sects and their numerous sub-sects was a creative Tibetan response to Buddhism in Tibet. The sects went their separate ways, each following vigorously and continually transmitting its own tradition and practice. This was partly due to lack of communication. But the basic difference among the orders centred on their different interpretations of 'emptiness', which is the basis of Buddhism, and with the rise of each sect there have been momentous theological debates whether the phenomenal objects really exist or not. These debates contributed greatly to the development of Tibetan religious literature. But, just as the Buddha was not conscious that he was propounding a new religion, so the founders of various sects did not deliberately set about establishing them. The sects grew from the interpretations of four or five extraordinary Buddhist scholars. Naturally enough, great numbers of monks in a particular region began to accept ready-made interpretations of Buddha's teachings, because it was easier to do so.

Gradually, as Tibet became increasingly religious, the various sects came to play significant political roles, like that of parties in more secular countries. The high lamas of Sakya, Kargyudpa and Gelukpa sects ruled Tibet at different periods of history, and naturally the ruling sect exercised the greatest power. However, it would be wrong to think, as many Westerners do, that all monasteries or sects exercised political power. Before the Chinese invasion only the Gelukpa ('Yellow

Hat') sect, to which the Dalai Lama belonged, had its representatives in Lhasa, and they had the biggest say in government affairs. However, as they formed one of the components of the Buddhist Holy Trinity, monks of other sects were highly respected and enjoyed considerable secular power, but only in local matters, and not in national affairs.

Of the four major sects, Sakyapa is the second oldest, commanding numerous followers all over Tibet. The others are Nyingmapa, Kargyudpa and Gelukpa. Sakyapa has great affinities with Nyingmapa, the oldest sect, which forms its basis. The head of Sakyapa has always been a tantric practitioner, like the Nyingmapa lamas. This means that he is allowed to marry and keep his plait of hair. A true follower of tantric doctrine is believed to be a voluntary impotent, for he does not discharge semen. However, if he feels it necessary to have a successor, he invites the soul of a dead holy person to enter into the womb of his wife. In former times the Sakya Lamas sent too many such invitations, which led to the division of the 'Celestial Family' into two parts. Later on, quarrelsome rifts generated by their ignorant staff created an unhappy relationship between the two divided families. The present unfortunate reigning lama (Sakya Trichen) is from the House of Dolma Phodrang; he is now in Mussoorie, India. Two other lamas from the House of Phuntsog Phodrang now work in Washington, USA. Unlike the Dalai Lama, the Sakya Lama's priesthood is hereditary.

The Celestial Family claimed its origin from the gods. Yuring, the elder son of Lharik (which literally means 'the race of gods'), descended to this world. Of Yuring's seven sons, the youngest, Masang, remained on earth and his grandson, Yangpang Kye, became the father of the Sakya Lamas. He was believed to have killed the body of a wicked man and thus saved his soul from eternal damnation. Then he married his wife, Silima. Since then the celestial line was popularly known as Khonrik, meaning 'those from out of a conflict' between man and gods. But the Sakyapa sect was not begun immediately after this. About thirteen Lamas of Sakya followed the Nyingma sect, the oldest and the then only religious order in Tibet.

Some scholars claim that Indian *tantra* was developed from the pre-Buddhist native religion of Tibet, Bon, which survived in Eastern Tibet until 1950. On the other hand, the Tibetans believe that their *tantryana* was exported from India. Pandit Gaya Dara from Nepal, on three consecutive missions to Tibet, taught Shakya Yeshi a new type of *tantryana*. Yeshi in turn imparted his newly acquired knowledge to Khon Konchok Gyalpo (AD 1034-1102), the fourteenth Sakya Lama. The High Lama compiled these esoteric teachings of the Buddha into a famous volume called *Lam-des* ('The Path and the Result'). *Lam-des* became the first bible for the monks of the Sakyapa sect. Since then it has been the sacred duty of every High Lama to interpret *Lam-des* to all his followers. When I was a child *Lam-des* meant a colossal congregation of monks. Monks, particularly the novices from Sakya Monastery whose branches were scattered almost all over Tibet, swarmed into our town. No monk was qualified to call himself a Sakyapa until he had heard the Sakya Kyap-Gon ('Lord of Refuge') reading *Lam-des*. A monk (*drapa*) owes his most reverential allegiance to the Kyap-gon who initiated him to *Lam-des*.

Three more sectarian volumes were mysteriously passed down by Sakya Kunga Nyingpo (AD 1092-1158), the son of Konchok Gyalpo. The Sakyapa scriptures state that Kunga Nyingpo retreated into meditation when he was twelve. Reciting a *mantra* of Manjusri, the God of Knowledge, he instinctively received his first set of knowledge, *Shenpa Shidel*. His second spiritual discovery was *Maha-kala*, consisting of three separate teachings. Bari, known as the Translator, is believed to have found the first of these three teachings on Mount Maha in India, and he presented it to Nyingpo. The second teaching was offered to him by his tutor, Shangton Choeber, who found it in the heart of a great Indian yogi during his cremation. The last, considered the most profound tantric knowledge in thirteen books, was presented to the Kunga Nyingpo by Maloo-lodo Dakpa. The authors of these sacred books of Sakya are anonymous. Contemporary Tibetans no doubt preferred mysticism to enlightenment, confusion to clarity. The mystic origin of these books made the sect appear more extraordinary and apostolic.

Two jealous lamas made an abortive attempt to murder Kunga Nyingpo, but he died a natural death. He was succeeded by four sons, two of whom became scholars of repute – Dakpa Gyaltsen and Sonam Tsemo. Gyaltsen received from his holy father a mystic knowledge symbolically called 'the Eight-petalled Lotus'. Each petal symbolized a teaching, and the whole lotus symbolized the Void, the essence and end of Mahayana Buddhism. Although his birth was associated with heavenly signs of greatness, he did not make any fresh scriptural contribution towards the sect. Religious lore says that after he was born he sat in a meditative posture saying: 'I am born in Salvation.'

One of the greatest Tibetan saint-scholars was Kunga Gyaltsen, popularly known as Sakya Pandita (1181-1251). He studied at the feet of his uncle Dakpa Gyaltsen and knew Sanskrit instinctively – an intellectual attribute which means a born genius. His knowledge of the tantric and *sutra* aspects of Mahayana Buddhism became legendary throughout Central Asia. According to Sakyapa writings, he was the only Tibetan who accepted a challenge from an Indian Brahmin to debate and discuss the two aspects of Buddhism. Sakya Pandita won. There is no other philosopher in Tibet whose works have aroused such secular and monastic attention. His best known work is *Sakya Lekshe*, a happy mixture of ethics, morals and civics for everyone. When I was in Sakya, I saw many a wise man settling petty disputes or family quarrels by quoting a line or two from *Sakya Lekshe*. When he began: 'As Sakya Pandita said,' his clients and their opponents bowed their heads in surrender. Such was Sakya Pandita's benign impact on Tibetan life.

Since the Sakya Lamas were the first priest-rulers of Tibet who established a working relationship with China, this is the right place to consider the rights and wrongs of China's suzerainty over Tibet. Tibetans lived in a world of their own, and this self-imposed isolation was undoubtedly one of the biggest factors contributing to our tragedy. Tibet was too inno- cent. When I read Heinrich Harrer's *Seven Years in Tibet* at school, I found to my sadness that not one person in the whole of Tibet could repudiate the Chinese claim over Tibet in 1949. The international legal status of our country was at the mercy of the big powers. We had neither the knowledge nor the desire to squabble over legal and political semantics. But if anybody threatened the land of snow, the Tibetans reluctantly took up arms. All we wanted was peace in both senses: we had no desire for war, and we wanted to be left alone. As I study Tibetan history, I feel proud of the Tibetan desire for self-determination. It is the history of an undaunted struggle to maintain Tibet's independence against the intrigues and invasions of China, and to a lesser extent of Britain, Russia and Nepal.

The first recorded event in Sino-Tibetan relations took place around AD 635. The thirty-third Tibetan king, Songtsen Gampo, married a Chinese princess, Wencheng, and then a Nepalese princess, besides his three Tibetan wives. When I was at the Chinese school in Sakya, the Chinese teacher would say, patro- nisingly: 'Ever since Princess Wencheng married Songtsen Gampo, the Chinese and Tibetans have been blood relations.' In one way it was an example of an equal if not weaker sovereign offering his daughter to a stronger one, as Tibet was militarily superior to China at the time. However, Gampo's was not a politically motivated marriage. The Tibetan chronicles emphat- ically state that the king married two foreign princesses in order to get the two most venerable images of Buddha for Tibet.

At the beginning of the eighth century, the Tibetan king

Tridhi Tsukten repelled the invading Chinese from Lhasa and conquered several provinces of China. Seeing his capital in danger, the emperor agreed to pay tribute to Tibet. When the emperor's successor failed to pay the tribute, Tibetan troops captured Chang'an, the then Chinese capital, in AD 763.

Ralpachen, the fortieth king and the greatest conqueror in Tibetan history, invaded Western China at the beginning of the ninth century. However, this time Chinese monks and Tibetan lamas mediated to bring peace. Khung Khu Meru (Lake Koko Nor) was declared the Sino-Tibetan border in the east, and the boundary was marked by stone pillars, erected in AD 821. Similar pillars were erected in front of the Imperial Palace in Chang'an and the Potala Palace in Lhasa. Mutual pledges were inscribed on these pillars both in Chinese and Tibetan stating that neither China nor Tibet should trespass the newly defined borderline.

Contemporary chronicles described King Ralpachen's expanded kingdom in poetic terms: 'Zhulongshen Mountain like a curtain of white silk was the (eastern) frontier with the Chinese King of Astrology; an iron pillar near the River Ganga was the (southern) frontier with the Indian King of Dharma; the gate of Pata Shadung was the (western) frontier with the Persian King of Wealth; and the ridge of sand resembling the back of Nyamangma was the (northern) frontier with the King of Beta'. That Tibet was a great military power in Central Asia from the seventh to the ninth centuries is an indisputable historical fact.

To understand the next phase of Sino-Tibetan relations, one must be aware of the tremendous impact of lamaism in every sphere of life in Tibet. Lamaism killed the fine militant spirit of Tibetans, and Tibet as a great military nation was gone for ever. This change from the conquest of other nations to the conquest of the human mind was extremely sudden. The religious Tibetan will pray earnestly: 'May I be born in the land of Buddhism, Holy Tibet' – an attitude that indicates the spiritual height to which Tibet had been elevated. Mahayana Buddhism had been safely uprooted from its birthplace, India, and transplanted miraculously well to the alien cultural climate of Tibet. There it flourished. Scores of pandits from India and Nepal spent their lives in Tibet, helping the Tibetan lamas to translate Buddhist scriptures from Sanskrit into Tibetan; Tibetans studied Buddhism in India and returned home to transmit their knowledge. Tibet had certain rare Buddhist scriptures which are not available even in Sanskrit. It is little wonder that Tibet came to be regarded as an 'abode of Buddhism', and that the Sakya Lamas, and subsequently the Dalai Lamas, were thought to be *Bodhisattvas*.

Political conditions before the Sakya Lamas gained supremacy in Tibet must be briefly stated. Lang Dharma was the forty-first King of Tibet. A fanatical follower of Bon, he destroyed monasteries, persecuted monks, and in short tried by every means to exterminate Buddhism, till he was assassinated. After his assassination Tibet disintegrated into petty principalities, both lay and monastic, and remained divided for more than three centuries. There was no Chinese interference during this period, though Tibetans near the Chinese border naturally had unofficial trade relations. This long period might have provided an excellent opportunity for the Chinese emperors to exploit the fluid political situation in disunited Tibet, but they left the opportunity to Chingghis Khan.

At the end of this period, in the early thirteenth century, the Chinese emperor Guizheng invited the Sakya Pandita to his court. Through his tantric miracles and immense learning, the Pandita converted the emperor to Lamaism, and became his personal Lord of Refuge. Assisted by a Chinese team, the Pandita translated a number of Buddhist texts from Sanskrit and Tibetan into Chinese, including *Lam-des*, the bible of the Sakya sect. Throughout his life he held the Buddhist world in Central Asia under his intellectual sway, and his fame enabled his nephew Phagpa to become the first priest-ruler (*Tisri*) of Tibet.

Like his uncle, Phagpa was a great scholar and mystic. After the Pandit's death in 1251, he succeeded as the national mentor at the Imperial Court. When the Mongol Kublai Khan over-threw the Song Dynasty, he adapted the Tibetan script to the Mongolian language, translated Buddhist scriptures into Mongolian, and promoted lamaism among the Mongols. Kublai Khan himself became a confirmed lamaist. Phagpa died in 1280, and the title 'Tisri' passed to another member of his family. Unlike the office of Dalai Lama, the Sakya lamahood was hered-itary. Twenty-eight such lamas in succession ruled over Tibet. They appointed their own subordinates without the imperial consent. They established their own government, functioning quite independently in Sakya. During their reign a number of Indian pandits visited Tibet, and Tibet's cultural relations with India became stronger than those with China. However, the tradition of sending a brother or son of the reigning Sakya Lama to China as China's national mentor continued throughout the Sakya era. China did not intervene in any way when in 1358 the twenty-eighth Sakya ruler was dethroned by the monk Changchub Gyaltsen, whose line ruled Tibet until 1435. Then there was another struggle for supremacy. Four kings of the Ringpong dynasty ruled in succession from 1435 to 1565, fol-lowed by three Tsangpa kings between 1566 and 1642. Within a short span of less than three centuries there had been three major struggles for supremacy in Tibet, all among the Tibetans themselves. The emperors at Beijing did not intervene in these political struggles, because Tibet was not part of their domain.

In an otherwise almost static society, the only dynamism came from the Tibetan religious sects. These sects, founded by the best brains in the country, were responsible for every great movement in our cultural history. In the fourteenth century, yet another sect was founded by Tsong Khapa, the Luther of Tibet. He reformed Tibetan Buddhism drastically, and established a new school known as the Gelukpa or the 'Yellow Hats', to which I have referred already. (The Dalai and Panchen Lamas belong to this sect.) Tsong Khapa was the most famous lama reformer; and his sect was the most popular in Central Asia from the fourteenth century onwards. Thus, when Zhu Yuan-zhang overthrew the Mongolian dynasty in China in 1368, he went in search of the famed Tsong Khapa. The Buddhist emperors of China respected the high lamas of Tibet, and certainly did not use them as political puppets. This remained the case until the advent of Western political ideas in China, particularly those of Western imperialism, which had arrived by the eighteenth century. It is a tragic irony that from then on China inflicted on Tibet what she herself was suffering in the hands of the Western colonial powers – so, for instance, there were continued attempts by China to increase Tibet's military dependence on her. Thus, if we survey Central Asian history through Westernized twentieth-century eyes, it appears indeed that the emperors of China used the high lamas for their political ends. This reading, however, seems disastrously wrong. Tsong Khapa refused the imperial invitation on the ground that he was ill, though at the request of a later emperor, Chengzu, he sent one of his disciples to China. The new sect spread like wildfire in Mongolia. In 1578 Sonam Gyatso, the third 'pope' of the Yellow Hats, received the title 'Dalai Lama' from the Mongol ruler Altan Khan. 'Dalai' is Mongol for 'ocean', and refers to the extent of Sonam Gyatso's knowledge. The Khan became a dedicated follower of the Yellow Hats, and his subjects readily followed his example. With the help of the Mongols, in the 1640s the Vth Dalai Lama established supremacy over the other sects; and so the Dalai Lamas ruled Tibet until 1950.

In 1652, the first Manchu emperor of China invited the Vth Dalai Lama to Beijing as an independent sovereign. The honour and the ceremonial reception given him were unparalleled in Chinese history. This tradition was maintained until the Chinese Empire fell. Sir Charles Bell described the XIIIth Dalai Lama's reception at Beijing in 1902: 'The Emperor met him one day's journey from the capital. Arrangements were made by which the Dalai Lama passed over the city walls instead of under, for the city walls carry traffic, and it is unfitting that any should pass over His Highness's head. When receiving the Dalai Lama in the Imperial Palace, the Emperor came down from his throne and advanced eighteen yards to meet him, a point of etiquette that will be appreciated by all who have lived in Eastern countries.' Here was the emperor of a colossal cultural empire bowing before the Dalai Lama of tiny Tibet. The reason is simple: the Dalai Lamas were the personal gurus of the Chinese emperors. China sought spiritual guidance from Tibet, and Tibet sought patrons for her lamaism from China.

The VIth Dalai Lama, Tsangyang Gyatso, was a romantic figure. He spent his youth composing erotic verses, drinking and womanizing, instead of devoting himself to the study and practice of Buddhism. His outrageous and staggering misbehaviour made the Tibetans and Mongols suspicious of his reincarnation. In 1706, the Chinese and Mongols murdered the young Dalai Lama, and installed a 25-year-old lama as the true reincarnation. The Tibetans refused to recognize him, and discovered a new incarnation in Lithang, Eastern Tibet. The Mongols seconded the Tibetan choice.

Fearing a Mongol-Tibetan alliance, the Emperor Kangxi dispatched an army in 1718, but the Tibetans and Mongols defeated the Chinese troops. Hence the Tibetan nominee was enthroned as the VIth Dalai Lama, disallowing Tsangyang Gyatso's tenure of office. However, Tsangyang Gyatso has now been reinstated as the VIth Dalai Lama, and his successor is known as the seventh. The imperial troops remained in Tibet until 1723, when the new Emperor Yong Cheng ordered their evacuation and handed back territory annexed by China during the crisis over the VIth Dalai Lama. The Chinese left behind two *ambans* (resident representatives of the emperor with a small military escort), posted in Lhasa.

In 1791 the Gurkhas of Nepal invaded Tibet and captured Shigatse. They were, however, defeated the following year by a

combined Chinese-Tibetan army. The victory pillar erected by
the Chinese in Lhasa states that the troops were composed of
men from Solong, a district in the Tibetan province of Gyarong.

After the defeat of the Gurkhas, the Chinese *ambans* naturally got a stronger grip on the Tibetan administration. *Ambans*
were posted at Shigatse, Tingri, Chamdo and Traya, and the
Tibetan officials, both lay and ecclesiastical, were ordered to
submit all vital decisions to them. The Dalai Lamas were highly
respected, once they reached maturity; between 1804 and 1876,
four of them (the IXth, Xth, XIth and XIIth) died at the ages of
nine, twenty-one, eighteen and nineteen respectively. It is possible that the *ambans* had a hand in these premature deaths, for
they could impose their authority on a regent more easily than
on a Dalai Lama. The Chinese Resident was also to assist in the
selection of the Dalai and Panchen Lamas, and an imperial
order was issued on the procedure of selecting high incarnates.
The *ambans* exercised active power from 1720 to about 1840, and
thereafter their power was nominal.

When the Limbu tribes of Nepal invaded Tibet, China did
not help the Tibetans to expel them; nor did she help when a
Sikh force of 5,000 under Zorawar Singh invaded Western Tibet
in 1841. Tibetan troops alone expelled both the invaders. In
1855, Nepalese forces invaded for the second time, under the
pretext that their subjects were ill-treated. The Nepalese were
victorious, and a treaty was signed by which Nepal gained extra
territorial rights in Tibet. Why China did not come to Tibet's
assistance seems clear: China and Tibet had made no military
pact. In 1863 the Chinese invaded Gyarong in Eastern Tibet and
annexed it to China.

In 1890, the British Government in India wanted to establish
trade relations with Tibet, but they were uncertain whether to
approach China or Tibet. Knowing that the Chinese authority
extended during the eighteenth century in Tibet, the British
contacted China, and in 1893 signed a convention with her,
without Tibet's knowledge. But when Britain applied for her

concessions, the Tibetan Government rejected the convention, and the British came to realize how little influence the Chinese had over Tibet in actual practice. Lord Curzon, who became Viceroy of India in 1899, was compelled to regard Chinese control over Tibet as a 'constitutional fiction – a political affection which has only been maintained because of its convenience to both parties'.

In 1904, Lord Curzon despatched a military mission under Colonel Francis Younghusband to impose a trade agreement. The Tibetan troops were defeated, and the Dalai Lama's Regent signed a convention with the British in Lhasa. Seals of the Dalai Lama, the Kashag (Ministerial Council), the National Assembly and of the three big monasteries were stamped on the Agreement, but the Chinese were not signatories.

The British military expedition and the subsequent convention made the Chinese realize that their power in Tibet had disappeared. So in 1910 China invaded Tibet, and the Dalai Lama fled to India. But Chinese control was short-lived; in China revolution broke out, and in 1912, the Tibetans drove the remaining Chinese forces out of Tibet. 'With that', writes the Dalai Lama, 'Tibet became completely independent, and from 1912 until the Chinese invasion in 1950 neither the Chinese nor any other State had any power whatever in Tibet.'

The International Commission of Jurists' report to the United Nations, *The Question of Tibet and the Rule of Law*, sums up conclusively: 'Tibet's position on the expulsion of the Chinese in 1912 can fairly be described as one of *de facto* independence and there are, as explained, strong legal grounds for thinking that any form of legal subservience to China had vanished. It is therefore submitted that the events of 1911-12 made the re-emergence of Tibet as a fully sovereign State independent in fact as well as in law of Chinese control.'

Even more than international law and Tibetan history, it is the Tibetan people who convince me that Tibet belongs to them. My parents, my relatives, my family friends and acquaintances

owed their entire allegiance, both political and spiritual, to the
Dalai Lama. Some of them vaguely knew also that the Dalai
Lamas in ancient times were the spiritual guides of the Chinese
emperors, who venerated them as any devout disciple vener-
ates his guru. When I tried to explain to Mother that the Chinese
claimed sovereignity over Tibet, she snapped with her practical
common sense and simplicity: 'And you believe the Chinese?
They tell lies with greater conviction than we honest people do
when we speak the truth.' Then I asked her what difference it
would have made to the ordinary Tibetans whether Tibet was
ruled by the aristocrats and lamas, or by the Chinese. She
answered: 'Tibetan rulers were bad, but the Chinese are worse.
Think back to when you were a little boy. When I pinched your
bottom hard when you were naughty, you cried a little and
stopped; but when others, especially outsiders, hit you a little,
you cried aloud and wept as if your parents were dead. Yes, the
Chinese are Chinese and the Tibetans are Tibetans.'

For 38 years Tibet enjoyed *de facto* independence. She took
no part in the Sino-Japanese War, refused permission to transport war supplies from India to China through Tibet during the
Second World War, and participated in the conference of Asian
countries held in Delhi. In 1948, she sent an official trade delegation with Tibetan passports which were recognized by India,
China, France, Italy, Britain and the USA. But most of these
steps – particularly those initiated by the Tibetan government
itself – were last-minute desperate efforts to establish international relations, and were thus too late. Surely, 38 years was
ample time for Tibet to make herself independent *de jure* as well
as *de facto*. This was a golden opportunity that Tibet missed.
Between 1912 and 1950 the Western powers were preoccupied
with the two great wars, and in China Mao and Chiang were
fighting for supremacy. Then who or what was to blame?

There were various causes: the fanaticism and ignorance of
the lamas; the irresponsible and pleasure-loving nature of the
aristocrats, and the utter simplicity and complete innocence of

the Tibetan masses. To offset this, the XIIIth Dalai Lama, who was in power from 1895 to 1933, was extremely progressive. He was forced to flee twice – once to China and once to India – and he learned much from his experiences. After the restoration of Tibet's independence in 1912, he made every possible effort to open up the country. But his small steps seemed giant strides to the unworldly Tibetans. When a plan was drawn up to build a road from the Indian border to Lhasa, via Phari, Gyantse and Shigatse, the people living along the proposed route appealed to the government for the immediate cancellation of the proposal. They contended that if vehicles replaced donkeys and mules, the *tralpas* would not be able to pay their taxes. The government could not do a thing. If this road had been built, it would have been a vital artery to the new Tibet.

The monks were no less ignorant. No sooner were the two English schools opened, one at Gyantse and the other at Lhasa, than they had to be closed down. Disguised as monk-scholars, Chinese and Russian spies used to stay at the Lhasa monasteries and spread the rumour that any Western influence (presumably Christianity) would be detrimental to the Buddhist *dharma*. Under their influence the Lhasa monks compelled the government to close these primary schools. The monks, obsessed with Buddhism, were unconscious of the fact that they were trying to preserve the status quo and perpetuate their privileged order. They sincerely believed that whatever they were doing was right and in the interest of lamaism – the Tibetan national aspiration.

Above all, the aristocrats, and specifically the government officials, were responsible for our tragedy. Indifferent to their duty, they indulged in petty political squabbles and loose living. It is said that, when the Amdo garrison fell to the invading Chinese army in 1950, an urgent message was sent to Lhasa. When the messenger arrived, he found that the officials concerned were playing mahjong, and he was told to wait until they had finished their game.

After the XIIIth Dalai Lama's death in 1933, there were years of ill-feeling between the monks of Sera Monastery and the Lhasa government, which ended in an armed clash. The Rinpoche (Abbot) of Reting Monastery was appointed as Regent. During his regency his monastic staff took the opportunity to make Reting Monastery rich and powerful, and it was rumoured that the Rinpoche wanted to continue his rule indefinitely. Finally, in 1947, his political antagonists put him under arrest, and he died under mysterious circumstances.

There was also a cold war between the progressive and the reactionary elements of the government. The reactionaries triumphed because they claimed to be the vanguard of lamaism. Tsepon Lungshar, the finance minister, led the 'Young Tibet Group' – a liberal democratic party. Lungshar, who had visited India and some European countries, including England, outlined some reform programmes with four or five of his colleagues in Lhasa. But this was leaked, and he was charged with treason; so his efforts to democratize Tibet fizzled out.

Another outstanding Tibetan tried to reform and save Tibet – the *geshé* Gyedun Choephal of Amdo. A brilliant Buddhist scholar in Tibetan and Sanskrit, he translated Sanskrit works into Tibetan, and wrote excellent treatises and an objective, readable history of Tibet, which he left incomplete while in prison. However, before his premature tragic death, he added a touching verse to his unfinished history:

Even though evidence is produced and truth proved,
Blinded are the eyes of malice and ignorance.
It is true that an envious man
Is angered by the greatness of others.

He had both political and intellectual antagonists; the latter were mostly monks. He visited Mongolia, Russia and India. He was accused of being a Russian spy, and consequently imprisoned. Later some of his writings on democratic reforms in Tibet were discovered. He was finally driven mad, and died in prison.

I do not say that Lungshar or Gyedun Choephal could have saved Tibet. However, I would assert that we Tibetans ourselves were responsible for our tragedy to a large extent. It would be unfair to condemn individual lamas, individual monasteries or individual aristocrats. The whole system was rotten to the core, and could not withstand twentieth-century pressures. It was ready to fall, and it fell disastrously.

FOUR

The Law's Delays

A FATHERLESS family is always vulnerable, and Mother was desperately anxious for us, especially my brother and myself to grow up. As a widow, ably looking after six children and at the same time carrying on a business, not to mention farming, she was a natural target for jealousy. In our tiny community, where everyone knew everyone else, there were always rival groups. The Tibetans sadly lack the virtue of forgiveness, and those who were able to forgive and forget were considered weak. Mother was constantly attacked on false charges and each time she was compelled to seek refuge in the law. Despite bribery and corruption, justice was restored each time. She fought two major cases and two minor ones – a record for a woman in Sakya, if not in the whole of Tibet.

Tibetan law was embodied in a book that used to be exclusively in the hands of a few aristocrats. Known as *Trim Yig Shelche Chusum*, meaning 'The Thirteen Decrees', it is believed to have been promulgated by King Songtsen Gampo in the seventh century. Originally it contained sixteen legal clauses, but in the seventeenth century three clauses were removed; these were two pronouncements on military strategy, and a special code of conduct for barbarians.

The Thirteen Decrees were accessible only to a few law-givers and officials, and were highly respected. Astonishingly, a book written in the seventh century could be deciphered without much difficulty in the twentieth, which shows how static Tibetan society had become. The revered book had never undergone any modification, apart from the removal of the three clauses. Although capital punishment was abolished by the XIIIth Dalai Lama, the book still includes vivid descriptions of primitive methods of mutilation.

The first clause expounds the duties of officials, who are advised to 'give up your own interests and take up the interest of others'. The clause proclaims the individual's right to follow his own sect. Different religious sects played vital political roles in shaping the destiny of Tibet, much as political parties have done in more secularly orientated countries, and this stipulation helped to preserve sectarian rights and check sectarian domination in particular periods of history. The power of a governor is clearly defined: he is authorized to collect taxes and donations as required for the government; but he has no power to grant land without consulting the central government, except during emergencies, such as floods or war. The decree warns the governor to see that his subordinates do not treat his subjects unjustly and cruelly. He is reminded that creditors are allowed to take only simple, not compound, interest.

The second clause deals with the holding of investigations, both the hearing and the trial. A fair hearing must be granted to all. The judge is first of all to examine the accuser's charges, and to ascertain that they are not trumped-up accusations. Only if both parties are intellectual equals (which must be assessed by the lawyers earlier) can they be heard and tried together before the legal commission; otherwise, accusation and defence must be heard separately. The Tibetan legal system, unlike the complex laws of today, sought to find the truth rather than to test the ingenuity of a hired lawyer, and put its trust in the integrity of the law officials. In a small society like Sakya, most people knew who was right and who was wrong even before the assizes opened. A wrong verdict meant the loss of the judge's reputation. 'Hot trial' (flogging during the hearing of a case) was resorted to when there was no other way of getting at the truth. As a lad I used to watch unfeelingly some criminal being whipped, while the two law officials would interrogate him during the intervals between the lashing sessions.

The third clause is on making arrests. A person is liable to arrest if he shows disrespect for the king, fights with weapons, robs or steals, rebels or spies, or if he violates the law in any other way. The murderer must be arrested and punished in public. The blacker the criminal the tighter the arrest, says the clause. The classification of crimes was based on the scheme of values prized and accepted by the Tibetan society, though a commoner might argue rationally that the life of a high lama is no more precious than his own.

The fourth clause places the black deeds in the order of descending seriousness: killing an incarnate lama, a high ecclesiastic, or a government official; stealing from the monastic or royal coffers; killing one's parents; desecrating holy objects; casting black tantric spells; arson and poisoning. Punishments for such crimes could be 'taking out of eyeballs, amputation of tongue or hand, throwing the criminal alive into water or from a precipice'. However, as the influence of Buddhism increased, capital punishment and mutilation decreased considerably, and finally the XIIIth Dalai Lama officially banned such un-Buddhist punishments. This clause was preserved because the Tibetans, like any cultured people, have a peculiar passion for the past, a respect bordering on veneration; the institutions established by the ancient mighty kings and the enlightened medieval lamas were not to be questioned. Another reason was that they believed that the spiritual world was progressively degenerating; hence past achievements could not be surpassed.

The fifth clause concerns fines, which were all defined in amounts of gold. Conversion from gold into currency used to be one of the most baffling jobs for the lawyer. These figures were rough guides only, and much was left to the lawyer's discretion and common sense. Mother recalls that most fines were imposed in terms of religious penances – three days of prostration before holy images in the temples, a thousand butter lamps, and so on.

The sixth clause lays down the powers of tax-collectors and travelling officials to prevent exploitation and curb their rapacity. Their privileges are legalized; and the *tralpas* are warned they may not provide the officials with more than the law accords them. The rights and privileges of officials on a journey are defined.

The seventh clause, like the third clause on making arrests, indicates the hierarchic order upon which society was built, grading indemnities for murder according to the social status of the person killed. A regicide might have to pay the same weight in gold as the assassinated king's body. The rate for the murder of a high lama, or nobleman next to the supreme ruler in the hierarchy, is 120 *sang;* for the lower nobility, between 20 and 60 *sang.* Six *sang* in each case are to be paid to the government. One fourth of the total life indemnity goes to the law officials for pens and ink, the rest to the family of the murdered person.

The eighth clause deals with injuries caused by abortive attempts to murder or kill. Injuries above the belt are fined more than those below it. An injury of about a 'finger square' is liable to three coins; the breaking of a bone of coin size, one *sho-gang.* Clothes and other articles stained with blood are to be replaced by the person causing the injury, who will also provide the injured party with six *khels* of *tsampa*, one *khel* of *chang*, and a leg and shoulder of mutton. Where the injury is accidental, the injured will receive the cost of medical treatment. Even the king has to pay the cost of medical treatment for anyone he has injured. The suspected murderer has to pay only one-third of the life indemnity. Anyone who shoots at a thief and kills him has to perform the customary death rituals.

The ninth clause describes some esoteric ways of settling insoluble cases, and is an amplification of part of the second clause. When the facts fail to come to light, when a case is beyond the lawyer's comprehension, or when evidence is lacking, the dispute is resolved by swearing, and by playing dice or picking out black and white pebbles from a bottle of water or boiled oil. A person is permitted to swear if he is respected for his integrity. Swearing is especially effective because of the Tibetans' profound belief in their faith.

The tenth clause deals with fines imposed on thieves and robbers. Those who steal from the royal coffin may be fined thousands of times the value stolen; from a monastic establishment, eighty times; from a commoner's house, eight to nine times. The stolen goods are to be returned intact in each case. If the thief does not confess when the evidence is against him, the government can impose extra fines.

The eleventh clause is devoted to divorce, which may involve not only a married couple but parents and children, and brothers and sisters in a closely-knit family. This decree is perhaps the most consulted clause of the Thirteen Decrees. If the husband is proved to be right he is awarded eighteen gold coins and a complete set of clothes. If, on the other hand, the wife is proved to be right, she is entitled to twelve gold coins and a daily wage of grain. (During Mother's time one such gold coin was valued at ten *sang*.) In addition, her dowry will be repaid. The sons of the marriage go with the father, the daughters with the mother. If the divorce involves division of the land, the sons will get the preference. The second type of divorce concerns the disintegration of an established family. When a son or daughter desires to live separately, a daughter gets a quarter of the amount given to a son. If one of them decides to become a monk or a nun, the family must provide him or her with provisions and clothing.

After eleven serious decrees, the twelfth, on adultery, comes as a relief. According to ancient codes, says the clause, such a person may be punished depending on three stages of sexual intimacy: first, wooing; second, the verge of sexual intercourse; third, the act of intercourse. Intercourse on one or two occasions may be condoned. If there have been more than 60 occasions, a fine of 60 *khels* of grain may be imposed on the adulterers. Some Western scholars have written that the husband has the right to cut off his unfaithful wife's nose or ear; one could question this sensational statement. Here is a rough rendering of the relevant passage in the book: 'Although it is decreed in some old law books formulated by the ancient kings that any of the limbs of the licentious may be amputated and he be banished, this is applicable only if a commoner commits adultery with the wife of a person of authority, ecclesiastical or governmental.' When a man seduces the wife of another he is required to pay the rightful husband three gold coins and one-fourth of the standard life indemnity. If a woman seduces the husband of another, she has to perform some social ceremonies; and the greater the social incompatibility the heavier the fines.

The thirteenth and final clause is a miscellaneous one. Nevertheless, it is important because it deals with ordinary human relations. The borrower of an animal is held responsible if the animal is lost or killed. He should also be held responsible if it dies within twelve hours from the time of its return, in which case he has to pay its total cost. An arsonist will be fined the value of the property burnt and will have other fines imposed at the lawyer's discretion. Turning from fire to water, Tibetan farmers found that the best way of harming their enemies was to flood their fields; it is the duty of the law officials, says the clause, to scrutinize such cases and ensure justice to the wronged.

The Thirteen Decrees end with advice to the custodians of the law: 'Remember that Kunchok-Sum is your eternal witness. Be careful of wily litigants and prejudiced mediators.'

The Decrees were formulated for Tibetans living at a certain period of history; nevertheless, as far as I can remember, the system sufficed even in the early 1950s. Tibet's self-sufficiency as a nation in every conceivable way never ceases to be a source of pride for me. She had her own scheme of values, her own institutions, and other marks of a highly sophisticated civilization. The Tibetans were so deeply entrenched in these values that they were unwilling to exchange them for anything better, and clung to the old at all costs. This is the heart of our national tragedy.

A discussion of Mother's legal experiences will demonstrate the Thirteen Decrees in action.

The Earth Bull Year (1949) was a time of unprecedented thefts in Sakya. A wealthy Nepalese tradesman was robbed; but the greatest shock to the peaceable citizens was the theft of some holy gold objects, stored in the Great Sakya Monastery. They shook their heads at such a sacrilegious, devilish deed, speculating about the thief's identity. Some nights my family could not sleep; they could hear an occasional gunshot from the wealthy houses, and the victims' desperate, hoarse cries for help. My mother used to watch from our housetop, excited, frightened, and wondering what would happen if the thieves came to our house. We had no man to protect us. Mother was told that she should hire some strong men to guard our house. She shrugged her shoulders and said: 'What can they steal from us? There are many rich houses for them to rob.' But they came nevertheless.

One dark, moonless night, Mother, who was an extremely light sleeper, heard the hinge of our yard door creaking as if blown by the wind. A few minutes later the door slammed and someone dashed out, his footsteps echoing in the stillness of the night. The sound travelled westward, said Mother. Next morning two lengths of cotton cloth were missing from the leather storage bag. Mother consoled herself with the practical Tibetan aphorism: 'Robbery should not occur. If, however, it takes place, the robbers should not be found out.' So she wisely kept the matter concealed, except from our relatives and friends.

However, soon our theft was the topic of Sakya gossip, discussed by loafers in the sleepy market, by labourers in the fields and even by the aristocratic intelligentsia. Evidence accumulated, much against Mother's inclination. The suspect was a respectable-looking carpenter who had distinguished himself in a recent repair at the Sakya monastery. He wore a big golden earring, a mark of prosperity. The evidence, casually collected, might not have appeared as valid and conclusive to a modern lawyer as it did to the Tibetans; but it was strong enough to warrant the carpenter's arrest. First, Mother knew that the thief ran towards the west, and the suspect lived in our neighbourhood, due west of our house. Secondly, the suspect's wife came early in the morning after the theft allegedly to buy a matchbox, but actually to check on our reaction to the theft. But the most valid evidence was the fact that a fortnight after the theft the suspect was found tailoring a huge white tent. Mother was able to get a piece of the cloth, which proved to be identical with our own. Added to all this, it was rumoured that the carpenter was connected with the infamous theft from the monastery – a rumour supported by the fact that he had worked there.

Mother had not intended to go to the law, and she regretted the persistent rumour. The government officials observed their usual silence and autocratic aloofness; except in murder cases they did not condescend to investigate unless petitioned. Faced with such strident accusations, the thief could not cope with his guilty conscience any longer. He had the temerity to call Mother to his residence, protested loudly against the rumour which injured his reputation, and threatened her with a lawsuit. In reply she admitted the loss of her two lengths of cloth, but denied any share in the rumour, and told him to go to court if he so desired. He then sued us.

I still have the utmost admiration for Mother's courage in pursuing any course she took up to the very end, and for the way in which she faced bullying and malicious attacks while we children were still too young to be of any help to her. She would say: 'I can put up with being robbed, but the robber can't live with his deed.' She often railed against the fact that, being a woman, she was bullied by the stronger sex. The Tibetans tended to ride roughshod over widows and women in general,

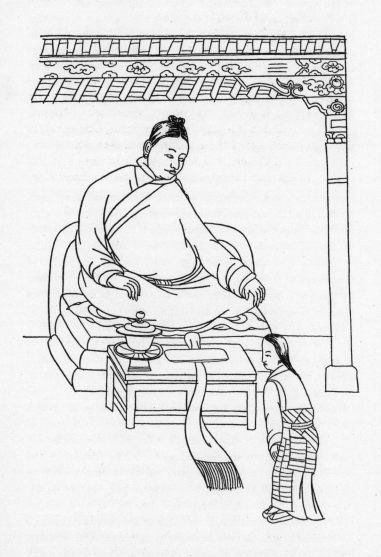

as happens in any patriarchal society. The weak government further encouraged this state of affairs.

Tibetan judicial procedure was peculiar to itself. Since the government was not departmentalized, there was no separate court as such. Judicial power was invested in the ill-organized government; though in recent times a separate court had been established in Lhasa. But in Sakya, as in other places, there was no separate judicial body. Thus when Cheme, the suspect, presented his petition to the Sakya local government, the governor appointed two senior officials (*donnye*) to investigate the case. These legal commissioners acted as judge and jury all in one. After the initial summons each disputant had to report separately to the Commissioners. With a great sense of pride and an air of wisdom, Mother used to describe the legal world's ceremonies, complexities and intrigues. The first presentation before the law officials is very important, she told us. You enter the court with bowed head, firmly yet not arrogantly – a faltering step would indicate your lack of confidence. Placing a *khadar* (white ceremonial scarf) before His Honour, you retreat a few steps, and with bowed head and bended knees unfold your case in the most honorific language. Your original statements must neither be altered nor added to. You must not contradict yourself, and must always substantiate your initial statements.

The law officials were not supposed to accept bribes, though in actual practice bribes were the only way of achieving results. Nearly every week Mother, with bribe in hand, had to go to each of the two officials. Mother recalls that one of the judges was 'an impartial holy man', but that his colleague had a 'big stomach' for bribes. If she offered three balls of butter or a basin of sugar, this second judge would reply: 'I shall speed up your case, and the matter will soon be in black and white.' When she bribed him with a 100 *sang* note, he would solemnly intone; 'You need not worry too much, as the evidence is increasingly guaranteeing your victory.' He would then add: 'I am sure you will win the case, but it is a matter of time.' Indeed it was a matter of time. The officials would unnecessarily prolong a case until they were satisfied with the bribes offered.

But when Mother took only a small bribe she would return home highly disappointed. The judge threatened her with a public whipping because she was hiding the truth. He would say: 'Woman, your accuser has made fresh charges which are all supported by clear evidence. You had better confess before it is too late. Otherwise we will lock you up in a cell and whip you until the truth is wrung from your crying mouth.' And with pretended indignation he would throw her humble offerings back at her. 'This is not necessary,' he would say, meaning, 'this is not enough.'

Nevertheless, there were some impartial and conscientious law officials. In Mother's case, Tsedor, the more honest of the two judges, rejected money, but accepted little presents. He was primarily responsible for expediting the case and restoring justice. Tibetan lawyers had no substantial fixed fee; they were entitled to one-fourth of the fines imposed on the guilty, which was very little normally.

After months of individual and collective hearings, Cheme was arrested. He was also suspected of the theft at the monastery. Owing to the lack of evidence even after his arrest, he could not be conclusively pronounced guilty. As the case progressed, it became more and more complex. Eventually the robbery at the monastery overshadowed everything else, while ours became a secondary issue. Cheme would still not admit his guilt, although the evidence against him was overwhelming. Therefore the 'hot trial' (flogging and hearing simultaneously) became imperative. A date was fixed, but unfortunately the thief escaped just before the scheduled day. It was discovered that his wife had sent him a hacksaw concealed in a bag of *tsampa*, and he sawed through the bars. Before a month had gone, news reached Sakya that Cheme was in Shigatse. Yet the government at Sakya did not bother to bring him back, just as if he were in a foreign territory. At any rate, the complex case was resolved: the thief was self-convicted and Mother became the undeclared victor.

We children rejoiced at the outcome, but Mother regretted that the case could not reach its proper logical conclusion. The aftermath was unpleasant. My sister Donkar recalls how frightened she was in Shigatse, when she accompanied Mother on business trips, because Cheme was said to have told some Sakyans that it was there he would have his revenge on us. But despite her fears Mother enjoyed the admiration of many, and even used to boast a little of her success, throwing out a few legal phrases. Her faith in the law became greater, and she would reply to any possible bullying: 'This is not a jungle or a desert. We have an impartial law in our land, codified by a pious, just king, and maintained by an enlightened lama.' Because of her constant contact with people of all classes, she was a glib talker and knew the art of dealing with men.

As the brightest member of her family, she became the mentor of our large circle of relatives. Even Grandfather used to say of her, 'Akyi is the only man in our family.' One day our Aunt Nyima rushed into our house, with tears in her eyes, and poured out her grievances to Mother. During a recent village meeting, a villager named Wadhar refused to accept a drink of *chang* from her bowl. Her husband, our Uncle Lakchung, at once demanded an explanation. Wadhar's reason for his refusal was that Aunt Nyima's 'bone was impure', meaning that she was low-caste.

Although caste in Tibet was not nearly as rigid and inhuman as in India, it certainly existed. Butchers, hunters and especially blacksmiths, were known as 'impure bones' – a term applied to the occupations which the non-violent Buddhists considered the most sinful. According to an eminent Tibetan historian: 'Because butchers kill animals, blacksmiths make weapons and agricultural implements (tools for violence), and because hunters shoot wild animals, these people were origi-

nally considered bad in the theological sense.' As Buddhism
rapidly became the pivotal force of Tibetan society, 'bad' in the
religious sense became 'bad' in the social sense also; but the
three groups were not ostracized. The 'impure bones' could not
share a common cup with the rest of the community, they married within their small homogeneous group, and their sons
were not permitted to pursue a monastic career. Apart from
these three stipulations, the 'impure bones' participated fully in
religious, cultural and social life. Our family had several friends
from the impure class, and they were always invited to our
annual religious functions and social get-togethers. They
shared the same room, joked, conversed, sang and danced with
the rest. Nevertheless the stigma was felt, though borne stoically.

This was the social background to Aunt Nyima's problem.
Mother accepted the challenge, since the case concerned the
entire circle of our relatives, no matter how distant. Most of
them were within a radius of two or three days' journey on
horseback. Mother's first task was to trace her maternal ancestry – an easy task, since Tibetans kept close family ties. She was
pleased to find no loophole whatsoever. The head of a large cultured, rich house in the town of Shab joined in on Mother's side;
he was a man well known for his loquacity and glibness.
Wadhar also had a wealthy relative in the Shab area. The two
men were friends, and devised a mutually acceptable compromise, which saved both parties' finances and Wadhar's face.
Wadhar had no evidence to prove the impurity, and to avoid
legal complications he agreed to acknowledge that his accusation was false and to retract it in public. The ceremony took
place in front of the outer gate of the Great Sakya Monastery, in
the midst of a crowd of onlookers. Wadhar poured three cups of
chang and placed a snow-white *khadar* around Mother's neck,
saying in a subdued voice: 'I am sorry I wrongly accused your
family. I retract my scandalous statement made to Mr
Lakchung. Your bone is pure.'

Judging from Mother's two lawsuits, Tibetan law was just. Though a case might take time and money and cause anxiety, the verdict seldom went against the innocent. The temporary justices of the peace might unnecessarily prolong cases to extract the maximum amount of bribes. But even corrupt judges knew that ultimately they had to restore justice, and that they must heed public opinion if they were to retain their reputation.

However, this same just law did not apply to the two foreign communities in Tibet, the Nepalese and the Kashmiri Muslims. During a religious festival a Nepali killed a Tibetan in an open fight. As he was immune from the normal judicial procedure, he was arrested and taken to Shigatse, where there was a Nepalese trade agent. After three years of imprisonment, he returned to Sakya. Since the Nepalese were outside Tibetan jurisdiction, they often took the law into their own hands. There was a time when even the nobility feared them. When I was a small boy I spent weeks in terror of them, after I had fought with my best friend, Lakpa Tsering, the son of a wealthy Nepali tradesman, caught him by his earring and tore a hole in his earlobe. Knowing their communal strength, I was scared and even Mother was frightened, but mercifully they left us alone.

There are various theories about the arrival of the Nepalese in Tibet. Some came as skilled silver or goldsmiths, to make holy figures; some were petty traders; others were the remnants of the Gurkha expeditionary force of 1855. Having defeated the Tibetan army, the Gurkhas dictated a treaty granting extra territorial rights for Nepalese nationals resident in Tibet. These people, known as Khatsars, had become completely Tibetanized; the majority of them could not even speak Nepali, nor had they ever seen Nepal and its king. But because they enjoyed extraordinary privileges they preferred to owe their allegiance to distant Nepal. Mother's Khatsar contemporaries were all products of intermarriage. When a Tibetan man married a Khatsar woman, he acquired Nepali citizenship. The

Khatsars were all Buddhists and merchants by occupation. Tibetans had a low opinion of them, and would warn the inexperienced: 'Be careful of the two-headed Khatsars. They side with Nepal when it is victorious and with Tibet when it is victorious.' After the 1959 uprising at Lhasa, the Khatsars were given a choice between Chinese or Nepalese citizenship. Surprisingly, only four families in Sakya opted for Chinese citizenship.

The second foreign community in Tibet consisted of the Muslims. In Sakya there were no permanent Muslims, but many Muslim tradesmen used to visit Sakya annually during the Dochen festival. In Kalimpong I have met a few Tibetan Muslims known as Khache. They have impressed me with their love for Tibet; and even more with their remarkable ability to preserve their communal identity, and at the same time to absorb Tibetan social and cultural customs. The Khaches had close social relations with the aristocracy. In Tibet, Buddhists and Muslims lived peacefully together, with no religious conflict. The Khache mosque was built right inside the Buddhist consecrated area of Lhasa. There were Muslim schools where Urdu and Tibetan were taught and the *Koran* was studied. Khache Phalu, a Tibetan Muslim, is a great Tibetan literary figure, author of a widely read philosophical treatise based on the common ideals of Buddhism and Islam. Khaches wore Tibetan dress, spoke perfect Tibetan and ate Tibetan food. Some of their men married Tibetan women, who were invariably converted to the Muslim faith.

On the basis of their Kashmiri ancestry, the Tibetan Muslims considered themselves Indian nationals. In 1961, about fifteen hundred Tibetan Muslims were transferred from Lhasa, Shigatse and Tsethang to the hill stations of India. A Khache whom I met in Kalimpong – an old man with a long silvery beard – was full of nostalgic memories of heavenly Tibet. He told me: 'We can't be more free even in India than we were in Tibet. Our only obligation was that some of our elders would attend the New Year celebrations and do obeisance to the Dalai Lama. We owe him and his government immense gratitude. Son, you will never have the happiness and freedom that we enjoyed in Tibet.'

FIVE

Love and Marriage

IT WAS three years since Father's death – ample time to recover economically from the expense of the funeral rites, and also from the grief we felt. By this time Abu and Donkar were in their mid-teens. One summer evening, to our dismay and bewilderment, Mother announced that she would have to remarry. She explained that, unless she had a strong partner who could saddle, load and unload our donkeys, she could not possibly continue our petty trade. Remarriage was essential if we hoped to acquire greater social status and income. In short, she was to remarry for our sakes, to build a great future for us. Moreover, a fatherless family was often bullied. Who would protect a weak woman with a bunch of children?

I took this shocking news to heart, and felt that she was betraying us. A mixture of anger, envy and sadness possessed me. The reactions of Abu and my sisters were equally emotional. Abu and Donkar told me with grave concern that a stepfather would certainly give us a stepfatherly treatment, citing a number of examples already familiar to me. As a child who needed love more than milk, I was exceedingly selfish and felt jealous. Abu was old enough to foresee a possible danger to our inheritance, no matter how little wealth and money we possessed.

Consequently, they urged me to ask Mother to abandon the plan. They thought that Mother would pay no heed to them, but would take notice of my childish tears and cries. 'Mother,' I pleaded, 'have pity on us fatherless children. Have you forgotten the last words of Father?' Mother broke down and wept bitterly. 'You are all unfortunate children; you do not have a millet-grain of luck. You did not do any meritorious deeds in your last life to deserve your good father.'

Despite our unanimous protest she did not change her mind, for she sincerely felt that a stepfather was desirable and necessary. We continued to be resentful for several days. Tibetan family life lasts from the cradle to the grave; and we could not endure the anticipation of an unfriendly and mean outsider in our family.

Our new stepfather, Wangyal-la, arrived without any ceremony. To our pleasant surprise, he proved to be exceptionally loving to all of us. After his early retirement from the army he had been employed as a donkey driver by a large agrarian family in Samling, about six miles from Sakya. His character harmonized with Abu's. He was humble, unassuming and quiet, and his inexhaustible energy and love of work were great assets to our family. He showed no sign of favouritism even after the birth of our half-brother, Sonam Rinchen (later to be called Kesang Tenzing). But, unfortunately, Wangyal-la died within the year.

Among the Tibetans there was a popular belief that a mole on the face made a woman deadly to her husband, and made a man formidable to his enemies. As if to prove the truth of this, Mother, who had such a mole, lost her second husband. Wangyal-la had gone with Abu to Kalimpong on his first commercial trip, and returned home shivering from head to foot with malaria. Abu too looked completely washed out; they had faced almost insurmountable difficulties on the return journey. Wangyal-la never recovered from the fever; but we bore his death stoically enough.

Apart from Mother's fatal mole, another factor responsible for our stepfather's death was our protest against his coming, which created a bad omen. Mother's life was a constant struggle against gods and men, against nature and *karma*, to win a place in the world for her children. Yet whenever she tried to assert herself beyond the limited horizon of Sakya, fate knocked her down and she found herself once again where she began. Occasionally she would protest: 'O Kunchok-Sum, what have I done to deserve all this misery? Surely I am getting more than my fair share.' At other times, in a mood of self-condemnation, she would cry: 'I have sinned against the *Sangha*. I have bewitched a potential Buddha and I am suffering for it now.'

After this tragedy Mother, still undaunted, had yet another hope for a brighter future – through her growing children. Abu and Donkar were still too young and inexperienced to go to Shigatse or Kalimpong by themselves, but they were entrusted to the charge of one of our family friends and made several trips with him, so that trading was not discontinued. Mother kept an 'apronful' of goods in the open market, and supervised the farming and household work in the mornings and evenings. Four of us had been born within five years without any gap, and Mother, like a gardener waiting for his flowers to blossom, was impatiently looking forward to the day when we would be grown-up. Then we should be able to ease her burden and gradually carry it on our own shoulders.

Whenever she saw any of us passing, she made judicious use of her stick, followed by lengthy advice. She would say: 'I am a mother with a difference. Every mother gives birth to her child and brings it up for a while. Then her duty is finished. I have brought up seven of you with my own hands and without a father's help. For the sake of your future security and happiness I have fought against tremendous odds. You owe me a debt that no other children have ever owed their parents.'

Now that Abu and Donkar had almost reached their majority, she hoped to see the end of the worries faced by a widow. As far as work was concerned, Tibetan majority began at fifteen. 'A boy of fifteen knows how to settle disputes and do business' was the usual maxim although the opinion and views of the young were neither valued nor encouraged, because they had no beard or grey hair. But Mother's hopes were shattered once again. This time it was not actually disastrous, though Mother viewed it very seriously. It was the turn of Donkar, my elder sister, to trouble her and cause yet another nervous breakdown.

Donkar was one of the most interesting characters in our family. She was affable, though she lacked sensibility. She was very intelligent, and would have laughed at a student of economics having to learn the obvious things which she knew instinctively, like the theory of supply and demand. She was an adept business-woman, but our family did not benefit from this talent as much as it might have done. She was well known for her overwhelming generosity to her friends, both male and female. Thus, when she was put in charge of the goods in the open market, her profits went to her friends. Later on, Mother could not trust her own daughter. Donkar was incapable of keeping a secret. But her crude sense of humour, characteristically Tibetan, and her cheerful disposition solved many of our family problems. In a society where shyness and modesty were feminine virtues, and where diffidence paid dividends, Donkar was too frank and unconventional. She was one of the prettiest girls in Sakya, and must have broken the record for the number of her boyfriends.

In Tibet lovers were far more down-to-earth than Romeo and Juliet. Although married couples were extremely faithful, the unmarried, particularly the young people, enjoyed much premarital licence. It was Mother's constant regret that she did not heed the saying: 'Girls and garlic should be sold before their scent dies.' Being the eldest daughter, Donkar was badly needed at home to assist Mother in her struggle to bring us all up. Mother would persuade and threaten Donkar, trying to make her give up her lover Tengyal-la, the son of an aristocratic family. Because Donkar was pretty he loved her, but because she was from a comparatively poor family he would not marry her. Indeed, his parents would never have permitted him to do so.

Obstinately, Donkar continued with him. Mother was driven to threaten her with the letter of the law, which forbade a couple to marry if they were nearer in blood relations than seventh cousins. Such a nuptial crime had a frightful social stigma, and in primitive times those committing it were cased alive in leather and thrown into the river. Mother told Donkar a white lie: that Tengyal was a distant relation of ours. All the same, Donkar had two sweet sons by him. Her future seemed hopeless and her family disgraced, which upset Mother immensely. In the end she escaped to India, where she married a Khampa freedom fighter; even before she arrived there Tengyal had married another woman.

Donkar's disobedience and misbehaviour were all the more objectionable because she had taken no notice of Mother's advice. Though in the West the giver of advice tends to be treated with contempt, in Tibet advice was much sought after and valued tremendously. When they wrote to the lamas, Tibetans asked for nothing but blessings; when they wrote to their elders, they asked for nothing but advice. 'Please advise me, the ignorant' was a cliché, and advice was given abundantly and extravagantly. Of all pieces of advice, the one most often given was: 'Be obedient and respectful to your parents.' It is in this context that Mother's violent objections to Donkar's unseemly behaviour should be seen. Since parents usually knew the weakness and strength of their children, and also loved them, parental control was indispensable. Advice had a special relevance to youngsters in Tibetan society. We did not get our primary preparation for life in school, as is the case in a modern society. Our mentors were those who had experienced everything except death.

In retrospect, Mother's iron determination, undaunted courage and strength of mind impress me enormously. But because of her single-minded determination she would be on the verge of either a nervous breakdown or a heart attack during the crises that occurred throughout my childhood.

However, she used to recover from her mental wounds in time
to prevent any drastic impediments to our progress. The storm
over Donkar's affairs slowly cleared.

One bright autumn day, I was listening to Mother turning
her silver prayer wheel and murmuring her prayers. She was
obviously not concentrating, but was pondering something I
did not yet know about. Finally she said, with deliberation: 'The
duty of good parents is to prepare their children for the journey
through life. When I have finished with your and your brother's
marriage, my duty will be almost completed. Then I can die in
peace.' Mechanically operating her rosary and prayer wheel,
she continued: 'The duty of good children is to perform all the
funeral rites with due ceremony when their parents depart for
the heavenly fields.'

Abu was then about sixteen, and this was the first indication that Mother was busy planning for his wedding. Her
plans were sound and rational. My youngest sister, Dawa
Bhuti, had had a nasty fall from a cliff near our house. Her left
foot was badly injured and she became permanently crippled;
thus her matrimonial prospects were gloomy. Nor could she
work hard at home. Mother put her in a nunnery, and sent
Sonam Rinchen, my half-brother, to a monastery. Mother felt
that Abu and I might not get along with a half-brother.
Besides, the age difference between the two of us and him was
wide, and so a common marriage for all three of us, according
to the Tibetan practice whereby brothers shared the same wife,
would be extremely difficult. These were the superficial secular reasons. Mother also had a profound philosophical reason
for dedicating Sonam and Dawa to the monastic life. She had
never forgiven herself for her criminal sin of pulling down
Father, once a monk, to the laity. Therefore she resolved to
donate two of her children to the *Sangha*. Monks and nuns
were believed to add to their parents' store of good deeds,
which would determine their next life. Besides, this was a
good opportunity for Mother to assert one of the claims made

in the lawsuits. For only 'pure bones' could enter a monastery.

As well as preparing for the imminent wedding, Mother wanted to establish our sisters independently. According to strict social custom, a girl before getting married had to have three basic articles of jewellery – a head jewel, a necklace and a jewelled box. These were the signs of womanhood. Although the quantity was more or less fixed, the quality of jewels varied sharply from the aristocrats to the middle class and the poor. Despite her disobedience, Donkar received a decent set of jewels. They cost about 1000 *sang* – practically a fortune. To make her independent Mother got some land on lease for her.

My second eldest sister, Yangchung, was an asset to our family – a 'jewel in the house', in the graphic Tibetan phrase. Smallest of the sisters, she had a great fund of common sense and a tremendous capacity for steady hard work. She was our family treasurer, and was to assist Mother until the new generation took over the responsibility from the old. Then she would be married into a good family; already there had been numerous offers.

As was the custom, Mother made several sets of clothes in advance for us to wear when grown up. Measurement was of little consequence. Not only dress, but furniture, kitchen utensils and agricultural implements were accumulated and preserved for that big day, which death sometimes prevented one from reaching. A pound of rice might be saved for years because a greater need might arise in future. A cotton shirt was worn only once or twice a year, and for the rest of the year was kept safely in a trunk. Some Westerners feel that the East is spiritual and the West materialistic, and Tibet is placed in the 'spiritual' category. I, as a Tibetan, find that we Tibetans are more materialistic than the average Westerner, and certainly more so than the Indians. There are a number of wealthy Tibetans who wisely ran away before the 1959 revolt and who have comfortably settled in India. When I was studying in Dr Graham's Homes, at Kalimpong, one of them, a millionaire, approached the principal and asked for a free scholarship for his daughter because she was 'a poor refugee'. If you step into a Tibetan refugee's hut in India, and then visit an Indian peasant's home, you will find that the refugee has collected more property within a decade than the average Indian farmer over a generation.

By now Mother was ready to discharge her biggest duty, and Abu was consulted. The brothers' common wife had to suit him; as younger brother I was of secondary importance. But his response was not encouraging. With the family, Abu was reserved. I seldom saw him smile, and Mother found him as obstinate as a bull. However, he was industrious. Whenever he had a little leisure, I would see him at his *chapé* (scriptures), chanting like a lama. Mother loved to hear him reading aloud, and would proudly say: 'He will surely give me some happiness in the evening of my life.' He was religious as a lad. He used to challenge his monk friends in religious debates, and he knew more than some of them. At his birth the astrologer had recommended that he should become a monk.

It was a tragedy that he never had an opportunity to develop his mathematical abilities. At the age of twelve he accompanied Mother to Shigatse on a trading venture. There he mentally calculated the correct price of a tin of paper-covered sweets, giving the correct number of sweets and the price of each one. This was hailed as a great mathematical feat in the markets of Shigatse. Calculation was usually a prolonged business. 'Sit down comfortably, take off your hat and roll up your sleeves' was the prologue to it. But Abu did everything in his mind with astonishing speed and accuracy.

Away from home, however, Abu's shyness and reserve were transformed into affability and charm. He was obliging to his friends, helpful to strangers and kind to beggars. His fellow-tradesmen respected him for his integrity. Mother thinks that he did not feel very happy at home, and says that he took advantage of her, as Father was not there to control him.

Abu began to follow Donkar in the field of romance. Taking no notice of Mother's advice, he wrote love letters to his girlfriend; as she was illiterate, she got the young intelligentsia of Sakya to read them for her. They memorized the letters, reciting them by the river when they came to fetch water, or discussing Abu's metaphors and flowery phrases. In short, his love affair became an open secret. The Tibetan love letter had its own strict rules, and did not contain many professions of heartfelt emotion. It took the form of a love poem; each line began with a different letter of the alphabet in succession so that a glance at the left side of the poem showed the thirty letters of the Tibetan alphabet in correct order.

Autumn was the season for love-making in Sakya, because of the opportunities that harvesting provided. The young people looked forward to this season with feverish excitement. When the whole valley of Sakya became a stubble plain with the wind whistling among the half-cut stalks; when the kites flew in the cloudless blue skies; when the flocks of migrating birds travelled across the sky from north to south; when the contented farmer carried loads of grain to his granary – this was the season of romance. The crops were collected from the scattered fields and brought to a clean dry spot near the suburbs. The boys and girls looked after the crops that were being thrashed and slept among the sheaves at night. As soon as the moon rose, the open-air love-making began. From all sides came whistling and counter-whistling – the language of love, or rather of the game known as 'stripping from bed'. Groups of boys went hunting for sleeping girls, hauling them from their beds of dry stalks. The girl was often taken aback – or pretended to be. Sometimes she was literally raped. In spite of our rigid social system, young unmarried people enjoyed free love. Yet in Tibet you never saw youngsters walking hand in hand. They were practical, not romantic.

The girl Abu had chosen was the only daughter of a *chang* seller, noted for her licentiousness. Abu did not approve of

Mother's proposed bride, and eloped with the girl of his own choice to Shigatse. Later they returned to Sakya and lived with the girl's mother. Mother's hopes were dashed to the ground; her plans were shattered. It was outrageous and incredible. She thought it was sheer ingratitude, the worst breach of Tibetan ethics. I remember her saying: 'I never thought that *he* would ever leave me alone and go to the dogs.' Abu and she were estranged for about five years. But when they met in India after their escape, she forgot the past and forgave him.

Since Abu and Donkar were disobedient in the matrimonial field, I missed all the gorgeous ceremony of a Tibetan marriage at home. However, I had the opportunity of seeing my uncle being married when I was a little boy. It happened with this couple that the wife was two years older than the husband, but age was of little or no consequence. What mattered was social status, and astrological predictions for a successful union. Theirs was one of the wealthiest families in the village of Chokhor Lhunpo, and so my grandparents had no problem in finding a suitable wife for their son. As my uncle was somewhat deaf, and his face was slightly deformed, I do not think that he could ever himself have taken the initiative of asking a girl to marry him. This is one of the strengths of arranged marriages. In Tibet this form of marriage was generally successful. As might have happened with Abu and myself, two or three brothers managed with one wife; or sisters took the same husband, though this happened less often. As for the paternity of the children, a few resourceful wives could remember whose they were. The Tibetans did not bother to find out who the father was as long as it was one of the brothers. Usually the child called the eldest man 'Father' and the rest 'Uncle'.

Mother was the chief agent in this marriage. The climax of the deal came when Mother offered 'begging *chang*' to the would-be bride's parents, who lived in Lhatse. The negotiations were kept secret, and anyone revealing them would have been considered an enemy of both families. The bride's mother received an honourable sum for 'giving milk to her daughter'. Like a Western engagement, the proposed marriage could be called off if either party wished. During the wedding, it was customary for the bridegroom's family to ask the price of the girl's jewellery and compensate her family accordingly. But in most cases payment was not accepted.

Contrary to Western practice, marriage had no legal or religious aspects. However, since the Tibetans are luck-addicts, an animistic rite would be performed on the roof on the wedding morning. This was not Buddhism, but one of the survivals of Bon, the pre-Buddhist native religion of Tibet. The law intervened only in cases of divorce. A divorced wife with a son or sons to her credit was entitled to one-fourth of the common property. If she had a daughter, she was entitled to about one-sixth. If she was barren, she was entitled to demand an undefined amount for what was known as 'wages for day and night'.

The astrologers declared that Friday at sunrise was the most auspicious time for the bride to leave her house, and Tuesday noon the time for her to arrive at her new home. Both houses had to ensure that the acquisition and reception of the bride did not entail any bad luck. Although the distance between Lhatse and Chokhor Lhunpo was three days' journey on horseback, the marriage party did not hurry. The unsuspecting bride was told that she was going on a pilgrimage to Sakya. She believed this white lie, until she was formally told the truth in the first ceremony held in beautiful tents pitched five miles from her destination, where her party met the bridegroom's.

The marriage ceremony and banquet were designed to promote good luck and fortune, and so the bridesmaids or the best man were rarely the closest friends of the bride and groom. It was more important for both families to ensure that their members attending the ceremony fitted into the lucky scheme. For example, the bride's name was Tashi Bhuti, Tashi meaning 'good luck' and Bhuti 'bringer of sons'. Both her parents were alive, and her family was well-to-do. Hence everything was in harmony with the lucky scheme. Any breakages or bad language at the ceremony and the subsequent banquet would be considered a bad omen.

The wedding day was cold and cloudy, and snow was about to fall. It was a bad omen if the bridal road was blocked by snow, but if it fell when the bride was in her new home it was a good sign, and a cause for greater rejoicing. So the party had to reach Chokhor Lhunpo before the snow began to fall. Everyone at the house was frantically busy, and the bride's party hurried to avoid the snow, even if it meant disregarding the astrologer's appointed time for arrival. They arrived in the morning, when they should have come at noon; but nothing untoward happened, and after a while the snow fell.

I was at the attic window watching the welcome ceremony, and saw the scene at the gate when the party arrived. The bride, on a white mare, was supported by two smartly dressed men. She was crying aloud, and her words were, as far as I can remember: 'I am not going to live in this strange bad place.' She had come to a new world, where the inhabitants spoke a different dialect from her own, where different customs prevailed, and where a different lord ruled. I saw her dismounting and dancing wildly on the threshold (not in joy, but, as I learned later, in violent protest). My grandmother desperately tried to hand over a pot full of milk and butter to her new daughter – the symbol of occupation. The bride kicked it away. Next she thrust her feet against the threshold, while two men tried to push her in. Suddenly they grabbed her and threw her like a sheep into the courtyard. Then she was dragged into a small room, where eventually she fell asleep through exhaustion. Her behaviour was not understood as a bad omen. In fact, if she had not had real cause to cry, she would have been expected to shed some crocodile tears for the occasion. For a bride not to cry was abnormal, and hence a bad omen.

The banquet continued for a full week, and the whole wedding party, including the guests, slept in my grandparents' house. Two or three members of the family combined to sponsor each day's banquet, which lasted from sunrise to midnight. Tea and *chang* were more plentiful than rain during the monsoon. Everyone from the youngest to the oldest joined in the drinking. Pretty girls were at your service. Each day of food and drink ended with the presentation of gifts and ceremonial scarves to everyone.

On the fifth day of revelry the bride's parents entertained all the party and handed over the dowry with stiff formality. A huge yak-hair quilt, spread in the middle of the room, was greatly admired. The bride's father then took out each article of clothing, one by one, from a nearby trunk and showed it round the admiring guests, some of whom had been drinking. It took some time to exhibit five sets of clothes, each set containing seven articles. Finally he ended the suspense of the excited audience by showing the jewellery, which shone in the dim lighting. To the head ornament the bridegroom added a turquoise in its centre – the equivalent of an engagement ring. As was the tradition, the bridegroom's father stepped out and asked: 'Can you please state the total cost of her jewellery? We shall pay you.' The bride's father answered: 'It cost us 1000 *sang* but we shall not take a single small coin from you. But please be affectionate to our daughter. She has been brought up on meat and butter.' The father spoke with an emotion which he tried to conceal, while the bride and her mother wept loudly.

Two months passed, during which time the bride enjoyed leisure and the very best food. Then, one auspicious day, she and her husband went to Lhatse to 'get permission from her house deities to leave them for ever'. Though less elaborate than the wedding, there was a small ceremony at the bride's house, followed by merry-making. The husband carried a skin bag of *chang* and another of *tsampa*; the wife a basket of wool and spinning appliances. They took a solitary trip of about one mile towards the direction of their own house, had their packed lunch, and then returned to the bride's house. This was the Tibetans' nearest equivalent to a honeymoon.

SIX

Shangri-la is Shattered

ONE EVENING in 1952 we heard that Acho Dawa, the husband of our next-door neighbour Namgyal, had arrived home unexpectedly. A mercenary by profession, he had been away for three long years in Kham, in eastern Tibet. Usually he would send a verbal message or letter, through a fellow-soldier or a trader bound for Sakya, well in advance. His daughter Mingmar would announce to us: 'My father is coming next month. He will bring plenty of presents for me from Kham and Lhasa. I will share them with my friends, but I won't give anything to anyone else.' But this time his return was a complete surprise to his family as well as to his neighbours.

As soon as we heard of his arrival, Donkar was sent to offer him 'welcome *chang*'. Tibetan welcomes and farewells were more than a handshake and a few apt words. We welcomed a new arrival with a kettle of *chang* and another of tea, and sometimes with presents too. We bade farewell in the same manner, adding a ceremonial scarf as a good-luck token. Acho Dawa was accorded the usual full ceremony, no matter what unusual circumstances brought him back.

Rushing home in a fever of excitement and perturbation Donkar accidentally knocked the *chang* container against the door frame and broke it to pieces. It was a bad omen. 'Who's chasing our sex-mad daughter?' asked Mother, jokingly; but Donkar, paying no attention, said excitedly: 'Acho Dawa says that the Red Chinese are coming to our land! The enemies of the faith have come!' Mother replied: 'Good news seldom comes true, but bad news always does.' We were just about to eat our dinner and begin our daily prayers when Donkar brought this incredible news. Mother did not eat her usual amount; but we all declaimed our prayers more earnestly and loudly than usual. As I went to bed that night I was both afraid and longing to know more.

The next morning Acho Dawa was surrounded by an anxious, attentive crowd. He told us: 'The sun of bliss will set from the land of snows. Our dreaded enemies are already knocking at the frontiers of Kham. They are the foes of our faith, and have destroyed the monks and monasteries in China and Mongolia. They are bloodthirsty monsters; they eat human beings and any animal they can lay their hands on. They are devils incarnate.'

His audience was thunderstruck by the vehement manner in which he gave this astounding news. The destruction of holy monasteries and the slaughter of revered monks were unbelievable. If the Red Chinese exterminated what we worshipped and adored most in our life, then they must indeed be devils and evil spirits incarnate.

Such was the news from the East. A few adventurous merchants and terrified soldiers from Kham were the only source of our meagre information. Whenever our elders talked about the Red Chinese, I visualized them as being other than human, ready to swallow up the Buddhists. If I gave any trouble, my sisters would warn me: 'Keep quiet! The Red Chinese are coming!' From time to time other aspects of Communism trickled through to us. Our impoverished neighbour Namgyal would say jokingly: 'I hear that someone is coming to distribute wealth. Who knows whose best clothes we shall be wearing?'

We learned that Acho Dawa had fled from Amdo, on the Chinese border, where he was stationed. He belonged to Tibet's crack troops, the Gyantse Regiment. He and his company were guarding a strategic bridge. One evening the local inhabitants gave them too much to drink, and while the Tibetan troops were incapacitated the Red Army simply walked across the bridge with the greatest ease. Acho Dawa felt that some of the local inhabitants were Chinese spies and fifth columnists. When the Chinese Communists invaded Tibet, on 7 October 1950, a number of Khampas, particularly those living on or near the border, collaborated with them. In Kham generally the people were dissatisfied with the Lhasa administration; and the inhabitants of the border area had always enjoyed the opportunity of flirting with the Chinese. They paid very little tax either to the old China or to Tibet, but their spiritual allegiance to the Dalai Lama was absolute. Unfortunately, local and tribal interests took precedence over national concerns. It was not until about 1954 that the Khampas came to realize that the Chinese Communists were not liberators but oppressors, and started the revolt which spread from Kham to central and southern Tibet.

Acho Dawa did not give us any objective account of the invasion. Like any other nation, we Tibetans exaggerated our own insignificant little successes and played down the enemy's landslide victory. We were constantly boasting about the Tibetan army's strength, courage and tenacity. There were fantastic stories of how a certain captain, or some gallant Khampa warrior, was bullet-proof. The big guns, tanks mortars and hand grenades of the Red Chinese could not kill our soldiers. This belief was popular among the Khampas, and many an honest Khampa has since told me about the true incidents he witnessed. Donkar's present husband, who is a Khampa, even told me: 'If you have a profound belief in your lama, and wear his relic to protect yourself against weapons, you will never be injured, even when the bullets hit your heart. They will bounce back.'

As the world knows, the ill-organized, ill-equipped, inexperienced Tibetan army was a mockery when pitted against the modern, well-equipped, well-disciplined veteran guerillas of the Red Army. The exact strength of the Tibetans consisted of 8,500 rifles, 50 pieces of artillery, 250 mortars and 200 machine guns. The credit for such strength as we had should go to the XIIIth Dalai Lama, who was more politically realistic than his predecessors.

That year I saw more religious functions than usual. The Sakya Monastery performed several *magdogs* (rituals to prevent war), at which gigantic *tormas* and effigies were burnt. The Sakya Lama himself headed some of these rituals. Some were performed by order of the Central Government; others were voluntary. When *dharma* was in grave danger, the guardian gods were invoked to prevent, divert, or minimize the rising forces of evil. Each *magdog* pushed the imminent danger further away in the minds of the religious Tibetans, though the Red Army was rapidly advancing. The Tibetans believed right up to 1959 that they would be saved by the gods and the Precious Trinity. But, alas, victory is on the side of the big battalions; and the gods were fast asleep.

Apart from the official rituals, individual families also performed small-scale *magdogs*. Mother invited four monks to carry out the rites at our house. Afterwards they bemoaned the atheistic evil forces engulfing Tibet. They discussed the various prophecies, all of which pointed toward this inevitable invasion. One prophecy said: 'Ultimately, Tibet will be under China.' It foretold a bloody war in which 'corpses of men and carcasses of horses will be as high as mountains'. A whole cosmic changeover in Tibet was also forecast. A time would come, said one prophecy, when 'children will no longer respect their parents or pupils their teachers, and civil wars will ensue'. In short, the monks said that everything synchronized with the Red Chinese invasion. They complained that the government had not carried out the prescribed remedies properly; for example, the officials had not built a life-size image of the guru Rinpoche, which would have prevented the Chinese invasion. Because the government was led by the Gelukpa sect, they contended, the officials would not respect Rinpoche, who was the guru of the Nyingmapas.

There were many volumes of prophecies (*lungten*) in Tibet. Some were believed to have dropped from the skies, or found in remote places. Others were written by lamas who claimed that a god had dictated them. Many were said to have been destroyed by the officials, because certain prominent people mentioned in them were painted in black colours. It is said that Lang Dharma, the anti-Buddhist king of the ninth century, was also foretold. In recent times the government had discouraged the reading of *lungten,* since they filled the over-religious public with panic and despair.

As a further drawback, the dates mentioned were ambiguous. A *lungten* would not say that the Chinese would invade Tibet in 1950, but instead in the Year of the Iron Tiger. In every 60 years there would be another Iron Tiger year, and so the prophecy was applicable to every generation. Thus the prophecy-dominated public was in a perpetual state of despondency.

In one *lungten,* written in the middle of the ninth century, King Ralpachen asked the guru Rinpoche what would be the future of Buddhism in Tibet. The guru predicted the advent of Communism, almost in so many words: 'The subjects will rule the kingdom, the king will be made a commoner. A sacrilegious act will be considered a deed of heroism.'

The king asked the guru how long the *chorten* (pagoda) at Kathmandu, in Nepal, would last. (This *chorten* is symbolic of Buddhism in Central Asia, and it attracts thousands of Buddhist pilgrims.) The guru replied: 'When the Emperor of China is suddenly assassinated, when Tibet's monasteries become empty, and when the great lamas roam like street dogs, the great *chorten* will crack.' Recently this holy *chorten* caught fire and was partially damaged, so the prophecy has been largely fulfilled.

Thus, even before the Chinese invaded, the Tibetans knew something of what was coming. We had no news reporters or political commentators, but our lamas seemed to have seen into the future, and written predictions which, had they been heeded, might have helped us to escape the catastrophe. They had been persistently telling us that if we did not do enough good deeds, collective punishment was inevitable. Today most Tibetans consider our national disaster as a natural and logical outcome of our collective *karma*.

The Sakyans observed a number of bad omens in 1952. One night some seers claimed that they had heard wailing from the holy Ponto Hill. I myself saw one bad omen, which occurred in broad daylight. A wolf was found roaming on the ramparts of the Great Sakya Monastery. Along with other boys I joined our superstitious elders in chasing it and stoning it to death on the exposed river bed. A wolf was such a bad omen that the nonviolent Buddhists, who usually hesitated to disturb even a fly, did not spare it. The dead animal was stuffed with hay and hung outside a monastery. It was later claimed to be the supernatural harbinger of the Chinese.

March was usually stormy in Tibet, but in 1953 the storms were far more severe than ever before. The elements waged war against one another. One afternoon a violent whirlwind raged across the Sakya valley. Donkar banged the door shut before the storm could smash it, and spat as a symbolic expulsion of evil. After a little while ten strange-looking khaki-clad horsemen rode past in a line. They were certainly not Tibetans: they were Chinese.

Shangri-la was shattered. The sanctity of its *dharma*, its lyrical peace and its simple contentment were at stake. A whole cosmic change was in store. The old order, like an ancient, worm-eaten building ready to fall, felt the first quake of the advancing alien force.

On catching sight of the Chinese, Mother prayed: 'O Kunchok-Sum, do not let me live to see what was never seen before – the nine unseen evils.' Being a boy, I always wanted 'to see what was never seen before'. Moreover, Acho Dawa had told us that the Red Chinese liked young people. But I was scared because I had heard that they forcibly took children from their parents, and I dreaded the prospect of separation. I slipped out of the house, however, and went to have a closer look at the strangers.

Some labourers carrying manure met the Chinese near the Dolma Palace. The most effective ritual that the Tibetans could perform against the enemies of religion was *dogpa,* which consisted of clapping the hands and cursing simultaneously. So the labourers clapped their hands. The Chinese were plainly pleased. Parting their chapped lips, they smiled and joined in, clapping vigorously. We thought they were being craftily deceitful, but later we learnt that clapping was a way of welcoming and congratulating comrades. The Chinese were exhausted, but tried to be lively. Their faces were powdered with dust, their lips dry and cracked; they wore khaki uniforms with storm caps and carried machine-guns. When I saw those tired, neatly-dressed soldiers my image of the Red Chinese was transformed. They were fairer (or yellower) than the average Tibetan, neater, and of course much cleaner.

They dismounted at the Dolma Palace, and then it seemed to me that they went to get blessings from the Sakya Lama. In fact, of course, they were merely being diplomatic. They also met the *Zodpa* (governor) and his cabinet. The chief of the delegation surprised the naïve Tibetan officials with his knowledge of Tibetan history. He told them with courteous gestures how in the thirteenth century Phagpa had been appointed vice-regent by the Chinese emperor – referring to the past glory and greatness of Sakya, which appealed to the provincial vanity of the officials. This brief historical reference was adroitly linked with the present purpose of the Chinese. The chief comrade hoped that the local government of Sakya and His Holiness the Sakya Lama would take a leading role in making a new Tibet. The Chinese comrades had crossed mighty seas, waded enormous rivers, climbed high mountains and marched an unimaginably long distance to serve the Tibetans. The 'liberation of Tibet' was the self-appointed task of the People's Liberation Army. The American and British imperialists must be driven out of Tibet and Tibet must at last gladly join her Motherland.

He explained that the Chinese Communists were in Tibet solely to help her to stand on her feet. As soon as the Tibetans were able to supply their own needs and rule themselves, the Chinese comrades would return home. They were looking forward to that historic day. At the moment the Tibetans could not manufacture even a matchstick (he apologized for the example). While serving the Tibetans, the Chinese comrades would take 'neither a needle nor a thread' from Tibet. It was the duty of existing officials to 'leap forward' in order to lead the masses. They should be the vanguard of peaceful liberation, he concluded.

This was the official Chinese policy, constantly reiterated and amplified according to the speaker's intellectual capacity. For our part we asked ourselves, 'Liberate us from whom? From monastic domination, from an outmoded weak government, from feudal lords?' But to press the question seemed to be sheer ingratitude. We would much prefer a better next life to any transitory present happiness. However, the Chinese assertion that 'the American and British imperialists must be driven out' baffled us. The Sakyans, like the majority of Tibetans, had never seen a white foreigner in their life. An 'imperialist' was a word we had never heard. We wondered where in Tibet these oppressive Americans and British had been hiding all this time. The Dalai Lama stated that there were only six foreigners in Tibet at the time of the invasion, and none was involved with military service. But perhaps Robert Ford, who later wrote *Captured in Tibet*, might be described as engaged in military service, as he was operating a radio transmitter in Kham both for military and civilian purposes.

The arrival of the ten Chinese charged the whole atmosphere of Sakya with fear and suspicion, further intensified when a large troop arrived, the largest group of men that we had ever seen. The sight was monotonous and terrifying. I wondered how that conglomeration of men could identify themselves, for everyone looked exactly the same. The khaki uniforms, the storm caps, the machine-guns, the rucksacks were all identical. The soldiers were short and spoke through their noses. The humorous Tibetans used to call them 'the impotents', because they never seemed to look at women. They would say, 'These soldiers are strong and sexless like our sterilized he-donkeys.' What was even more amazing was that they never separated from their guns. They were always alert and vigilant. 'The Chinese carry their guns with them wherever they go, even to the lavatory,' became a local saying.

We were impressed by their iron discipline, neat appearance, high mobility and complete uniformity. When we saw the first disciplined body of men, we thought they must be under a particularly tyrannical general. But as the number of troops moving towards northern and western Tibet increased, we realized that the whole army was like this. I never saw or heard of any case of misconduct by a Red soldier. In Sakya the Chinese never raped a woman, bullied a peasant or even maltreated anyone – in the early 1950s, at any rate. I must admit that I admired the Red soldiers, and sympathized with them for the iron discipline that made strong young men behave like lambs. They presented a great contrast to the slackly-disciplined Tibetan soldiers. (According to Mr Kunsang Paljor, who was educated in Beijing and subsequently worked for the Chinese Press in Tibet until 1969, the soldiers in Tibet are the cream of the People's Liberation Army. They have been specially selected, and they get better pay and quicker promotion than other troops, besides other privileges. They are also the most disciplined, which accounts for their good behaviour.) The function of an army is to fight, and if there is no war soldiers usually grow fat like pigs; but this was not so of the Red Army. They worked on roads and planted vegetables for themselves. They showed great kindness to the Tibetan peasants in the most

conspicuous ways, helping the farmers in the fields and bringing water when it was scarce. Nevertheless, the Tibetan peasants did not trust this seeming kindness, and it was only the
aristocrats, foolish for all their cleverness, who did so.

Chinese troops continued to pass through Sakya on the way
to western and north-western Tibet. As roads had not then been
constructed, most of these troops were infantry. At night they
would camp on the vast open space in front of the Great Sakya
Monastery, looking like white ants, and next morning they
would disappear like ghosts. The official explanation was that
the People's Liberation Army was going to defend the frontiers
of China, 'our Motherland', braving all hazards and hardships
on the roof of the world. We were constantly reminded that we
should be grateful for the PLA's sacrifices, and must co-operate
with them. Occasionally we would hear whispered rumours
that there was a war going on towards Ladakh in the west, and
that Holy India was fighting for us. The elders would close their
eyes and pray: 'May the Red Chinese be defeated!'

Most ordinary Tibetans had no illusions about the smiling
comrades, and turned a deaf ear to their persuasive propaganda. However, since the Red Army paid liberally for transport, there was no shortage of willing donkey-drivers and
muleteers. Abu often hired out our three donkeys. While carrying army goods, he suffered no unpleasant experiences at the
hands of the soldiers. In this they were quite different from the
ill-disciplined Tibetan 'Defenders of the Faith'.

This burden of transport would be lightened when roads
opened in Tibet. In 1955 the Sakya local government, 'at the
request of the Chinese', announced that about fifteen young
labourers would be sent to Dhamshong as the town's contingent for the construction of an airport. The public was unwilling, and there were protests. Mother forbade us to go. Finally,
some young beggars and orphans agreed to be sent, and on
completion of the airport they returned to Sakya as if from
Eldorado. The Chinese had paid them lavishly in silver dollars.

They also brought with them new songs, composed and sung at Dhamshong, which hailed the new era that had opened in Tibet's history. My sisters loved to sing these new songs, and I was fascinated by the labourers' tales of aeroplanes flying like birds and alighting on the ground they had prepared. They had seen the 'winged horses'. This was far more mysterious to us than anything Westerners had ever thought about Tibet. It was an incredible reality, a tangible mystery. Seeing is believing, and now fifteen labourers from Sakya had seen aeroplanes at Dhamshong. Like other young people, I thought that exciting times were awaiting our generation. The young agreed that China was the greatest nation on earth, but the old abhorred the 'black magic' of the Chinese. The monks tried to make their miracles seem less miraculous, asserting that the formulae for making machines were to be found in the tantric texts.

There are now six airfields in Tibet, serving the Chinese military headquarters at Chamdo (eastern Tibet), Lhuntse and Lhokha (southern Tibet), Gyantse and Shigatse (midwest Tibet), and Ngari (extreme west Tibet). I doubt whether anyone would be naïve enough to think that these are for Tibet's use.

Thus the young Tibetans were seeing what their parents had never seen, and doing exciting, interesting jobs which would contribute towards the making of a new Tibet. I shall never forget the day when Mother decided to send Abu to do road work near Sakya. He beamed with joy and bubbled with excitement. How I envied him! Before 1959 wages were high, but the work was not hard for the industrious Tibetans.

The Communists' efficiency at organizing was obvious, even in those early honeymoon days. The road workers were formed into groups, and ten groups made up a labour organization. The Chinese exploited the illiterate labourers by inducing a chronic sense of competition (supposedly one of the principal evils of capitalism), bred of jealousy and constant fear. At that time China was seething with Mao's 'Great Leap Forward'. Its echoes reached the road camps, and 'progress' was the slogan in every youthful mouth. It seemed that if there was no progress the Tibetans would be perpetually damned. The Chinese ingeniously made 'progress' synonymous with rapid road construction. They suggested that labourers should be set a daily target, and – in order to apply Chairman Mao's thoughts – they had always to exceed it. So about ten yards of roadway would be set as the target for a group of ten, and it was expected that they would construct about half as much again. Thus intense competition was encouraged between individuals, between groups and between labour organizations. The Tibetan labourers danced admirably to the Chinese tune. After the day's work, they were rounded up for a mass meeting in which incentive prizes were distributed. Individuals were presented with Mao badges, and groups with banners. The Chinese supervisors praised certain labourers and certain groups for their flaming patriotism.

The workers found joy in singing. 'Progressive' elements in the camps composed Tibetan songs exalting the invincible might of the People's Liberation Army, hailing the cause of progress, and showering Chairman Mao with thanks and praise. The songs said that Tibet would advance with the speed of a motor car and that truckloads of happiness would be brought to the Land of Snows from revolutionary China. The Chinese also taught the labourers their own songs, such as *A Huge River has Huge Waves*. The song is set in the war against the Japanese. A heroic Communist soldier is so thirsty that he cannot fight. His lady comrade arrives and sings him a beautiful song about a huge river flowing through a deep gorge, with mountainous waves dashing against the rocks. The hero quenches his thirst at this illusory water, and continues to fight. I don't know whether the workers understood what they sang, but they sang it with gusto.

I asked Abu why the Tibetan youngsters worked so hard for the Chinese. He said: 'Do you remember how when you were small the bullies used to encourage you to challenge a boy of your own age and make the two of you fight like cocks? The Chinese use the same methods.' In fact, the highways were completed well before time.

Some of my left-wing friends cite the highways in Tibet as classic examples of the 'progress' achieved under Mao's leadership. But were they built for Tibet's economic progress, or to enable China to realize her ambitions? The question can be answered by a survey of the roads so far built.

Between 1954 and 1965 the Chinese built two long highways in Tibet. The Chamdo-Lhasa Highway starts from Chengdu, and passes through Dartsedo, Derge Gonchen, Chamdo, Showa, Gyanda and Ganden to Lhasa, passing through Shigatse, Sakya and Lhatse. It links Xinkiang with Tibet, and it also touches Indian territory at Ladakh. The road cuts right across the Tibetan plateau, linking the military headquarters.

The Chamdo-Lhasa Highway has three branches. One leads south to Tsepla, across the border from the North East Frontier Agency. In 1962, during the Sino-Indian conflict, the road served its purpose, giving China the advantage over India.

The second branch starts from Shigatse, passing through Gyantse, Phari and Chumbi, and ends on the Tibetan side of the Nathu-la Pass, the scene of a bloody incident in 1967, when the Chinese tried to frighten India. The strategic significance of this offshoot is equally obvious: it almost reaches Sikkim. From Phari it is a day's journey on foot to the Bhutan border, and China has laid claims to both Sikkim and Bhutan. This road takes the shortest possible route to the border areas; it does not attempt to serve the Tibetans living in remote and inaccessible places.

The third offshoot of the Chamdo-Lhasa Highway also starts from Shigatse; it passes through Shekar, Tingri and Nyalam, and ends at Kathmandu. At the moment China has a flourishing business with Nepal along this Lhasa-Kathmandu road. In the background she carries on her propaganda, which really amounts to subversive activity. Nepal has certainly become the biggest base for China's self-appointed 'revolutionary task' in the Indian subcontinent.

The urgency with which these highways were built is indication enough of China's military designs. As soon as they invaded Tibet the Chinese began road construction. Between 1952 and 1959 the native labourers were highly paid, but after the 1959 uprising in Lhasa, I saw with my own eyes how the Tibetans were used like slaves on the road. Thus, at the expense of Tibetan sweat and toil, these strategic highways and their offshoots were built in a very short time, enabling China to establish tight control over Tibet, and at the same time to reach the sensitive border areas before anyone else. The Tibetans always called these highways *magmi-lamka* (military roads), since only military trucks plied along them. In Sakya I did not see any civilian traffic. There were no passenger buses; only military trucks loaded with khaki-clad soldiers and well-concealed goods.

Throughout history, China has persistently tried to gain domination over Tibet, as I have shown in my account of Sino-Tibetan relations. In the past, the tremendous physical barriers – high mountains, hills and huge rivers, and the long distance between Lhasa and Beijing made any colonial conquest meaningless; but the roads made it a reality. As many writers have pointed out, Tibet has been converted into a Chinese military base, and the roof of the world has become a springboard for the Chinese Communists.

By the mid-1950s, the section of the Xinkiang-Lhasa Highway passing through Sakya was complete. There had been much talk about the coming of vehicles. Then one afternoon we heard a loud rumbling noise. I rushed out and saw people on their doorsteps and roofs, while the timid peered out of their windows. My suspense soon gave way to wonder. I saw two houses with glass window-panes, moving on wheels, and was amazed that the fast-moving wonder houses should run so obediently on the narrow track. They turned, twisted and straight-

ened in a way that not even the most well-trained horse in
Sakya could, and I wondered how those mindless machines
could be so much more obedient than any yak, donkey, mule or
horse. I knew that we had to shout at the animals, push them
around and hit them in order to drive them, and even then they
would go astray. But these metallic houses without a mind or
soul went perfectly on the road. I was not particularly astonished at their speed – being the first vehicles on the road they
were driven slowly and carefully. Mother and some of the older
folk slammed their doors, Mother saying, 'Now I am seeing all
that was unseen before. This is not a good sign. Why did I live
to see it?'

As the two military trucks stopped, excited children ran
from every direction towards the fantastic spectacle. Mother
tried to hold us back, but I struggled free and ran with them.
The youngsters crowded around the two trucks as though they
were holy objects from China. The drivers gave us cold smiles.
I touched the standing vehicles that did not seem exhausted
even after the long journey from Shigatse. The elders had often
stirred my imagination with their tales of holy miracles, but I
had never seen any with my own eyes. Now I was beholding a
real miracle.

In the 1950s the young all over Tibet were possessed by
wonder and expectation. Just as the few foreigners who
glimpsed Tibet found it mysterious, so we found these two
vehicles miraculous. It was as if we had been locked up in seclu-
sion for ages, and then had suddenly come into contact with the
outside world. I had heard fascinating tales about vehicles,
aeroplanes and electricity from Abu, who went to India once a
year on business; but I thought they were like the intangible
miracles of Tibet, seen only by the few faithful.

The completion of the highway meant that the journey from
Beijing to Lhasa had been cut to less than twenty days of safe
and comfortable travelling, as compared with more than three
months of hardship on the caravan routes. The old were indif-

ferent, if not unhappy. They used to say, 'We are not going to
spend the rest of our lives running about the world. We don't
think your government will take us to the holy places in your
vehicles. Even if they do, pilgrimage without penance is not
meritorious, so your wheeled houses are of no use to us. But
they are useful to you, since your country is so far off.'

Under the so-called peaceful liberation policy, extending
from 1951 to 1959, the Chinese Communists made no direct contact with the masses. This is surprising, as one would normally
expect the Communists to urge the proletariat to 'shake off their
yokes'. But the only contacts that the common Tibetans had
with the Communists were at the road camps and on journeys.
The Chinese used the Tibetan people intelligently for their
military preparations in Tibet. The blue-uniformed comrades
encouraged the Tibetans to work industriously on the roads,
but they made no effort to indoctrinate them. They seemed to
know that the Tibetans were stubborn and conservative, and
that they would not exchange their own worst vices for the best
Chinese virtues. They were deeply rooted in Tibet and in anything that was Tibetan. The majority were quite unreceptive to
new ideas, especially to Communism, which directly opposed
the spirit of their way of life. Admittedly there were a few
Tibetans who responded to the Chinese call; in Sakya about six
young beggars and orphans became 'Chinese'. But the great
majority detested the Chinese *pompola* or overlords (a term later
changed to *lhoshang*, a coinage meaning 'comrade'). However,
they were a silent majority: they would not embrace communism, but neither would they revolt against the Chinese, at least
until they were organized and led.

China had two courses open to her. She could have taken
Tibet by military force, and imposed a military dictatorship
without any difficulty. But this was considered non-communist
in spirit, and was also against world opinion. She chose the
second way: on the pretext of 'Peaceful Liberation' and by
granting special autonomous status to Tibet, she could buy time

to get a hold over the country. This was done by using the masses on road work, and by persuading the élite to believe in the social utopia of Mao's heaven on earth. If China were to rule Tibet successfully, the intellectual backbone of the country had to be lulled, wooed and deceived. In this way the possibility of a revolt would be minimized, and the illiterate masses would follow the aristocrats, whom the Chinese had converted into the 'vanguard of revolution'.

SEVEN

Schools Old and New

WHILE THE Chinese Communists were busy building highways and airfields – and wooing the upper strata of Tibetan society – they did not interfere much with our traditional way of life. The aristocrats believed that even under the new system they could retain their privileges if they co-operated with the Chinese. The commoners still cherished high hopes of living the same orderly life governed by the wheel of *karma*.

This was the general climate of opinion when Mother told me one day that on the following Monday I would be going to school. Having been born on a Monday, I should start any fresh venture, big or small, on that day; for that was, and still is, the most auspicious day for me. The astrologer's predictions were flattering and encouraging. He said I was gifted with great natural ability for learning, and if this ability were properly exploited I should become a reputable monk-scholar. I should therefore pursue a monastic career. But Mother politely declined the suggestion. She told the astrologer apologetically that due to her sinfulness she was deliberately making the wrong choice, but that she had her own mundane, ambitious plans for me to build up the prosperity of our family.

I waited anxiously and impatiently for the great day to come. I was indescribably pleased with the prospect of going to school; once I could read I would be admired by the simple rustics, envied by my enemies, and respected by society at large. When the long-awaited Monday dawned, I was scrubbed, dried before the fire and liberally oiled, especially my hair and face.

And when the sun rose over the Sakya valley Abu took me to the ancient temple of Manjusri, the God of Knowledge, one of the holiest temples in Sakya. I prostrated myself before the benevolent smiling god three times, praying silently as taught

by Abu, and beseeching him: 'Strike open the eye of wisdom with your dagger!' Small as I was, I felt charged with blessings and full of confidence after my pilgrimage to the source of knowledge.

Then I presented myself before the teacher chosen by Mother. He was a young official named Kunga Topla, who held the post of Minister of Fuel in the Sakya government, and was renowned for his strictness and learning. Abu brought along some presents and a *khadar* for him. There was no fixed fee: the amount was left entirely to the means and generosity of the pupil's parents. Most teachers were willing to pass on their knowledge for very little reward. I used to give Kunga Topla some sugar when Abu returned from Shigatse or Kalimpong, or some cheese and butter when our cows were in milk. When I left school I offered him a hundred-*sang* note. That was all he got for teaching me.

In Tibet there were no organized or established secular schools. Instead, an aristocrat or government official would teach some eight or ten boys in his own house. Kunga Topla taught twelve boys. Very few girls went to school, and nobody went to a teacher unless he had a specific use for education. The aristocrats' sons were educated, because they had to inherit their fathers' positions. The leading *tralpas* educated their children, because they would be involved in constant transactions with the government. And, since the petty tradesmen in Sakya were compelled to sell their goods on credit, they needed someone to scribble notes. Lamas were not supposed to be scholars. They were supposed to study Buddhism, and then practise it for the quick attainment of Buddhahood. Therefore it is not surprising that the monks were taught to read only the printed forms of the alphabet (*uchen*). If a monk was found learning the second form, handwriting (*ume*), by his fellow-monks, he would be severely criticized for harbouring earthly ambitions, and accused of wanting to join the government service.

The daily routine of our school was monotonous. We had to reach school 'before the sun struck its rays on the mountain peaks'. This timing was rigorously observed. Whichever of us twelve boys reached school first was allowed to slap the faces of the other eleven with a large piece of cut bamboo, the second boy could enjoy slapping the next ten, and so on. The method of slapping on the cheeks was an institution in itself. We had to blow out our cheeks to receive the slap. The bamboo was flat and smooth; in operation it was bent, and one end flicked on to the inflated cheeks. We were so used to it that we hardly made a sound when we were slapped.

When we were seated in an orderly single row on the terrace facing the sun, we yelled at the top of our high-pitched boyish

voices a hymn of Jampaiyang, the God of Knowledge. After this we recited some tongue-twisting *mantras* in Sanskrit – appeals to Jampaiyang, beseeching him to assist us in our quest for knowledge. Our teacher lived in an exceptionally high building of four storeys, so that the townspeople could hear our morning prayers loudly and clearly, and we became a dependable clock for them.

Next, we memorized spelling and grammatical rules. Higher education meant memorizing the whole dictionary and two or three textbooks of grammar. The pupil left school with a prodigious memory, but little else.

The next session began at about ten o'clock, after the leisurely morning meal. The rest of the day was devoted to calligraphy. The Tibetan intelligentsia had an idiotic obsession about handwriting, and would judge a passage by the way it was written rather than by its contents. The creative energy of the pupil was channelled towards the painstaking imitation of his teacher's handwriting. This system had a damaging and unwholesome influence on our language, which lacked fresh, original expressions. Even our best work contained clichés and platitudes.

There were no classes in the Western sense, but basically we had four grades, based on the types of handwriting. First of all we learned to read the print from the script (*uchen*). Then we learned to write the large *ume* characters on wooden boards – a tedious and eye-damaging exercise. The board was powdered with chalk dust, in which the teacher would mark out the characters; we then had to trace over the marks in ink. The characters were huge at first; as we progressed they were made smaller. When our handwriting had acquired sufficient firmness and shape, we switched from board to paper – a promotion indicating that we had half-completed our education. Despite this undue emphasis on calligraphy, we used to take delight in practising it. The sons of the aristocracy would spend about seven years on their handwriting.

Naturally, our occasional tests were handwriting contests. All we had to do for the examination was to copy the teacher's model handwriting as accurately as possible. As with our morning arrival, the first in the examination had the pleasure of slapping all those below him. Since the boy who came last had no one to slap, he was forced to slap a mask tied around a pillar. We would all roar with scornful laughter, while the poor urchin was almost in tears. But we bore no lasting grudge against one another; it was a matter of give-and-take. If the teacher was in a good mood, he would jokingly advise the humiliated student: 'If you want your revenge, you had better start working harder.' If the teacher was in a bad mood, he would knock the boy down with his wooden writing-board.

In modern terms, our teacher was a mental case. He was a kind-hearted, short-tempered and volatile character, and every now and then he seemed to be on the verge of madness. He resigned early from his post and took to meditation. We used to be all the more scared because of his instability. One morning on the terrace we began to play when we were supposed to be

reciting our prayers. Infuriated, the teacher kicked me so hard
that I found myself hanging like a bat on the edge of the tall
building. Corporal punishment was considered the only effective means of disciplining a naughty boy. We feared our
teacher, not because he was a tyrant, but because he was our
guru; so we respected and loved him as well. When I had
escaped to India and went to school in Kalimpong, I was surprised at the resentful manner in which the students took even
a gentle admonition from their teachers. Small as we were in
Sakya, we took every thrashing from the teacher as an act of
kindness, and never felt hurt mentally. We consoled ourselves
with the thought that, because the teacher cared for us, he took
pains to thrash us for the sake of discipline. In Kalimpong I
found that this attitude was quite beyond the comprehension of
Westernized students.

Athletic sports were unknown. Our popular diversion was
'playing army', for which we would band together and challenge a group of boys from a different school. Sometimes we
threw stones at each other from a distance, and sometimes we
fought with our fists. The townspeople would scold us for pretending to engage in war, the most dreaded of all disasters.
They thought it a bad omen.

One day, while engrossed in our calligraphic designs, we
were brought down to earth by a surprise visit from a group of
blue-uniformed comrades. The visiting 'working personnel'
showered us with their cold comradely praise and distributed
sweets among us. They were a special delegation from the
Shigatse primary school, and brought us a message from the
students there. We all crowded round to read it and to admire
the handwriting and the expressions it used. The message soon
became a popular handwriting model. Its contents were pure
propaganda, and I am certain that the Shigatse students did not
write it. It began with effusive revolutionary greetings, and
went on to announce the creation of a similar Chinese-run
primary school in Sakya. The students of Shigatse were glad

that we were receiving some sort of traditional schooling, which would enable us to 'leap forward' when the Sakya primary school opened. The letter concluded with the usual call to strive hard in order to transform the old stagnant Tibet into a new dynamic socialist society. Our path was our Motherland's.

The sudden visit and the friendly message caused a sensation in Sakya. Mother was very much alarmed. She said that I was already caught in the Chinese net, and that distributing sweets and noting our names was 'not a good sign'. So she asked our teacher for ways and means of getting me out of the Chinese trap. My teacher was sincere and frank as usual. Like the other aristocrats, he had a superficial understanding of the Chinese plans for the advancement of Tibet, which the uneducated masses dismissed as 'not a good sign'; but he could not fathom the Communists' policies. He simply advised us that I should join the Chinese school. His argument was sound. The Tibetan and Chinese governments had signed the 17-Point Agreement of 23 May 1951, and we as individuals would have neither more nor less than the provisions laid down there. When the venerable government of the Dalai Lama agreed with the terms and conditions, who were we to disagree? (Probably my teacher did not know that the Chinese Communists had made the Tibetan delegation sign the Agreement at gun-point.) So we had to accept the new regime whether we liked it or not. According to the alien ideology, he continued, whoever 'leapt forward' would stand a better chance in the new situation and, conversely, whoever refused would inevitably fail, if not actually suffer.

This was my teacher's firm opinion, shared by most of the Tibetan intelligentsia. Although the upper strata had everything to lose, they co-operated enthusiastically with the Communists in the early 1950s. The Tibetan government was a stranger to the maxim that the end justifies the means. Though some people were familiar with the practical concept in their daily affairs, the government was idealistically based on

Buddhist religious principles, and at no time did it resort to Machiavellian expediency. Furthermore, its dealings were essentially at home, where it was expected to set an example. The government was practically a religious body, and an unquestioning belief in its actions was rooted in the Tibetan mentality. No traditional Tibetan would have believed you if you had told him that the government sometimes lied. How could the citadel of integrity tell lies? When the Chinese subtly started to violate the 17-Point Agreement, the Tibetans got the biggest shock of their political lives. It was pathetic how naïvely the Tibetan nobility believed the Chinese. A Lhasa aristocrat recently told me, 'The Chinese Reds were the fox; we were the ass.'

When the Chinese invaded Tibet, they had to create almost a new political language. The Tibetan language has the richest terminology in Buddhism, but it is inadequate for modern communication. The Communists established a Tibetan research centre in Beijing, where Marxist literature was translated into Tibetan and new words were coined. Although the new language was clear and simple, its contents were totally alien to the Tibetan intelligentsia, who could have made little of terms like 'national minority', 'autonomy', 'foreign imperialists' or 'Motherland'. Did they really understand the full significance or implications of the 17-Point Agreement? Most of them did not bother to read the books on Marxism, Mao's thoughts, or even the Chinese blueprint for the future of Tibet. My teacher was typical: he used the books to decorate his room. They had no intellectual curiosity, and preferred to study their time-worn scriptures. If they had read the books put out by the Chinese they would have been wiser, and might have had some idea of what was going to happen.

The aristocrats' knowledge of Chinese Communism was fundamentally what they heard from the polite comrades, who persistently quoted the clause 'Officials of various ranks shall hold office as usual' from the 17-Point Agreement, and 'From each according to his ability and to each according to his need' from the Communist bible. These two concepts were driven hard into their heads, and I heard many young aristocrats in Sakya explaining them with commendable originality. Before, it was the fortune of birth that determined one's status in society. Now the Chinese would defy the law of *karma* and change this hereditary system, so that everything would be determined by one's ability. 'Even a beggar's son can become the Governor of Sakya if he has the ability' became a cliché. This proposition had little to disturb the aristocrats. Democratic reforms, the Chinese assured the credulous members of the ruling class, would be carried out 'from above and not from below'; it was up to the upper class to reform – or even not to do so. As far as education and natural ability went, they were still miles ahead of the masses, having generations of learning to their advantage. Consequently, if they studied Communism and sent their children to school, they would undoubtedly occupy the best positions even in the new society. Names and titles might vanish, but in substance they would continue to enjoy the same privileges.

As well as these intellectual allurements, for about seven years the Chinese invaders literally threw away *dayin* (silver dollars). Every man has his price, and I do not think that there was any Tibetan heroic enough to refuse. When the Preparatory Committee for the Autonomous Region of Tibet and various Communist youth organizations were inaugurated, officials of all ranks enjoyed their share of dollars.

So it was not surprising that when the Sakya primary school opened in 1955, most of the 82 students were sons and daughters of aristocrats and officials. The aristocrats, who were supposed to be the vanguard of the 'Peaceful Liberation', virtually gave no chance to the commoners. They sent their children to the new school and encouraged their relatives and friends to send theirs. The word 'new' acquired a special flavour during this period. The simple, unlettered masses doubted, suspected and even detested the Red Chinese, 'who have been ordered to smile'; while, for their part, the Chinese did not bother with the conservative, stubborn masses of Tibet for the time being. Our homely school was closed down. I left it with mixed emotions. I was sad to leave my teacher and fellow-pupils, as we were all attached to one another by a mixture of respect and love, fear and gratitude; but I was also anxious to join the much-publicized new school. Like the government officials, I knew I would be able to leap forward well ahead of the others. It was an opportunity to show my ability; even though I was only the son of a nameless petty tradesman, I might win a place in the new order.

The inaugural ceremony was unforgettable. Gathered together were 82 children of my own age, the biggest crowd of boys and girls that Sakya had ever seen. Everybody was in his or her best clothes, and some of the aristocrats' sons had even had the audacity to cut their hair in the Chinese style. The Chinese patted them on the back, and the monks shook their fists at them. We saw for the first time the Chinese Communist revolutionary way of celebrating a new epoch. Colourful posters in Tibetan letters, almost six feet high and handwritten magnificently, had been stuck all over the walls; and a gate of welcome had been built. We children were given plenty of sweets for enduring the long speeches.

Of all the speeches, that of the Sakya *Zodpa* was the most memorable. He began in his usual dignified manner by a familiar quotation: 'To improve your minds you should persevere in learning.' Then he went on: 'Even if you cannot learn more than one word a day, you will have learned a hundred words in a hundred days. Under the invincible leadership of the Chinese Communist Party and its Chairman Mao, education justly becomes the determining factor. If you can prove yourself worthy, you can become the Sakya *Zodpa* regardless of your background.' Then he got stuck, like a record player. He repeated the last word several times, uttered many 'ahas', and finally, distrusting his eyesight, looked harder and closer at the paper. His distinguished audience of Tibetan officials, school-children and Chinese 'working personnel' were flabbergasted. It was unbelievable that the governor, the highest official, could not read his own handwriting! It became a big joke; but later we found out that the Chinese comrades, as was common practice, had written the inaugural speech.

The primary school was an old dilapidated palace pur-chased from a Sakya princess. During this period of wooing the Tibetans, the Chinese made few breaks with tradition. There were only two classes: the upper wrote advanced calligraphy on paper; the lower used wooden tablets. I was in the upper class. After being in a simple, tiny school, I found the Chinese-sponsored school well organized and well staffed. However, by Western standards its curriculum was narrow and standards were low. Our major subject was Tibetan, still taught along the traditional lines, and minor subjects included basic Marxism, arithmetic, world geography and Chinese history.

Our elderly Tibetan teacher was a retired high-ranking offi-cial of the fast-vanishing old hierarchy. I remember two inci-dents particularly in which he was concerned. For a few days he dropped hints that some officials were being offered more silver dollars for sitting on a comfortable chair than he was for labori-ously teaching us. I sensibly took up the hint, and wrote a flat-tering composition on this burning issue. Next day the teacher wrote on the blackboard: 'Some of you little students are quite correct in writing that some officials are getting more *dayin* for sitting on a chair and doing nothing than others are for teaching what really cannot be bought with money.' He was so pleased with my 'innocent, frank suggestion' that he showed it to his Chinese colleagues, thus exposing his 'unpurgeable old green mind'.

The other incident was less happy. I was always fighting, and on one occasion I threw stones at Jango Bhula, the son of a powerful aristocrat, and chased him into the class room.

Without asking a single question my teacher caught me and thrashed me there and then. Jango, after being patted and consoled, accused me of stealing his bamboo pen, which I had not done. Being sensitive to injustice, I asked why the teacher had not thrashed the aristocrat's son as well. He felt that this was outrageous on the part of a nameless commoner's son, and warned me, as if I were a grown man, that it would be my fault if he resigned. He had not applied for the post, but had been requested to teach by the Chinese and ordered to do so by the Sakya authorities. Mother had a lot of trouble trying to pacify him, running about, bowing down, and giving bribes.

Our arithmetic teacher, a veteran of the Red Army, spoke through his nose in a broken Tibetan that made us laugh. We took the whole summer to master addition and subtraction. Even his mathematical examples were propagandist. I can hear him now, saying in his nasal accent: 'I have five eggs. I offer three to the People's Liberation Army. How many have I left?' As soon as he had chalked the question mark on the blackboard, he turned around to look at the students. If he saw anybody playing or being inattentive, he would set about him with a thin long bamboo.

Another unforgettable character was our political lecturer, Comrade Nyima. He was a thin, dark, Tibetan youth, who spoke in the much-admired Lhasa accent. Everything he said was in praise of the People's Republic of China, of the Chinese Communist Party and its Chairman Mao, and of the new ideology. We learnt from him that China was the greatest socialist society, that it had the largest population in the world, that its leader was the greatest revolutionary in human history, and that its army consisted of the most heroic crusaders of Socialism. Marxist-Leninist Communism was the only way to collective happiness. In the ultimate analysis, all nations on earth had to reach the utopia of the socialist classless society via the Chinese Communist Party. He would elaborate eloquently on the stages of the road to this utopia – the agrarian revolution,

the industrial revolution, peasants' associations, and co-operative groups. The classless society, or 'Commune', was the ultimate goal. China was then on the third phase, and Tibet must
leap forward in order to catch up with her mighty Motherland.
When we attained our final goal, explained the zealous teacher,
everyone would live in one gigantic family. There would be no
problems. We would have no worries about food, clothing and
houses, as everybody would wear the same clothes, eat the
same food and live in the same house. There would be perfect
equality. By the time we reached the classless society, the industrial revolution would be complete, and practically everything
would be done by machines. In fact, a time would come when
our meals would be brought by machines right up to our
mouths. When Nyima talked about the various stages of the
revolutionary road, they sounded like the different phases of
meditation, and the ultimate Commune seemed like *nirvana*.

Whenever I heard the phrase 'classless society' (*Chitsog
Ringlung*) I at once visualized a Shangri-la – except that Nyima
did not say: 'We never ever grow old in the *Chitsog Ringlung*.'
This was the vision of Chairman Mao's heaven on earth, the
proletarian paradise; but it was also the opium of the intellectual. We were enchanted by the miracles of machinery and the
promises of a proletarian paradise. Those were the days of
excitement, challenge, ambition and youthful idealism.

To prove that, unlike Shangri-la, this prescribed future was
no illusion, delegates from all over Tibet were invited to visit
China. Sakya sent a lama and a lay official. They were treated to
a conducted tour of the best part of Communist China, and saw
all the showpieces – factories, mines, 'protected' monasteries,
people's cultural palaces. They had never seen such things in
their lives, and came back choking with admiration for the
Chinese scientific and technological miracles, though by
Western standards China's technology in the 1950s was not
worth talking about. The lay delegate, Bartso, was a close friend
of my teacher, and was convinced that China was heading

towards a heaven on earth. He seemed to have developed a veneration for Chairman Mao; one day, to my utter surprise, I saw a green rubber figure of Mao placed on his household altar.

To us, one of the most extraordinary things about the Sakya primary school was the Chinese cult of physical labour, which was to replace the devotional exercises that the religious Tibetans performed. The farmer was to become the glorified new aristocrat, and to work and produce was to worship the Mighty Motherland. Even Chairman Mao worked in the fields; we saw him doing so in a film. Mao had said that we must oppose book worship and cultivate work worship, so every afternoon we worked on a nearby field. Before we started, the taskmaster, a demobilized soldier, would read extracts from the *People's Daily* – for example, some school in China had 'turned a barren hill into a sea of forest'. We must emulate them. While working himself, the taskmaster would observe who was working hard. Industrious and progressive students would be admitted to the Young Pioneer Corps.

I was one of the progressives. Our taskmaster, who was fond of me, told me that I should be overjoyed because I had been selected for membership of the Corps. Mother doubted and suspected such innovations, and warned me that I was going more and more 'under the Chinese'. But, being wise, she adopted a wait-and-see policy. The children of the aristocrats were eagerly joining the Corps, and she reasoned that if there was any harm in joining, the educated officials would not allow their children to do so.

For a time, Comrade Nyima discontinued his lectures on Mao's philosophy and devoted a few talks to the Young Pioneers. He went briefly over the historical background of the organization; however, he dwelt mostly on the patriotic, heroic and revolutionary crusade that some early Pioneers undertook during the wars against the Japanese and the Kuomintang Reactionaries (Nationalist Chinese). We must emulate our young heroes and martyrs, and set an example to the rest of the children in Sakya. Above all, we must follow the Chinese Communist Party and its invincible Chairman Mao; we must serve the people and build a great Motherland. At the same time we must always vigilantly fight the people's enemies, imperialists and reactionaries. As a missionary would try to make us 'truly Christian children' at school, so Nyima said that the basic aim of the Corps was to make us 'true Communist children'. We must be steeped in Marxism-Leninism, devoted to physical labour and accustomed to the idea of Commune living; and we must love the Party more than our parents. Having fulfilled these conditions, we were finally invested with the Red Scarf of Honour.

Through his lectures exalting the symbolism of the Red Scarf, Nyima created a high concept of it in the impressionable minds of us children. It was a unique badge of pride and honour, which every child should strive to acquire. Other children began to envy us, and some of the aristocrats used all their old influence to gain their children admission to the Corps. We enjoyed various privileges: at meetings we were placed ahead of the others, and we were given extra sweets and praise.

But as we seemed to drift closer and closer to the godless Communists, the monks became more and more hostile towards us. They used to call us the 'leading mules' – rather an apt description. In every group of mules there would be one or two that got special treatment and wore bells and dyed yaks' tails around their necks. One afternoon I was walking along the river bank, proudly wearing my red scarf round my neck, when I met a group of young lamas. At once they gave chase, caught me, pulled the scarf tight round my neck and almost strangled me to death. Once when the Young Pioneers were marching near the Great Sakya Monastery, the lamas stoned us from the ramparts. Although the 'working personnel' were displeased with this reactionary behaviour, they did not make the slightest verbal protest; the time was not yet ripe.

Our chief instructors, invariably young aristocrats, were the progressive members of the Youth League, another Communist organization for indoctrinating young people. My sister Donkar was a member of the League. If the Young Pioneers proved themselves worthy of the high honour of wearing the red scarf, they would be permitted to join the Youth League when they were sixteen. The League did not attract as many members as the Young Pioneers, and so the Chinese used the local government to enrol members. The young aristocrats were asked to volunteer, and some bright-looking middle-class young people, Donkar among them, were ordered to join. She felt that, if she disobeyed the old lords, perhaps a time might come when they would be in a position to victimize her; if she disobeyed the new lords, she might suffer also, at some future date. The League's activities included weekly meetings, and singing and dancing at the new festivals. Its members were paid handsomely.

We were also paid for attending school. Each student received 30 *dayin* a month, and a complete Tibetan costume each year. Wearing our smart new clothes we were once taken for an anticlockwise walk around the Great Monastery – a deliberate act of sacrilege, as only the clockwise direction was permitted. Most of the students came from wealthy families and did not care much about the salaries and gift of clothing; but I was thrilled. There was a song about the gift of *dayin:* 'From the Revolutionary East showers of silver dollars rain over the land of snows. The mountains of silver dollars are higher than the snow-capped peaks of our land.'

In April 1956 the Preparatory Committee for the Autonomous Region of Tibet was inaugurated at Lhasa. When the Sakya branch of the committee was opened, we had a grand festive day. An enormous portrait of Mao Zedong was set up, flanked by the portraits of the Dalai and Panchen Lamas. Multi-coloured posters in Tibetan adorned all the walls. Long speeches were made, and the schoolchildren and the officials applauded unfailingly. We also heard the news that a giant aeroplane had circled over Lhasa for some time, dropping beautiful multi-coloured leaflets in Tibetan and Chinese. I read some of them, all the more impressed by virtue of their having dropped from the sky. They read: 'Greetings on the occasion of the establishment of the Preparatory Committee for the Autonomous Region of Tibet.' Many of the senior officials of the Sakya government were offered good posts in the Sakya branch of the committee. So far, at least the officials and aristocrats were enjoying life.

Even after leaving my first school, I kept in close contact with my teacher, Kunga Topla, and when he entertained his guests, I used to help him. Social life in Sakya was at its peak. The aristocrats played mahjong, spending *dayin* freely. They discussed the latest meetings of their organizations and talked about the bright prospects for Tibet, enchanted by the new concept of a Communist Shangri-la.

EIGHT

Limits of Indoctrination

ONE AFTERNOON I came back from school and found the whole family crying and moaning as if one of its members had suddenly died. For a few moments I stood not knowing what to do. Then Donkar told me what had upset the whole household: 'The government has put me down to go to China!'

I had heard earlier that a batch of ten or twelve youngsters from Sakya would be sent to China on free scholarships, but before the final announcement was made the whole town had been kept in suspense. It was our misfortune that Donkar was one of the selected candidates. It seemed to us as if she was going to be sent to the gas-chamber rather than to the Motherland, for to us separation from our family was like death itself. We dreaded and feared even the short occasional business trips to Shigatse, only 40 miles away. Every possible safety precaution would be taken. The astrologer was consulted; blessings were sought from a high lama; and rituals were performed. To send our eldest sister to distant, unknown, uncertain China was an impossible proposition.

From the beginning the Communists were extremely careful about their image as the people's saviours. Thus they got the local Tibetan government to do all the unpleasant and painful things, such as forcing the bright Tibetan youth to go to China for indoctrination. No one else from Sakya volunteered to go for free schooling in the Motherland. The Government compelled families who had six or more children to send one of them to China. Mother recalls that the list was prepared on fair grounds;

because she had three sons and three daughters, and especially because Donkar was a clever-looking girl, our family was eligible. However, Mother was determined to keep her daughter at home, and appealed to the highest political authority of the Sakya local government, the *Zodpa*.

She went before him bringing a basin of sugar and of course a *khadar*. But bribery alone was not enough; a well-prepared, reasonable petition was needed to win a case. Mother harped continuously on the fact that she had a houseful of children to bring up, and needed Donkar, as the eldest, to help her. It was also unfair that Donkar should go with eleven boys and without a companion of her own sex. The answer she received showed the prevailing Tibetan intellectual mood, brought about by Communist propaganda.

The *Zodpa* said: 'I think you should send your daughter for your own good and hers. Remember woman, once she completes her education in Beijing, she will come back as a new aristocrat. She will have the right to work in the Sakya government. In Lhasa I have already seen women in colourful aprons working among the nobility in our sober offices where no woman was ever seen previously. The Chinese Communist Party have benevolently declared the emancipation of women, and His Holiness the Dalai Lama has assented to it. I think you should not miss this golden opportunity; you will regret it later if you do. Our government has been impartial as usual. You can certainly afford to send one child to China when you have so many. Your daughter, I hear, is clever, and I think she should do very well, bringing benefit to herself and credit to our Sakya Government. We cannot risk sending any urchin or beggar who might disgrace the name of sacred Sakya. You must send your daughter.'

But Mother persisted with her petition, each time bringing fresh excuses. By far the most weighty reason for our ultimate success was that Mother had already made an agreement to give Donkar away in marriage, and neither the Tibetan government nor the Chinese had the right to break the bond of the marriage which was about to take place. Donkar was reluctantly released.

Finally, the Sakya government managed to levy the 'child tax' on eight families. When the eight boys left Sakya, we rejoiced over our good fortune, but also sympathized with the others' misfortune. The parting ceremony was as mournful as a funeral service. The parents and relatives gathered and wept, as did a large crowd. As I miserably watched them leaving Sakya, I thought: 'Where will they be? Far away from Sakya in some strange place in the vastness of China. Will they ever return home to our sacred Sakya?'

After the first batch had been sent, there was less reluctance and remonstrance shown over the free scholarships in the Motherland. Nor was it surprising, for by then the blue-uniformed Han working personnel had been successfully courting the upper strata, and many young people had joined the various Communist youth organizations. When I was at the Chinese school, Comrade Nyima used to try to induce me to go to China. He would speak nostalgically of the Beijing Institute of National Minorities, where he had been educated. 'In China,' he said with pride, 'the roads shine like mirrors. You hardly see any pedestrians, but more vehicles than the entire Tibetan population.'

When the order came from Lhasa in 1956 to send a second batch of children, younger than the previous batch, Nyima did not hesitate to recommend my name to the Tibetan and Chinese authorities. But Mother vetoed the proposal. I was in a quandary. I did not really want to leave my mother, sisters and brothers, to whom I was passionately attached; but at the same time I fervently wished to see the Chinese 'proletarian paradise', which had inflamed my imagination ever since I had come into contact with my Chinese comrades. If I did not go now, I thought, I would be far behind those who were going to receive the best socialist education that China could afford. My problem was providentially solved when the plan was abandoned. The explanation I heard was that the younger children could not adapt themselves to the comparatively hot Chinese climate, and the earlier experiments had failed due to the deaths of a number of the children.

Since coming to India, I have met many of the young Tibetans who were educated for at least five years in China and who are now in exile. Among them are two whom we knew intimately in Sakya. One of them, Garshi Tsewang, was educated in China for nearly five years. After the abortive Lhasa uprising of 1959, he was sent back to Tibet as a member of the working personnel and was posted in Sakya, where he worked for nearly a year as an interpreter. Towards the end of 1959, when the much-publicized 'democratic reform' was over, his family decided to escape and they asked Tsewang if he wanted to join them. One evening, wearing his blue uniform, Mao badge and blue cap, Tsewang slipped out of Simchung House, the Chinese headquarters in Sakya, and escaped with his family to India, where he now lives a free and contented life.

The other cadre who escaped to India was Thubten-la, who was also an interpreter in Sakya during the democratic reforms. Having worked for nearly a year in Sakya under his Han boss, Thubten-la was transferred to Shigatse, where his wife was then living. He lost no time in packing up, and escaped with his wife in 1960.

So from our small town alone, two young Tibetans who had been indoctrinated in China for at least five years 'betrayed' the Chinese rulers. They told us that most of the Tibetan youth, indoctrinated in China and now working under Han bosses, would have escaped if they could. 'Just as you are forced to undergo *thamzing* (mutual accusation), or study basic Marxist-Leninism, or denounce your religion, we are also forced to do what we did in Sakya. There is no other way if you can't escape,' said Thubten-la. So I knew that Norzin-la, the Tibetan girl who was employed as our Chinese interpreter, was acting when she appeared to take her part so seriously; there was no other way open to her.

The young Tibetans studying at the Beijing Institute of National Minorities between 1952 and 1956 were pampered with the best of Chinese dishes – four dishes per meal, and three meals daily. When the first batch of youths arrived at the Institute in 1952 from Lhasa, they refused to sleep in bunks one above the other, because the holy relics they wore round their necks day and night would have been desecrated; so they were given a special dormitory with beds side by side. A Buddhist temple was consecrated for the Tibetan students, and the Communists imported *tsampa*, yak's meat and butter from eastern Tibet for them. They also received an extravagant amount of pocket-money. This high-class treatment continued right up to 1956.

The course at the Beijing Institute of National Minorities was basically the same as that which we had at the Sakya primary school. However, instruction was in the 'revolutionary language' – Chinese. At the beginning, Tibetan was taught as a minor subject, but by 1957 the weekly lessons had been reduced from six to two. The Chinese language lecturer would assert chauvinistically that Chinese was 'the most revolutionary and widely-spoken language in the world'. The Tibetan students retorted that they were destined to serve the Tibetan people, and the Tibetans would not understand 'the most revolutionary language'. Despite this argument, if any Tibetan student was found speaking in his mother tongue he was punished by being made to stand for two or three hours on a bench, and by *thamzing*. History as approved by the Party was by far the most controversial subject. The Chinese teacher would begin with these words: 'Ever since Princess WenCheng KungJu married the Tibetan King Songtsen Gampo, Tibet has been part of China.' The fact that the Tibetan king married a Nepalese princess as well was well known to the Tibetans, who would comment: 'Then Tibet became part of Nepal as well, because Songtsen

Gampo also married a Nepalese princess.' But since 1959 debate has been strictly prohibited in classrooms, and anywhere else.

Chinese chauvinism knew no limits. The teachers at the Institute would exclaim: 'What do you backward Tibetans know? Nothing! The Han race is the bravest, cleverest and most able in the world.'

Tension between the Chinese and the Tibetan students at the Institute became more marked, culminating in an astounding 'poster war' in April 1957. Many of the Tibetan students became nationalistic when they went to China. In 1956 there were 824 Tibetan students at the Institute. Ngawang Thondup, who was in the first batch of Tibetans to arrive in Beijing, recalls: 'When you are far away from your homeland, you lose all your petty internal differences in the larger national interest. Many of us became nationally conscious only during the process of indoctrination, because before that we faced no such provocative challenge. But when we arrived in China, we united to face the challenges. Sect, province and social class were all irrelevant. The important point was that we were all Tibetans.'

The Tibetan students had three serious grievances. First, a few months earlier, Zhou Enlai had stated in a speech made in Qingdao that 'the Tibetans must follow the example of other national minorities, like the Manchurians', who had lost their cultural identity and been absorbed into China. The implication was that they should wear Han clothes and speak the Han language. This was in direct violation of the Sino-Tibetan Agreement of 1951. Second, the weekly Tibetan lessons were reduced from six periods to two. Third, a Chinese lecturer pointed disrespectfully at the picture of the Dalai Lama's Potala Palace, with the words: 'This is a landlord's house.' When the Tibetan students demanded to know who was the landlord, the lecturer spelled out, 'The Dalai Lama'.

Although the Chinese official news spoke of nothing but unprecedented progress and prosperity achieved in Tibet since the 'liberation', some of the older students heard that the

Tibetans in eastern Tibet were openly revolting against the Chinese overlords. Seeing the Chinese Communist policy against Tibet slowly unveiling itself at the Institute, the students had no doubt about the Chinese colonial oppression in their country. During their indoctrination the Tibetan youths had learned valuable lessons in organization, efficiency and resourcefulness, and planned their poster war to good effect.

One night three huge posters, containing the three grievances written in Tibetan and Chinese and illustrated by caricatures, were stuck prominently on the walls of the dining-hall and auditorium of the Institute. The students had previously agreed on who should get up to speak if the Chinese demanded it, and also that all Tibetan students must be united in their protest. Next morning the students crowded round the startling posters. Immediately after breakfast the special gong for an emergency meeting was furiously sounded. All the students of the Institute, numbering over two thousand, anxiously gathered in the auditorium. The Principal demanded to know who had put up the posters, which indicated 'local nationalism and a reactionary tendency to separate Tibet from the Motherland'. As planned, Ngawang Thondup and another Tibetan youth got up to speak. The Tibetan students, who were all occupying one section of the hall, applauded loudly, and students from Inner Mongolia and Xinjiang joined in. The two speakers elaborated in Chinese on the three main issues raised in the posters.

A heated discussion between the Tibetan students and the Hans raged in the packed auditorium. There was much shouting and counter-shouting of slogans. The Principal diplomatically called a halt to the battle of words before it degenerated into an open clash between the Hans on one side, and the Tibetans, supported by students from Xinjiang, Manchuria and Mongolia, on the other. The Principal brought the meeting to order, and concluded: 'I shall refer the matter to higher authority. I shall also investigate your three points of protest. But I can assure you that it is Party policy to abide by the 17-Point Agreement, to respect the Dalai Lama, and to allow you to preserve and improve your mother tongue.'

Soon after this incident the Institute closed for the vacation. The Chinese authorities tried to avoid dealing with the issues, and to sow dissension among the Tibetan students and break their unity, which was built on a strong feeling of nationalism. They did not meet with much success. During the holiday the Tibetan students started a *Lhamo* Association, for presenting traditional Tibetan operas – a cultural activity which made them still more nationally conscious. Although the Chinese realized the danger posed by the *Lhamo* Association, they found it difficult to ban it for some time, as it had a cultural character. However, at the beginning of 1957 political struggles began all over China. The Institute was badly affected, and those responsible for the poster war were hauled up and punished.

Ngawang Thondup, however, managed to escape to Tibet soon after. On the pretext that his mother was seriously ill he was able to get three months' leave of absence. The authorities thought he might not return to Beijing, so he was required to obtain the signature of a high dignitary who would guarantee his return to the Institute after the allotted three months. Even today he feels guilty that he had to betray the teacher who signed that guarantee. Since he did not return to the Institute, a caricature of him received a *thamzing*. The Tibetan students were pronounced guilty of 'local nationalism and reactionary tendencies'. Many of them did heroic things during the investigation; Thangmey Kesang Dekyi, for example, a sixteen-year-old girl, swallowed a roll of paper containing the names of the girl members of the *Lhamo* Association when the Chinese began unearthing the nationalist movement. During this purge the 'criminals' were made to wear paper hats with 'local nationalism' inscribed on them. According to Tibetan custom, wearing a paper hat was considered the most degrading punishment a criminal could be given.

Perhaps such nationalist activities were only possible in the honeymoon days when China was pursuing a deceptively liberal policy towards Tibet. Furthermore, it was during this period that Mao uttered his famous slogan: 'Let a hundred flowers bloom, let a hundred schools of thought contend.' However, conditions in both China and Tibet have changed for the worse since that brief time of freedom.

Since 1956 the Tibetan cadres have been trained in China without any Tibetan influences and under much stricter regimentation. Whether their indoctrination was any more successful may be assessed from the experiences of a Tibetan who escaped to India in 1969. Kunsang Paljor, the cadre in question, was sent to Beijing in 1956 at the age of sixteen, when there was no more special treatment for the Tibetan students. Indoctrination was directed first against religion. The students asserted that, despite the Chinese Communist view of religion as poisonous, the Tibetans would continue to practise their faith, and that freedom of faith was within the framework of the Sino-Tibetan Agreement of 1951. The Communists told them that the old superstitious ignorant Tibetans deluded themselves with religion, but that young students like Kunsang Paljor should not do so. If one had studied Marxist-Leninism diligently, said the Chinese, one would at once see the hollowness of religion.

At first Kunsang Paljor intended to study only the Chinese language seriously, but when he had picked up enough knowledge to read the Chinese papers and periodicals he began to take a keen interest in Chinese politics.

The extent of Kunsang's aptitude and academic qualifications can be gauged by the type of assignment the Chinese authorities gave him on his return to Tibet in 1961. He worked as a journalist on the *Tibet Daily News*, the Communist organ in Tibet, and probably knew more about what went on in Tibet in the 1960s than anyone now outside the country. When he came back to Tibet, he was shocked to see the unhappy serious faces of his fellow Tibetans, remembering their smiling faces and laughter before he went to China.

Kunsang's example may be a hopeful pointer to the future. Here was a bright young Tibetan, who was indoctrinated in Beijing for six years, who came back to Tibet only to be enlightened on the unspeakable plight of his fellow Tibetans, and who finally made a daring dash for personal freedom when he could no longer endure Chinese Communist oppression. He admits that, as an intellectual, he was paid well and his own life was comfortable enough; but what he could not tolerate were the sufferings and privations of his own fellow-countrymen, and the darker aspects of Communism which are deemed essential to pave the way to the Marxist material salvation of mankind. According to Kunsang, the Chinese Communists used to say scathingly to the Tibetan students: 'The more you are educated along Mao's lines, the more reactionary tendencies and local nationalism you develop.' This he felt was an apt assessment of the Chinese-trained Tibetan cadres. For the Tibetan students, the indoctrination has been a means of education and sharpening the mind, while the Chinese Communists considered it an end in itself. Kunsang says: 'If you know how the Chinese Communists deceive other people, you can deceive them in the same way. That's what I did. It never occurred to the Chinese Communists that I would ever escape to India; I merely paid them back in the same coin.'

NINE

Thoughts of Escape

THE SUMMER of 1956 was particularly pleasant. The snow was melting like butter even on the highest peaks, and the Sakya river was flowing full and crystal-clear. We often swam in its waters. The Sakya valley was vivid green and very beautiful. The pastures were carpeted with lush green grass, and flowers with gorgeous blue and yellow bells stood out against the natural carpet. The arable fields were equally beautiful. The barley stalks were tall and strong, a sure sign of a good harvest; the mustard fields were dazzling with their bright yellow flowers; and the sweet peas were already blossoming. How anxiously we waited for the sweet peas to become half-ripe! Then we would go in groups to raid the flowers – breathless chases, when our hearts beat faster and louder than our sprinting feet.

The memories of that summer are associated in my mind with the exciting news I heard at school. I remember hearing Comrade Nyima reading a current issue of the *Tibet Daily News*, which described the first meeting of the Preparatory Committee for the Autonomous Region of Tibet, presided over by the Dalai Lama. Of the three decisions taken, the one that most interested me was this: 'To train cadres, including ecclesiastical and temporal officials, within the shortest possible time and on a large scale, and to plan to train 2,000 cadres in schools in Tibet within the year.' An improvised school for the cadres was opened in Sakya by the end of 1956. The Chinese called it 'Working Cadres School', but we humorously nicknamed it the 'Old Men's School', for the concept of adult education was unknown to us.

Sixty young men, from all parts of the Sakya region, were paid 60 *dayuans* per month, plus free food, lodging and clothing to attend. The local people were not taken in, and argued: 'The Uncles (Chinese) won't give you all those *dayin* for nothing. After the pleasure purchased with the silver dollars, you're sure to get pains.' But for the time being the young men had a fabulous time contributing to the social life of Sakya. Being young and carefree most of them were spendthrifts, throwing away their silver dollars. The sleepy bazaar suddenly became alive and hummed with business. In addition, the young of both sexes had many new faces, handsome or pretty as the case might be, to choose from. Previously, romantic or casual affairs had been confined to the town itself; but when the Working Cadres School was started, there were many good-looking young men coming from round about. It was at this time that my sister Donkar gave birth to an illegitimate son.

Sakya in 1956 was an interesting and exciting town, where remnants of past greatness and the apparent progress of the present peacefully existed together. The Great Sakya Monastery, consecrated when the Sakya sect was in its heyday, still rang its calm, heart-soothing bells on the gentle wind. Nearby was the Shetok, the stately building that once housed the government of Tibet in the fourteenth century, and was now the seat of the Sakya local government. Every now and then you could see a bored official peering from one of its windows. There was also the Simchung House, a white, prosaic, symmetrical new building, on whose roof fluttered the huge red flag of the Chinese administration.

In those days I was extremely happy, living a life full of new interest, excitement and hope. So it was with a great sense of shock that we heard that the 'peaceful liberation' was postponed for six years by the Chinese. Our own school was closed

down, as was the Working Cadres' School, after its few months
of happy existence. In short, everything that the Chinese had
started was hurriedly dismantled – the offices of various
Communist youth organizations, the local branch of the
Preparatory Committee, the hospital. The two Chinese teachers
who taught us arithmetic and physical training could hardly
conceal their joy, and most of the Chinese 'working personnel'
were equally pleased. After all, they had been sent to Tibet
under compulsion, separated from their loved ones, and only
sustained by the occasional censored letter.

Sakya once again became a memory-haunted backwater.
The narrow streets, above which the old houses leant towards
each other, were deserted. The once-flourishing market was
asleep; there was more noise from the chirping sparrows than
from the voices of the customers. The monastery regained its
sanctity and silence. The Simchung headquarters was desolate
and abandoned – for a while at least. The young people became
listless and dispirited. The aristocratic activists were out of
their well-paid jobs. My own teacher had to cut down on his
lavish expenditure. While employed by the Chinese, he drank
tea sweetened with sugar every afternoon, but now he was
forced to go back to the traditional diet; and he had to stop
smoking cigarettes and return to his good old native pipe.
Parties were few and on a small scale. The fervent, vigorous
pseudo-intellectual life was dead, and socialism, once a staple
mental diet, was discussed no more. The young government
officials, who had been in the vanguard of the peaceful revolution and had interested themselves in their new, enthralling
posts, lost all their zeal and enthusiasm after the Chinese magi-
cians departed. They resumed their traditional lethargic life –
quite reluctantly, I think. A few sold their recently acquired
watches, for seconds, minutes and hours were the masters of
the time-bound Chinese, not of the Tibetans.

However, the mass of the people, who had obstinately
resisted the socialist fever of the 1950s, and the monks, who

were implacably opposed to the Chinese, breathed a sigh of relief when 'the enemies of the faith' departed. The old and faithful thanked Kunchok-Sum for not allowing the Chinese Reds to succeed with their 'peaceful liberation'. Indeed, the masses did not want 'liberation': the Chinese Communists imposed it upon them. The mere fact that the Chinese had left Sakya was an unspeakable relief to ordinary people. They thought that the alien enemies of the native faith would leave the Land of Snows, the bastion of Buddhism, and that they would be allowed to worship and work alternately as before. Mother even sent Abu to Shigatse on a normal business trip, despite an unexpected drop in the value of currency.

The Chinese had to postpone their 'liberation' because there was no 'revolutionary situation' and the conditions were 'unripe for reforms'. Realizing that the so-called liberators were actually oppressors, the Khampas, who were the first to be 'liberated', had already formed the resistance movement known as the 'Four Rivers and Six Ranges'. The first fighting took place in Batang and Lithang on the eastern border, and the conflict spread like wildfire towards Kham proper and central Tibet. The Chinese allegation that the revolt of the late 1950s had no popular support has no basis in fact, but it was the only ideologically plausible excuse they could give. If the revolt even in its initial stages had not been generally supported, the small 'upper strata reactionary clique' would have been like a tiny bee buzzing frantically against the might of the Red Army. Furthermore, to allege, as the Chinese did, that most of the rebels 'were coerced or deceived or forced directly by the feudal lords to resist the Chinese' was an imaginative lie. Even if such an attempt had been made, the rebels could easily have run away to the security of the People's Liberation Army; for Tibet was already infested with the armoured khaki-clad ants of the Chinese.

Opposition to the Chinese was due to the fact that to the Tibetans religion was everything. To the poor it was the only living comfort and hope for a better next life, and to the rich it was the only ideology which gave their life meaning. That the Communists were the foes of our faith was common knowledge well before the Red Army marched into our country. The commoners had another advantage over the elite: since they were illiterate, they were unreceptive to new ideas. They could not read the deceptive 17-Point Agreement for themselves, neither had anyone else read it to them; nor could they understand the new concept of the Commune system. They dismissed all these with a shake of the head and the cryptic phrase, 'not a good sign'.

I am not implying that social reforms were not needed in Tibet – far from it. However, the common Tibetans were by and large content with their life, though the contentment was bought at great cost. The Tibetan people had their own concept of happiness, which was essentially spiritual. Chairman Mao had a new concept of happiness, which he thought would be welcome to the Tibetan masses. Now that I know a little more about the great leader of China, I wish that Mao had seen for himself the exact situation in Tibet. If he had known that the Tibetan people were unhappy with his kindly-conceived 'liberations', he might have withdrawn his comrades from Tibet. After all, why should the saviour of the masses give them more suffering?

I also think that, step by step, Tibet would eventually have transformed herself. The XIIIth Dalai Lama introduced a considerable number of reforms, as already described. The XIVth and present Dalai Lama had plans for democratization which the Chinese invaders did not allow to mature. Knowing the honesty and sincerity of the Dalai Lama, I have complete faith that he would have tried to reform Tibet. As long as Tibet shut its door to the outside world, there would have been no talk about social changes; but this situation could not possibly have lasted. Social changes were inevitable, even if there had been no Chinese invasion.

Leaving speculation aside, once the Chinese had gone, the people in Sakya hoped that the postponement might finally lead to a cancellation of the 'peaceful liberation'. We piled hope upon hope, possibility upon possibility. When Abu came back from his business trip to Shigatse he brought the news that the 'Delhi *Gyalpo*' (*gyalpo* means king) was coming to Lhasa to make a treaty between China and Tibet. This referred to Nehru, who had been invited by the Dalai Lama in late 1956.

Nehru was perhaps the only outside world statesman known generally among the Tibetans. I remember seeing photographs of him respectfully kept in a trader's house in Sakya. On asking who he was, I was told that he was the 'wisest man in the world, like Sakya Pandit was in his own time'. The news that he was coming to Tibet was indeed glad tidings. We hoped that he might prove our political saviour, and help us to get out of the intricate mesh of the Chinese liberation. He was our only hope. And no Tibetan would ever have dreamt of the policy which he in fact adopted towards Tibet – a policy which synchronized neither with the prevalent intellectual mood, nor with the Indian people's wishes. It was governed by three factors: 'The preservation and security of India; our desire to maintain friendly relations with China; and our deep sympathy for the people of Tibet.' So all that the Tibetan people received for the trust and faith they put in Pandit Nehru and Holy India was a cold, passive sympathy.

Of course at the time none of the Tibetans had the slightest comprehension of the great chess game that Pandit Nehru and Comrade Zhou Enlai were playing. Tibet was murdered, and upon its grave the Panch Shila, or five principles of co-existence, the clauses of the Sino-Indian Agreement of 29 April 1954, were engraved. I recently told a Tibetan labourer working on the roads in India that India had recognized Chinese sovereignty over Tibet, and he cried out that we had been betrayed. Not only did the Dalai Lama and the nobility trust India, but, far more importantly, the common people of Tibet did. We were taught to refer to her as 'Holy India', and nearly every scripture we read had a few words of Sanskrit at the beginning. But Pandit Nehru did not come, and we were disappointed.

After the postponement of the 'peaceful liberation', for six years the situation in Tibet progressively deteriorated. One sign of this was the unprecedented number of Khampa 'pilgrims', mostly from Amdo, who came to Sakya. They stopped there for a week or so, selling Chinese tea and cups, and seeing the monasteries. After this they would set off again towards the north of India. Most of them lied and said that they were 'pilgrims', but a few were frank enough to tell us the truth: they were refugees from Amdo and Kham. They recommended us to start selling our property, collect silver dollars, and make our way to India while there was still time. They warned that, if we stayed, we were sure to end up in the same boat as the Amdos. Instead of heeding their friendly advice and making careful preparation for an early escape, many Sakyans preferred to buy Chinese cups and other goods, storing them away for special occasions that never came.

Meanwhile Khampas in small groups continued to move towards India via Sakya. The biggest contingent was a group known as the Jagod Tsang. Before their arrival there was general apprehension; the Chinese Communists had portrayed the Khampa freedom fighters as notorious bandits whose sole business was looting, plundering and rape. They had a certain amount of justification. Most of the Khampa guerillas were engaged in a praiseworthy national war of liberation, with little means at their disposal, and were supplied by the local inhabitants with their daily necessities. Some, however, used the name of a holy war to engage in nefarious activities, especially near the Indian border.

The Jagod Tsang group seemed fairly well disciplined and organized and had acquired some military characteristics. The fighters were tall and tough-looking warriors, mostly middle-aged men, who looked big and fearsome in comparison with their Chinese counterparts. They encamped on a large grazing ground a mile outside the town, in tents guarded by fierce-looking sentries. They claimed that they had been fighting hard in several places for the glory of our *dharma*, and had many victories to their credit. Explaining their future plans, they assured us that they were going to attack some stranded Red Army units in western Tibet. They demanded pistols and rifles from the rich, and replacements for their weak, tired horses, and they received more food supplies than they could carry. Despite their assertions, we suspected that they were making an honourable retreat to India, since prospects of victory were slim. They had retreated from Kham while the resistance movement was fighting its last losing battle in the area. After a few months they left Sakya.

At about this time the Sakya Lama also left, travelling incognito. We were told that he was going for a religious retreat in a remote meditation sanctuary among the rocks and slates of Mount Taktsenma. Such retreats were quite usual for the High Lama. In spite of travelling incognito, he had the full traditional send-off. I saw the procession. A double column of colourful riders was headed by religious musicians playing the vibrant tunes we loved to hear. Next came young monks carrying religious banners and umbrellas signifying the holy status of the High Lama. They were followed by grave ecclesiastical dignitaries, conscious of the divine presence and oblivious of us, the spectators. Preceded by monk officials and followed by lay officials rode the Sakya Lama, the Lord of Refuge, in a comfortable palanquin carried by four strong men in yellow brocade. Anyone who caught sight of his face through the small window of the palanquin was considered supremely fortunate. The government officials were all in gorgeous Chinese brocades, fashioned as Tibetan etiquette demanded; they condescendingly bowed their heavily capped heads and shook their long earrings.

This spectacular procession of piety and splendour passed peacefully along the cleanly swept path, sanctified by burning and smouldering pine needles – a spiritual purification that enabled the *Bodhisattva* to pass without being accidentally contaminated. Along both sides of the road were the Sakyans, humbly bowing low to receive blessings from the Lord of Refuge. Though the haughty bodyguards tried to prevent it, the devout onlookers prostrated themselves on the spot. Even we children were overawed. None of us knew that we were saying a grand goodbye to our young lama and teacher.

A week later, a nomad friend of ours from Khawu, near the religious retreat, brought down our monthly supply of fuel – about fifteen yakloads of sheep and yak dung. He told us that the nomads in Khawu saw His Holiness and party crossing the pass leading to India. Although they could not be absolutely certain, they guessed that the Sakya Lama was seeking refuge in India. Mother's attitude was: 'If our Lord of Refuge leaves sacred Sakya, we shall never be happy.' We believed that the Sakya Lama, like any High Incarnate in Tibet, saw the past, present and future as clearly as you can see yourself in a mirror; hence his departure was a pointer to a fearful future. Mother declared that we must follow the Sakya Lama, as he was our lama and leader for this life and the next, and we could not live a proper life without him.

Abu, on the other hand, though extremely religious for his age, showed signs of disagreement. He had been to India, and knew that it was not a land of milk and honey. If you could not work you would not get food in India; it was not like Tibet, where you could never starve, no matter how poor you might be. Like most Tibetans, Abu felt that the Chinese occupation was like a 'red cloud over Tibet', which would vanish any time. Lastly he defended his standpoint by saying that the Chinese Reds would not inflict suffering upon the poor. We were an insignificant cypher to them. There was no difference whether we were under old or new masters; we had been born low and would remain low. We were unconvinced by Abu's arguments. In addition, he was a disobedient son, who had heedlessly deviated from the traditional norms. During this period of uncertainty he got entangled with a brewer's daughter. Mother violently disapproved of his choice, and he just as violently loved his fiancée.

Rejecting his views, Mother went ahead with her plans. She had partly accepted the Amdos' sincere advice, and had been hoarding silver dollars, selling nearly all our goods and changing our Tibetan currency into *dayin*. She was also far-sighted enough to arrange our escape before the Chinese returned to Sakya, but Abu let her down. However, Abu's attitude seemed to be justified when we heard that the Sakya Lama had written two letters, one to the local government and the other to the monastery, ordering everyone, especially the officials, to remain in Sakya. The letters were written and sent from the Indian side of the India-Tibetan border as soon as the party arrived at its sanctuary. His Holiness stated that the oracles in his retreat had told him to leave Sakya temporarily. However, he hoped that Tibet would soon get rid of the Chinese Reds and that he would be able to see Sacred Sakya again, intact, both spiritually and materially. The letters were mainly to convey the order that none should escape. The Sakya government, under the wise leadership of the *Zodpa*, must function as before. Every official must return to his work in the government building, and its windows must be open so that the public could feel secure and not panic. The same applied to the monks. The Great Monastery must function as before. All prayers and rites must be held as usual; the monks must not leave their duties to drink gallons of tea; and the musicians must play their usual tunes from the monastery roof, so that we could sleep as soundly as before. In short, His Holiness's absence should create no confusion and disorder in Sakya.

What is one to make of these strange letters? When, years later, I met the Sakya Lama at the Sakya Settlement in India I asked him why he sent them. He explained that he was very young when he left Tibet and did not know much; nevertheless, he would consult his advisers and send me a written answer. I have not received it yet; but I would imagine that His Holiness, or more precisely his advisers, thought that the Chinese occupation was just a 'red cloud over Tibet' and that one day the sun would shine again. These ill-advised letters typify the unceasing hope of the Tibetans, which stems from fortitude and perseverance in adversity. It also stems from ignorance – the highest and supposedly the most enlightened authority in Sakya thought that Tibet would somehow regain her independence, and soon, too. This conviction is the reason why some lay Tibetan may stop me in the bazaar and ask when we are getting our *rangtsen* (independence), as if some sort of a legal case were still going on; and why my ageing mother waited each day for *rangtsen* as if it were going to drop from the skies.

Those who are stranded in Tibet must be waiting even more impatiently. After the flight of the Dalai Lama in March 1959, whenever a noisy Chinese aeroplane flew over Sakya we used to bow down at once and pray that it was His Holiness returning to us. The mentors of the Sakya Lama thought along the same lines. They reckoned that the Chinese occupation would not last long, but that even during this estimated short period of darkness and distress the Chinese were likely to harm the person of the Sakya Lama. He was the most precious jewel of Sakya, its pivot; therefore, no risks must be taken as far as he was concerned. As for the others, they must remain, partly to guard the town and partly to look after the fruit of our forefathers – all the 108 monasteries round about, including the famous Great Monastery of Sakya.

So everyone in Sakya stayed put and waited for the Chinese. The letters did not directly affect the public, for they

were addressed and secretly delivered to the government officials and monks; but they affected them indirectly, since the
mindless masses would follow their superiors' example. It
was tragic that the High Lama unwittingly rounded up his
subordinates for the Chinese, who must have considered it a
highly patriotic act from a 'reactionary traitor'. When the aristocrats and monks found themselves in prison, they said to
themselves: 'Had we not received that order, we should have
been safe in India by now. But it was due to our *karma*, and we
must not complain irreverently against our High Lama.' Sakya
is only about fifteen days' trek from the Indian border, and
any of our learned lamas and aristocrats could have escaped
easily.

When Lhasa was falling to the Chinese, after the flight of
the Dalai Lama, a woman with second sight claimed that she
saw Chinese soldiers on the holy Ponto Hill. This omen was
confirmed when the Chinese general, after successfully suppressing the Lhasa uprising, sent a few soldiers to Sakya. The
night of their arrival was one of the most tense and sad
moments that its citizens had ever experienced. Mother said: 'I
have never been more terrified and sad since the day I was
born.' By then we knew that our venerable government had
collapsed, perhaps never to recover. It suddenly struck us that
Tibet was no more our country; that we were no longer free
Tibetans; that we were under alien overlords, the Chinese
Communists. The Land of Snows, the land of lamas, the land of
eternal mystery had passed away. Losing one's country was
like suddenly losing one's parents. When we heard that the
Chinese had captured Lhasa, all of us in Sakya felt the shock of
that great loss. Everyone who visited us that day asked Mother
in a choking voice: 'What shall we do now, Akyi?' Many people
in Sakya were so upset that they literally fainted.

That night Mother did not sleep. She leaned against the
wall and peered fearfully through the window, watching
every movement in the disturbed town. When we woke the

next morning, we found her face swollen and her eyes red with weeping. There had been more movement in the village than usual, she told us. At midnight she had seen two close associates of the Sakya Lama passing our house, leading horses heavily laden but without any bells. She knew that they were going to India, and envied them their good fortune. She was worried that the whole population might go, leaving us alone for the Chinese. Since Abu – who knew the way to India and was the only man in our family – stubbornly refused to escape, we were helpless. By an infallible decree of *karma* we were perhaps born to be the prey of the godless Chinese Communists.

Next day the Chinese called for a mass meeting. To Mother's surprise and relief, she found that only the two persons she had seen escaping were missing. The meeting was proclaimed as a jubilant occasion for the Tibetan people in general and for the 'serfs' in particular. The army chief told us, as Beijing's spokesman, that the revolt was engineered by the Tibetan 'upper strata reactionary clique'. The nobility and monasteries of Tibet had joined hands with the foreign imperialists and had started an abortive rebellion. Having failed miserably, Tibet's serf-owners had robbed the Tibetan people of their beloved Dalai Lama. When we heard this we breathed a sigh of relief, and murmured: 'Thank God, the Precious One is safe. Now we shall be all right.'

Having condemned the reactionaries, he told us how the heroic units of the People's Liberation Army in Lhasa had suppressed the rebellion in 47 hours – not even two full days, he emphasized. Suddenly he became very modest. The credit for this decisive victory went not to the PLA alone but also to the Tibetan masses. While the PLA were sweeping the rebels from their Lhasa stronghold, the Tibetans followed, bringing them food and other supplies. There was a sudden burst of laughter from the crowd at the very idea of Tibetans bringing food to the fighting Chinese soldiers. The girl interpreter, Norzin-la, pointed to the section of the crowd where the laughter had come from and demanded the reasons for it. No one replied; everyone's eyes were glued to the ground. Later we found out that it was an ex-soldier of the Tibetan army who had started the laughter.

Knowing the Tibetan commoners' response to the Chinese 'liberation' during the previous eight years, I am positive that the Chinese claim that they were supported by the Tibetan people in their suppression of the revolt is utter nonsense. Even if we could have done no more than throw a handful of dust at the enemies of our faith, we would have done it with all our heart and soul. Far from supporting the Chinese over-lords, the Tibetan people would have launched a countrywide revolt, if only they had had dynamic leadership. In May 1959, the people of Sakya protested peacefully against the Chinese plan that the Governor should be 'tried by the masses'. The Lhasa uprising in March 1959 was a spontaneous revolt sparked off by desperation. The people in the capital were naturally better informed of the current political situation, and being more educated they were able to organize themselves and offer at least a token resistance. If we had had modern means of communication, the entire Tibetan people could have been mobilized. Unfortunately, our government officials were not able to identify with the Tibetan masses. The situation was a new one, demanding new leaders with new ideas. Tragically, our leaders (if they deserve the term) were not pre-pared for the new situation, nor did they have much freedom to deal with it.

Once the revolt in Tibet was over, everybody felt their life was broken beyond repair. Like most Tibetans, Mother was desperately exploring the possibilities of flight. So far no one in Sakya had been brave enough to make a break for freedom. The pioneer venture was left to the Phunubpa family, a large, pros-perous clan in the village of Samling, three miles from Sakya. They owned, to use a Tibetan expression, 'yaks and sheep on the hill and horses and donkeys in the vale'. When we heard of their escape, we envied them because we wished we had tiger-like sons in our family, and we prayed that they might not be caught. It was Chinese official policy not to send any Red Army men after common Tibetans escaping, though they sent parties of soldiers after the upper strata. When they heard of the Phunubpas' escape, the Chinese 'working personnel' orga-nized a search party consisting of eight Tibetan progressives and activists armed with rifles. They found the Phunubpas in an old summer sheep-shed on Mount Taktsenma, and told them that they had been misled by reactionary elements and should return home. Not believing them, the brave Phunubpa men gave them a few bold strokes, and the search party came back wounded and bleeding. The Sakyans hailed the Phunubpas' resistance as an act of valour and manliness. When I was naughty, Mother would challenge me: 'If you are brave, why don't you behave like the sons of Phunubpa?'

No doubt the Phunubpa family was well equipped and manned for the escape; but they certainly demonstrated to the Sakyans that it was better to risk everything for the sake of per-sonal freedom and even to die than to exist under the Chinese. Soon many were to follow their example. Next to flee was Rasha Lama-la, the tantric practitioner and our weather con-troller under the old order. As usual, a search party was sent, but they returned empty-handed. Later, we learned that such parties never really searched, not because they were lazy, but because they themselves were planning to escape. In our final and successful escape the commander was a 'progressive', who had been on several such chases and who, instead of chasing the fugitives, worked out a good route for his own future flight. Unfortunately, Rasha Lama-la's party ran into a Chinese patrol on horseback. The Indian border was only a day's journey away, and they could already see the mighty Himalayas, beyond which lay freedom. Thinking they were out of the dan-ger area, the party rashly travelled during the day.

When the unfortunate party 'returned', as the Chinese put it, the people of Sakya were summoned to welcome them. As they reluctantly arrived in front of the Great Monastery, the fugitives looked tired and dispirited. We were supposed to applaud, but we all clicked our tongues to express our pity. We all thought that the chief organizers of the escape, if not all, would be imprisoned; but to our surprise and relief none was imprisoned immediately. Instead, they were all taken to the Chinese headquarters at Simchung House, where the comrades gave them refreshments, followed by a sermon, which was later repeated to us all in a mass meeting. As she herself longed to escape, Mother was keenly interested in knowing what the Chinese would do if you were caught. The Chinese told the fugitives: 'You all belong to the common masses of Tibet and you should have no fear whatsoever. It is time for you to raise your heads and enjoy an equality undreamed-of by your parents. We presume that you have been misled by reactionary elements, and have carelessly listened to evil rumours. Now return to your senses and settle down happily. You will not be punished, even for your insane attempt to escape.'

All the same, Rasha Lama-la and Phuntsog Rapten were persistently questioned as to why they had schemed to escape. Phuntsog Rapten was later sentenced to prison; but a 'progressive' friend of the lama warned him in time, and he managed to escape successfully to freedom.

Seeing the readiness of the people to escape, the Chinese called a special public meeting. It was so different from the old days, when the lords would have passed some pedantic decree without a word of explanation. The new overlords would persuade us, explain to us, and try to convince us through their arguments and dialectics. They painted such a horrifying portrait of India that many changed their minds. 'Have you any idea what you are doing when you plan to escape?' Comrade Norzin-la interpreted. 'India is one of the hottest countries in the world – so hot that you do not need to boil water for tea. You have been born and brought up in the icy mountains of Tibet; yet you want to jump out of the glacier into the furnace. If you decide in a thoughtless frenzy to leave your own beautiful Tibet and betray the Mighty Motherland, you are deliberately going to your doom.'

Next they turned to the poverty of India. 'Are any of you rich enough to live in capitalist India? A capitalist society is heaven for a few affluent capitalists and hell for the masses. The teeming millions are eternally locked in misery and famine. India is perpetually starving, as you serfs used to starve under the evil feudal system. She has to borrow food from the imperialist United States and other similar countries. Apart from the staggering capital repayment, she cannot pay the interest on all her debts. Would you like to go to this starving, unjust country?'

The next point concerned India's calamities and diseases. 'Because India is burning hot,' argued the Chinese, 'you sons of snow are susceptible to all the diseases found there. And the diseases of heat are many. Malaria will finish you off before your allotted time.' (Malaria was one of the most dreaded diseases of India known to the Tibetans, and any Tibetan visiting an Indian hill station in summer would be susceptible to it.) 'Most of those who escaped have already died. Unless you have money, you cannot get medical treatment in a capitalist society – unlike here. Every year India faces floods, and millions are drowned in them. Are you going to dig your graves in India by foolishly leaving your own land?'

The final point was a threat. 'Under this sky,' said the spokesman, raising his fist and his voice, 'you cannot escape from the Chinese Communist Party and the People's Liberation Army, just as you cannot escape from death. And what is India to us? Nothing! We can march in whenever we please. India is bound by the 1954 Agreement on the Five Principles of Co-existence. Accordingly, the Government of

India will extradite all Tibetan self-exiles, who are Chinese nationals.' (In fact, the Indian Government did round up Tibetan refugees at the beginning of 1959, before the Dalai Lama escaped to India, but fortunately did not send them back.) 'The duty and ultimate goal of every Communist is to overthrow the bourgeoisie and to create an international republic. Asia is our special task. The patriotic people of China cannot rest until we have liberated our neighbours. Now, however, if you wish to escape in spite of our sincere advice, you can go during the day so that it will be easier for you,' he concluded contemptuously.

The meeting cast doubt where there had formerly been certainty, and placed those who had decided to escape in a dilemma. Fortunately for the Chinese, an ex-monk who had escaped earlier returned to Sakya to collect his wife, and confirmed everything that the Chinese had told us. His experiences made good propaganda, and he was sent to tour the areas round Sakya, telling the people about his disillusionment with India. 'I thought India was a land of *khushi* (freedom), and so I escaped. My first taste of *khushi* was right at the border. A corrupt local policeman kicked me here for nothing.' (He showed his bottom to his audience.) 'I thought I could get plenty of food in India, but I had to live on this small piece of bread for a whole day.' (He showed a sample piece.) 'You have to buy even water in India! Most of the Tibetans who escaped have already died of malaria. I have been suffering from it, too, but thanks to the Chinese Communist Party I am getting free medical treatment and careful personal attention from the Chinese doctor, and I am all right. I hope none of you will be mad enough to escape to India.'

To be sure, Mother was not convinced, but owing partly to the 'unhappy India' campaign, and partly to the stricter restrictions imposed, it was extremely difficult to get into contact with trustworthy people going to India. So far the Chinese had done nothing drastically harmful to the commoners. Above all, oracles at the oldest temple in Sakya city and at our late father's abbey declared that we should remain in Sakya. Probably it was not yet time for us to escape. In any case, we decided to try our new life under the Chinese Communist Party.

TEN

The Reactionaries are Crushed

ONE COLD, bleak morning we were awakened by the servant of Paljor Khang, one of the third-ranking officials in the Sakya local government. On his master's order, the servant bought an Indian fountain pen and an exercise book. Mother was inwardly rather annoyed at such an unusually early purchaser, for he had arrived even before our fire was lit. With a conceit arising from his having access to his master's secrets, the servant confided in Mother that Mr Paljor was going to attend a 'political education' (*lobjong*) session conducted by the Chinese. Traditional writing implements were not only cumbersome but 'old' as well. The 'modern' pen and book would make His Excellency appear more progressive, and the Chinese would be pleased.

The ecclesiastical and government officials, the aristocrats and the affluent took their pens and books to the Dolma Palace as if to school, without the slightest suspicion of what the Chinese really meant by *lobjong*. Later in the morning, when we were helping Mother to lay out her goods in the market, we saw the grave students, accompanied by their personal servants, walking with dignity towards the Dolma Palace. We all got up and bowed our heads – for the last time.

A fortnight after the beginning of 'political education' it became clear that *lobjong* meant imprisonment. The nobility had failed to understand the language of Communism even after eight years of constant contact with it. Two lay second-rank officials, Dragpa Tsedor and Jango, who had been spending their holidays near the Indian border, returned to Sakya to attend *lob-jong*. Just before the Chinese arrived, Dragpa had gone to see his relatives in a village only a day's journey from the Indian border. At the Chinese request the Sakya governor wrote to him and Jango, ordering them to return to Sakya immediately for political education. Jango was on holiday at his estate two days' journey from Sakya. One afternoon we saw them returning on horseback, sumptuously dressed and accompanied by their usual retinue of servants. They were immediately arrested. Had they known the actual situation, they could easily have crossed the border in broad daylight.

For the first two weeks the political prisoners did not feel alarmed. They were left to themselves in the Dolma Palace, though sentries were already posted. During this period their families, their relatives and their friends called to see them at the 'school', bringing plenty of delicious food. The Tibetan aristocrats used to eat the best food and wear their best costumes when they met together, in a contest of riches. It was an expensive custom for the commoners, who had to give food and drink to their superior friends on such occasions. I went to see my old teacher, Kunga Topla, who had been arrested with the others, taking with me a small tin of sweets round the gate, where two soldiers checked the presents. Someone who later escaped from the prison told me that they enjoyed two weeks of feasting – the last feast of their pampered lives. It was an ironic situation: here were 'criminals' allowed to commit more of the sins against society for which they had been imprisoned.

After the second week visitors were strictly prohibited. Before long we heard that the 'reactionary upper clique' was under trial. Most of us were helplessly sympathetic with the prisoners, the people's 'exploiters'. The abiding common link between them and us was that we were all Tibetans, living in the Land of Snows, eating *tsampa*, wearing the *chuba*, and praying '*Om Mani Padme Hum.*' The difference between the Chinese, who imprisoned our own Tibetans, and us was as great as between sheep and wolves. Mother would say: 'The Chinese Reds first courteously came and then shamelessly robbed us of our country. Now they have the audacity to imprison our own men in our own land, like a street dog occupying your yard and then barking at you.' Others would say: 'Our eyes and ears are imprisoned. We are like a dog with broken limbs.'

However, some of the *tralpas* thought that the wheel of *karma* had at last turned against the sinful aristocrats, and that imprisonment served them right. Their attitude was: 'They have sucked so much juice from us that now they can't digest it. The evil they have done to others has bounced back at them.' Those who had a personal grudge against the aristocrats were pleased. But without exception everybody resented the fact that the lamas had been imprisoned.

Once the Chinese had closed the prison doors to the outside world, we had no clear idea of what went on inside. We were all upset and waited anxiously for the prisoners' release. It was not, however, until we reached India and met some of those who had escaped that we came to know the wretchedness and torment of prison life. About ten prisoners managed to escape after two or three years' hard labour, and four made a hair-raising escape from prison itself.

I got most of my information from Tashi, one of the four who escaped directly from prison. Far from being an aristocrat, he was a bootmaker, living in a village about four miles from Sakya, and had been to India a few times on foot. He was informed on and imprisoned for spreading reactionary rumours that India was a free and happy land, and for planning to escape, which he finally succeeded in doing.

Tashi told me one of the most thrilling escape stories I have ever heard. Being young and a 'progressive', he and three other prisoners were given the privilege of fetching water from the distant river Daachu. They were always escorted by an armed Chinese guard. Each of them must have thought of escaping, but none thought he could trust the others. However, one day the bravest of them took the biggest risk of his life; he suggested that the four should escape. They worked out a rough plan, and the same night they swore that if any of them violated their pact in any way, he would be killed by the other three.

One afternoon the four volunteered to go for water. When they reached the river, one of them yelled with pretended excitement; 'There's a huge fish under this boulder! Come and have a look!' The Chinese guard also rushed inquisitively to the scene. Suddenly the tallest prisoner caught him round the neck; the others hurriedly disarmed him, bound him with their belts, and placed him behind a huge boulder. They took his gun and sprinted towards Mount Taktsenma. When they reached the foot of the mountain in the late evening, they saw torches everywhere and heard gunfire from all directions. Sakya was in a commotion. That night they hid like deer among the rocks. After a long, exhausting journey, they arrived half-starved at the Indian border. Tashi was extremely proud of their heroic deed and of the automatic rifle they had taken from the guard. They were the only Sakyans to have fought with a Chinese.

Tashi gave me detailed information about conditions in the Dolma Palace. On the first day of their political education, the 'students' were told to do nothing but think. Before they could ask what they were supposed to think about, the interpreter added: 'Just think deeply and widely on what you have done, please. Next week we would like to know your thoughts.' The following week a mass meeting of all the prisoners was held in the inner court of the palace. An angry, scornful army chief, introduced as Zhou Zhang, spoke at length to this effect: 'We, the Chinese Communist Party, are both the earth and the sky. Everything and everyone is between the two. Now you are under our thumb. Just as you cannot escape from death, so you cannot escape from this prison. For generations you have sat on thrones and given orders; for centuries you have ridden on other people's backs. Up to the present day you have done nothing but suck the Tibetan people's blood. The tide of history has washed all this away. Now you will change places with your serfs and slaves and pay for what you have done to them. The rod with which you whipped the people will be used against you: this is the retributive justice of our Party. The Chinese Communist Party has snatched the power from the ruling clique and has transferred it to the people of Tibet. So your sun has set forever, and the people's has risen and will shine forever.

'During the past nine years you have spared no effort to delay, postpone and if possible nullify our democratic reforms. You have betrayed the Motherland, Tibet and the Tibetan people, and have organized an abortive, secessionist, rebellious movement with imperialist collaboration. Fortunately, the heroic soldiers of the People's Liberation Army and the patriotic Tibetan masses have completely crushed the reactionaries. I know that most of you have actively participated in the rebellion. You have sent the Sakya Lama to India and helped the Khampa bandits with food supplies. Our party policy is that self-confession gains leniency, so the more you confess the sooner you will be free. You are under trial by the People's Court, and the people are your witnesses.

'Now I want every one of you to write down the crimes you have committed from the earliest days you can recall, especially details of your connection with the rebels.'

The 'students' were stunned and mortified. They looked at one another with vacant, lost eyes, completely taken aback. The learned tutor of the Sakya Lama, hearing all this, went out of his mind. He jumped up, yelling and shouting, and began to dance his lama dances. Two guards kicked him, dragged him away, and threw him into a cell, where he continued to make noises like an animal late into the night. The Chinese thought he was still defying them, so he was taken to Simchung House. A pro-communist Tibetan, who was cooking for the Chinese there, saw the poor man hung upside down the whole night. When he was taken down the next morning, he fell dead on the ground.

In the so-called People's Court the act of rebellion was the most serious of all crimes, since the rebels and their associates were downright traitors to the Motherland. In Sakya, no one was directly involved with the nationalist movement. However, there were people connected with the Sakya Lama's escape, with Ponta Tsang, a Khampa leader who was a special political officer from Lhasa in Sakya, and with Khampa guerillas who passed through Sakya en route to India. All these were scrutinized most thoroughly. You might not have been a high-ranking official in the old hierarchy, but if you were connected with the 'traitors in any way, no matter how unintentionally, you were a first-degree criminal under the people's law'. As such you would receive top punishment at the hands of the Chinese Communists. The usual crimes, such as exploitation and oppression of the masses, faded into insignificance.

The Chinese put pressure on every prisoner to confess his connections with the reactionary, traitorous Sakya Lama, and the Khampa Freedom Fighters. They set traps to get information, and their clever use of psychology was not at all obvious to the simple Tibetans. At the weekly mass meetings the Chinese officers would claim that they knew everything that had been done by the prisoners, who would feel compelled to admit everything. But the Chinese were never satisfied 'until they took out your heart'. On one occasion, the Abbot of the Great Sakya Monastery courageously turned the tables on the Chinese. He said: 'I have confessed whatever I am guilty of. Now I understand it is the custom of your Party to say I have done things I have not done. So now I apologize to the people for everything done or left undone. I am guilty of everything on earth.'

Both inside and outside the prison, everyone was employed to spy on everyone else. A former prisoner whose family is now stranded in Tibet told me about it: 'One day the interpreter told me that Comrade Zhou Zhang, the Chinese commandant, wanted to see me. To my surprise, the chief was smiling and grinning. Shaking hands with me and patting me on the back, he told me to sit on the chair beside him while the interpreter stood. Then he offered me a cigarette, which I politely refused. I did not say that I had taken a vow not to smoke, but told him I had throat trouble. He suggested kindly that I should see the doctor. All this time I was dreading to hear what was coming. Without further delay, he said: "Comrade, I want you to watch your friends and your room-mates. Keep an eye on how they work and how they think. I can promise that you will be released if you report faithfully." I thought over all this while eating, while walking, while going to bed. I knew it was a per-fidious thing to do, so I decided to compromise by reporting only trifles. I kept a close watch over the others, particularly my room-mates, but they seemed even more cautious and suspi-cious than I was. In fact, one of my room-mates tried to sound me out by asking me what I thought of our predicament.

'Two weeks passed and I had nothing to report. Then one afternoon, while on hard labour, I saw that Kunsang was engaged in private worship, secretly turning his rosary in his pocket while working. I reported this to the chief comrade, who told me that I was showing signs of progress and would soon be out of prison.

'Another day a clean-looking Tibetan with a Chinese hair-cut was thrown into our prison. He said he was formerly an interpreter but had been purged for harbouring bourgeois habits. He hinted a number of times that he was fed up with the Chinese, and appeared to be quite frank. We were all suspicious of one another, though not especially of him. He was a very helpful commentator on the *Tibet Daily News*, which we had to study for two hours after work every night. He voluntarily took the lead and explained the issues most eloquently. His quick release was a tremendous loss to our study circle.

'But the very next day Jamyang, one of our group, was sum-moned by Zhou Zhang and accused of having complained that the *Tibet Daily News* did not contain news but was a monotonous report of progress made by the Chinese in Tibet. This baseless complaint, said Zhou Zhang, indicated that Jamyang was still longing for the dark ages of serfdom. Zhou Zhang sarcastically told him that he could now wait for the return of the old order 'until the black crows get grey hair'. Jamyang was immediately put into a single cell. So it was evident that the former interpreter was really a spy.'

My friend told me that another favourite method of extorting confessions was by interrogating every criminal prisoner individually for hours. During the interrogation the Chinese frightened the prisoner out of his wits by such statements as: 'Your friends and relatives have confessed that you sent the Sakya Lama to India. Now where and how did you do so? How can you hide your crimes?' The terrified prisoner naturally thought that this must be true, and 'confessed' everything. Apart from such interrogations, the prisoners had to study Maoism, and participate in political struggles, confessions and accusations among themselves. In other words, they were forced to do whatever we in the world outside were encouraged to do.

The process of charge and countercharge was known as *thamzing*, a Chinese coinage which means in Tibetan 'attack and struggle'. The accused person was brought before a mass meeting in which the accusers stood up and made their charges. This was considered the most effective way of enlightening the masses, and it also, in the Communist language, 'raises up the people's heads and makes the oppressors bow down.' *Thamzing* was vigorously applied inside the prison. The usual accusations were that the 'criminal' had not confessed his black deeds, or that he was still harbouring the old aristocratic thoughts. When Abbot Jampel Sangpo was undergoing *thamzing*, one of the lamas, Kyukpa Jinpa, was so petrified that he committed suicide. He jumped into a deep toilet, where he had hidden a knife in the excreta, made three cuts on his forehead and two on his neck, and finally stabbed himself in the heart. When he was found to be missing there was a great commotion in Sakya. Chinese guards, with loaded guns at the ready, ran in every direction, and saffron-robed progressives poured out of the Great Monastery in search of Jinpa. By then the prisoners had been transferred from the Dolma Palace to the Monastery.

The people in Sakya took this shocking news to heart. The lamas formed one of the constituents of the Buddhist Trinity, and when they were persecuted the masses mourned silently. The Chinese could not convince them that the monks were social parasites and exploiters of the people. When they refused to accept this, the Chinese had no alternative but to condemn anyone clinging to the 'old superstitious beliefs'. Well before Communist influence had reached Tibet, the ordinary Tibetan regarded the aristocrats as social parasites; he knew that the wealth of the nobility was the fruit of his sweat and toil. But he did not begrudge the monks what they took from him, because they spent their lives praying in the monasteries for the general good.

We heard from time to time that the prisoners were on starvation diet, a rumour confirmed when my sisters saw them eating half-ripe corn while weeding. When Mother heard this she cried. I later heard about the deplorable food from ex-prisoners now in India. They told me: 'In the beginning we were given a small mug of the worst *tsampa* per day, such as we would have given to the donkeys in the old days, with the words: "You have been giving this kind of *tsampa* to your serfs and slaves for countless generations. Now you eat it." In fact, we never gave this type of *tsampa* to our servants, though there was a distinction between their food and ours. Later on, when we were rationed to a handful of soaked beans, that mug of poor *tsampa* was something to be longed for. I ate fifteen beans in the morning with two mugs of water, another fifteen for lunch, and ten for dinner. Some of us ate the soles of our shoes. I longed for the mere sight of a drop of *tsampa*. We wanted to die, but the

Chinese would not let us. They had to torture us physically and
mentally.'

With this totally inadequate amount of food the prisoners
were to work twelve hours a day. The monks were employed on
the most degrading jobs. The people of Sakya had to endure the
sight of their revered lamas, among them the Abbot Jampel
Sangpo, carrying human excrement to a newly made vegetable
garden, where they were made to mix water with their load and
sprinkle it all over the garden, and the Tibetans took it as a
deliberate desecration of their faith. When we saw the aristocrats before whom we were accustomed to bow, and the high
lamas whom we venerated like gods, working in the fields, we
wondered if we were going mad.

I have since learned that even worse things took place when
the prisoners were deported to Shigatse and Lhasa. They were
used like animals, and even the octogenarians were made to
work. Most of them were used on road work and on reclaiming
waste land for cultivation. Each was set a daily task of digging
sixteen square feet. If he exceeded this amount, he would be
called a progressive, and the duration of imprisonment would
be curtailed. If, on the other hand, he could not finish it, he
would suffer punishments like standing outside for three hours
in the cold night. Since the Chinese were constantly on guard,
no one could rest even for a few minutes.

When the time came for the prisoners' deportation, the
faithful Tibetans came to get a last blessing as their venerable
lamas were dumped into trucks. Many Sakyans were in tears. It
was even more moving to see the aristocrats and their wives,
children and parents gazing at one another from a distance.
Even if they had been permitted to speak to one another, I doubt
whether any of them could have uttered a word, so strong was
their grief. Our old rulers had lost all their dignity and vitality.
Their heads were bowed down as if their necks were broken.
Now that they were departing from the land where they had
been born and had held sway, leaving behind all their loved

ones without a word of farewell, they appeared paler and sadder than ever before. In the old days, a three-day journey by foot from Sakya to Shigatse was marked with ritual ceremonies and precautions. Many Westerners think that Tibetans loved a wandering life and disliked a settled one, but this was only true of the nomads; the rest of them led a settled life and were not fond of travelling. Furthermore, parents, children and grandchildren spent their lives together in a close-knit family circle, and other relatives kept very close. Thus deportation was a second death.

After the lamas and officials had been imprisoned for two weeks, the Chinese in Sakya confiscated all our guns and swords. They did not seize the weapons blatantly, but put out an announcement: 'The People's Liberation Army advise the people to deposit weapons of any kind with the Han (Chinese) Working Personnel. This precaution is necessary in view of the fact that the weapons may fall into the hands of the enemies of the people, which would be doubly dangerous. When the reactionaries are crushed, owners can reclaim their weapons. Meanwhile, please deposit everything – even a small dagger – in our safekeeping.'

Wealthy households, especially those of the merchants, possessed pistols, and rifles, and every family had a sword and several daggers. Tibetans used to wear a small dagger at the waist, but the Chinese confiscated even these. We willingly relinquished the long sword that our late father had carried on his travels. Those who made the witty excuse that they needed their swords to cut off the heads of the people's enemies were told to relax: the invincible People's Liberation Army would do it for them. Others said pathetically: 'The Reds need not get scared of us. They have big guns and have imprisoned our brains. We are already dogs with broken limbs.'

After the confiscation of weapons, we heard the disturbing news that the Sakya *Zodpa* would be the first person to suffer *thamzing*. Rehearsals were already being held at the Great Monastery, with saffron-robed young progressives taking the leading roles. When the date for the trial of the *Zodpa* was jubilantly announced, the people of Sakya decided to plead with the Chinese for their beloved leader. The organizers were four responsible citizens; one of them, Dawa Thondup, came to us to deliver the message. He said: 'It is believed that the Chinese respect the masses, so we should all go and plead for the *Zodpa*. As everyone knows, the Sakya *Zodpa* is the most merciful ruler that we have had in recent times, and it is our duty to save him from public flogging and humiliation. In this way we would be showing our gratitude and repaying him some of the debt that we owe him as our leader.' This statement was quite true: the *Zodpa* was the most respected and loved authority in Sakya, admired for his strong sense of justice and care for the *tralpas*. When the Sakya Lama asked him to escape, the *Zodpa* declined the invitation with the words: 'I cannot run away and leave this monastery and its subjects.'

On the morning of the *thamzing* men and women poured into the Great Monastery from far and near, each bringing a *khadar*, as they had been asked to do. That morning they were going to plead for their beloved *Zodpa*, because when he was in power he had accepted pleas from his subjects with understanding and mercy. *Shungo* was the traditional way of pleading. When a subject was punished heavily, his influential relatives and friends could plead on his behalf before the supreme political ruler for mercy; their plea was preceded by the offer of a *khadar*. Often the *Zodpa* would show mercy; but the Chinese would not listen to the pleadings of the masses. The old rulers were humane and far more merciful than the Chinese, for they were bound only by religious principles. Admittedly they were free to accept bribes and sometimes to show partiality too. But the inhuman, mechanical application of Communist ethics was infinitely worse than the Tibetan shortcomings. The Chinese were bound by official Party policy, and no authority in Sakya had the power to deviate by a hair's breadth from the Party line. Their duty was to carry out the officially approved programmes systematically and conscientiously. They could do no more than passively sympathize with Tibetan aspirations, and obviously many of them did so.

Abu and I were the representatives from our home. We joined the crowd at the Great Monastery, and then moved towards the Chinese headquarters. But before we could show our *khadars* as a token of respect, armed guards began to surround us. We were all in a panic, but Abu and I managed to escape, and threw away our *khadars* in the monastery latrine, as the Chinese were arresting anyone with a *khadar*. The thrifty hid theirs in their trousers. Most of the crowd fled, and those arrested were soon released. However, the four organizers, though poor, were treated as criminal traitors. They were publicly flogged by the progressives, at the instigation of the Chinese, and were later deported for hard labour to an unknown destination. Although our effort was in vain, it proved that the people, though uneducated, had not lost their sense of justice.

After Kyukpa Jinpa's suicide, all penknives were confiscated from the prisoners. However, Jango – the official who had unwittingly returned to Sakya for imprisonment when he could have escaped to India – managed to hang himself by fastening his belt to the ceiling of his cell. It was surely due to his *karma*, the people concluded. He was held responsible, justly or unjustly, for sending the Sakya Lama to India, and his suicide was taken as an admission of guilt. He left a note which read: 'I confess that I alone am responsible for sending the Sakya Lama to India. Please do not inflict too much suffering on my daughter Choden.' The Sakyans sympathized with him all the more for this heroic note. Afterwards all belts were confiscated, which meant that the prisoners were often embarrassed by having nothing to hold their robes together.

Finally, the Sakya *Zodpa* managed to take his own life. He tore his monk's robes into strips and made a rope to hang himself with.

When we heard of the two suicides one after the other, we breathed a sigh of relief and pity. It was ten times better to die than to suffer mentally and physically for the rest of your life. The agony of suicide was mercifully short, whereas the Chinese would have inflicted far worse suffering day and night until their natural death. Mother thanked God and uttered in the name of the dead: '*Om Mani Padme Hum*. May they never be born again under the Chinese Reds!'

ELEVEN

The Education of the Masses

I HAVE already mentioned Norzin-la, one of our Tibetan 'monitors', who, together with Chinese teachers, was responsible for 'education of the masses' – in other words, brainwashing. Norzin-la was a popular girl interpreter, a graduate of the Beijing Institute of National Minorities. She wore her long black hair in the revolutionary style, with two plaits behind and a short fringe over her forehead, and she used to wear the ugly blue Chinese uniform. She had the sharp, clear-cut features and oval charming face of a typical Tibetan beauty. Despite the years of training at the Institute, she still retained some of her native charm and love of laughter. She went everywhere with her Chinese boss, who was an orthodox disciple of Chairman Mao and could never make any statement without turning to the Chairman for moral support.

Among the native progressives the most outstanding figure was Namgyal-la, a middle-aged, hump-backed man with a glib tongue. He was not a native of Sakya. Having committed a murder in Lhatse, he ran away and settled in Sakya a few years before the fall of Tibet. In Sakya he took a number of odd jobs, including some in the monastery. After the monks and the nobility were imprisoned, he was the chief collaborator with the Chinese. It was widely and credibly rumoured that every night he was seen going to the Chinese headquarters at Simchung House. He was the most 'revolutionary activist' in the whole of Sakya, 'leaping forward' well ahead of the masses. When the new administrative machinery was set up, he was appointed

Chairman of the Sakya *Zhou* (district). And the vagabond Namgyal became Namgyal-la, with an honorific suffix added to his name.

The Great Sakya Monastery, previously a supreme place of worship and pilgrimage, was now used for the sacrilegious purpose of indoctrination, which denounced the very sanctity of *dharma*. After the reactionary nobility and ecclesiastics were safely imprisoned, we were summoned to a mass meeting. 'The wolves must be separated from the sheep' was the slogan. Norzin-la told us: 'You must know who are our enemies and who are our friends. Our enemies are the ecclesiastics, the officials and the feudal lords. Our friends are the proletariat. Unless we isolate our enemies from the masses, they will try to oppose our democratic reforms. If you leave the wolves with the sheep they will continue to eat the sheep. Therefore, the wolves must be separated from the sheep.' This business of new enemies and new friends was beyond our comprehension at first. All we understood was the order that we were to snap our traditional connections with our superiors.

Furthermore, we strongly resented the order. Unlike many other countries, the social connection between the rulers and the ruled was close in Tibet. Once such a relationship was established, it invariably matured into friendship. Though the two parties were not on equal footing, nevertheless there was no superiority or inferiority complex. We enjoyed family friendships with half a dozen aristocrats and still more high lamas. The butchers, supposedly the lowest class, had friends from the upper strata. As I have said, when the old rulers were imprisoned we visited them with presents; thus it was almost impossible for us to cut our connections completely, all of a sudden. Despite the strict restrictions, our family, like many others, continued to have clandestine relations with the 'new enemies'. When the Dragpa family was virtually starving, Mother twice gave them *tsampa*. Nyima Tsering, an old servant of the Jango family, was a second-ranking official in the new hierarchy; nevertheless, he continued to help the family in Tibet, and when he finally escaped to India he brought many of his master's valuables and gave them to members of the family there.

As time went by, the restrictions were enforced with increasing severity. A popular nickname for the Chinese policy was the 'wet hide helmet'; as it dried out, the hide helmet became tighter and tighter until it crushed your skull. The innocent families of political prisoners were ostracized by the rest of the Sakyans. If we met any of them face to face we had to practise the new proletarian snobbery and turn away our heads.

When the wolves were thus isolated from the sheep, we began our next lesson which was to be the core of our 'education'. The Chinese working personnel and the native progressives had been widely heralding the forthcoming event. In July 1959, a mammoth mass meeting was held in the Great Monastery, presided over by Tang Hanju, the Party's man in Sakya. His interpreter was the beautiful Norzin-la. We all sat on the flagstones of the courtyard, while our new rulers sat on comfortable chairs under the shady painted canopy of the monastery's inner gateway. Namgyal sat among them, forcing his small head upright against the humpback that was 'a result of the evil system', and crossing his short legs in imitation of our aristocrats. People in the crowd muttered under their breath: 'What's that vagabond doing on a throne? Society has now really turned upside down. The unworthy has become the worthy.'

Tang Hanju got up and Namgyal applauded vigorously, gesturing to the crowd to follow his example. When the echoes of the protracted applause had died away, Comrade Tang began to speak.

'Within a short period you people of Sakya have achieved a great deal. You have been introduced to your enemies and your friends and can now basically recognize them. This is the first key step to any people's revolution. We have now isolated the people's enemies. However, this does not mean that you can now relax, thinking that all around you are friends. You must be constantly on guard against enemies and never be deceived by them. We will always drive them from the ranks of the people whenever we find them. Only then can we carry out the long-awaited democratic reforms in Tibet. Our present revolutionary task is Three Strikes and Two Reductions.'

The audience looked dumbfounded; what he said sounded like Sanskrit *mantras*.

Comrade Tang continued: 'Who are the three we should strike? We must exterminate the rebellion; we must exterminate the feudal government; and we must exterminate landlordism. With whom should we compromise? With those rulers and rich farmers who did not take part in the rebellion. Their rents and interest will be reduced by 80 percent. These are the Two Reductions. We, the Han working personnel, have seen the revolutionary force and fervour of the Sakya people and have no doubt that you will thoroughly implement the political campaign of the Three Strikes and Two Reductions, as resolved by the People's National Congress and the Preparatory Committee for the Autonomous Region of Tibet.

Namgyal again applauded vigorously, and we followed him.

In the revolutionary (the equivalent of holy) language of the Hans the campaign was called 'San fan, shuang jian'. With the pride and pleasure of a lama airing his Sanskrit, Norzin-la occasionally uttered the words 'San fan, shuang jian' in her Tibetan accent before the uneducated masses.

We spent the summer of 1959 first studying the theory of the political campaign and then putting it into practice. The masses were divided into discussion groups of ten families. Since those with education had been imprisoned, scribblers of my category were in high demand. Each group had to have a secretary and a potential progressive. As we studied the Three Strikes and Two Reductions, Norzin-la and her Han boss went around inspecting each group; after a few days we were surprised to find

Namgyal busily engaged in a similar inspection. On the first day Norzin-la sat in the centre of each study circle and explained the Three Strikes and Two Reductions, with special reference to Sakya. She would ask a question and answer it herself without letting us try – a sign of an imperfect dialectical approach.

'Who adopted the resolution of the Three Strikes and Two Reductions?' asked Norzin-la rhetorically. After a short pause she continued in her clear musical Lhasa dialect: 'The Preparatory Committee for the Autonomous Region of Tibet passed that resolution on 17 July 1959. What are the Three Strikes and Two Reductions? The Three Strikes are anti-rebellion, anti-feudal structure and anti-slavery. The Two Reductions are of the rents and interest of those old rulers who have not taken part in the rebellion. Why should we launch this political campaign? Unless we carry out this campaign, we cannot achieve long-cherished democratic reforms and cannot march on the revolutionary road towards Socialism and Communism. How can we reform when there are reactionary rebels, when the feudal serf system is not abolished, and when the people do not have personal freedom? Unless and until we have exterminated these three basic evils, we cannot succeed in our democratic reforms. Why should we make special concessions to the exploiters? The people might feel that exploiters deserve no concessions; but we have to make a clear distinction between patriots and rebels. On the land owned by patriotic estate-holders and their agents who have not betrayed the Motherland, the rents and the interest are to be reduced, so that 20% goes to the landowners, and the remaining 80% to the tillers of the soil. I hope everything is clear to you. Let me see how much you have understood. You can explain the Three Strikes and Two Reductions in relation to your own Sakya.'

Norzin-la seemed exhausted by her repetitive discourse and relaxed in the centre of our study circle, staring at each one of us in turn. As we were unused to speaking in public and were also afraid of making mistakes which might bring untold consequences, we sat dumb, looking at one another, digging one another with our elbows and muttering: 'Why don't you say something?'

At last Norzin-la became angry and demanded: 'Why can't you speak out? Are you afraid?'

Finally a promising progressive, a woman called Tsering, made a nervous speech in reply. 'Thanks to the Chinese Communist Party and its Chairman Mao, our days of fear are gone forever. Now I can speak out my thoughts because I have been granted freedom of speech which our fathers and forefathers never heard of. I feel the present political campaign is vital to our long-awaited reforms. The first strike is against the reactionary traitorous rebels: we must kill all the rebels in Sakya. The rebels include all those government officials, monks and estate-holders who have sent the Sakya Lama to India and who have helped the Khampa rebels. The second strike is against the forced labour imposed by the old reactionary government. The third strike is against the slavery system. By this strike we can liberate all the slaves of the nobility.'

Tsering astonished us all by her eloquent grasp of the subject, though later we learned that she had received special tuition from the Hans. Norzin-la praised her for her appreciation of the political campaign; however, she corrected a misunderstanding by explaining that the implementation of the Three Strikes did not mean the physical extermination of the persons concerned. 'Killing would not solve the problem. We would rather reform the rebels through hard labour; we can use them on some construction project which will benefit the people. Killing the reactionary clique would not necessarily kill the evil system.' This correction seemed too subtle for our uncultivated minds to understand, but we all nodded in agreement.

Everyone in Sakya was forced to learn the political campaign by heart, and everyone at last knew it as thoroughly as 'Om Mani Padme Hum'. To the middle-aged and the old, the indoctrination was incomprehensible, and the thought-content was totally alien. One of the Chinese asked an old lady, Moh Tsering Bhuti, who were the three principal serf-owners. She replied: 'The Party'. She had never heard of terms like 'serf-owners'. Han explained patronizingly: 'Honourable mother, the three principal exploiters of Tibetan society are the local government, the monasteries and the estate-holders.' Realizing the enormity of her mistake, she apologized profusely and assured the comrade that it was not intentional. On another occasion, when another grandmother was asked: 'Against

whom should we launch the Three Strikes?' she replied unwittingly: 'The Party!'

Naturally, the young did not make any glaring mistakes.
We were asked more critical questions, probing deeply into our
indoctrination, such as: 'Do you think that the Three Strikes and
Two Reductions are necessary?' Once we had learned the knack
of answering – which was basically praise for the new system
and abuse for the old – it was easy.

When we had satisfactorily passed the oral test, we were
told to practise what we had learnt. The operation of this political campaign was most important, said the Chinese, and they
added: 'If you don't kill the wolf, how can you have its valuable
skin? If you don't exterminate the serf-owners and their agents,
how can you have their property and land? Hence, *thamzing* is
essential.'

The preparation for the political struggle was emotionally
painful. Every single person was thoroughly interrogated and
scrutinized. We had to dig out all past sufferings under the old
rulers, no matter how small. The secretary noted down all the
charges and grievances. From this data the Chinese worked out
who had most oppressed the people. The most 'oppressive
oppressor' among them would be the first to face the People's
Court.

As a group secretary, I observed that ex-criminals and their
relatives took the campaign very seriously indeed, as was quite
understandable. In our group, Tsering was the most revolutionary activist. Her husband had murdered a man called
Thakla in Sakya, and the government justifiably punished him
severely by confiscating all his property and by banishing him.
Tsering was illiterate, and could not understand why she and
her husband had suffered under the 'dark, cruel and barbarous
feudal system'. All the same, she was a skilful debater, and
could twist any point to make it suit her argument.

She made charges to this effect. 'I do not deny that my husband killed Thakla' – the murder was committed in broad day-

light when the harvesters were all around – 'but you must
understand the circumstances. Thakla's cows were found eating our scanty crops in the fields during harvest. If they had
eaten all our crops, we were sure to starve to death. Is that not
right, Comrades? My husband was so worried that on the spur
of the moment, in a fit of anger and grief, he killed the owner of
the cows. Under the old evil system we could not eat the fruit of
our labours, and so we could hardly manage to live on what we
grew. If cows feasted on our crops, what were we to live on? I
bribed the law officials with all my valuables, but they did not
help my husband. He was given more than two hundred lashes
on his bare bottom. After they had nearly killed him they confiscated all our property and banished him in disgrace and
humiliation. Was that not an evil and barbarous system,
Comrades?'

Whenever she shouted such rhetorical questions, we were
supposed to second her by shouting 'Ré' (yes), and shaking our
fists. Though uneducated, the people displayed a surprising
sense of justice; when Tsering tearfully complained of injustice,
many of them laughed aloud. One frank woman, Chungla,
went so far as to tell her: 'After your husband took another
man's life, can you blame the authorities for punishing him?'
But Chungla was reprimanded for her bourgeois tendencies.

Those who had old personal grudges, like Tsering, unhesi-
tatingly told of their sufferings, though most of the accusers had
a hard time substantiating their charges. Many people in our
group made the lame excuse that they could not remember any
particular affliction, because they experienced 'sufferings as
countless as the hairs on our head, or waves in the ocean', a
phrase coined by Namgyal, which became a cliché during the
political struggle. But each individual had to record his sufferings, and it was the duty of the secretary to note each family's
experiences in detail.

Tsering one day reminded Mother of our 'numerous sufferings under the despotic aristocrats', referring to our old legal

cases. She added: 'Akyi-la, if you can tolerate those sufferings inflicted by the despots, we as fellow-proletariats cannot bear them. We must retaliate. It's a golden opportunity, and you must narrate them.' In short, any dealings with the political prisoners, whether friendly or hostile, had to be proclaimed in public. It was impossible to hide anything, because in a small place like Sakya everybody was a witness to everybody else's affairs. The progressives would accuse you of hiding your sufferings and showing unnecessary mercy to the oppressors.

It was often debated in our group whether it was just to blame the old authorities, because they were fundamentally governed by an archaic barbarous system. (To the Han working personnel our old system was synonymous with 'barbarous', indicating the old imperialistic prejudice of the Chinese.) The more intelligent of our men, especially the ex-monks, said that we should condemn those who had deviated from the old norms, but this was dismissed as a 'benevolent rightist view'. 'We are against everything that is part of the old system, and against everyone who stands for it' was Namgyal's attitude. Many admitted that the former rulers had bad habits. But in fact, if we paid our taxes, no one punished us arbitrarily. The rulers neither helped nor harmed us; they simply left us alone.

When the 'books of sufferings' were submitted to the Chinese, they declared that Dragpa was the 'most oppressive oppressor' and must be the first man to be tried by the masses. Dragpa was a surprising choice. First, his family had only recently joined the ranks of the aristocracy, and his father was known for his benevolence in Sakya. His son, Tengo, was the only Sakyan educated in Lhasa, a fashionable, intelligent young man, who had been carried away by Chinese propaganda during the 'peaceful liberation' period, and actively co-operated with the Chinese working personnel. I do not think he had any bad intentions; he was simply deceived. But the people and the monks of Sakya felt that he was selling the Holy City to the Chinese. As such, he became very unpopular and was abusively called 'the enemy of the faith'. The people of Sakya felt that Tengo's active co-operation with the Chinese during the early 1950s had had far-reaching consequences, and thought that it was he who had brought the Chinese to Sakya. So they wanted their revenge. Later on, the Chinese realized this and refused to give the mob permission to strike against Tengo.

By accusing Tengo's father, Dragpa, the people were getting their own back on the man who had unwittingly helped the Chinese in 1955 to open their school and organize Communist youth movements. When it was announced that Dragpa was to be tried and voluntary accusers were called for, the progressives were not considered enough for a grand *thamzing*. Norzin-la picked out the two best speakers from our group and compelled them to accuse Dragpa in public; they were Tsering and another woman who said she had been raped by Dragpa. The preparations for the *thamzing* were like the rehearsal for a play. Norzin-la was the director. She taught us how to accuse the exploiter properly, and how to shout slogans and shake our fists in the air.

As well as shouting slogans, we had to sing a revolutionary song which ran as follows:

Socialism is good, socialism is good, socialism
   is good for the people.
Foreign imperialists ran away with their tails
   trailing on the ground.
We must follow the Chinese Communist Party, and
   reconstruct the mighty Motherland.

If anyone was found not singing or shouting at the proper time, he would be questioned immediately: 'Why are you not singing? Are you not happy when the people are?' As we queued up in two long lines on the open ground in front of the monastery we sang this song several times and shouted slogans. This was done to arouse our animal instincts, so that we might appear 'as aggressive as tigers before the helpless wolves'. The main slogan was: 'We the people of Tibet must unite to exterminate the reactionary upper strata.'

The procedure for *thamzing* was as follows. The courtyard of the Great Monastery was used as the arena. Under a painted canopy the people's tribunal sat on comfortable chairs facing the huge crowd. They included Han working personnel and native revolutionary activists. Leaving a space in front of the tribunal for the performance, we all sat cross-legged on the hard flagstones of the courtyard. Red Army men armed with machine-guns were posted everywhere, even on the monastery roof. We often wondered whether they were guarding the political prisoners, or all of us. Why should the Chinese be scared of 'a bird in the cage'?

After the thunderous slogans, the political struggle began. Tang Hanju, the Party chief, explained the meaning and aims of *thamzing*, and then stated the crimes of the accused. Norzin-la interpreted. 'Today is a historic day for you. So far you have been serfs and slaves of a few lords and lamas. On this historic day, under the leadership of the Chinese Communist Party and Chairman Mao, you have overthrown your exploiters, your oppressors, and have risen up as free individuals. The aim of this political struggle is to teach you former serfs and slaves to shed your inbred fears of your former masters and regenerate yourselves as fearless liberated new men. This is the first step towards the establishment of the people's democratic dictatorship.' The crimes of the accused were that he had associated himself with the reactionary Khampa leader, called Ponta, and that he had helped other Khampa rebels with weapons and horses. There was no need to mention his perpetual exploitation of the masses. The greater part of this character assassination was done by Namgyal, who seemed to have searched high and low for every possible fault in Dragpa, as he did in other cases too.

After the accused had been painted black beyond recognition, Namgyal shouted for Dragpa to come out, and the enter-

tainment began. The accused was dragged out by two armed
guards. The Chinese way of tying a man's arms behind his back
was as cunning as their policy. A strong rope was first put
around the neck, and each free end was spirally wound round
each arm down to the wrist. Then the arms were tightly tied
together at the back, so that the neck was pulled back and the
arms were forced outwards with excruciating pain. Victims
who managed to escape have told me how agonizing this form
of torture was. Compared with this, our old way of simply tying
a criminal's hands behind his back was merely a token punishment. Later on the Chinese exhibited the old cumbersome hand-
cuffs as 'torturing implements'. The Chinese method was
infinitely worse, for the more a prisoner moved the tighter the
rope became.

Tied in this most painful fashion, Dragpa was made to bend
down as low as his knees, facing the people. One of the progressives shouted: 'We, the people of Tibet wish to exterminate
the reactionary upper strata', and the people repeated it thun-
derously after him, raising their right arms and fists in the air.
(This gesture was symbolic of the revolutionary force of mass
unity.)

Then Namgyal got up dramatically and began his accusations. 'Dragpa, listen now! Can you recognize me? I am liberated Namgyal, who was once a serf. Under the leadership of the
Chinese Communist Party and our Chairman Mao, I am today
getting this glorious opportunity. Before I make my accusations
I want to show you the invincible united strength of the liberated masses. Look! See!' He caught the wretched man by his
hair and showed his agonized face to the public, but they hid
their faces. 'On behalf of the Sakyans and myself, I accuse you
of carrying out reactionary rebellious activities. When the reactionary rebel, Ponta, came to Sakya, you not only associated
yourself with the rebel but you actually supplied his bandits
with weapons.' Suddenly he asked the audience: 'Is it true or
not?' 'Ré!' we all shouted.

Pointing an accusing finger at Dragpa, Namgyal made the standard formal accusation: 'Wolfish man, I have charges against you as countless as the hairs on my head and the waves in the ocean, but I can't deprive the masses of the opportunity to bring their charges against you. Therefore, here I end, much against my will.' And the next person followed.

Such charges would be dismissed as false and baseless by any recognized court; but in the People's Court the accusers were also judge and jury, and conviction was automatic. Since the primary aim was to imbue the people with proletarian consciousness and disgust for the feudal past, and also to 'de-class' the ex-rulers, it was not thought relevant to check the accuracy of the charges. When there was a shortage of accusers, the working personnel welcomed anyone with any false or fabricated charges. In Sakya there were many who volunteered to accuse, but they were so incompetent that they indirectly defended the accused. For example, a poor tailor accused a lama of giving his guild more than the official record allowed. 'When our guild was employed by the monastery, we could not manage with the traditional grant of *tsampa*. We asked for more and you gave it to us; but why did you give us more *tsampa* than the book permitted?'

During this period of *thamzing* an anonymous couplet became popular throughout Tibet.

> *Nothing to look forward to but ceaseless thamzings*
>   *every week;*
> *So when death calls us we will be too late!*

Mao had said that political struggles would never cease until classes disappear from society, and ours was only just beginning. We had one *thamzing* after another, of every type – the extermination of rebels and their associates; the extermination of feudal government and its running dogs; the extermination of landlords and their agents. If the Chinese working personnel observed any aristocrat not yet humbled, or discovered any counter-revolutionary, they called for a *thamzing* as we used to call the butcher to slaughter our sheep. The people who organized the peaceful mass demonstration in defence of the Sakya *Zodpa* were given the worst *thamzing* of all. If any of the reactionary upper classes escaped, their effigies were erected for the purpose of *thamzing*; but we always prayed that we might not be forced to denounce the Sakya Lama and other high lamas, for we firmly believed that a word against your lama would send your soul straight to hell. Fortunately, while we were there we were not compelled to denounce them.

The next political campaign was *dukchu*, meaning 'tears of sorrow'. Norzin-la told us: 'In order to find the cause of your long misery, not in *karma*, as you were deceived into believing, but in the evil system of serfdom, you must freely expose your old injuries; you must freely declare your sorrows and sufferings; you must wash them away so that you can feel the new state of liberation.' By this decree we were compelled to cry out our sorrows in public. The proceedings for this campaign were as thorough and systematic as the previous one. Each family was forced to write down 'all the past experiences of oppression under the evil system of serfdom'. The old system was blamed for everything, including natural calamities. For example, the evil system was responsible for Father's death; it was not because of his past *karma* but because the old government did not build hospitals for the people. This argument might appear rational, but to the Tibetans it was utter nonsense. According to the Chinese, the concept of *karma* had been driven into the Tibetans' heads for thousands of years and had become part and parcel of their psyche, which must be completely destroyed in order to create a new one. The root cause of our sufferings lay in the old system.

A special meeting dedicated to past sorrows was held in Sakya. A representative from each family was to relate the 'life of oppression and suffering' whose root was to be sought not in the delusion of *karma* but in the evil system. We were instructed

to 'recount with true anger and sadness'. Anybody who did not
shed tears and cry aloud his injuries and sorrows was suspect,
for it was presumed that the people (excluding the rulers) had
had a life of continual oppression and suffering; thus any commoner who did not shed crocodile tears while pouring out past
sorrows was not of the people. If you could contrive to faint
after purging yourself of all your past injuries and sufferings,
you would be regarded as truly revolutionized. The *dukchu*
campaign roused the Tibetan sense of humour, and there was
much fun and laughter among participants and audience alike.
The fainting business, of course, was a great help.

The best performance was put on by a man well known for
his joviality and humour, who was chosen to be the first speaker
on the day we 'washed away our sorrows' with Chairman
Mao's thoughts. As instructed, he began his autobiography of
ceaseless sufferings and sorrows by crying aloud with burning
anger and hatred: 'The life of the common man in the past was
the continuous endurance of abject poverty, inhuman oppression and unbearable sufferings. Mine was worse than the average ...' His voice tailed away and he pretended to faint on the
ground. We burst into uncontrollable laughter, and stretched
out our hands to help him. He was taken off to the Chinese dis-
pensary.

Namgyal began to commiserate with the sufferer. 'We have
seen, Comrades, how misery-loaded his past life was – so much
so that he could not describe it because of uncontrollable emotion. The very remembrance of inhuman oppression and
unbearable suffering makes even a strong man like him collapse
into unconsciousness.' The Chinese did not dare to announce
the doctor's diagnosis, but the 'patient' was out of hospital that
same day.

The Sakyans were full of admiration for this pioneer actor,
and most of the 'sorrow-narrators' followed his example. After
wailing out the introductory remarks taught by the working
personnel, the narrator would unobtrusively glance to left and

right to find a safe place to fall. As he made his cautious recon-naissance, those of us sitting near him would say: 'He's going to faint. Get ready!' Some people had the nerve to whisper to the narrator which direction he should faint in. Unfortunately the Chinese came to know about our play-acting and reprimanded some of us for counter-revolutionary behaviour. After this, the working personnel made sure that we narrated our life of sor-row from beginning to end, and that we shed tears. It was easy to concoct some story of suffering, but difficult to cry when you did not actually feel sad.

Within a short period of three months we had been 'enlight-ened' as to the fact that the root cause of all our sufferings lay in the harsh realities of serfdom and not in the illusion of *karma*. The corrupt decadent system was responsible for every wrong and for every imaginable trouble. Neither we nor our *karma* was responsible; the old system was. We had also been enlightened that the reactionary upper strata – the government, the monas-teries and the nobility – were not only traitors to the Motherland but were the three biggest wolves in the whole of Tibet. We found it hard to believe that the government and monasteries were oppressive exploiters; however, regarding the nobility we had little doubt. From time to time we were warned that the indoctrination we were undergoing was only a preliminary; there was much more to study.

Thus a strong feeling of antagonism had been built up between the people and their leaders. Now it was time to split the common people and to divide them into further classes. This was the preparation for the ceaseless class struggle in which not only did the poor maliciously criticize the rich but children were forced to criticize their parents and their teachers, and friend criticized friend. Our individual characters and identity were to be extinguished in the fire of revolution, and we were to foster, from collective living, new uniform characters whose only object of worship would be an impersonal Motherland, personified by a living deity, Chairman Mao.

For the demarcation of various classes, the Chinese announced the policy of 'self-estimation and public verdict', which sounds much more poetical in Tibetan. We were made to estimate the worth of our property and land in terms of money, and also how much labour we paid for each year. This latter consideration was the determining factor in our class segregation. Owing to the historical and socio-economic conditions in Tibet, there had been no Marxist division of classes into capitalists, bourgeoisie and proletariat. The Chinese analysis of classes in Tibetan society was fairly accurate: the ecclesiastics, the government officials of all ranks, and the nobility, with their estates and retainers, were the three main exploiters; and the agents of the three were the secondary exploiters of the masses. At the top end of society the Chinese analysts had no problem, since the upper strata were distinctly marked. With regard to the middle and lower classes, they calculated in this way: if 40-50% of the total annual labour was hired, a family was classified as rich farmer, or upper middle class; with 30-40% hired labour, it was lower middle class; and with 30% and below, it was classified as poor farmer, or proletariat. Because of our petty trade we made the uncoveted grade of 'lower middle class farmer'. The upper and lower middle classes were only 'friends of the proletariat'. I used to feel uneasy when the masses had special meetings from which the two middle classes were excluded.

The Chinese selected a few progressives from among us to represent us in the new governing machinery of the people's democratic dictatorship. Sakya was made a *zhou*, a Chinese word for district; and the chairman of the *zhou* was, as we expected, Namgyal, who became Uyon (Chairman) Namgyal-la. As I mentioned at the beginning of this chapter, he was a convict runaway. If a murderer could be nominated as our new titular ruler, we could have no faith in the new set-up. It made no difference whether he had committed murder in the old society or in the new: the important point was that he was a criminal. When the Mutual Aid teams started in Sakya, Tsering, the wife of another murderer, became the leader of our team. Such people were nominal rulers only, because their power, if any, was to lead the masses in carrying out the Chinese indoctrination programmes. They did not have the authority to call even an emergency meeting without the prior permission of the Chinese working personnel.

As the overthrow of 'serfdom' was one of the achievements on which the Chinese Communists prided themselves, it is worth taking a closer look at our old social system, now destroyed and vanished without trace. Having overthrown the old world, they devoted the whole period of 'democratic reforms' to the creation of a new cosmology, with all the essential characteristics of the old: the horrors of hell (the old order) and the happiness of heaven (the new era). When I heard the Chinese depiction of the 'evil serfdom', I was reminded of the early theologians, who must have done similar pioneering work in creating and then reinforcing the idea of hell as we Tibetans know it today. Without exaggeration, some of the orthodox comrades seemed to be suffering more when they described the oppression of the Tibetan masses under the old feudal order than what we actually suffered by living under it. According to the Party propaganda, the 'serfdom' upon which our old society was built was the most evil social system that ever existed in human history. Broadly speaking, according to the same propaganda, there were only two classes of men in the Old Tibet: the 'serfs' and the 'serf-owners'. The serf-owners used their serfs and slaves, said the Chinese, far worse than we used our donkeys; at least we had our Buddhist compassion for animals, whereas the landlords and high lamas meted out unprecedented and unmitigated cruelty to the Tibetan.

The Chinese Communists have blown up the small social evils of the old order to such monstrous proportions that an objective consideration of the facts is imperative. In every exaggeration there must be a grain of truth, yet my parents never suffered the degree of cruelty and rapacity that the Chinese ascribe to Tibetan 'serfdom'.

In the first place, the terms 'serfdom' and 'feudalism' are not really applicable in the Tibetan context. Tibet had been a world in itself right up to 1950, and our old social system was entirely different from that of feudal England, for example. Judging from our family's experiences I think feudalism in Tibet was quite different from other types, and different in a better way. Our family was not exceptional; we received neither royal favours nor bureaucratic support.

The Tibetans had developed a system of government hitherto unknown to the world – a government in which religion and politics ran parallel without conflict of any kind. The term 'theocracy' is inadequate to describe it. Although there is no example of such a utopian government in Indian history, Tibet imported this basic idealism from India, along with most of her spiritual and intellectual resources. The Tibetans sought harmony and balance between the spiritual and temporal needs of men. Had it not been for this happy marriage of religion and politics, Buddhism would not have flourished in Tibet.

At the apex of the pyramidal structure were the Dalai Lamas, who, as a fact of history, were enlightened and benevolent. Even if one did not accept the doctrine of reincarnation, one had to agree that the Dalai Lamas had been most carefully selected, trained and brought up according to the strictest Buddhist standards, literally from childhood; and the products had been the closest approximation of the Buddha possible to Tibetans. However, since the high lamas spent more of their time in meditation cells than in offices, the administrative work had usually to be entrusted to their lay and ecclesiastical officials. Admittedly, some administrators and bureaucrats misused their power for selfish gain or created friction between the lamas; but similar shortcomings are inevitable in any free society. During the Dalai Lama's absence or minority, the most learned and enlightened lama of the Gelukpa sect became the regent. As the Tibetan saying goes, 'If your son has the ability, the Lion's throne is not sealed off.'

By far the most effective counterpoise to the hereditary nobility were the monk officials or *tsedrungs*, who came from all sections of Tibetan society. The different monasteries selected their brightest little monks of eight or nine and sent them to the Tse School, where they were trained and educated until they were eighteen. Admission to this elite school did not necessarily guarantee a post after graduation; to join the government services the monks had to pass certain prescribed examinations. The *tsedrungs* were celibate, and so had no families who might tempt them to exploit the ruled, as was the case with the aristocracy generally. The usual government policy was to appoint one monk and one lay official to any post, to act as a check on each other. Though both were Buddhists, their outlooks differed vastly: one had a large family with a history, property and land, whereas the other had only his duty to care for. Of course, there were exceptions: some monk officials were far more worldly than their lay counterparts.

Tibetan feudalism was not instituted: it evolved. Until the first century AD, the entire land was the property of the State. However, when King Lha Thori embraced Buddhism, which gradually became the state religion, the central government began to donate land to the *Sangha*, both for construction and cultivation. In the early stages, the kings of Tibet made a decree by which seven families were to look after the material needs of each monk. But as Tibet became more and more religious, the community of monks became more organized, more worldly and less ascetic. And when religion got the upper hand in the administration of the country, more and more monks and monasteries were granted land for their maintenance. The monasteries either leased their land or employed workers. According to Chinese propaganda, 37% of the total arable land in Tibet was owned by monasteries.

Chokhor Lhunpo, my late father's monastery, shows the

system in operation. There were about sixty monks, and their monastery collectively owned about 35 *khels* of land (a *khel* is about two and a quarter acres). The produce of the land was the chief source of monastic income, supplemented by offerings from the lay followers. This monastery was businesslike and employed the inhabitants of the area on its farm, instead of leasing the land to tenants. My mother's family, the Trungras, was

one of the ten families who worked on the monastic land. The terms and conditions for labour were fair enough. The Trungras were given about five *khels* of land and a six-roomed house; in addition, if a wealthy family offered a silver coin to each monk, the family also received the same amount. The duty of the ten families was to look after the monastic land jointly. Usually each family sent one of its able-bodied members for five months each year to carry out seasonal tasks such as ploughing and reaping on the monastic land. Mother often went to work on the monastic fields as a girl. The work was lighter and more enjoyable than the work that she and her sisters had to do on their parents' land, and when the harvesting season approached the children had to draw lots, because all of them wanted to go and work on the monastic fields as the family representative. The monastery gave each worker one *dré* of *tsampa* per day, and the workers could take as much tea and *chang* as they wished – there was no limit.

The distribution of monasteries was fairly uniform throughout the country. However, the manorial estates were mostly concentrated in central and southern Tibet, because most of the aristocrats lived in and around Lhasa. According to the Chinese Communists, 25% of the land belonged to the aristocrats. Before the centralized government headed by the Dalai Lama was established, a number of autonomous principalities existed in Tibet. During the takeover, the non-violent lamas found it difficult to strip the princes of their privileges and rights, and so their lands and subjects were left almost untouched, provided they agreed to pay a certain amount of tax to the venerable government. The ancestors of Ngapo Ngawang Jigme, now one of the puppets of the Chinese, were kings of Tibet over a thousand years ago. His family owned 2500 square miles of land, and 3500 serfs.

The old aristocrats, as they were called, formed only a small segment of the Tibetan aristocracy. The number of landlords was increased in two ways. First, when a child was chosen as a reincarnation of the Dalai Lama, his parents became the Tibetan equivalent of millionaires overnight. The post of Dalai Lama was not an enviable one, but certainly his family made a fortune. They would be given two or three large estates with workers attached to the land, and their sons were elevated to prominent posts in the government. There were six such holy families in Tibet. Secondly, national heroes were awarded estates and promoted to the higher echelons of government service, which also increased the number of landlords.

No Sakyan aristocrat had manorial estates. In Sakya the two palaces had numerous 'subjects' and large estates. We were the subjects of Phuntsog Phodrang, as our late father was an ex-monk from Chokhor Lhunpo, which belonged to the Sakya Lamas of this particular house. It was not only customary but also necessary to pay your personal allegiance to a particular high lama or a lord, and in return for your allegiance you were assured of protection. When Mother was confronted with our legal cases, Phuntsog Phodrang extended its royal influence to help her. As recognized subjects of Phuntsog Phodrang we were entitled to live in a five-roomed house for a nominal 'working' rent: every year we had to harvest eight *khels* of fields for the palace. We were, however, given rations for harvesting. Since our family did not work permanently, the adult members were required to pay 1½ *sang* per year, in token of our allegiance to the lama.

The Lama employed his subjects in various capacities, either permanently or part-time. Ngandek, the elder brother of my late brother-in-law, Sherab-la, served in a permanent capacity. He was appointed as a cook and was given his food, together with a set of clothes every year; but he received no wage. However, his family taxes were reduced considerably as a result of his permanent service. After a few years Ngandek was appointed as an attendant to the newly born Sakya Lama, and when the Lama became older he became his personal bearer. As such he virtually ran the palace, and his reputation spread in Sakya. There were other subjects working under harsher conditions. For example, one of my aunts lived rent-free but had to look after a large number of fields in a village called Gochung. Although she was given the usual allowance of land for looking after the palace fields, she was always in debt.

To what extent were these 'serfs' free? They had every right to petition their lord to be relieved from his service. His answer would depend on the plausibility of the petition, the petitioner's influence, and the size of the bribe and his own temperament. However, if he objected, the serf often fled to remote parts of Tibet or to India. This was possible, since Tibet had no efficient police system at all. The Chinese Communists used to tell us in Sakya that the serfs had no freedom of any kind, but this is utter nonsense. The official labour would be carried out by one or two labourers, and as long as the recorded work was executed, the family was perfectly free to do as they liked.

According to Chinese propaganda, the government owned only 38% of the land. These statistics are suspect, as the government would have eventually gone bankrupt if decentralization had been allowed to continue at this rate. The government leased its land directly to the *tralpas*, respectable and responsible tax-paying citizens whose constant cry was: 'We live on chaff and pay taxes in grain.' The non-taxpayers were called *duchung*; when these families became full-fledged *tralpas*, the government made them accept land and pay taxes accordingly. When our family produced children we were told to become *tralpas*. However, since we were already subjects of Phuntsog Phodrang, we were exempted from tax.

The *tralpas* were not taxed so that the government would have money to invest, but to maintain the standing army, and to meet running expenses. A *tralpa*'s duty was to provide soldiers and transport for the travelling Lhasa officials; as the - number of 'enemies of *dharma*' increased in the east at an alarming rate, the army had to be strengthened, and the taxes were increased. The taxes were calculated on the basis of a soldier's annual wage for every four *kangs* (a *kang* is about 135 acres).

The taxes were worked out by our village arithmeticians. If you had seen them at work on a bright sunny day in their usual rendezvous, a big, weedy, fallow field, you would have mistaken them for dice players. As the happy-go-lucky, unlettered *tralpas* chatted and joked boisterously in groups, the two mathematicians sat opposite each other, engrossed in their calculations. Between them lay their untidy mathematical apparatus. Date and plum seeds, all dry and shiny through frequent fingering, were used for single units; small engraved pieces of wood for ten units; and copper coins for a hundred units. While one of them chanted the numbers and calculated at the same time, the other silently watched the calculations and checked when and if necessary.

In Sakya a government agent called the *Ganpo* was responsible for transport taxes. His duty was to receive messages heralding the arrival of an aristocrat from the mail runner, and to make preparations for the lord and his retinue of servants. I used to see him striding along a country lane, ostentatiously playing with the message scroll. He would go from house to house, shouting 'Come for a meeting at once!' When an inquisitive farmer stopped him for an explanation, he might say: 'The Governor of Shekar Dzong is en route to Lhasa. Horses, food and fuel must be supplied. I know His Majesty is extremely short-tempered, so you had better hurry up.' While the travelling officials stayed, the local *tralpas* had to serve them and provide horses and escorts for a three-day journey.

Apart from these taxes, emergency taxes were sometimes imposed. During my parents' lifetime, only one such tax was collected – the 'ear tax'. Every citizen was required to pay two *tamkas* if he still had both ears! It was levied by the XIIIth Dalai Lama to pay for rifles purchased from the British government in India.

TWELVE

Democratic Reforms

'Bring me the keys at once, woman,' said Namgyal, not in the cultivated, respectful language in which we always addressed our superiors and elders, but in the rudest language that a Tibetan proletarian could possibly use. He was speaking to Dragpa's wife. She hurriedly presented him with a huge bunch of keys, sticking her tongue out as she did so – which, in Tibet is a highly respectful gesture to the new master, Uyon Namgyal-la. He snatched the keys from her and kicked the door open. With him were other local activists and three scribes, of whom I was one. Bringing up the rear were Norzin-la and her Chinese boss. We glanced through the well-furnished rooms and quickly stopped at the dark storeroom for some dried fruit and pastries – tasting for the first time the fruit of our perpetual toil. Then we carefully locked all the windows and doors, and glued strips of paper with huge rectangular Chinese characters on every one of them.

At this time the property and lands of the reactionary upper strata were being confiscated for later distribution to the have-nots. This was in retaliation for the Tibetan rebellion, which was considered to be treason by the Communists. No layman or lama in Sakya was directly involved with the Tibetan revolt; nevertheless, all the ecclesiastics and aristocrats, except for two families, were found guilty of the highest treason – 'reactionary rebellion to separate Tibet from the Motherland'. The lamas' guilt was in their acts of *magdog* (war-preventative rituals against the 'enemies of the faith'). The Chinese comrades emphasized that *magdogs* would not harm them in any way, but said that the evil intention, though useless, betrayed the Motherland. A few high officials were connected with the rebel leader Ponta. Ecclesiastics and officials alike were guilty of 'sending the Sakya Lama to the foreign land' (India). This charge was unfair, for only those intimate with the lama among them knew that he was heading for India and not for a spiritual retreat, as we had been told. Anyway, the angry Chinese comrades showed no judicial discrimination. Four responsible *tralpa* houses were found 'guilty of helping the Khampa bandit Jagod Tsang and his gang', who had passed through Sakya on their way to India.

The houses of the reactionary upper strata were not long kept locked and sealed. Having killed the wolf, we could now have its skin! Along with the others who could read and write, I was kept busy making inventories, while the local progressives counted each article. I must admit I enjoyed feasting on all the stores of food. However, I witnessed a pathetic incident in the Jango house. After Jango's suicide his family had been thrown into the groom's quarters near the gate, inside the walled-in stable yard. I saw one of the progressives looking down haughtily from the window of the altar room, the best-furnished room in the house. As he looked he whistled with pride and every few minutes arrogantly spat into the yard. Below, at the door of the groom's quarters, stood old Mrs Jango, sadly looking up at him. I wondered what she was thinking, but I was not mature enough to put such a question to her. Anyway, I could not have dared; for we were strictly prohibited from associating with the upper classes.

Later, in India, I asked some of the free aristocrats what they thought of the confiscation of their land and property. The pious Buddhists among them looked at it philosophically. Nangpa Drarong, the sponsor of my grandfather's mission to Chang Thang, told me: 'Ever since I was twenty-two I have wanted to practise Buddhism faithfully. I knew that clinging to worldly possessions was the biggest hindrance on our way to perfection. Therefore I wanted to give most of my wealth to charity, keeping just enough for myself and my family. But these pious aspirations were all in vain. I was locked up in the perpetual darkness of human existence; so, spiritually, I am grateful to the Chinese for giving away my wealth to charity. Now I have nothing to cling to – my family, friends and relatives are all stranded in Tibet. I am liberated from possessiveness and can devote the rest of my life to the faithful practice of *dharma* with no obstructions.' Though a thorough layman up to the age of 65, he became a monk after escaping to India, and now leads an admirably religious life in Kalimpong.

Another man, whose family is still in Tibet, told me: 'I can now afford to be frank and objective, seeing that I have lost everything. Our property was certainly not entirely the fruit of Tibetan labour. Our father was an official in the Sakya local government, but he received no salary. We had to pay government taxes just like any *tralpa*. We had, as I have said, a large family, and everybody, brothers and sisters alike, worked side by side with our labourers and servants. Our actual exploitation consisted of occasional bribes that our father received, employing two servants, and hiring labourers in the working season. I would not have minded if our wealth had gone into Tibetan mouths, but the Tibetans were given the useless things – old furniture, ceremonial dresses and agricultural implements. The Chinese took away the core of our wealth, gold, silver and precious stones.'

This is perfectly true. As soon as we opened the locked and sealed houses, Norzin-la and her boss collected all the valuables, which included jewellery, gold and silver objects, and precious stones. The confiscated valuables were kept in the People's Treasury at the Phuntsog Phodrang Palace. Towards the end of the year, the donkey driver of the palace, Acho Mingmar, was accused of stealing some of them. We used to hear rumours that the gold, silver and precious stones were transported to China; but of course the Chinese were most secretive, and nobody in Sakya really saw the valuables being loaded into trucks and taken away. However, recent news reports that Tibetan images have been on sale in Hong Kong, Japan and Kathmandu leave me with little doubt that China is earning a great deal of foreign exchange by selling Tibetan treasures in the international markets.

In spite of the wide publicity about the distribution of wealth, all that the proletariat received were clothes, furniture and agricultural implements. The upper and lower middle classes did not get anything, nor did we desire it. However, my sister Donkar, who was classified as a proletarian, received two old silk shirts, a pair of old ornate shoes worn by some senior lama on festive occasions, a huge cumbersome ant-eaten box, two tables with missing legs, one wooden saddle, an old blue brocade *chupa* and an odd glove unmistakably belonging to Sakya Bamo. The costumes of lama actors, worn once a year during the festivals and treasured in monasteries for the rest of the time, were also distributed. She did not get a single piece of turquoise or gold or even a tiny pearl; nor did anyone else of her class. On receiving her share, our next-door neighbour, who in the Chinese language was called a 'serf' but who was in fact a sweeper of the Phuntsog Phodrang Palace, told us: 'The uncles (Chinese) ate all the meat and gave us the bones.' The Tibetan proletariat were not so stupid that they could not see the obvious, and so they grumbled behind the backs of the Chinese.

The overlords had a countrywide network of spies, and they immediately knew about this discontent. They launched a new political campaign, with 'A needle is better than a bar of gold' as its slogan. Norzin-la told us: 'If you have a bar of gold, what is the use of it? You cannot mould it into a ploughshare or use it for any productive purpose. On the other hand, if you have a needle, just a mean, tiny needle, you can sew with it. A golden needle is useless for sewing. The age-old craze for the most useless metal, gold, is an imperialist insanity. We must struggle to destroy the insane concept.' We were told officially that the valuables of our commonwealth would be sold and the money used for the industrialization of economically backward Tibet.

In spite of the gifts, most Tibetans clung to the age-old belief that 'fruit produced without labour cannot be digested except by lamas', and that no matter how much the Chinese might give they would still be what they were previously, as decreed by their *karma*.

Before the distribution, the Chinese took the opportunity of exhibiting the wealth of the richest house in Sakya, Phuntsog Phodrang, the oldest palace of the Sakya Lamas. The entire wealth was displayed, not arranged in an orderly way, but spread out as widely as possible. Then the people were summoned. To see the treasures we had to commit the sin of walking over holy pills (*jinlaps*), which the local activists had deliberately spread on the flagstones of the courtyard. *Jinlaps* were mystical panaceas, blessed by the high lamas and eaten faithfully by their followers as a cure for any sickness. They had to be kept in high, sanctified places. The moment you desecrated them by walking over them, you not only committed a sin but also destroyed their mystic vitality. The Chinese working team caught some Sakyans stealing not priceless valuables, but *jinlaps*. Along with others who tried to avoid walking on the *jinlaps*, they were cornered and closely interrogated.

The enormous wealth of Phuntsog Phodrang was the accumulation of centuries. The spacious courtyard was full to overflowing, and the inner rooms were packed with priceless valuables. The most recent treasures had been brought from Kham in the early 1950s by the Sakya Lama and his brother, who had gone on a pilgrimage round the many Sakya branch monasteries in Kham. Norzin-la was there with a loudspeaker, giving a running commentary on the results of exploitation. 'People of Sakya, take a good look at the unimaginable wealth that belonged to only two men! It is far greater than the total value of all the Sakyans' belonging put together! The owners are supposed to be living Buddhas, and with that holy mask they have sucked the people's blood. Think deeply and widely whether these Sakya Lamas can be living Buddhas or not. If they are what they claim to be, why did they not practise their *dharma* like Milarepa? They should have gone to the caves to meditate.'

In spite of such concrete proof, most Sakyans made allowances for the lamas. They said: 'Why did they hoard so much? I wish they had kept just enough for the celestial household and spent the rest on holy monasteries. Perhaps they never knew they owned so much. After all, they did not go to their coffers. These were in the hands of their treasurers, whose power was almost unlimited.'

The upper and lower middle classes included the petty traders and pedlars of Sakya, ourselves among them. Soon after the distribution of wealth the Chinese Communists opened a branch of the People's Bank in Sakya, and told the traders to invest all their capital in it. Mother was terribly upset at what she thought was a polite way of confiscating all our money, and her fears about the Chinese keeping it were quite justified. Once it was deposited we could not take it out again. If we wished to take out even a small amount we would be asked why we wanted it. The money virtually ceased to be ours. Mother used to ask what was the use of the receipt, which was nothing more than waste paper and might be used more usefully for lighting the fire. She tried to hide half our small capital, but she was found out and received a severe public criticism.

As regards the nomadic herdsmen the Chinese Communists followed a special policy. The democratic reforms were not applied to the nomads; if they had been, all the yaks, sheep and goats would have been divided up among the poor herdsmen. But the nomads were used to their free way of life, and would have gone on doing with their animals as they pleased. In the vast wilderness of Chang Thang, the land of the nomads, the Chinese Communists found it most difficult to get a firm grip.

The Party's efficient, ruthless administration was incapable of operating in the Tibetan Wild West. So the comrades left the nomads' property alone for the time being, though they registered every yak, sheep and goat owned by them in 1959. No herdsman was permitted to slaughter more than a certain number of sheep each year. If he exceeded the number he would be charged with anti-Motherland sabotage – a very serious crime in the new set-up. Both the herdsmen and the livestock owners were heavily taxed. Their dairy products, collected as 'national patriotic wealth' for the people's commonwealth, were all consumed by the khaki-clad men of the People's Liberation Army and the blue-uniformed working personnel in Tibet. In 1964 the Chinese exchanged about ten thousand Tibetan sheep for Nepalese rice – the sheep were confiscated from the nomads.

THIRTEEN

'Eat Less, Produce More'

SOON AFTER we had completed the basic task of the Three Strikes and Two Reductions, the accent was changed to hard labour for greater production. 'Only greater production,' interpreted Norzin-la at a mass meeting, 'can guide our progress, and co-operation is absolutely essential for it. Comrades, we have already seen evidence of the miracles that co-operation can perform. When the masses of Tibet rose and united like an indestructible iron ball under the leadership of the Chinese Communist Party, the evil system that exploited and oppressed the people for centuries was crushed in a few months. This is the living proof of the unfathomable power of mass unity. Now if you can divert that power of your zealous patriotism and revolutionary fervour to co-operation among yourselves, we can transform backward Tibet into a happy prosperous Communist society and can contribute much towards the reconstruction of our mighty Motherland, China.

'Because we have crushed the reactionary upper strata and achieved our basic victory, we should not relax and rest there. Far greater tasks lie ahead. Through economy and frugality we must struggle to bring about maximum production. Comrade Mao has said sagaciously that we must economize to make economic progress. This is no time to rejoice over one victory; that will come later. Now is the time to forget rejoicing and begin to build Tibet anew with our bare hands.'

This crash programme was known as *Thonpe Dronchung*, which really means: 'Eat less and produce more.' The key step towards the realization of this objective was, as Norzin-la implied, through Mutual Aid Groups, *Rogre Tsogchung*. These were small and simple co-operatives of ten farmers, which had obvious administrative advantages to the Chinese overlords. Through the co-operatives they got a firm grip on the masses by means of their agents, the progressives. In the initial stages the local activists spied on us, and later everyone was compelled to spy on everyone else. Sentimentality was not to play any part in our collective national political life. We must discard all our old values and embrace the new ones with open arms.

The only real freedom left to us was the freedom to choose which co-operative we would join. However, a qualification must be made even to this: we were not permitted to elect our own leaders. Without a word of approval from the masses, the Chinese made the new appointments, evidently based on the performances by the progressives during the earlier political campaigns. The chairman of our co-operative was Tsering, whose activities I have already described. Most of the members of our co-operative had been together in our study group, during the indoctrination period. Our secretary was a former monk, from the proletariat; like the titular chairman, he was a mere puppet, dancing to the tune set by the Party, and directed by the Han working personnel. Through the co-operatives the Chinese Communists made us work, talk, eat, cry and sing as their almighty Party wanted. Our upper classes were in the inner prison, and we people were in the outer prison. Like the political prisoners, we were subjected to hard labour and continual indoctrination. The Chinese exploited our labour power to their own best advantage, and at the same time, indoctrinated us ever more effectively through their agents in our co-operative. They worked on the old principle, 'Divide and rule'.

The co-operatives demonstrated what miraculous results enforced co-operation could bring about. In the old days the farmers had very little employment in summer, apart from watering the fields and tending their animals. But the Chinese

Communists gave us a number of bright, practical, new ideas, which kept us busy throughout the summer. In spite of the fact that we had three rivers that flowed in the summer, in the past there had always been an acute shortage of water for irrigation. The old decadent government, obsessed with pious and idealistic aspirations for its subjects, did not care to direct the farmers to build bigger and better canals. The Chinese at once saw to it. The newly formed co-operatives were employed on enlarging the Tenzin Canal and constructing a new dam, which took less than two months. With the irrigation highly improved, we harvested very good crops that year. The people were astonished at the combined power of co-operation and compulsion. Of course we had to wait until the harvest time was over to see whether the innovations ordered by the Chinese were for our benefit or for theirs.

Though the results were good, they were achieved under deplorable conditions. Ten families amalgamated their agricultural and weaving implements and made them joint co-operative property. The secretary laboriously registered each day's attendance, so that nobody could escape from working. When we were enlarging the canal, the Chinese working personnel forced us to work insanely hard, by making the various co-operatives and the individual labourers compete against one another. Each co-operative was given the daily task of digging a section of the canal, measuring roughly twelve feet long, six deep and five wide, through hard, stony ground. It was the duty of the co-operative's chairman to make sure that the target was exceeded. Thus the competition resolved itself into seeing who could exceed the target by the greatest amount, and not who could reach it. When the sun was about to set, the Chinese working personnel and Uyon Namgyal-la would examine each co-operative's performance and declare the result on the spot. The first received a thunderous applause; the last, humiliation and disgrace. At a special public meeting the protagonists and the antagonists were isolated. A young man called Nyima Tashi was declared to be the most industrious, patriotic worker, and was presented with a photograph of an aeroplane. The laziest, a middle-aged woman called Sonam Dolma, was punished by having a drawing of a pig stuck on her forehead, symbolizing laziness and lack of patriotism for the Motherland.

During this hard labour several inexperienced workers got terrible sores, like overworked donkeys. When Mother heard that our friend Sherab-la had got such sores, she said: 'O Kunchok-Sum, what is the world coming to? I have heard of donkeys getting sores on their backs through too much labour, but have never before heard of human beings getting them.' We could not accuse the Chinese overlords of forcing hard labour on us; they did not actually say: 'If you don't work as we order you to, we will shoot you'; but in the ultimate analysis it was nothing less than forced hard labour.

Besides the irrigation projects, we were made to bring every strip of arable land under cultivation. Narrow edges that had lain waste beside the fields for generations were tilled. Tracts of waste land that had previously been kept for grass were brought under the plough. Basic scientific farming techniques were taught, and immediately applied. The old government would circulate a bombastic note decreeing a certain thing, but the decree remained on paper, neat and beautiful, and the illiterate subjects would not hear of it. The Chinese Communists, on the other hand, would first of all call a mass meeting, in which they explained their decree, persuading, urging and convincing. If anyone violated it he received a punishment far worse than his predecessors ever did.

Included in the politico-economic campaign was the killing of all the dogs and flies in Tibet. This was directly opposed to our religious sentiments, and in Sakya we openly expressed our resentment. The old people were encouraged to catch flies, and a reward was offered to the one who caught the most; but this appeal was in vain. The dogs were stoned by our local activists, instigated by the Han working personnel. The Chinese explained that the dogs and flies were parasites in our economy, and that both were hygienically harmful. But most people did not accept this scientific view, and took it as a deliberate act of violence and part of the Chinese aim to destroy Buddhism. The Tibetans loved their dogs, and some families even used to perform death rituals when their dog died.

During our lunch break and after work in the evening we had to attend indoctrination classes – a total of about two and a half hours a day. Labour and 'education' must march forward together, side by side, not because the Chinese comrades cared for our intellectual and physical welfare, but because they wanted to indoctrinate us and then use us for the reconstruction of the Motherland. There was no more talk about machines working for us, as there had been in the mid-50s. It was made abundantly clear that we Tibetans must develop the Motherland with our own hands. The strength of the united masses was incomparable, both physically and politically. 'If you have zealous patriotism and revolutionary force you can conquer sickness by the hard struggle of physical labour', we were told. We had time for two things only: forced hard labour, and indoctrination. We were exhausted mentally and physically.

In the old days there had been a time for everything – for merrymaking as well as hard work. The seasonal work days were exciting, enjoyable events in the farmers' calendar, and the labourers used to look forward to feasts washed down by *chang*, and to songs and laughter. The Tibetans had an unlimited capacity for hard work; but hard work without adequate food was veritable torture. The Han working personnel were constantly at our elbow, urging us to work and work and to sing, too! Norzin-la and the other Tibetan interpreters felt that we should be as joyful and free as uncaged birds, when we really felt miserable. They had been taken to China when they were small, and there had been taught only Beijing's view of old Tibet as 'a reactionary, dark, cruel and barbarous feudal serf system'.

Once Norzin-la asked our co-operative: 'Why are you not singing while building your own canal? You should be singing happy songs, since you yourselves have become kings and queens.' Tsering, our chairman, whose tongue had sharpened considerably, retorted: 'Norzin-la, we are feeling even more patriotic than happy. If we were to sing, we would waste our time and energy and would not be able to compete with the others. Retrogression would be an unacceptable defeat for our co-operative. We must leap forward to develop our Motherland.'

It was true that songs would not come when the workers' spirits were imprisoned by the fear and anxiety of competition. But the songs must be sung, insisted the Chinese. The workers used to mutter: 'When we want to cry, we have to sing!' It was hard to sing our working songs at high speed; the traditional songs of different seasons were set to the natural rhythms of a particular type of work, such as digging and shovelling, but we were made to work far faster than the natural rhythm. Furthermore, the words of the songs had been changed, because some of them were in praise of the old order.

As we sat down to our rationed meals, the memories of past working days came back. At the beginning of the *Thonpe Dronchung* campaign we used to laugh at the quality and quantity of our meals. Our tea was watery, black and butterless, in contrast with the old thick buttered tea made in a churn. The girl who served our co-operative with this watery tea would shake the teapot and say sarcastically: 'Wait a bit! The tea is so thick with butter that it won't come out of the spout!' Though most Tibetans drank *chang* in the past, we were not allowed to drink, for drinking was anti-Motherland sabotage. The former heavy drinkers used to say: 'In this revolutionary era *chang* flows in the canals', and knelt down to drink water from the canal like horses. Thus we laughed at our own plight. We also joked about the earlier political campaign, and noted sarcastically that the 'two reductions' we had been told of turned out to be on *chang* and tea. Later on we were not allowed to make such remarks. Our chairman had reported some of our members, who were 'advised and corrected' – the first – warning.

A working person was allotted a monthly ration of 22 lb of *tsampa*, half a pound of oil or butter, a third of a brick of tea, and a little salt. Only the tea was sufficient; the rest was a starvation diet to us. Old people and children received even less. We hardly saw meat, because of the dialectical argument that ran thus: if you killed your animals that worked and reproduced, you were killing the national economy; and if you killed the national economy, you were committing anti-Motherland sabotage. So we tightened our belts every day.

I am not implying that Tibetan workers in the past drank thick buttered tea and strong *chang*, or that they ate chunks of boiled meat and special meals every day; it was only on special seasonal working days that they were given extra food. But the Chinese overlords did not only deprive us of these traditional prerogatives; they also took away our basic necessities, and drove us to depression and despair. In our own co-operative the prophetess Yudon fainted with hunger. When the Han working personnel came to investigate this, they put the blame on the greed of the upper and middle-class farmers.

The whole co-operative protested to the Chinese. 'In the old days,' we told them, 'if we needed more grain, we borrowed from the upper classes and the rich. Now that we have exterminated both, we have no one else but the Party to approach. Please lend us grain from the People's Granary.' The reply was a polite no. The working personnel explained that the upper and middle-class farmers still possessed enough grain to lend to the poor; the People's Granary must be kept in reserve for emergencies. One of our members answered in desperation: 'The Party has repeatedly told us that everything now belongs to the people. You say that the earth is the people's and the sky is the people's. What is the use of calling everything the people's when we don't have the right to use it?' He was reminded that 'people' meant the majority who were starving, and it was the Party's duty to save them. Finally, Yudon was lent barley grains at the official interest rate of 10% per annum.

On another occasion a proletarian asked Norzin-la: 'You tell us that the sun of the lords and lamas has set and that the sun of the people has risen. When is our happy time coming? Will it ever come in our lifetime? Otherwise why should we work so hard with so little food, and suffer more than we used to in the past? If you believe in *karma*, you can at least pray, and assume that your hard work will be rewarded in the next life. But you say that when we die, we die, and that's all. We have only one short life, and if we are compelled to spend it on hard physical labour, we are already in hell before we die. Who is going to get our share of pleasure and enjoyment? And when?' He was told that part of his happiness was coming pretty soon, with 'our own first harvest'.

The 1959 harvest was excellent, due to the new farming techniques and extra care taken throughout the summer. Apart from building canals and pools for better irrigation, and tilling waste strips, we were made to weed our fields often and make more manure than usual. We were all excited about our crops. But when the grain was ready for storing in our granaries, the Chinese informed us, through Uyon Namgyal-la, to keep it ready for weighing in the open field before we took it away. Mother exclaimed: 'This is our own crop. Why should the Party weigh it? The old government never did so.' Great heaps of barley and peas were separately piled. The grain was well matured, big and hard.

Like the rest, we thought that we would have enough for the following year and would not face the same acute shortage of *tsampa*. But Norzin-la and the local activists, including Namgyal, weighed every grain of barley, following closely the priority list that the higher authorities had made. They weighed first the seeds for the following season; secondly the tax called *Gyalche Chidru*, meaning 'grains of patriotism'; and thirdly our

rations, amounting to 22 lb per working person per month. The
rest was to be sold to the government, whether we liked it or
not, and the money kept in the People's Bank, never to be used
or even seen by the owner. Nobody escaped from the Chinese
orders which were carried out efficiently and ruthlessly. I need
not comment on whether 22 lb was sufficient monthly diet for
someone working about ten hours a day and undergoing indoctrination for two or three hours more.

The people in Sakya were very dissatisfied with these starvation rations. They argued that there should be plenty of grain,
because the aristocrats' granaries were untouched and the
year's harvest was excellent. But our voice was raised in vain.
Though Norzin-la and some of the Han working personnel
might sympathize with us, they had no authority to give even
an extra handful of grain; the order must come from the Party.

Immediately after the harvest was over, the Chinese exaggerated the results, as usual. They claimed that the yield was
about ten times the seed, due to the people's industry and the
Party leadership. It followed that if we could produce a bumper
crop in the first year of our liberation, there was no reason why
we could not double this year's yield in the following season.
We were made to sign a pledge to the effect that we would
obtain a yield of twenty times the seed in the next season. Many
voices were raised in disagreement. How could we guarantee
that we would obtain such a yield? The farmers explained to the
Chinese that it was in the hands of nature whether we would
get a bumper crop or not. It depended largely on the unpre-
dictable weather. If hailstones fell, our crops would be ruined
and we would get a far smaller yield than in the year then ending; but, on the other hand, if we were fortunate enough to get
timely and adequate rains, we might get better crops and might
possibly be able to break the previous year's record. But the
Party should not force us to sign where conditions were beyond
our control, unless the Motherland had devices to prevent hailstones and to bring rain.

However, this was dismissed as 'a disgraceful defeatist attitude and a conservative superstitious outlook'. Said Norzin-la: 'As long as you have enough patriotism for our Motherland, you will always find means to overcome difficulties no matter how mountainous. You should never underestimate the power of the united masses.' The signing of the decree was meant to strengthen our will to work even harder the next year. Eventually, we were persuaded to pass a resolution that we would work twice as hard as in the previous year, and to harvest a yield twice as much as in the first year of our liberation. Everybody murmured: 'If the Chinese are going to force us to work twice as hard next year, then they must be plotting to kill us all.'

So the much-acclaimed democratic reform was practically over in Tibet. Our family tasted the 'people's democratic dictatorship' for over a year; and though still young I had the unique experience of seeing Chinese Communist rule in practice. Born and brought up as I was at a most critical juncture in our history, I was able to taste both the religious old Tibet and the progressive new Tibet. Looking at both regimes as impartially as is humanly possible, I am critical of both. The Tibetan government, for all its religious pretensions, was decadent, inefficient and feudal. It stubbornly believed that its basic duty was to work for the collective Buddhahood of Tibetans. The Chinese regime, for all its revolutionary pretensions, is fundamentally colonial, inhuman and tyrannical. Theirs is the most sophisticated and diabolically ingenious form of colonialism that has been evolved in history, but neither the rulers nor the ruled are happy. Both live in perpetual fear, insecurity and suspicion, eternally on their guard and under attack. The Communists presume that equal income equals collective happiness, but we found that this was not so. Like the religious old order of Tibet, they believe that the whole world is wrong and that only they are right. All the same, they have some impressive qualities. I admire their iron discipline, their machine-like efficiency, their single-minded devotion in all their undertakings, and many of their revolutionary ideas, both on paper and in practice.

Leaving aside the complex legal question of the Chinese pseudo-historical claims on Tibet, are the common Tibetans happier and better off now than they were previously? Everyone would have welcomed a truly democratic reform; but my account should enable the reader to judge whether the Chinese 'liberation' amounted to democracy or not. I am in sympathy with most of the reforms that the Chinese Communists carried out in Tibet, but I would question their ulterior motives. I agree that the wealth of the lamas and lords was mainly the fruit of the Tibetan masses, and so the distribution of wealth among the poor was in theory correct and welcome; but, as I said earlier, the Tibetan proletariat received mainly useless objects, while the real wealth was taken by the Chinese. Similarly, I agree that it was right for the land to go to those who tilled it. The distribution was done in a very fair manner: the land owned by the upper strata was confiscated and distributed; the land owned by the medium farmers was paid for and distributed; finally the confiscated and purchased fields were classified into three main groups according to their fertility, and were divided in the fairest possible way. But all this was of little use when our crops were appropriated, and we were made to work extremely hard on near-starvation rations.

Tibet is no longer a country; it is a mere geographical expression, part of the 'Mighty Motherland'. Our labour and natural resources are exploited for the glory of China and the Hans. In short, the Chinese Communists are milking Tibet as well as the Tibetans.

FOURTEEN

The Triumph of Materialism

ONE DAY our co-operative was harvesting Donkar's tiny field, which was in a beautiful spot near the foothills of Mount Taktsenma. We managed to finish it before lunch, and sat down for our meagre meal. In the old days the farmer used to press his labourers to eat and drink much more than they could possibly manage. A popular custom, called *shabdag*, obliged you to drink a huge cup of *chang*, and if you left one drop in the bottom of the cup you had to drink two more as a penalty. Such extravagance was no longer allowed; we must now live a life of frugality and productivity. With that rich tradition, laughter had also gone. There was none of the usual horseplay and crude natural humour of former days. The jokes we pretended to make must conform to the Party line. As we sat soberly around the burning stove, drinking butterless tea and going slow with the day's *tsampa*, we saw Norzin-la and her Chinese boss, Comrade Li, walking briskly towards us. We presumed that they were on their normal 'educational drive', and secretly regretted that they would not leave us our lunch-hour free.

Tsering, our chairman, welcomed them on our behalf, and Norzin-la asked us if we were tired. This was just a formality; as anticipated, we all shook our heads, and then nodded hard. The chairman cautiously looked around to see that everyone had gestured in the affirmative and added, as a sign of progressiveness: 'Even if we had been tired, it's our own harvest and our own work.'

Meanwhile, Comrade Li was minutely observing the field

just harvested, and seemed to be fascinated by some invisible object. Recovering from his contemplation, he asked jerking his finger towards the centre of the field: 'Why have those barley stalks been left near that pile of stones?' We knew that he had been meditating upon the god of the field. In Tibet a few white stones would be piled up in the centre of every field; they were the visible abode of the guardian of the field. While reaping, we would always leave a few stalks uncut near the cairn as a grateful offering. Comrade Li was not interested in our 'useless superstitious absurdities', and began to moralize. 'I see you have left those stalks for your gods. But I am afraid that the invisible gods will not eat the grains; the hungry, useless birds will. You do not have to undergo self-torturing penance or meditation to discover this truth. You simply observe and find out for yourselves.' He smiled sardonically.

The older co-operative workers, Moh Tsondru and Tsering Bhuti, found it hard to endure his mockery of what was sacrosanct, and Moh Tsondru was trembling with righteous indignation. The two comrades must have seen this, but they continued unperturbed.

'Now,' continued Li in his monotonous shrill voice, 'if you leave ten stalks in every field, you can imagine how much grain is wasted. Suppose every field in Sakya was left with that amount! Chairman Mao has said: "Economize and progress." You cannot afford to give grain to the birds that do not work for society. So I hope you will shed your illusions and live a life of frugality and productivity.'

After this introduction he got down to the main business. He took a small red notebook from his front pocket, looked through some marked pages, and threw open the day's topic for group discussion. It was: 'Religion is the poison of the people.' (Since opium was almost unknown to the Tibetans, the word 'poison' was an apt substitute.) Norzin-la was well prepared on the subject. She drew her examples and illustrations from the locality, and though we might not be convinced by her because of our deeply rooted 'superstitious' faith we knew what she was talking about. Such comprehension merely served to increase our helpless rage. For generations we had been worshipping our images and idols, thinking them more real than our next-door neighbours; and now the Chinese had come to shake our beliefs to their foundations.

Norzin-la said mockingly: 'You are worse than children to think that mud idols have a mind. They are made by you and feared by you. You believe that the Sakya Lamas are living Buddhas, and attribute supernatural divine power to their names. If you are still stubborn enough to think so, lock up the Sakya Lamas in an empty room without any clothes and food and see if they can survive a week. They have been exploiting you from the thirteenth century onwards, and deceiving you like sorcerers.' She stopped and signalled to Tsering, our chairman, to air her views, which meant nothing more than amplifying what had already been said.

Tsering's 'views' indicated that she had been exceptionally attentive. We were not supposed to give an exact echo of the official examples and illustrations of the Chinese; we received more credit if we could show resourcefulness and inventiveness by applying the topic personally to ourselves. The political educationist would then applaud and say approvingly: 'You are a progressive and revolutionary activist. Well done! Keep it up!' Tsering invariably won high praise. She cleared her throat with a few unnecessary coughs and began: 'What the comrade says is perfectly true. Every morning I fill up the seven brass cups with holy water and offer them to the gods on my altar. But when I go to empty the cups in the evening I find that they are still full. Kunchok-Sum has not sipped any water. How foolish and backward I have been to waste butter on the lamps before my altar, when I don't have butter for my tea!'

When Tsering finished her dreaded turn, she could hardly conceal her triumphant, relieved sigh. Next to speak was Sherab-la, our friend the ex-monk, whose views were highly commendable in the light of our political lectures. After him everybody was compelled to 'air his views', and no one escaped what we called 'the digging of the heart'. Finally it came to Moh Tsondru's turn. She was renowned for her childlike frankness and over-religious ardour, and when the time came for her to speak she hesitated and came to a dead stop. Norzin-la, showing a trace of sympathy for a fellow-Tibetan, prompted her: 'Come on, Grandma, you must have some thoughts in your head. One of the characteristics that distinguishes human beings from animals is that humans can think, no matter what. Let us share your own thoughts. It does not matter if you cannot express them in the new language, but at least let us hear you speak.'

Our chairman and her progressive revolutionary activists were showing signs of restlessness. They were worried that our co-operative might be 'left behind' – the opposite of the 'leap forward' – and be penalized for conservativeness. Those sitting near the old woman dug her gently with their elbows; others winked at her, hinting that she should 'air her views'. She seemed to have understood all the various signs and signals, but to be labouring to hold back inexplicable or hideous thoughts too dangerous to be shown.

At last her swelling thoughts burst free in a torrent of anger and sincerity. The enfeebled old woman, possessed by the truth she believed in, shouted in an angry, choking, trembling voice: 'We know that the holy figures are made of mud by our religious painters; we know that the images do not physically drink water from the cups. You need not tell us about these superficial things and poke fun at our faith. But you don't know what we know ...' Her voice faded for a few moments while she struggled with thoughts she could not express. Then she continued more calmly: 'We believe that our holy figures are not human beings; they are the symbolical physical representations of our true faith. Thus the intangible is made tangible. They are the containers of our faith, the pegs upon which we can hang it, like the wooden pegs upon which we hang our ladles. Through them we can grasp it more firmly. We know that some lamas do not need any images, because they do not need any material help. Why do you stick portraits of Mao all over the walls of your rooms?'

She was interrupted by mocking laughter from the Chinese, who were showing a bewildered fascination for her sincerity. But Moh Tsondru, carried away by her conviction, took no notice. She was determined to finish.

'As for wasting our economy on religious offerings,' she went on, 'the more generously we offer to Kunchok-Sum, the richer we become, both spiritually and materially. I have never heard of any Tibetan being reduced to beggary through his religious offerings. I don't think that the members of this co-operative should lie. The lamas never asked for offerings; we voluntarily offered them in exchange for performing rites. I personally feel more satisfied if I make an offering to some great lama than if I spend my savings on food for myself.'

Although Moh Tsondru's outrageous views unmistakably unveiled 'an unpurgeable old green mind', the deceptively polite comrades praised her lavishly for her candidness. Norzin-la, like a patient, devoted teacher, explained all over again: 'You have not yet properly understood the people's infallible ideology. This is the most glorious period in the entire history of Tibet, when you can raise up your heads. The parasitic lamas have been deceiving you for so long that you have grown accustomed to their deception and exploitations. However, you will slowly understand. We will help you, and so will the progressives from our co-operative. We are sorry there is no more time today, but we know how eager you are to reap your own first harvest. Thank you everybody. See you again.' They left, scoffing.

Yet many of the young were convinced by the Chinese. They would say: 'The Chinese have been really well educated, especially in the way they argue. You can't refute their points, and what they say appears real and true.' The older generation remained firm. No matter how persuasively the Chinese atheists tried to demonstrate the futility of religion, most of the members of our co-operative adopted a kind of mental blindness against the inroads of agnosticism. Our attitude was: 'The godless Chinese, who do not believe in the infallible law of cause and effect (*karma*), tell their lies with greater conviction than we can tell the truth.'

The antireligious drive was carried out in Sakya with the usual revolutionary fervour. The programme was well calculated. Traditionally, the harvest season was followed by a number of extravagant thanksgiving rituals, and equally extravagant merry-making. Conversion to atheism was partly aimed against such drains on the economy. But the main aim was to destroy the basis of Tibetan civilization, or anything that gave the Tibetans a distinct identity of their own. After the Dalai Lama's flight, it was the unstated official policy of the Chinese overlords to create in us Tibetans a detestation of 'the repulsive old rotten society' and a cynical contempt for the holy life-blood which nourished our beings. In 1959 they gave us shock after shock, blow upon blow, with no time to recover.

In order to prove that our faith was nothing more than self-delusion, and that the entire fabric of our Buddhist universe was a thin tissue of primitive superstition, the Chinese dismantled the Sakya Bamo, one of the most dreaded she-spirits in Tibet, and converted it into a scarecrow. Mother used to take me with her to the abode of the Sakya Bamo to make our monthly offerings. The she-spirit was believed to reside not in an image but in a life-size effigy with a hideous-looking mask. The Chinese conveniently transferred her to their newly made vegetable garden where she was put on sentry duty, to frighten away the birds.

By this contemptible act, the Communists were certainly successful in shaking the flimsy religious foundations of the young. We asked one another: 'What has happened to our potent gods? Are they scared of the all-powerful Chinese Reds? Or are they really mere mud images as the Chinese say?' I have no doubt that the young in Tibet have been converted into atheists by now, for the Tibetans are not inherently Buddhist. The older generation, Mother's contemporaries will gradually die, and the new generation will be perfect atheists. They will see the sad memory-haunted remnants of a dead civilization, and will ask their parents, 'Who made all these big buildings?'

While the youngsters, including some of the young lamas, were succumbing to the Chinese campaign, some of our elders privately explained the mysterious operations of the collective *karma*, which applied to all Tibetans. In our countless former existences, extending through aeons of time, we have been born and reborn not only in different parts of the world but also on different planets – for the Buddhists believe that there is life on other planets too. In our past innumerable existences every one of us Tibetans had committed bad deeds, which were the cause of our national plight.

Throughout the season of 'our own first harvest' and the winter that followed, the Chinese Communists were preoccupied with exposing our 'superstitious beliefs'. In the old days we happily hibernated in the long, cold winter. But now we were forced to see our orderly Buddhist universe collapse into chaos, both in mental and physical terms. The Chinese Communists, full of revolutionary zeal and utterly without any human sentiment, deliberately set out to prove to us that what we pathetically believed in was nothing more than a mirage, and that one of the three components of our Trinity – the monks or *Sangha* – were nothing but professional parasites. The native revolutionary activists, the progressives and the patriotic elements under the direct supervision of the Han working personnel, did a tremendous amount of research on the monastic economy. Their aim was to estimate how much the monks of the Great Sakya Monastery 'appropriated' per year. They prepared six scholarly charts, under the separate headings of tea, butter, *tsampa*, barley grains, meat and salt, showing how much the monastery consumed annually. The figures were absolutely staggering. The economic charts, like our venerable *thankas*, were hung on the painted walls of the monastery.

One day the people of Sakya were called to have a good look at these astonishing charts. Most of them could not read, but literate progressives, like guides to some historic building, read and explained the 'incalculable sums of exploitation'. Upheld by their unalterable faith, the vast majority switched on their mental blindness, as if to say: 'We don't expect the Chinese Reds to say anything else.' Some of them said: 'This is another Chinese lie. They are experts in arithmetic, and so they can add any number of digits just as they please.' Others were indifferent to the past, saying: 'Those are mere figures on paper. The actual essence was digested long ago and thrown into the latrines as excreta, and the excreta is probably on the fields helping to produce more. What is the use of showing that?'

The Chinese Communists classified the monasteries as one of the three principal exploiters in the old society. Their philosophy of materialism had no scope for our abstract spiritual values. The Tibetans had a set of values diametrically opposed to those of the Chinese Communists. It is useless to ask why the Tibetan people did not embrace a revolutionary ideology which would redeem them, instead of clinging to the opium of Buddhism. In its day Buddhism itself was a revolutionary religious ideology. Having embraced Buddhism, and having subsequently Tibetanized it beyond superficial recognition, the Tibetans created a whole spiritual universe for themselves. The social, legal and political systems and institutions were all derived from the central *dharma*. As for the monks themselves, few of them lived up to their ideals. Most were mediocre, though sincere and religious enough. Their material dependence on the working population was not parasitic according to the Tibetans for in the old world they had a specific function which they discharged conscientiously. But there were some hypocritical monks who, under the guise of religion, exploited the masses, as the Chinese Communists say. To them, entering the *Sangha* was a religious vocation which provided a lucrative living, and they led as worldly a life within the confines of a holy monastery as the lay Tibetans outside, if not more so. Only in such cases were the Chinese justified.

After they had ridiculed, mocked and scoffed at our faith, and after they had indiscriminatingly humiliated and condemned our holy monks, the Chinese Communists ironically declared 'freedom of religion'. They made it clear that religion was a poison, and that anybody clinging to it was following a suicidal course in the new set-up. Norzin-la, in her musical Lhasa accent, told the monks: 'You are now perfectly free to do whatever you choose to do. You can be a monk by day and a layman by night. You can be a monk for a week or for any length of time and a layman at other times. But one thing must be made clear: you have to stand on your own two feet and work for your living. The people are not going to support you any longer. They are politically enlightened now.'

As the Chinese Communists had demonstrated how utterly futile and deluded they considered religion to be, most of the monks were not so foolish as to remain in an insecure monastery, either for their faith or for their own good. They had to adapt themselves to the new situation or perish. Previously there were about five hundred monks in the Great Sakya Monastery, but by the end of 1959 only 36 aged monks remained. They were given their share of land, animals and agricultural implements. Although the Monastic Ordinance forbade them even to touch an agricultural implement, let alone work with it, the reverend lamas had to labour like mundane farmers.

After 'our own first harvest' was over, Mother and I went to see Aunt Mingmar in Gochung, a village some way from Sakya. On our way back we saw two of our most senior monks, grey-haired and matured with wisdom, struggling hard to keep two mindless, stubborn oxen to the line of the furrows. One of them pressed down the bumpy ploughshare, which 'massacred countless sentient beings', closing his eyes as he did so; while the other tried to make the unwilling animals move without hurting them. The calm, dignified expressions on their shiny healthy faces, expressing a rich inner life, were in the process of acquiring the dust of mundaneness. Their clean saffron robes, indicating the past security of their monastic life, were picking up the earth of the laity. Mother wept. I suggested to her that she should rest until she stopped weeping; otherwise the working personnel might ask her why she was crying. The Chinese comrades would hardly believe that they were tears of joy over the new era. As she wept in the wilderness she indignantly exclaimed: 'Why do the Chinese devils give our monks the freedom to do the impossible? This is a sure way to rack our souls.'

Of the remaining monks, about a hundred were imprisoned, mostly for clinging to Buddhism. The rest went to their homes, and many of the young ones proceeded to get married. Marriage was actively encouraged, and celibacy was vehemently discouraged. Those who married were congratulated privately and applauded publicly, and the honourable title of 'progressive' was conferred upon them. Those who hesitated to take partners were derisively labelled as 'backward', or 'left behind', or 'conservative with an unpurgeable old green mind'. It was under such circumstances that Sherab-la, the young monk from our co-operative, asked Mother if he could marry my sister Yangchung. He told us that since his elder brother had turned himself into a reactionary rebel by escaping to India, his own future was gravely jeopardized. Though a poor monk, both in rank and wealth, he was likely to be imprisoned for his unavoidable connection with his own brother, and unless he could give the comrades substantial proof of his faith in the new set-up he was in danger. So he married Yangchung.

The 36 monks who continued to live in the Great Sakya Monastery could not begin to look after it, let alone the other 107 smaller monasteries in Sakya. At least a hundred monasteries stood vacant, without a soul to look after them. They were abandoned, and as time passed would fall into decay. When we were in Sakya, the Chinese did not deliberately destroy any of these monasteries. However, I heard from a Sakyan who reached India in 1964 that the Rinchen Gang Nunnery, the only nunnery in Sakya, had been demolished and its planks used for building a new Chinese house.

Early in 1959 we were not restricted from worshipping in the monasteries and temples; but as we became progressively more 'educated' we were told not to go to monasteries or to invite monks to perform annual family rituals. If we indulged in any of these 'absurdities' we would be accused of longing for the old order and rejecting the new. In the mornings Tibetans used to perform the ritual of *kusang* (burning pine needles and sandalwood twigs); but by the end of 1959 you no longer saw sacrificial smoke rising from the house terraces. Hardly anyone went to the monasteries. 'What's the use of seeing mindless mud images?' those who dared to be 'superstitious conservatives' were asked.

Monks could no longer be invited to perform the traditional rites. They were warned that they might continue to deceive themselves if they so desired, but they might not deceive the people. In Sakya there was no one foolhardy enough to defy the Chinese indirect orders, which were in reality far worse than the direct ones. If we were given an express order that we were not to practise Buddhism, we would try to extinguish our hopes and obey the order. At least we were less liable to commit mistakes that might cost us our lives.

Idealists might argue that religion is a matter of the mind, not of rituals, monks and images. But this is true only of those who have reached extraordinary spiritual heights. In Sakya there were only two or three fully enlightened lamas who did not use any material object to practise their faith. They lived on water and flower seeds, and locked themselves up in empty caves to meditate. Such lamas had acquired skill and experience in the practice of *dharma*, and might be able to follow Buddhism inwardly and Communism outwardly. But we unskilled Buddhists needed some conventional medium through which we could attempt to grasp the ultimate reality, and on which we could concentrate to perform our devotions. Far more important was the fact that all our culture, traditions and customs were derived from religion, and that to deny religion was to uproot our life.

Although my family did not risk performing rituals outside our home, we, like others, continued to worship in secret, making daily offerings of butter lamps and holy water. But one day Norzin-la, who had become friendly with Donkar, paid us a visit. She was invited to our family altar room, since it was the only clean place. On seeing the burning butter lamp, she scolded us like a mother telling off her child: 'Why do you waste your butter like that, by burning it in the air? You don't even have butter in your tea!' And she patronizingly looked into our cups filled with black butterless tea. Mother apologized profusely for her 'mistake', and promised not to repeat it. Norzin-la replied understandingly: 'Ama-la (honourable Mother), it's really not your fault. The evil system has become a part of you since you grew up under it. Anyway, you will slowly change.'

After this frightening incident, Mother shifted part of the altar to the dark storeroom, and we made our daily offerings there. She wondered where else she could hide her offerings, and was worried about the fact that if she died under such atheistic conditions without proper funeral rites, her soul might perpetually haunt the earth and never find the 'clear white path'. Sowa Norbu's case – he died in 1959 without any of the traditional funeral rites – was a pointer to the future. The thought of damnation haunted her day and night. She decided to risk an escape, which would deliver her either to freedom, or to a quick death under the Chinese Communists.

FIFTEEN

Flight to Freedom

'I CAN'T bear this torture any longer,' said Mother bluntly, late one night three days before the proposed escape. She continued in a sad subdued voice: 'Now that we have been tasting the new life for months and have learned the ways of the Chinese we know exactly what it is like and what it is likely to be in the future. There is no hope either for our present earthly life, nor for our life in the next. If we can't have either life we are no better than animals. At first how graciously the Chinese assured us of freedom of religion, but how cleverly and gradually they have now deprived us of that most vital freedom! I don't know how you children feel, but I cannot exist without practising my faith. I feel empty, insecure, discontented and spiritually despairing. My inner happiness is ruined. I feel unhappy about the present state of our life and even more unhappy when I think of my next life. What hope is there for me when I am not allowed to prepare the future path along which I alone have to travel after death?'

After this revelation, Mother went on to recite a long list of complaints which were familiar to us all. Being simple rustics, the Tibetans lamented the acute shortage of food more than anything else. In the past everyone had enough to eat, though admittedly there was economic inequality. In Mother's words: 'Now the Chinese have made everybody a beggar. In the old days, if we did not have enough *tsampa*, we could borrow from the rich. From whom can we borrow *tsampa* now? If we go to the Party they will accuse us of anti-Motherland sabotage and warn us to practise *Thonpe Dronchung*. I have never heard of *tsampa* being rationed before. My parents never told me how much I should eat; I ate to my satisfaction. Even the servants had free access to the *shibso* (*tsampa* container). Now I have to lock up the *shibso* – a thing unheard of in the past!'

On a little over eight ounces of *tsampa* we had to work the whole day and attend indoctrination classes for nearly three hours every night. There was no holiday except on China's national days. Even when we worked until we 'defecated and urinated', we could not get back the fruit of our sweat. With our sweat, toil and life 'the Motherland must be reconstructed'. There were no signs of happiness and rest on the horizon. Life was to be even harder than we had yet experienced; and this was later confirmed by refugees from Sakya.

'If some Tibetan commoners in the past were serfs of the ruling classes, now all Tibetans are serfs of the Chinese overlords,' said our new brother-in-law, Sherab-la, who was also present at the top-secret meeting. He pointed out that if we Tibetans could not enjoy the fruit of our labour, at least the collective fruit should remain in Tibet. And why should we be slaves to China? In the past Mother and my brother Abu went to Shigatse or India without permission. Courtesy required the servants of aristocrats to ask for leave, which was generally granted. Under the Chinese, when Mother wanted to visit her younger sister, who was a nun in Lha, a day and a quarter's journey from Sakya, she had to petition Uyon Namgyal-la, who in turn handed the matter to the remote higher authorities. After a thorough cross-examination, she was granted a slip of paper. This was the 'freedom of person' in the Chinese Communist style.

Under the Chinese Communist regime we lost our peace of mind completely – a loss felt most acutely by our elders. In Mother's words: 'The new life is like the miserable life of a poor wretched student under a tyrannical teacher. For the student, such a life is good discipline and a profound training, which he can put up with for about five or six years; but how can we bear to live under a tyrannical teacher until our dying day? We live on tenterhooks day and night, awaiting our turn to get a *thamzing*, imprisonment, or deportation to China. If I pass the day in safety I cannot pass the night without fear; or if I pass the night without fear, then I am afraid during the day. I don't feel at home in Tibet any more.'

The leader of the proposed escape party was Nyima Tsering, formerly a servant of the Jango family, and next to Uyon Namgyal-la in the farcical new hierarchy. His qualifications were class background and above all progressiveness. As a second-ranking man, he was often sent to pursue escapees, but he never brought any back. Instead, he secretly studied the 'reactionary road' leading beyond the Himalayas. As he told me in India: 'I never wanted to stay under the enemies, no matter how much they tried to win me over. Who wants to use a stone as a pillow?' My brother-in-law, Sherab-la, was his friend, and it was through Sherab-la that Mother first came to know about Nyima's secret. Since our family did not include a strong man, it was extremely difficult for us to get into any escape party; but with lavish presents, and backing from Sherab-la, we managed to get into Nyima's. We were happy but scared. The dangerous plan was kept a strict secret. Mother told us about the escape only three days before we left. She could not trust her youngest sister Nyidon or her eldest son Abu. We left quietly, without their knowledge.

After the decision, Mother was nervous and suspicious. A knock on the door gave her palpitations. She tried her level best to conceal her almost uncontrollable fear in public, but she felt that the Han working personnel, informed constantly by the native progressives, were casting suspicious eyes on her. One day, Norzin-la visited us and said quite sincerely: 'Ama-la, I am sure you are not going to India. Don't ever go, please. You will never feel happy there. At present you may perhaps be upset with your new life because there are so many drastic changes taking place, but this is only a transitional period, and soon you will be very happy. Why should you leave your own country and seek refuge in an alien one?'

Mother thought that some of our local activists had made a tentative report about us. Apart from our nervous behaviour, our secret preparations may have made them suspicious. Our three donkeys were groomed and well-fed. At night we moved some of our valuables to the solitary village of Gochung, where our aunt lived. We got ready special provisions for the journey. Harvest was recently over, and we had the weighed seeds for the next season and our official rations for the following year at our disposal. Due to our experience of near-starvation under the Chinese, we were obsessed with the idea of food for the escape. Of the three donkeys, two carried nothing else but food. When we arrived in India one of our greatest regrets was that we had not brought some of our family treasures instead of *tsampa*.

Suspicion was mounting, and we were forced to leave earlier than scheduled. The night we escaped is as fresh in my mind as if it were yesterday. The date was the twelfth day of the Ninth Month, which corresponds to mid-November, 1959. By this time the Chinese had established guards for 'the protection of the people', whose actual function was to prevent people from escaping. I left home early in the morning with our three donkeys. Driving them along, I met a man carrying a basket of cow dung near the bridge. He smilingly asked me where I was going, and I told him I was going to get some dry fuel from a friend in the village of Tashi Bhuk. Shaking his head with wonder he asked me: 'Can you manage?' I was then only eleven years old. Meeting a person with a load was a propitious sign for a traveller, and I felt happy.

My sisters Dawa Bhuti and Yangchung left home next, on the plausible pretext of watering the fields. By decree we had to water the reaped fields and plough them, so that the dry grass roots and stout stalks would become manure during the winter. Mother and Donkar left home at dusk. They told the neighbours that our cow was missing and that they were going to search for it. Our rendezvous was Rinag, the Black Hill opposite the Ponto Hill. I drove the donkeys to Gochung after dusk. While they were being loaded, my aunt's tears were rolling down her wrinkled cheeks, and she overwhelmed me with good advice. All I can recall of it, however, was that we were to write to her if India was a happy place.

Not everybody reached Rinag at the same time. I found my mother, sisters and younger brother waiting there. I felt sad that Abu, our eldest brother, was not with us at such a crucial time, for we had no man to help us. Mother carried Donkar's little son Tsering Dorji, and Donkar carried her one-year-old baby, later named Nyima Tashi. Donkar's fiancé was already in India. Yangchung and Sherab-la, the newly married couple, both carried heavy loads. Dawa Bhuti's foot had been injured through a nasty fall, so her load was lighter. I could only manage a bag. Our family was heavily dependent on our Aunt Mingmar, her husband Palchung-la, and our partly deformed but strong uncle. These three had jointly inherited Mother's family home. In all, there were nine families, a total of 32 people.

Nyima Tsering took some time to arrive, and his delay caused tremendous anxiety. Donkar cried: 'Mother, we'll go back. No one will know.' But Mother ignored her. It was a cold, bright moonlight night. We had planned to travel at night and hide during the day, and had calculated on having moonlight all the way. About midnight, while waiting on the Black Hill, I instinctively turned towards Sakya. There was not a flicker of light in the town. I gazed at the monasteries scattered all over Ponto Hill; they looked beautiful, silhouetted in the moonlight. I could see my favourite monastery, Dechen Ling ('Heaven of Peace') near the top of the hill, overlooking the town. I remembered how often Mother had taken me there to be blessed by one whom I now think of as the only true follower of Buddha in Sakya. He had no monastic titles; his name was simply Pukpa

Tsultrim-la. Having locked himself up in a small room, he practised his faith day and night quietly and unobtrusively. He
employed no servant, owned no property. As was his custom,
he gave us what he had accepted from the previous pilgrim, and
what we offered would be given to the next. If he refused to
accept offerings, his disciples would have been upset; so he
accepted them and gave them away again. Fortunately, he died
soon after Lhasa fell. I wondered when, if ever, I would see the
Heaven of Peace again.

At last Nyima Tsering and his family arrived, and we began
our long march to freedom. The older people took off their fur
hats and faced Sakya, bowing low in supplication to its
guardian gods. I heard them whispering their heartfelt prayers
into the wind: 'O third eye of wisdom that passeth all understanding, look after our great and holy monasteries, so that
Sakya may remain in name and substance. Guard and guide us
in our endeavour to escape.' I, too, had a last look at Sakya. I
was leaving my birthplace and childhood home, my friends and
relatives, the place where my father had lived and died. Again
we were stabbed by the knowledge that we were turning our
back on all that nature had taught us to love and value. As we
drove the loaded animals up the hill, fear pursued us – fear of
the invisible Chinese at our heels. We spoke in low whispers.
The animals did not wear their usual bells; there was only the
sound of their hooves. Even the donkeys must have known that
this was an unusual journey. They were driven uphill like a
herd of sheep, by untrodden paths, and they missed their driver
singing and whistling cheerfully after them.

As dawn was breaking, some of the men went in search of a
safe hideout in the caves. Before the sun had risen both we and
the animals were well hidden. We were disappointed at the distance we had covered during the night. From our hideout
Nyima Tsering told us that he could see the village of Yalung,
which meant that we had taken the whole night to cover about
five miles by the normal road. Safety came first, and we did not

mind the circuitous route, the dizzy precipices, or the steeple-like hills.

The first day we could not sleep. We were haunted by the fear of being caught, and tried to decide what to do if we were. Nyima Tsering called together the men of our party, and they discussed in low tones what retaliatory measures they could take if the worst came to the worst. They unanimously vowed that we would never return to Sakya, but would fight and die if we could not escape. That was not only the best and most honourable way, but it would also be the least painful, and a speedy end. The strategy for a possible skirmish was also planned. As soon as we saw pursuers, the women and children were to drive the animals on as fast as they could, and the men would guard the rear and attack the pursuers. But with what? Nyima Tsering had had a position of some importance with the Chinese and had been able to get a long sword; but the others had nothing but four huge sickles meant for cutting hay. (As I mentioned earlier, all our swords, daggers and guns had been confiscated soon after the Lhasa uprising.) In our helplessness we were compelled to acknowledge the far-sightedness of the Chinese. I am sure that our men would have offered firm resistance and sacrificed their lives had the need arisen. Nyima Tsering said: 'If our freedom fighters can attack the well-equipped, seasoned veterans of the People's Liberation Army with slings and swords, we ought to be able to kill a few working personnel and Tibetan traitors.' Having been in a number of search parties, he knew the Chinese Communist tactics and their methods of hunting fugitives.

While the men were planning strategy, the women chatted about what they had brought with them and what they had left behind. Mother seemed satisfied with the precautions she had taken at home. Before leaving, we had burnt all our old papers, and had left a message explaining why we had escaped. It was hoped that this message would act as a safety valve if we were caught. Its contents were to this effect: 'We have heard a rumour that the lower-middle-class farmers and the monks will soon be imprisoned. We hope this rumour is not true, but ever since we heard it we could not feel at home, and finally found it impossible to remain. However, we are not betraying the Motherland and the Party; we are hiding in the hills. We shall return home when the rumour is proved false.'

The whole day we planned and whispered together. We did not make a fire, because the smoke would be a signal to our pursuers. In fact, we never had a cup of hot tea or any other beverage until we safely reached the Indian border. Our hideout was beyond the Black Hill, on a steep rocky hillside. It was not a grazing hill, and so we did not see any yak or sheep nearby. All around us were dark brown rocks of all sizes and shapes; their sharp edges looked fresh and raw. Here was nature at its purest, untouched by the hand of man. The hill must have contained copper, which will no doubt eventually be mined by our fellow Tibetans and used for the 'reconstruction of the Motherland'. The hill did not attract even a bird. There was no noise except the sound of silence. At times we could hear our own beating hearts, or small stones falling down the steep hillside, blown by the strong wind which seemed the only living force there. At the sound of a falling pebble, the women immediately prostrated themselves in prayer, and the men jumped up, clutching whatever weapon they had. Towards evening Donkar's baby cried and had to be gently muffled in case anyone should hear. Donkar was trembling with fear, and others were indignant in case 'her bastard might land us in Chinese hands'.

At last the sun set. The animals were quickly loaded, and soon we were on the second night of our long march to freedom. If we could not cover a fair distance, we were bound to be caught by the pursuers the next day. So it was a crucial night, the night which would decide whether we were to escape or not. Crossing the rocky hillside, we descended gently into a valley, a summer pasture for the nomads. There was a small half-frozen mountain stream, from which the animals quenched

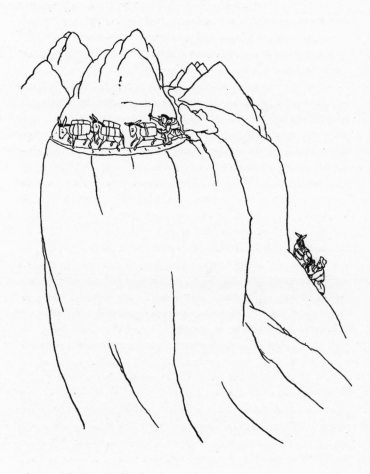

their thirst. Through this silent valley, slightly less cold than the surrounding hills, ran a rough path made by cattle and sheep moving annually from their high summer pastures to the lower winter one, and back again. We drove the pack animals and ourselves at a fair pace, following the course of the stream. There was a brisk wind blowing, but it did not slow us down. A bright moon shone, and numerous reflections glittered up at us from the ice of the stream.

The night was crystal-clear, and the stars were our compass and our clock until we reached the foothills of the Himalayas. When the pre-dawn stars appeared from the north – shining, we wistfully imagined, directly above Sakya – we children were tired and could hardly drag our blistered feet along. Drowsiness was worse than fatigue. We had had no sleep the previous day and night, and the adults were compelled to make a short halt on a grassy bank. The halt was intended to be so brief that we did not unload the donkeys, which at once lay down uncomfortably. We fell asleep.

Round about dawn Lhuwa Umtse-la, the tallest man in our party, furiously woke everybody. He caught me by my plaited hair and shook me, saying in a low, controlled but nervous voice: 'Wake up at once! The Chinese are coming after us!' Shaking off my drowsiness as quickly as I could, I found to my relief that the Chinese were not in fact right on our heels; but that a divination had confirmed pursuers coming after us. Lhuwa Umtse-la was believed to be extraordinarily favoured by the fierce she-spirit known as the Sakya Bamo, and kept a miniature of her in his charm-box. From the day we left Sakya he was in constant contact with his guardian, who saw what we did not see and knew what we did not know. Whenever he was engaged in his divination, we would anxiously crowd round him, like a lost platoon round its radio receiver. He prayed before his charm-box, and performed the same divination that Mother had carried out with her rosary when our father had gone to Chang Thang. When my brother Abu and his wife came to India later, they confirmed that on the second day of our escape about seven pursuers on horses were sent after us. They came right up to our encampment, where they found an empty vacuum flask which Mother had left in her panic and haste. 'Is the Sakya Bamo still alive?' I wondered.

After this alarm we had a safe journey, until we lost the track on the fifth night. It was a little past midnight, and we were keeping to the hillside at a high altitude. Suddenly the leading donkey stopped dead, with its long ears erect, looking down into what appeared as a deep well. It was an impassable gorge. We had to make a long detour by descending and then climbing up the other side, and when we reached the undulating plateau it was already dawn, and we had to hide. There was no time to cross the mouth of the gorge, so we hid in it for that day and resumed our trek after dusk. Mother thinks that it was by the sheer grace of Kunchok-Sum that we managed to come through the uncharted hills, mountains and valleys, and safely arrive in India. Nyima Tsering knew the 'reactionary road', which we covered within two nights; but after this we were left alone to search out our own way to freedom. It was unbelievable that donkeys could climb such steep hillsides, where only mountain goats normally clambered. Sometimes the path was so narrow that the men had to stand on the very edge of the precipice and help each pack animal to pass safely along the track, taking care that the pack did not hit against a projecting rock and cause both animal and man to fall to their deaths together.

Our routine was slightly altered when we had completed ten days of trekking across the wilderness of the Tibetan plateau. We sighted the Himalayas at sunrise, and our desire for freedom became so strong that we continued our march in broad daylight. I shall never forget my first sight of the majestic Himalayas. Range upon range, like a gigantic rampart, they ran from the infinite east to the infinite west, without beginning or end. Their massiveness made them appear impassable to me.

They were in distinct layers, rising one behind the other. Lowest were iron-hard, dark brown rocks, exuding a brownish moisture which formed the foothills linking the Tibetan plateau with the mountain ramparts. A little higher than this sombre colour was a huge green belt running right across, which we later discovered was a primeval forest of tall and graceful pines. In contrast were the great snow-capped peaks, each one appearing higher than the next. And over all milky clouds, like white silk canopies, hung majestically down from the heavens. Curls of mist filled the shaded valleys.

As soon as the Himalayas came in sight we made our way straight towards them as if to a target. They reassured us, and we felt secure now that we could not be lost in the snowy wilds. Our route had also improved considerably. We felt that we were almost out of the danger area, but we still avoided the temptation of following the normal routes on the plateau, and kept to the hillsides like a herd of deer.

On the fourteenth night we neared the foothills of the Himalayas. We came to a huge pasture, full of grass over six feet high, of a type which was dried and used for making brooms in Tibet. Concealed within the grass was the bed of a dried-up pool, which must have been full in summer. We hid ourselves during the day there – our last hiding place, if Kunchok-Sum granted it so! We still did not dare to make tea, because Nyima Tsering knew that the border area was infested with armed khaki-clad Chinese. We contented ourselves with dried yak's meat and *tsampa*. That day we heard two vehicles pass nearby; the coughs of the exhausts and the noise of the engines echoed and re-echoed in the silent hills and valleys until the trucks receded into the distance. Nyima Tsering guessed that they were heading to Tenke Dzong, where there was a Chinese military headquarters.

That whole day we waited impatiently for the sun to set. We were excited as the prospect of freedom drew nearer, and filled with mounting anxiety as to whether we could make it or not.

But most of the men were confident, and resolved to be more vigilantly watchful on this crucial night, which would either deliver us to freedom or crown us with the Chinese 'wet hide helmet'.

In the late afternoon, when the tall grasses cast their elongated shadows towards the east, we began our quiet preparations. But then Nyima saw six Chinese soldiers moving towards us from Tenke Dzong. We stopped our preparations and lay down flat on the sandy bed of the pool. I heard no sound of hooves, only the throbbing beat of my heart against the ground. A wave of cold sweat passed over me, and my teeth chattered. I knew that this was the end of our long trek and that we would have to return to Sakya, where some of the elders would long for death. Some of the women were sobbing quietly, and I thought that they might sob until their tears filled the pool, but it would not move the heartless Chinese.

Nyima, immovable and intently watching through the grasses, lay flat and spied on the advancing horsemen. Once or twice, backing cautiously from his position, he made a wry face and put his fingers to his mouth signalling to us to shut up for our lives' sake. We continued to pray and hope as he watched the advancing soldiers. At last he began to give us reassuring, cheerful glances, and we felt a little relieved. After what seemed a long time he got up. The six soldiers, smoking and talking, had passed by our hide-out without seeing us and ridden along the newly built road. Evidently their business was not to hunt us. This was the most ecstatic moment so far in our fortnight's trekking, a fitting prelude to the almost unbearable joy we were to experience the next day on the Sepubula Pass in Lachen.

We did not begin our journey from the pool among the grasses as early as we had intended, as we had to give the comrades time to reach their destination. It was pitch dark when we resumed our march, for it was the end of the month, when the moon shone half-heartedly a little before dawn. Nyima Tsering could also recognize some of the prominent landmarks of this area, because he had crossed the Pass a few times when his master Jango had gone on pilgrimage. All I can remember about this part of our journey is the cold and the fatigue. Everybody was exhausted. Donkar could not climb the pass, so she was put on one of our donkeys. Her baby had stopped crying, and we feared it was dead through the icy cold. One of the men rubbed the numbed, unconscious body, and managed to revive it.

There was a powerful gale, which drove back even our strongest animals. The wind was much more powerful than anything we had experienced in Tibet. The weather was deteriorating rapidly, and a snowstorm was blowing up; so we were forced to make a short halt and wait for the gale to subside – if it ever would. The wind made a high-pitched whistling sound, and it had the penetrating force of a sharp knife-edge cutting cheeks, ears and eyes. It raged for what seemed like hours, almost paralysing the children and the weaker adults with cold. I had cramp in my legs and fell on the hard ground. The stronger ones among us kept us alive by rubbing our numbed bodies with their hands. The wind calmed a little after dawn; we learned later that this gale was the usual prelude to dawn in winter. Then we slowly moved up.

Unlike other passes, the Sepubula, as we called it in Tibetan, was neither high nor steep. It was unexpectedly gradual and undulating. Our plan was to reach the pass before sunrise, but we were delayed by the cruel gale, so when the sun shone we were still struggling hard to reach the border. Nyima and some of the men were so excited that they ran the last stage to the top of the pass.

When we arrived, we found them jumping wildly around the cairn of stones, which held together tall prayer flags fluttering in the wind. There were neither Chinese patrols nor Indian border police visible. We all joined in the jubilation. Not one of us had a proper prayer-flag, but this was too rare an opportunity to miss. Lhuwa Umtse-la tore up a maroon silk shirt and offered it as the best substitute; under normal circumstances tearing a silk shirt would have been an insane act, for silk was highly valued in Tibet. We thanked Kunchok-Sum for guiding us to the border. Some of the women threw handfuls of dust in the direction of the 'enemies of the faith'.

Meanwhile our laden animals were all lying on the pass, as if to say: 'We have done our duty!' Before pulling them up by their tails and driving them down, we had our last look at Tibet, the country that was ours but had been taken from us by the Chinese. That was one of the saddest moments of my life. The joyous expressions faded from our faces as we looked at Tibet and prayed for a speedy safe return. Like the others, I closed my eyes in prayer, and the prayer that I raised high on the Himalayas when I was a boy of eleven still sounds in my memory: 'May we get our rightful independence as soon as possible!' I opened my eyes and had a last long look at Tibet, asking myself: 'Shall I ever see you again?'

Then we began our descent to India.

PART II
1960-1995

SIXTEEN

Freedom in Exile

WHEN WE decided to escape to India, the freedom we sought was a practical one: within the framework of law, we wanted to be masters in our own homes. To quote Mother: 'We wanted to be left alone to do our own worshipping and living.' From the beginning we were convinced that this was possible in India, but at the same time we saw some of the drawbacks. The wide gulf between the rich and the poor became increasingly evident as we progressed. Corruption and bribery were every bit as common as they used to be in old Tibet. In fact, our old rulers were less hypocritical, as they openly accepted bribes, whereas the Indian authorities proved more subtle: at the first check-point a policeman delayed us, until we understood what his gestures meant – 'I want money.'

Most of the refugees wanted to hang around on the safe side of the Himalayas, so that it would be easy for them to return when Tibet became independent. The earlier arrivals, ready with comforting news, cheered us up; and we decided to stay in Sikkim indefinitely. One day we had a surprise visit from an officious middle-aged Tibetan, one of the sad remnants of the old order. He condescendingly introduced himself as a personal representative of His Holiness the Dalai Lama. The moment we heard the name of the Precious One (Yeshi Norbu) we all rose instinctively to our feet and folded our hands in a position of prayer. The representative asked us to be seated, and gave us the reason for his distinguished mission in the most high-flown Tibetan we had ever heard. He must be a sophisticated Lhasan,

I thought. 'By the grace of our Yeshi Norbu,' he began with an air of assurance, 'we are sure to get our independence. His Holiness has sent me to deliver the heartening news to you that the United Nations has helped, is helping and will help us to get our independence. By the universal calendar of 21 October 1959, 45 nations supported our cause; only nine did not.' Even now I seem to hear him repeating 'forty-five' most emphatically; the number stuck in my mind.

Nyima Tsering, overconfident as usual, said: 'I told you so!' and every elder expressed his gratification at our unanimous decision to remain by the Himalayas with, so to speak, one foot in Tibet and the other in India. We had the foolish hope that by the end of 1960 we would be back home. Some of our fellow-fugitives had deliberately left half of their families in Tibet to look after their property; they were overjoyed and congratulated themselves on their far-sightedness. Mother regretted that she had not left Donkar in Sakya, as she had at one time intended to do. The atmosphere was full of good omens for the Tibetans, and some of our party actually went to Gangtok, the capital of Sikkim, to make purchases for going home. They returned with the good news that consumer goods were cheaper and more plentiful there, and suggested that Gangtok would be a better stopping-place. We could get odd jobs there and make money with which to buy things to take back to Tibet.

So we made a leisurely move to Gangtok. Once there, however, we discovered that jobs were not as plentiful or easy to get as we had been told. Finally we managed to get some work on the road. Feverish military activities were going on in India's northern borders, including the building of roads and military barracks. Peaceful, harmless Tibet was no longer India's neighbour; instead there was aggressive China, ready to spring and strike from the roof of the world. India had been slow to realize all this. Before 1950 a similar relationship to that of the United States and Canada had existed across the border between India and Tibet; but that situation was over, and now India was spending millions of rupees on defending the hundreds of miles of her northern border.

Knowing nothing then of the political realities, we found road-building a practical temporary solution to our immediate problem. I have no idea what the thousands of Tibetan refugees could have done without work on the roads, or what India could have done without our manpower on the Himalayas. Most of her own labour force is unfit for work in the mountains, and even today there are numerous Tibetans working on the roads and living in tents. The Himalayan climate is ideal for us and we are used to strenuous work. With thousands of other Tibetans, Mother and my sisters worked on the road in Gangtok. I, together with our three faithful donkeys, was entrusted to our Aunt Mingmar's husband, Palchung-la, and he and I profitably employed ourselves in transportation. We were paid for our labour in hard cash, which we could spend in any way we chose. There was no Norzin-la and her Han boss at our elbow, pushing us to work harder every day in order to demonstrate our 'patriotism for the Motherland'. There were many freedoms in India, including the freedom to starve.

Our tents were pitched on some dry paddy fields three or four miles from Gangtok. The area was crowded with Tibetan refugees, and newspaper reporters frequented it to gather so-called 'atrocity stories'. One afternoon our camp was visited by one of them, a hawk-featured man with heavy spectacles. Being unused to facing reporters, our elders were extremely suspicious and afraid to speak. Some whispered from behind: 'He must be a Chinese spy. Otherwise, why should he ask us questions like the Chinese Reds?' It took the Sikkimese interpreter some time to convince us that the reporter wanted us to 'tell the world of your sufferings'. Finally, Nyima Tsering, with characteristic Tibetan inaccuracy, told the interpreter that thousands of Tibetans had been tortured, hanged, strangled, drowned, burnt, buried alive, and suchlike. This was too much for the interpreter, who demanded evidence of all that Nyima

had naïvely accused the Chinese of doing. Nyima was at last compelled to come down to brass tacks, and described our own personal experience in Sakya under the Chinese occupation. Then the reporter was pleased, and gave us big sympathetic grins.

When the reporters pressed us for facts and figures, we were upset that they would not believe we had suffered so much. We wished at times that we could turn our hearts inside out and show them. We knew that we had suffered in a diabolical manner, and yet the questioners were sceptical and incredulous. We thought that the world would believe in our honesty. We are a dying people, and lies seldom come from the mouth of a dying man.

We passed the winter of 1959-60 peacefully in Gangtok, waiting for the Dalai Lama's order to return home. The mirage of independence kept us in an unending state of suspense and expectancy. Summer approached. By tropical standards the heat in Sikkim was pleasantly mild; but having been brought up in the cold, bracing, clear air of Tibet we found it uncomfortable. We thought that we would get malaria, the most dreaded Indian disease known to us. So our family, together with a few others, decided to leave for Darjeeling, the queen of India's hill stations. We were warned that Darjeeling was meant for the rich and, though we might enjoy the climate, our stomachs would go short. But Mother said: 'As long as we don't suffer from disease we won't starve in India. We can resort to begging if necessary.' Looking back into the past, I can hardly believe that we drove our donkeys right up to Darjeeling, disregarding exasperated car drivers, who blew their horns until we were almost deafened. I travel now quite often between Darjeeling and Kalimpong, and while doing so I always look out for our old campsites.

When we reached Darjeeling, everything and everyone seemed strange. I remembered the Chinese 'Unhappy India' campaign, when we had been taught that only the rich enjoy a luxurious life in capitalist India. We had nothing to do there and no one to approach. During nearly three months of idleness and despondency we finished eating all that we had brought from Gangtok. The question now was: do we beg or starve? There seemed to be no alternative, since to Tibetans beggary was the last resort, degrading both socially and morally. I have never been so upset as when my young sister Dawa Bhuti and I went once to the village near Darjeeling to beg for food. The two of us brought back a small bag of rice and wheat in the evening. Seeing us looking like urchins, Mother started wailing and embracing us. She cursed the Chinese Communists, and we all cried aloud.

Recovering from her emotion, Mother said resolutely: 'Never go begging again! We will sell everything we have.' She took out her *patuk* or headdress jewellery from a package wrapped up carefully in several layers of Tibetan cloth. The headdress was the traditional wedding gift from her parents, and in its centre was a piece of turquoise, signifying the sacrament of marriage, that her husband had presented to her. Apart from the monetary value of the jewellery, it had immeasurable sentimental value for her, as a priceless relic of her parents and our father. Yet she now sold it so that we could eat.

What struck us most in India was the monetary economy – the terrible value of money. Every day Mother would exclaim: 'O God, our rice (or some other commodity) is finished!' In the old Tibet, an average family such as ours faced at most two food crises a year. We stored enough provisions for the whole year, and we were not worried every week as to where our next meal would come from. Now we had to buy our necessities weekly, if not daily. Another discovery we made was that, in a modern society, if we did not have work for one week we were sure to go hungry the following week. In traditional Tibet the people worked leisurely through the farming season, producing all they needed, and for the rest of the year they relaxed at home. In Darjeeling, since we had no income, we finished the money we had from the sale of my mother's jewels very quickly, despite Mother's newly acquired frugality.

After nearly five months in Darjeeling we managed to find regular though strenuous work on a tea plantation, carrying firewood from the forest to the tea factory. Before long, however, I became very ill with a high fever, which Mother feared was malaria. The attack was so severe it was several years before I regained my full strength. By that time Donkar had heard that the Dalai Lama was going to open a school for Tibetan refugee children in Darjeeling, and, as I was eligible for the school both by age and family background, it was decided I should apply.

Ever since the Dalai Lama made his miraculous escape to India, the education of young Tibetan refugees has rightly been a special anxiety to him. Soon after his safe arrival in India, one of the first constructive moves that the Dalai Lama made was to start an improvised school for young refugees in Mussoorie. Subsequently, a special education office was established, which tried to organize two more schools in Simla and Darjeeling. By 1961 a total of 800 students had been enrolled in the three schools.

Realizing the immediacy and the magnitude of the educational problem, the Dalai Lama asked the Indian Government for assistance in educating the ever-increasing number of refugees. Prime Minister Nehru, who was by then disillusioned with China's earlier professions of friendship and moved by the tremendous national and international sympathy for the helpless Tibetans, gave immediate consent to an enlarged educational programme.

By 1962, however, the Tibetan refugee school in Darjeeling was hardly more than a children's camp. When I was finally admitted there it was first of all as an invalid. There were three Tibetan teachers, who busied themselves in teaching Tibetan and looking after us. Educational facilities did not exist. To begin with, I taught myself English, working industriously with limited means. I used the same exercise books three times over, and treasure them now as souvenirs of a period of sanity and insanity combined. Looking at one of them recently, I found a single short sentence repeated over and over again, until there was no more room on the page. Even the outer cover was not spared; it was first written on in pencil, and then with a fountain pen over the pencilled letters – an exercise in English in the traditional Tibetan style. Having used the book twice for English exercises, I used it a third time for Tibetan calligraphic practice. If this had happened in Tibet, I would have got a pile of books for my conscientious application of Chairman Mao's thoughts on economizing!

I studied with a burning intensity. The school was like a battlefield, and every word I could master was like knocking off an enemy. Each day I swallowed more and more tongue-twisting new words and practised them on the American and English volunteers who worked at the school, goading them for correct pronunciations and meanings. At mealtimes I had my books beside me, devouring food and knowledge. Somehow I never felt tired or bored. I used to compare my lot with others – for instance, compared with the forced labour in Tibet under the Chinese overlords, my study was a delight; and compared with the hard life Mother was leading in India, my own state was heavenly. Besides, Tibet's tragedy was still clear in my memory, and I felt that I had to justify the advantages and benefits that I was fortunate to enjoy. Despite my industry, I would not have learnt much had it not been for the young American and English volunteers. What progress could I make when I was learning English by the Tibetan method? I managed to get hold of an English primary reader which I highly valued, and which I copied calligraphically in the Tibetan style. The volunteers came to my rescue. These strangers, who had no racial, religious or national affinities with us, but only a common human bond, loved and cared for us when we most needed them. We children were skinny, pot-bellied, pale and yellow-complexioned through malnutrition. We had sores all over our bodies, due to unhygienic conditions, and an inability to adapt quickly to our new environment. But the foreigners treated and nursed us like real parents, without a patronizing air or any sign of revulsion at our unhealthy state; whereas our own kin, the sons and daughters of Tibetan aristocrats and wealthy Tibetans, studying in colleges or working around Darjeeling, did not come to help us. Perhaps they were ashamed of us.

In the rescue team were two ladies who really understood my craving for learning, and with whom I still keep in close contact – an Englishwoman, Mrs Jill Buxton, and an American, Mrs Marlene Mitchell, née Thompson. Both promised to send me to a better school. At that time, Mrs Mitchell was a charming, attractive Pan-American air hostess. She helped at the camp for nearly six months and was both our nurse and our teacher. When she finally left Darjeeling we children cried bitterly, and she was also in tears.

Mrs Buxton, whom we called 'Enchi Ama-la' (Honourable English Mother) really was a second mother to me, and it was through her kindness that I was finally sent to Dr Graham's Homes, Kalimpong, in January 1963.

I left the Tibetan school in Darjeeling expecting great things of Kalimpong. I imagined the Homes to be a normal 'English school', like the excellent private, mostly missionary schools, where India's elite are educated. At first glance the Homes fell far below my expectations. When I arrived there I was shocked to see fair, khaki-clad Anglo-Indian children walking barefoot. I thought they would be in blue uniforms, caps and ties, like the students of the 'English schools' in Darjeeling. Superficial impressions are often misleading, and in retrospect I feel that there could have been no more appropriate school than the Homes for me. If I had been sent to an elitist school I could not have maintained my humble heritage, and it would have been difficult for me to identify myself with my family and ordinary Tibetans. The other 'English schools' tend to create a distinct upper class in India, the Westernized elite. I found the Homes a wonderful institution which Mrs. Buxton knew would suit me and would not spoil me. I have never regretted her choice, and see it now as a rare second chance in life.

My formal education thus began when I should have left school, as I was nearly fifteen. As I became more involved in another culture, so I became more and more remote from my family. One morning, for instance, I was engrossed in my class work, when suddenly, looking up at the blackboard, I saw out of the corner of my eye my mother and sister peeping innocently through the class room window and smiling proudly at me. God knows how they had found the exact class. Since I was Tibetan, the teacher told me to ask the strangers to go away. I was trembling with rage and shame and told them to go as if I did not belong to them. As the school gong sounded for the morning break, I rushed out to drive them from the school premises, and found them comfortably encamped beneath the majestic shade of the tall clock tower. The other pupils were curiously crowding around, staring at them. Still pretending that I had no connection with the Tibetan picnickers, I ordered them to leave the compound at once. They looked so poor and dirty that I was ashamed to acknowledge my own family; now, looking back, I feel far more ashamed of my own conduct. I know that poverty is no crime; in fact, I sometimes find myself taking pride in it. Had it not been for my parents, I argue, I would not have been born, so I no longer feel ashamed of my family. All the same, I find it difficult to hold a free conversation with them. There just seems to be no common interest. Mother thinks that I do not talk because I have grown wise prematurely. Later on, Mother and Yangchung often visited me and annually spent a day at school at our May Fair, one of the red-letter days.

In December 1968 I successfully crossed the first big hurdle in my new life, the High School final examination. From school I went briefly to New Delhi to work for the Tibetan Industrial Rehabilitation Society, a bold, new experiment to set up industrial settlements in Northern India. Then, after seven months of working for T.I.R.S., I went on to Delhi University. With that, in a sense, the story of my family experiences under Chinese rule ends.

Since 1967 Mother has lived with Yangchung, whose husband, Sherab-la, died that year from tuberculosis. Yangchung now works to support them both, and they live happily together. In fact, since Abu disinherited himself, I, as second eldest son, should live with Mother and support her. So far I have not done so, and my obligation still remains unfulfilled. Mother has been extremely understanding; she has never told me to stop studying and start working. Yangchung weaves colourful Tibetan aprons from sunrise to sunset without a day's break. Her only outing is on a Saturday morning, when she goes to buy their week's necessities. She weaves about seven aprons monthly. Out of their small income, almost a third is sacrificed on religion; this includes the cost of two sticks of incense and a butter lamp burnt daily. On the fifteenth or thirtieth of every month, or sometimes on both these holy days, they invite a lama to perform certain rituals, and make the best dishes they can afford for these festive occasions.

Mother's house in Kalimpong measures only fifteen by twenty feet, and is in the dirtiest part of the town. Right in front of the window are two outdoor toilets and three pigsties, perpetually polluting the air that Mother and Yangchung breathe. The area is congested with the growing Tibetan population. Larger families have two rooms; the smaller families make do with one. Dogs hang about the doorsteps waiting for scraps, and some of the bolder ones step right into the room. Flies swarm, especially on hot days, taking full advantage of their Buddhist hosts' tolerance and non-violence. The whole atmosphere seems to me conducive to the rapid spread of tuberculosis. The only saving grace is the weather. I should like to move them to a cleaner place before one or other of them catches some dangerous disease.

What amazes me most is their cheerful disposition. They never seem to bemoan their poverty; they laugh at it heartily. Whatever they do not possess has to be improvised; and yet my sister jokingly calls it by the proper, honorific Tibetan name. For instance, she calls the jute mattress 'the woollen, dragon-patterned carpet'. This kind of sarcasm appeals strongly to the Tibetan sense of humour and causes much laughter in our diminishing family circle. The evenings are nostalgically similar to those we used to enjoy in timeless Tibet. Mother is engrossed in her daily devotions, turning her prayer-wheel in one hand, counting the beads of her rosary with the other and meditatively murmuring her prayers. Yangchung sits down to prepare the warp for tomorrow's weaving, and I sip some *chang*.

Due to her advancing age Mother has become extremely religious. She has taken vows before some high lamas not to eat meat or eggs and not to drink *chang*. She rises at 4 a.m. and goes to the local monastery for her devotional exercises. Apart from cooking, she spends her whole time preparing herself for the next world. She tells me she feels very old, though she is not yet 60. She is very happy over her achievements in exile which, according to her, are in the order of significance: blessings from the person of His Holiness the Dalai Lama; pilgrimages to the Buddhist holy places in India and Nepal; and lastly, the modern education that my youngest brother and I are receiving. Living from hand to mouth does not seem to sadden her in any way.

She and Yangchung have been standing on their own feet, albeit precariously, ever since we escaped. 'Aid or charity,' says my mother, 'is a debt which the receiver has to repay in his next life.' Unless compelled by necessity they do not accept even the little milk powder that the Tibetans resident in Kalimpong get as foreign aid. When I told them that I would be working for a foreign voluntary agency in New Delhi, they never even hinted that I might get them some help. They have kept their characteristically Tibetan self-reliance, which others are losing through being given charity.

Since our escape Tibet itself has been the scene of an unin-
terrupted revolution, ceaseless purges and liquidation. For
about five years there was firm enforcement of the democratic
reform, with more *thamzings*, indoctrination meetings and
work, and less food. Then came Mao's 'great proletarian cultural revolution', when the centuries-old Tibetan treasures were
destroyed within hours. The rampaging Red Guards broke
almost everything that was breakable, and burned anything
that was inflammable which had been connected, no matter
how remotely, with 'the relics of the feudal past'. When Mao at
last tried, without success, to halt any further destruction, the
Red Guards' mission was almost complete. After the cultural
revolution came a bloody aftermath of internecine factional
fights.

The three years of chaos and anarchy provided an opportunity for the suppressed Tibetan people to revolt against their
Chinese overlords. In Lhasa an organized revolt was led by
Chinese-trained Tibetan cadres; but all freedom movements
were suppressed in no time by Chinese occupation troops stationed in Tibet. After the immediate suppression there were
investigations which led to a new wave of terror, called the
'class-cleansing campaign', which brought political imprisonment, mass purges, and executions. By now the commune
system has been established in most parts of the country.

Refugees from the border areas continue to trickle across the
Himalayas, bringing more tales of terror. However, very few
have managed to escape from the interior of Tibet. The last
refugees from Sakya escaped in 1964. That year a Nepalese
national of Tibetan stock, called Doringsher, was permitted to
leave Sakya. His elder son had been imprisoned as a reactionary
capitalist; but the family managed to contact the Nepalese
consul-general at Lhasa and were allowed to leave Tibet
after settling their property. Our co-operative, still under the
voluble chairmanship of Tsering, gave Doringsher's wife an
official letter to hand over to us, urging us to return home. But

unfortunately she was afraid to bring the letter to India, and after reading it she threw it away. She confirmed that the letter was 'typically Red'. It said that our crops for the past three years were safely stored away; our house and belongings were untouched; and the members of the co-operative were happier and healthier than ever before.

Similar propaganda is put out by Radio Lhasa in a special programme for Tibetans in exile, broadcast daily. Apart from the comradely lies and fervent calls to refugees to return home, it occasionally includes interviews with Tibetans whose relatives are in exile. The last time I heard one, a certain Mrs Youdon was telling how much progress and prosperity had been achieved in the autonomous region since the liberation. She was sorry that her brother and relatives had been misled by the reactionary upper strata, but the Party and the people would unconditionally pardon the refugees if they returned to the new Tibet.

Despite the rosy picture of Tibet that the Beijing propagandists paint, the Tibetans continue to undergo unmitigated sufferings. Each new political campaign sweeps across the Tibetan plateau like a cyclone. Hardly any corner, no matter how remote, is spared. So although I have not heard from Sakya for eight years, I can assume with certainty that the Sakyans have suffered like the other Tibetans.

SEVENTEEN

Cultural Revolution as Cultural Destruction

THE SUMMER of 1983 still lingers in my memory. It was a happy reunion. I had just returned from the USA after completing my Ph.D. at the University of California, Berkeley. My mother, brothers and sisters were overjoyed to see me after nearly six years.

We received a pleasant surprise – a telegram which made this reunion even more complete. It read, 'Your aunty from Tibet has arrived. Please come and get her.'

The telegram, dated 16 May 1983, was sent by Abu's wife living in Sakya Tibetan Society, Puruwala Village, Himachal Pradesh, where the exiled Sakya community had settled. It was evident that our aunt had come with one of the Puruwala groups that had visited their relatives in Sakya early that summer and had then come back to India. This was one of the happiest pieces of news since 1959. After more than twenty years of separation, divided families and separated relatives on either side of the Himalayas were able to re-establish their ties.

When we received the telegram we wondered which aunty it was. In 1959 our mother left behind her two younger sisters in Tibet, Aunt Dechen Tsomo and Aunt Nyidon. The former was a nun and lived in a nunnery, a day's journey by foot from Sakya. The latter, though living in Mother's ancestral village (Chokhor Lhunpo), was not informed of our escape because she married a man Mother did not approve of.

It was Aunt Dechen Tsomo. Following Deng Xiaoping's

liberalization policy in 1979, Beijing slightly opened up Tibet, first to a few Asian and Western pro-Chinese VIPs, and subsequently to a number of Tibetan exiles wishing to see their families and relatives in Tibet. In the winter of 1985, for example, nearly 10,000 Tibetans from Western Tibet were also allowed to attend the Dalai Lama's Kalachakra initiation at Bodh Gaya, Bihar. Our aunt told us that since 1980 she had been trying to get a Chinese permit because, as she explained, 'Before dying, I wanted to see Ache (sister) Akyi, who defended the purity of our family lineage.' However, it was not until early 1983, when a more reasonable local boss replaced the old fanatical one, that she obtained the required permit.

Life in Sakya had been particularly hard. This was confirmed not only by our aunt but also by several pilgrims who visited Sakya Lhakhang Chenmo. Our aunt had aged beyond recognition. She was emaciated and half-blind. When she first arrived in Darjeeling, she at once burst into tears. 'Are you Ache Akyi?' she cried, touching our mother and then hugging her. 'I have suffered all there is to be suffered in human existence. At first we were all numb with fear and tension. Then hard labour, all day and late into night, kept us working like donkeys. There seemed to be no end to our suffering. In 1979 things began to ease a little. Now life is much better but we never know how long this might last. The Chinese never seem to keep their word.'

Aunt Dechen Tsomo left Sakya on 18 May 1983. She asked one of the Tibetan refugees visiting Sakya to take her to India where we were living. He was one of the thirty-odd Tibetans from the Sakya Tibetan Society, Puruwala, to have so far visited his relatives in Tibet since 1980. The Chinese Embassy in New Delhi had then gone out of its way to facilitate the Tibetan exiles' visit to Tibet. In 1979, the Chinese insisted on the Tibetan exiles carrying Chinese overseas passports in which the Tibetan applicants had to describe themselves as 'Overseas Chinese'. The Tibetans rejected the Chinese identity. This is not an isolated incident. Tibetans living in Western countries have expressed similar objections. Tibetan identity is so strong, both historically and psychologically, that no Tibetan likes to be called Chinese. History knows us by the name, 'Tibetan'. Then Beijing directed its Embassy in New Delhi to issue a special form in which the applicant did not have to declare his or her nationality. The move was intended to help avoid the kind of impasse that led to the scuttling of the first batch of Tibetans' plan to visit Tibet in May, 1979.

But so far only three or four Tibetans from the Sakya area have managed to visit their relatives abroad. Aunt Dechen managed to get a permit only through what she called 'the back door'. That is, she did not personally know the boss who issued passports but knew someone related to him. So she approached the latter with a small bribe, and sure enough he granted her the precious permit. Actually Sakya could easily fall into the border area jurisdiction because it is close to Sikkim, which enjoys a more liberal Chinese treatment than the rest of Tibet. The Tibetan areas bordering Nepal, for example, have been declared special border areas where no permit to visit the Indian sub-continent is necessary. That is why large numbers of Tibetans from Western Tibet can come on pilgrimage to Bodh Gaya every winter.

The reason why Sakya has been receiving a much harsher treatment than Western Tibet, to which it geographically belongs, is quite simple. Aunt Dechen told us that in the early 1960s, several Tibetan refugee spies with sophisticated American-made equipment were caught in the Sakya area. This episode probably referred to the CIA-Gyalo Thondup collaboration in which many well-intentioned Tibetans lost their lives. However, in late 1979, the CIA-Gyalo Thondup bases in Darjeeling, Delhi and Kathmandu were dismantled. But, once declared a security zone, Sakya could not easily be taken off the black list. And the Chinese continued to impose more restrictions on movement in the Sakya area than elsewhere in Tibet.

Before the Chinese arrival, Aunt Dechen Tsomo had had a meaningful life. It even had the shades of the Buddha renouncing his princely life! Being the favourite daughter, she was taught at home by her father – who was a *ngapa* (lay tantrist) – to read the scriptures. She was groomed as the heir apparent to the family property because the only son was slightly deformed and deaf. But when she was twenty, she ran away in search of her ideal nunnery, Za Rinpoche, about which she had heard so much. Za Rinpoche was far to the west of Sakya.

Before she could reach her destination, my father came on horseback and caught her near La, a village about a day's journey from Sakya. He persuaded her to give up the silly idea and return home, as directed by her parents. When she proved adamant, he offered a compromise. Za Rinpoche was too far from her home, he told her; she had better enter a nearby nunnery. In Sakya itself there used to be two big nunneries, Rinchen Gang and Trab Zang. She rejected both as degenerate. Then he asked her to enter Walung Gonpa, a new nunnery which is a day's journey from Sakya. In fact it was close to where he had caught her. She agreed.

Walung Gonpa was fairly new, built in the 1930s, by three rich farmers. Like most hermitages in Tibet, it was situated on a hilltop, far above the village of La, which is in the valley. There is an ever-flowing stream near the nunnery. It was very quiet, peaceful and beautiful. Knowing the non-violent nature of the inhabitants, wild animals and birds would hover around like pet animals.

There was a four-pillared central hall where all the nuns, numbering about thirty, prayed together. Around this hall were about fifteen or sixteen quarters. Usually two nuns lived together, as guru and disciple; Aunt Dechen Tsomo lived with a senior nun called Dhamcho Zangmo. Conceived as a centre for meditation and retreat, Walung Gonpa had no resident lama. All the nuns were equal in status but when they prayed together, they sat in neat rows on the basis of seniority and one of the senior nuns usually led the prayers. This leadership (*umtse*) rotated among the senior nuns.

Walung Gonpa was affiliated to the famous Nyingma Lama Cholung Rinpoche who resided in his monastery far away in western Tibet, Tod. As was to be expected, Aunt Dechen was full of admiration and veneration for her guru. Like most other accomplished lamas, he excelled in what is called in Tibetan jargon 'the five sciences' – philosophy, astrology, medicine, poetry and painting. Besides, he could do carpentry and metal work. Local legend has it that he built his own monastery, Cholung Gonpa, by himself. It was a fairly big monastery with thirty or forty quarters for nuns who used to come there for the special initiations.

Thus, both Cholung Gonpa and Walung Gonpa were built in the 1930s. It shows how religiously active Tibet remained right upto the mid-twentieth century when most nations were frantically trying to modernize. It also conforms to the general pattern of building monasteries in Tibet: private initiative and public donation. There is a popular myth that the so-called Tibetan religious kings during the seventh and eighth centuries were largely responsible for the propagation of Buddhism in Tibet. This myth has come down to us from the medieval lamaist hagiographies and transmitted by the modern Western writers on Tibet. There is no historical foundation to this myth. During the so-called Dharma-raja (*Chos-rgyal*) period only 12 temples were built. The vast majority of about 4000 monasteries were built after the disintegration of the centralized royal power (842-1249). And when the Dalai Lamas came to power in the seventeenth century, they began to expand their own sect, Gelukpa, using the state power at their disposal and often converting other sects, especially the Kargyudpa monasteries, to their own sect. The three other sects managed to sustain and expand their monastic life primarily through public support.

The same pattern of building monasteries through private initiative is discernable in exile also. Most of the organizations which helped to rehabilitate Tibetan refugees were Christian or belonging to the Indian government, both of which refused to build temples or monasteries as a matter of policy. But Tibetans continued to build replicas of their beloved local monasteries in India, Nepal and Bhutan, numbering about 146, purely through private initiative. Lamas would go begging for donations to build monasteries. Rich Tibetans, out of piety and social prestige, made large donations towards the construction of monasteries.

The same goes for the propagation of Tibetan Buddhism in the Western world. There is not a single meditation centre abroad started by the Dalai Lama's exiled government. In the West individual lamas, specially Trungpa Rinpoche, Lama Thubten Yeshe and Tarthang Tulku, are largely responsible for the establishment of numerous Tibetan Buddhist meditation centres and the propagation of Tibetan Buddhism. I mention all this because since Tibet was commonly seen as a theocracy, people might get the wrong impression that the Tibetan government was responsible for building such a large number of monasteries in Tibet, perhaps the largest in the world.

I might digress a little on the nuns in Tibet as they have been neglected in Tibetan studies. Though smaller in number than the monks in Tibet, they used to be quite a significant factor in Tibetan religious life. They personified the relative equality that women enjoyed in Tibet. According to 1981 figures, out of a total of 5143 monks in exile, 392 are nuns. Out of this total, 191 are Nyingmapa. This is another point to be noted: most nuns in Tibet tended to follow the Nyingma tradition. As in Aunt Dechen's nunnery, most nunneries were headed by a male lama, though there were exceptions. For example, Samdhing Monastery's head lama was a woman. She was probably the only female incarnate in the Tibetan religious hierarchy. Our aunt's name is derived from the name of the fourth reincarnate Jetsun Chonyi Dechen Tsomo, the most famous in the lineage of Dorje Phagmos. The story goes that one of the Samdhing Dorj

Phagmos transformed herself and her monk attendants into eighty hogs when the Dzungur Tartars came to raid the Samdhing Monastery in the seventeenth century. Dorje Phagmo is believed to be the reincarnation of Tara, the Mother of all Buddhas.

Aunt Dechen Tsomo told me of the rigorous training she underwent in Tibet. The Nyingma monks and nuns go through a much more rigorous spiritual training in meditation than any other sect, with the possible exception of Kargyudpas. But the Gelugpas view them as unreformed and uncouth since their religious life is so integrated with the folk world.

In Buddhist Central Asia, lamas have chartered two major approaches to enlightenment: the use of the body and mind as the most efficacious instruments of enlightenment. The use of the body involves *tantras*, and the use of the mind involves the study of *sutras*, as best exemplified by the Gelukpas. In general all four major sects (Nyingma Kargyud, Sakya and Geluk) claim to lay equal emphasis on both *sutra* and *tantra*, but where they differ is in their emphasis. The Nyingmapas stress on meditation from the beginning and the uses of physical senses as the most efficacious instruments of enlightenment.

Our aunt received about eight major teachings from Cholung Rinpoche. Her biggest regret was that she could not do the three-year and three-month meditation course that is compulsory for any fully ordained monk or nun following the Nyingma tradition. When she was about to take up this course the Chinese arrived in La and she had to abandon it.

There is a systematic method used for each of the teachings she received. As stated earlier, all the nuns of Walung Gonpa had to go to Cholung Gonpa to receive their teachings from the Rinpoche. The lama would give a set of teachings, after which the nuns were to practise through meditation. The lama would explain in great detail the deities they were supposed to visualize in their meditation. The meditation itself was closely monitored by the lama to whom each meditator would report her findings and feelings. Thus the lama could tell where they were heading.

What the Nyingma method suggests is a deeper internaliza-tion of religious values and higher levels of consciousness. The meditator is trained to watch every passing thought and report even dreams which reveal the levels of consciousness. Aunt men-tioned, for example, two dreams she had had during a year and a month of meditation which had prophetic meanings. In her dream she saw an old woman standing near one of the pillars of the central hall. Sure enough, next morning the nunnery received the news that a local woman in the village of La had passed away. At another meditation session she dreamt of my father on a black horse just before he died. In other words, it is possible to judge whether a certain meditation course is successful or not by watching one's subconscious. The assumption is that meditation in general heightens the meditator's level of consciousness and greatly increases his or her extra-perceptive capacity.

How did Walung Gonpa support itself? The sources of its income were diverse. The nunnery used to get regular commis-sions from the surrounding villages to perform rites for which the nuns were given tea and money. Sometimes local villagers used to invite them home to perform rituals as was the custom. In such cases they were fed and given two *dré* of grain (about 3 kg). During harvest time they went round the villages begging for grain. They also received regular economic support from their parents. Aunt Dechen's parents stitched her clothes and provided her with all the necessities when she was in medita-tion retreats. Her teacher's parents, being close by, provided fuel and *shi-sha* meat, of dead sheep and yaks. They ate only this type of meat, not the meat of animals killed for the purpose of eating. This once again indicates the degree of rationality reached in Buddhism with regard to non-vegetarianism. Meat is not bad in itself but the killing of animals is.

Throughout her narrative, Aunt Dechen emphasized how happy she and her teacher were at the nunnery. It was a life of peace and contentment. As for life after death, they became increasingly confident as they progressed in their religious practice. This seemed to be the best use of this precious and short lifetime, she said. Their contentment with the hermit life may be gauged from the fact that in 1960 they managed to escape to Nepal but missed their hermitage so much that they went back to Tibet. They hoped that they might be left alone in the rocky hermitage. They continued to live there until the Cultural Revolution in 1966.

Then one day in July 1966 Aunt Dechen saw, while fetching water from the stream, a group of people, including two Chinese men, in blue Mao suits, marching towards the nunnery rather briskly. She concluded intuitively that it could not be a good sign. They had been warned before by the villagers to leave their hermitage and settle with them in the valley below. Now Aunt Dechen sensed that they would be forced out of their beloved hermitage. But when the crowd arrived at Walung Gonpa, it did more than what was feared. First the men rounded up all the senior nuns who were like resident gurus to their juniors and shouted at them: 'Are you still clinging to your superstition? Are you still refusing to join the mainstream of the people and earn your own livelihood? Thanks to Chairman Mao and the Chinese Communist Party people are now enlightened. They will no longer be fooled by your mumbo-jumbo. The great Proletarian Cultural Revolution will now sweep away the last remnants of ghosts and spirits.'

It was apparent that these men had been briefed before they came to Walung. As soon as the Tibetan cadre finished his thundering speech, the blue uniformed Chinese motioned to the crowd which automatically split into two groups. The bigger group rushed to the main hall and started breaking up the statues and the walls. The smaller group ransacked the nuns' quarters and brought out all the religious artifacts and scriptures which were then loaded onto the senior nuns. Thus fully loaded and made to look as ridiculous as possible, the senior nuns were driven to the village in the valley. In each of the villages of La they were stopped for *thamzing* and then again driven to the next. Like the nunnery, the whole village was ransacked. Religious artifacts were taken out, the villagers' long hair was forcibly cut short. Prayer-flags were pulled down. The whole point of the exercise was to humiliate the believers and drive them into submission to the new doctrine. Whatever was sacred yesterday was made into objects of utter ridicule and the objects of veneration and pride were trampled on. The whole orderly cosmology was reversed; the earth replaced the sky, and the sky the earth. Aunt Dechen wept.

While the senior nuns were taken round the village, the juniors were ordered to take part in the dismantling of the central hall where once the precious images stood. When some nuns refused to obey the order, they were made to watch the iconoclastic vandalism.

From what Aunt Dechen told us, the Chinese followed basically the same method as they did in 1959 when we were in Sakya. The crowd consisted of two categories of young Tibetans: those who were working for the Chinese administration in La and the so-called progressives, who showed an unusual enthusiasm for Chinese initiatives and volunteered for any daring activities. They destroyed the nunnery and took away all the wooden planks and beams with them.

For a few days the senior nun Dhamcho Zangmo was locked up along with other so-called reactionaries. When she was released, Aunt Dechen Tsomo had already moved to the village in La. The destruction of the nunnery preyed on the nun's mind day and night. After the *thamzing*, Dhamcho Zangmo could neither talk nor sob; she looked forlorn. Aunt Dechen remarked that her guru's spirit was broken since that traumatic event. And a year later she passed away one bright morning. She not only died in the morning, which is considered auspicious, but before she died, her sister from a nearby village was present.

After that Aunt Dechen Tsomo did not feel at home in La; she went back to her ancestral village, Chokhor Lhunpo, where her sister Nyidon and her three daughters were living. Here also she found the same destruction: the Ugen Lhakhang with the beautiful golden image of Padmasambhava, the big Tsog Khang (central cathedral) where the monks once gathered daily for prayers, and the Nyunned Lhakhang where villagers once used to fast together on holy occasions, were all razed to the ground. A new building for administrative offices and officers' residence was erected, where Tsog Khang once stood. Religion suddenly gave way to crude utilitarianism and gross materialism.

Similar cultural destruction was evident in Sakya. Before there used to be altogether 108 monasteries and temples in that small town. By the time Aunt Dechen visited the holy city in 1968, only the famous Sakya Lhakhang Chenmo (central cathedral) was intact; all the rest had been razed to the ground. Some ruined remains are still visible in Rinchen Gang and Demchok. Otherwise, the destruction was so thorough and complete that one can no longer locate even the previous sites of monasteries and temples. One has to ask where such and such monastery used to be.

In Sakya, the Cultural Revolution was carried out systematically. First a few Red Guards arrived and had a meeting with the Chinese administrative personnel and the local 'progressives'. Next, they went round Sakya announcing the Great Proletarian Cultural Revolution. They rhetorically asked, 'Who will volunteer to destroy the centres of superstition?' When, apart from the local progressives (*yar-thonpa*), the majority showed a reluctance to come forward, a huge crowd from another village, Dongka, arrived at Sakya and destroyed most of the famous monasteries and temples. Once the destruction began, a number of youngsters from Sakya joined. It was evident that the Chinese appealed to what might be called the Tibetan 'wood hunger'. As mentioned earlier, wooden material for building houses in Sakya, as in most parts of Tibet, has always been very scarce, and many Tibetans went on destroying the monasteries whose wooden structures they were then free to take. Gold, silver and precious jewels which studded the statues were carefully collected by the so-called Commission for Cultural Relics before the Red Guards arrived on the scene. Thus even in Lhakhang Chenmo, which is physically intact, all the precious stones, gold, silver and metal articrafts were taken away. Most informants allege that the Chinese transported to China most of the precious metals and jewels from the 108 monasteries in Sakya. What you saw, even in Lhakhang Chenmo, were naked statues. As any Tibetologist would know, Tibetans as a rule never left holy statues and images naked; they always adorned them with precious metals and jewels. Papier-mâché statues were thrown into the river and scattered in the Sakya bazaar. If anyone tried not to walk over such holy objects, he or she was at once questioned and given *thamzing*. In other words, anyone manifesting religious sentiment was punished during the Cultural Revolution.

When people met anywhere, instead of greeting each other, they had to exchange quotations from Chairman Mao's *Red Book*. That is, one person would recite Maoist quotations and as soon as he stopped the other person had to continue where the first speaker had stopped. If anyone failed to recite the right quotations, he or she would have to face *thamzing*. In place of the sacred mantra, 'Om Mani Padme Hum' carved on rocks, the Red Guards now inscribed quotations from Chairman Mao's *Red Book*. In short, Mao replaced the Buddha in every respect during the Cultural Revolution. It was during this time that one of my Tibetan teachers, Kunga Topla, was killed by a firing squad, for allegedly tearing up Mao's picture. Pukpa Narma also met a similar fate when she was found making a mistake in inscribing Mao's quotations on a rock.

By the early 1970s, tales of death and destruction, violence and chaos caused by the Cultural Revolution were in circulation among the Tibetan exiles when the first edition of my book, *Red Star Over Tibet* went to press. Apart from a few passing references, I had not gone into great detail because the accounts I heard then had seemed rather exaggerated. However, after personally hearing my aunt's first-hand experience of the Cultural Revolution's devastating effect at the grass roots level, I now feel more inclined to believe in some of the accounts brought out by Kunsang Paljor and other young Tibetan cadres who escaped to India in the late 1960s and the early 1970s. It is clear that the Cultural Revolution was much more intense and devastating in Lhasa than in other parts of Tibet. As I shall explain later, this was because the Chinese Red Guards saw the Cultural Revolution in Tibet essentially as an opportunity not only to spread communism but more importantly, to Sinicize the Tibetans who had successfully retained their cultural identity over centuries.

Kunsang Paljor, who was then working for *The Tibet Daily News*, says that as many as 8130 Chinese Red Guards from twelve educational institutions in China proper came to Lhasa and only three Tibetan schools in Lhasa were involved in the beginning of the Cultural Revolution. It appears that these Chinese Red Guards came not only with an ideological mission but also with a Han-man's burden in Tibet – the Sinicization of Tibetans in the name of Mao Zedong Thought.

As Hong Yung Lee points out, the Cultural Revolution in China proper was a complex phenomenon. It has variously been interpreted as a power struggle; an ideological struggle over policy issues; a crisis of legitimacy; a confrontation between Mao and the bureaucracy; an ideological struggle between proletarian revolutionaries and capitalist revisionists; and an expression of Mao's megalomania. To be sure there was some evidence of local power struggle between the bureaucrats and the Red Guards as there were differences between the policies of the Maoists and the Liuists in Lhasa and Shigatse. But the overwhelming impression one gets from the Cultural

Revolution in Tibet is one of systematic destruction of indigenous cultures and forced attempts to impose the Han culture on
unwilling Tibetans in the name of the Great Proletarian Cultural
Revolution.

Thus, the Red Guards' major project and the main emphasis
of the Cultural Revolution in Tibet was the destruction of the
'four ancients' (*rnyinpa-bzhi*): ancient ideas, ancient culture,
ancient traditions and ancient customs. These four ancients
abounded in Tibetan society, pervading almost every sphere of
life. They were seen – ideologically, culturally and politically –
as obstacles to Tibet becoming an integral part of China. The
Cultural Revolution was seen as a golden opportunity for making this Chinese dream of the Sinicization of Tibetans come true,
complete with revolutionary backing and Maoist ideological
legitimism. Such a project might sound ludicrous now but that
was how the fanatical Red Guards imagined it to be. This kind
of reasoning came quite naturally to the Red Guards because to
them Mao Zedong appeared as the greatest Marxist thinker, the
greatest Chinese revolutionary, and so on. Mao was simply dei-
fied as the Buddha. But the problem with Mao and his Cultural
Revolution was that they had strong Han cultural dimensions
which were equated in Tibet with modernity, progress and
revolution, as we shall see.

When the Red Guards went on a spree of attacking temples
and monasteries in Lhasa, Kunsang Paljor says that it was clear
that the Chinese youths knew what to destroy and what to save.
All the valuable contents of such rich temples as the Tsuglak
Khang, Ramoche, Norbulingka, Tengyeling, Zong Kyap
Lukhang, etc., were neatly packed, ready to be carted away to
some 'safer' place. Only then were the Red Guards let loose to
destroy. The scriptures in the Tsugla Khang were made into a
bonfire which burned for several days in Lhasa. When the
Chinese tried to wrench off the metal pinnacle of Ramoche
Temple, the local Tibetan residents requested them to leave it as
a beautiful landmark of the city. But the Chinese Red Guards

refused, saying: 'If this pinnacle is taken off, it will produce thousands of bullets, with which we can oppose our enemies, and ensure peace and security.'

Cultural destruction was not confined to religious institutions alone; it penetrated private homes as well. Colourful prayer-flags which used to adorn almost every Tibetan rooftop and small altar or family chapel in most Tibetan homes were destroyed. In many instances private houses were ransacked, and if 'old' Tibetan items or artifacts, even those without religious significance were found hidden, the heads of the families were punished. For example, in Lhasa when the Red Guards discovered that Mrs Benshod had hidden 1000 *sang* (Tibetan paper currency notes) in 100 denomination, she was forced to wear the notes fashioned as a hat and was dragged to the marketplace for *thamzing*. There the Red Guards shouted: 'Even now she is trying to restore the old reactionary government.'

Another Tibetan called Dakpa (who belonged to the blacksmith profession in the old society), then an employee of the *Lhasa Daily News*, was also paraded and humiliated in the streets of Lhasa for retaining 'old ideas' because traditional Tibetan dresses were found in his house. In Nagchu and Gyantse, the Red Guards forcibly cut off the Tibetan braided hair so that they would look more like the Chinese. Tibetan personal names were changed into Chinese ones: Tenzin became 'Mao Sixiang' (Mao's Red Thought), Khechog Wangmo, 'Da Yuejin' (Great Leap Forward). Similarly, some place names were also changed: Tsuglak Khang, Tibet's holiest temple became 'Zhaodai Suo' (Guest House No. 5); Norbulingka, the Dalai Lama's summer palace, 'Renmin Gongyuan' (People's Park).

One may well ask what have old names, traditional hairstyles and dresses got to do with revolution, if not a systematic attempt to Sinicize the Tibetans in the name of the Cultural Revolution? This is what I mean when I say that in Tibet 'revolutionary', 'progress and modernity' were all explicitly equated during the Cultural Revolution (and continue to be so implicitly even now) with the Han race, Han culture and Han language. In the late 1970s a group of young Tibetan refugees founded a Tibetan Communist Party (1979-81), probably to make the point that even if the Tibetans had become Communists in order to bring social change in Tibet, they would do so in the Tibetan way. Cultural imperialism is no substitute for social revolution.

The Chinese Cultural Revolution covered the period from May 1966 to January 1969, during which almost 90 percent of Tibet's monasteries, temples and historical monuments were razed to the ground. This was, we have observed, not purely due to chaotic conditions and factional violence. There was a method in this apparently mindless destruction: what was economically valuable was carted away, and what was historically connected with Imperial China was saved. Thus, the Gaden Monastery (from which the Dalai Lama's old government originated) was utterly razed to the ground, whereas the ruins of Sera and Drepung monasteries could still be seen. Similarly, the Red Guards ransacked and destroyed much of Tashilhunpo Monastery but left intact the *Amban*'s chamber in the monastery. Such a well-planned destruction shows that the Chinese Red Guards in Tibet were not just ideological fanatics, but also Han nationalists bent on the Sinicization of Tibetans.

When some Western journalists were permitted to visit Tibet in the late 1970s, they described it as 'the graveyard of a murdered civilization'. The tragedy is that while the Tibetan race took nearly 1000 years to build a rich, complex Buddhist civilization and culture, it took just three years to destroy it. It was a great loss to human civilization, no matter how feudal and reactionary it might have appeared to the Chinese Red Guards.

EIGHTEEN

Reform and Resistance

WHEN AUNT Dechen Tsomo arrived at her ancestral village, she was fifty-one. Her previous lifestyle was totally disrupted, and she faced a crisis. She could work for the next ten or fifteen years but what would happen to her after that? She decided to adopt one of her sister Nyidon's daughters, Mingma. Had it not been for this arrangement, she told us, she would have suffered even more. The new regime had very little compassion for the aged. Before 1979, the commune and the mutual-aid teams rigorously maintained work points against which one's ration was measured: 12 *dré* of *tsampa* per working person per month in Sakya. If one could not work, no work points were registered; and the aged and the invalid received little or no ration. In this way, Shergi Se in Sakya, an old nobleman, was starved to death.

Things began to ease a little after 1980, especially after Hu Yaobang's visit to Sakya in May that year. The eighteen remaining monks at Sakya Lhakhang Chenmo were allowed to resume their religious practice. It was also announced that up to 50 monks would be allowed to enter the monastery. However, the future prospects seemed rather dim since the Chinese had put a ceiling on the number of monks and raised the age of entry to 18 when most of the novices would have ceased to be celibate. Moreover, monks were no longer allowed to practise religion in private homes; religion was confined to the monastery. However, streams of pilgrims from all over Tibet kept visiting the famous monastery, Aunt Dechen said. People in the surrounding villages began putting up prayer-flags on their rooftops and asking lamas to perform rituals in their homes. The pilgrims' offerings amounted to about 200 g of gold with which a butter lamp was made and offered to Sakya Lhakhang Chenmo. It was then rumoured in Sakya, Aunt said, even 'progressive' Tibetans working for the Chinese were surreptitiously practising Buddhism.

Even though Sakya Lhakhang Chenmo was basically intact, the Chinese had ordered restoration work. According to Lhawon Tsewang, who visited Sakya thrice, Beijing had allocated Reminbao 7,500,000 for the restoration work. A team of experts from Lhasa were doing the restoration in 1983. They replaced four wooden pillars with concrete ones. But the Chinese had sanctioned money for restoration only on the main cathedral, and not on the 107 monasteries that had disappeared during the Cultural Revolution. However, the local people volunteered to rebuild some temples such as Utse, the Temple of Manjusri. We got a few letters from Lo Chungla, my younger brother's teacher at Sakya Lhakhang Chenmo that he and some other monks were repairing the damaged statues and images. In 1983, Beijing returned to Tibet 37 trucks of broken idols, and a representative from Sakya was called to identify its missing images.

Since 1959 the Chinese had built in Sakya three schools, a bank, a hospital and a hydro-electric plant. In Tashi Gang there was a primary school with seven teachers. Aunt Dechen said the most useful of these to the local people was the hospital. She had an eye operation free of cost. One might have expected the schools to be the next most useful but Aunt explained that since only the progressives' and the cadres' children tended to get job opportunities, not many parents were interested in sending their kids beyond the primary. From Chokhor Lhunpo only one boy went to the middle school in Sakya. As for electricity, it was used in offices only.

As part of the policy of leniency, poorer families received some help from the state. Since 1980, 12 or 13 families in

Chokhor Lhunpo had received various kinds of material help. My eldest aunt's son, Danor, for example, got two carpets, two woollen blankets and a couple of utensils. He was the poorest among the relatives left behind in Tibet.

I have tried to show the current economic and cultural conditions at the grass roots level, mainly through the experiences and observations of my aunt. Between 1979 and 1985 the Dalai Lama sent, as part of the Sino-Tibetan dialogue, five fact-finding delegations to various parts of Tibet. It might be interesting to compare their findings with my aunt's experiences in Sakya. As might be expected, the findings of Dalai Lama's delegates were more critical – partly due to the regional variations and partly due to their official status.

The Dalai Lama's first delegation left India on 5 August 1979. Their aim was to 'try to understand the new leaders of China, and greet the six million Tibetans in Tibet'. Although the delegation spent more than three months in Tibet, they did not publish their findings. They brought back miles of film footage, some of which was shown on television by the BBC. In Dharamsala they showed films lasting for ten hours and gave reports for nearly eighteen hours. Those interested in Tibet in the West must have seen the more telling scenes of the film on the BBC TV network. One had indeed to see the film in order to believe the message it unfolded. Judging by the sad faces and patched dresses in the crowd, the economic conditions must have been bad, but more than that, it appears people were more starved of religion during the last three decades. This means that, like in medieval Europe, religion continues to be the most precious thing in Tibetan life. The Red Guards succeeded in destroying about 90 percent of the material manifestations of Tibetan religious life but they have failed to kill the Tibetan people's innate religiousness.

The first delegation reported the following to the Dalai Lama: the people's belief in Buddhism was far from shaken; the vast majority still cherished the Dalai Lama and dreamt of an independent Tibet under him; and their economic condition was incredibly poor. Among the Chinese leaders, the delegates met Li Xiannian who told them that China was 'willing to sort out the Tibetan problem through talks and to discuss any possibilities for the future.'

The second delegation consisted of five educated young Tibetans. They travelled through various parts of Tibet for more than three months. Their brief report said that the 'ordinary Tibetans still lead an indescribably poor life' and that all Tibetans 'desire the restoration of Tibet's independence'. What was most striking about their report was the strong evidence of persistent religious faith in Tibet. The delegates, who in their three-piece suits, looked far from lamaistic, were received and treated like high lamas everywhere they went. The mere fact that they represented the Dalai Lama seemed to have transformed them into objects of worship. Once some members of the delegation were having their hair cut in Kham. When their hair was thrown out, people scrambled to get strands of it as if they were precious holy relics of some high lamas.

The delegates also reported that 99 percent of all monasteries and temples in Tibet had been destroyed. In towns there were more new houses than old ones, 'yet no ordinary Tibetan lives in those houses'. All district headquarters were headed by Tibetans, 'although decisions are made by the Chinese supposedly working in other capacities'. The delegates did not meet 'one single individual who was happy, who said something pleasant about the conditions, or who did not have a story of oppression and suffering to tell'. Nor did they see a single Tibetan who had received a university education over the last 31 years. In Kham and Amdo, the Tibetan language was not taught in any school. However, in central Tibet it was taught at primary school level for three years. Finally, the delegates could not fail to observe an insidious process of Sinicization which posed a direct threat to the future of Tibetan civilization. Those who understood Chinese were held up to be very progressive, whereas anything Tibetan – language, dress, behaviour, culture – was considered a sign of backwardness.

The second delegation's long journey into various parts of Tibet ended with the so-called 'Lhasa incident' on 25 July 1980. A massive crowd had gathered in front of the guest house where the delegates were staying. Perhaps being inspired by the crowd, one of the delegates shouted, 'Tibet is independent' and the crowd responded emotionally. This was the second incident of its kind. During the first delegation's visit to Lhasa, an old woman had made a similar declaration; she was accused of undermining national unity and arrested.

The third delegation consisted of seven members headed by the Dalai Lama's sister, Jetsun Pema. They also travelled for three months in the summer of 1982. But unlike the previous delegations, this one faced some structured obstacles. This tended to confirm the earlier reports that the Chinese achievement in the field of education fell far below expectations. The spread of education was so uneven that the delegates' request to see the various areas upset Beijing's plan of confining them only to the showpieces. What, therefore, the third delegation brought back was a bag of statistics given by the Chinese. The delegates were briefed that there were 430 primary schools with 17,000 students, 55 middle schools with 10,000 students and 6,000 schools run by parents with 200,000 students who now received government grants, 22 high schools with 2,000 students and four colleges with more than 560 students. But the delegation was allowed to visit only 85 schools with 39, 844 students. Of these only 17,660 were Tibetans constituting 44 per cent. Similarly, out of 2979 teachers only 1024 or 30 per cent were Tibetans. None of the schools visited were 'comparable in standard to schools run by Tibetans in exile'.

The contacts between Beijing and Dharamsala had been suspended since July 1980 when a huge crowd demonstrated in support of Tibet's independence. This incident was widely reported in the international press because a large group of foreign correspondents, based in Beijing, were visiting Lhasa at the time and witnessed the event. China took such a serious view of the mass demonstration that the second and third delegations were asked to cut short their visits. This provided an appropriate opportunity for the Dalai Lama to ask the Chinese leadership if they wanted to talk. They agreed. A high-level, three-member delegation from Dharamsala left for Beijing on 24 April, 1982.

The fourth delegation in the series spent about a month in the Chinese capital, exploring various proposals for the future of Tibet. As we have seen, the Dalai Lama had always tried to link up the conditions for his return with the future status of Tibet. If China did not meet his minimal demands, the possibility of his returning to Tibet was ruled out. The delegation was briefed by the Dalai Lama personally before its departure and its main purpose was to sound the various options already discussed in Dharamsala.

Finally, in the summer of 1985, a six-member delegation was sent to investigate the conditions in north-eastern Tibet or Amdo, as we call it. This is the birthplace of the present Dalai Lama. The report they brought back was most frightening. As one of the delegates (Thubten Samphel) wrote, 'I don't know what the dinosaur felt when it knew that it was getting extinct but to me there can be nothing more frightening than the prospect that one's people, language and culture within a few generations will be mere exhibits in the museum, just as the dinosaur is today.'

The fact is that the Tibetans in north-eastern Tibet are already engulfed in a sea of Chinese. According to official Chinese statistics, the total population of Qinghai (Amdo) is 3,895,706 out of which 2,359,979 are Chinese and 754,254 Tibetan. Before 1949, there were only a few Chinese businessmen at Labrang Tashikyil in present-day Gansu province. Now approximately 75 percent of the population of this traditional bastion of Tibetan culture is Chinese. The Dalai Lama's birthplace, Taktser, consists of 40 families, of whom only eight are Tibetan, and the rest Chinese. The delegates found a distant relative of the Dalai Lama, a young man in his mid-thirties. He, his wife and children spoke no Tibetan. Sinicization had taken its toll. In Lhasa the Chinese outnumber the Tibetans.

The fifth delegation report posed this question: Will the Tibetans face the same fate that the Manchus and Mongols have already met? Early this century, the Manchus were a distinct race with their language and culture; today, only two or three million Manchurians are left in Manchuria, where 75 million Chinese have settled. In inner Mongolia, Chinese outnumber the Mongols by 8.5 million to 2.5 million. It is true that Manchuria and Mongolia are more suitable climatically for Chinese settlers. But we must remember the fact that the Chinese mass media announced in early 1976 the first arrival of permanent Chinese settlers. By the end of that year some 780 Chinese had arrived in Tibet. Most of them were to become farmers.

Those sympathetic to the Chinese view, find the Dalai Lama's discourse on the Chinese government's unstated policy and practice of population transfer difficult to accept. They ask how could the Hans, who are the inhabitants of low-lying, rice-growing interiors, survive on the roof of the world? The variation in terms of geography and climate is too vast for the Hans to adjust to. There may be an element of truth in this on the surface. But a deeper scrutiny reveals, as does a recent British publication, *New Majority : Chinese Population Transfer into Tibet* (1995), a new reality that is difficult to refute.

The simple fact is that there are nearly one billion Hans, among whom there may well be a handful of daring individuals or families looking for new frontiers away from the over-populated Han areas. And when out of one billion a 'handful' are added up in a sparsely populated country like Tibet, their numbers appear quite high. Moreover, Tibet is a vast territory, measuring approximately 600,000 sq. miles. This vast territory is not just a mountain desert; there are a number of relatively fertile valleys and arable areas, especially in eastern Tibet (Kham and Amdo), and southern Tibet. In other words, while the whole of Tibet is obviously not suitable for Han settlement, there are considerable tracts of Tibetan territory much warmer and more fertile, which attract the Han settlers. This is basically what has been happening in Amdo and Kham since 1959 – the Han appropriation of Tibetan lands for agriculture. In central and western Tibet (U-Tsang) the pattern of Han settlement is different. Here, the Hans outnumber the Tibetans in the urban areas such as Lhasa and Tsethang where the colonial administration and the new industries are located.

The Chinese dominate not only the administration but are also beginning to dominate the economy as well. For example, in the Lhasa market there were 756 Chinese businesses and only 305 Tibetan ones. Similarly, Tsethang had 277 Chinese businesses and 120 Tibetan ones by 1994. Thus, even Chinese statistics admit that the total number of Chinese immigrants in Tibet and the total Tibetan population are more or less equal: 4.34 million Tibetans and 4.2 million Chinese.

The fifth delegation might perhaps be the last. There has been a hardening of the Chinese position in the seven-year long Sino-Tibetan dialogue. In 1986, the Dalai Lama proposed to send a sixth delegation but had to cancel because of the Chinese demand that they carry overseas Chinese passports. Earlier, delegates did not have to carry such documents. What is at issue is the basic Chinese condition for the continuance of the Sino-Tibetan dialogue: the Dalai Lama and his followers must recognize that Tibet is part of China, and they must consider themselves as Chinese. This is unacceptable to the Dalai Lama and the Tibetan exiles. It hardly leaves any room for negotiation. As for the Dalai Lama's possible return to Tibet, the Chinese have told the third delegation that he would have to remain in Beijing, not Lhasa. The Chinese have recognized the undeniable fact that the presence of Dalai Lama in Tibet would prove to be a major destabilizing factor. He might indeed become a rallying point for another rebellion. The Dalai Lama, whether in or outside Tibet, continues to pose a dilemma to China.

Despite the drastic changes in Tibetan economy since 1959, Tibetans continue to face tremendous economic hardships. Phuntsok Wangyal, a member of the second delegation, reported that the Chinese official figures claimed the annual ration per person to be 550 lb but in actual fact it was 350 lb. Others reported even less – 90 to 120 kg of barley per person per year. None of the delegates failed to report the destruction of monasteries. One of the difficulties is that there is no consensus about the number of monasteries and temples in Tibet before 1959. The Dalai Lama estimates the number to be 6,200 and his sister around 4,000. The number of monasteries is known only in certain well-known localities. For example, in the Lithang Valley, there used to be 118 monasteries and temples of which only one remains. In Sakya there used to be 108 monasteries and temples out of which only one remains. In other words, the Chinese sought to destroy religion as a way of life but left some ten famous religious institutions connected with imperial China intact. These are Jokhang, Potala, Sera, Drepung, Derge Gonchen, Sakya Lhakhang Chenmo, Tashikhil, Tashilhunpo, Gyantse Pagon Choten and Kumbum. These monasteries have received central funding for repair work.

China acted almost immediately after the first delegation's return from Tibet. In February 1980, Zhou Enlai's 1957 article concerning nationalities policy was widely publicized in the Chinese mass media. This article reiterated Deng's basic line on the nationalities question. It remains a mystery why Chen Boda rejected it for publication in *Hongqi* in the 1950s. The article does not deviate from the party line in any substantive way. It does not accept any of the Tibetan exiles' political demands, be it federation or greater autonomy in Tibetan-speaking areas. However, it advocates a Dengist liberal policy.

Secondly, the fifth plenum of the 11th CCP Central Committee (February 1980) ordered its secretariat to work out the details of some economic concessions. In May, the Party General Secretary, Hu Yaobang, led China's own fact-finding mission to central Tibet. After touring for nine days, the Hu Commission issued a six-point directive on Tibet. The first point reiterated the definition of regional autonomy, the only departure being its stress on a more flexible policy. 'Anything that is not suited to Tibet's conditions should be rejected or modified as well as anything that is not beneficial to national unity or development of production.'

The second point made some major economic concessions to the Tibetans. It exempted them from paying taxes and meeting state purchase quotas for the next three years. Products of the peasants and herdsmen may be purchased at negotiated prices. The third point advocated a more realistic economic policy based on ecological realities in Tibet and the producers' wishes. The fourth point promised more Central funds which would be used to improve people's living standards in general.

The fifth point was interesting, inasmuch as perhaps for the first time, a Chinese Communist document paid tribute to Tibetan Buddhist culture. 'The Tibetan people,' it stated, 'have a long history and a rich culture. The renowned ancient Tibetan culture included fine Buddhism, graceful music and dance as well as medicine and opera, all of which are worthy of serious study and development. All ideas that ignore and weaken Tibetan culture are wrong.' In so doing the Communists identified the areas of Tibetan culture that might be preserved and studied. While pointing out the need to 'make vigorous efforts to revive and develop Tibetan culture, education and science', the document stipulated that all such endeavours must be based on 'socialist orientation'.

Finally, the sixth point promised greater Tibetan participation in the administration. 'Full-time cadres of Tibetan nationality should account for more than two-thirds of all government functionaries in Tibet within the next two or three years.'

On 24 June 1980, seventeen days after the Central authorities announced their directive, the Tibet Regional People's Government issued an eight-point directive. It affirmed, specified and elaborated Hu's six-point directive. It dealt primarily with economic and administrative matters and did not touch on such political issues as the quantum of autonomy, or the degree of Tibetan participation in the local administration. It declared that for 1980 and 1981 (later extended to 1988) Tibet was exempt from agricultural and livestock taxes. For the same period, industrial and commercial taxes were also waived. With effect from 1 July 1980, the state would pay the salaries of private (people-run) primary teachers. Communes and brigades would be encouraged and aided to develop ethnic handicrafts and other products. They may sell or exchange such products either locally or establish direct external clients. Towards this end, it was announced, rural trade fairs would be restarted and border trade resumed with Nepal, India, Bhutan and Burma. Production teams could have 5 to 7 per cent of their total irrigated land as private plots.

By far the most drastic reforms were introduced in the spheres of labour management. From now on, declared the document, government at all levels may not issue orders for production output and crop plans. Production teams, working groups or households 'shall decide their work system as they see fit'. That is, they can start fixed working groups the year round, or assign farmwork to individual groups on a temporary or seasonal basis. The rigid commune system that controlled everybody's life was broken at last. This self-management system marks a clear departure from the tightly structured and centrally imposed labour organization operative since 1959. Apart from their economic benefits, the new labour laws gave considerable freedom to the Tibetan people who detested the commune system.

After the six-point directive was announced a series of

meetings were held in Lhasa. They had two things in common: all were attended by the so-called 'patriotic personages from the upper strata' (i.e., the former ruling classes, both high lamas and aristocrats). And at each such meeting the same call was made: 'Build a united, prosperous and highly cultured new Tibet.'

The mobilization of the upper strata is reminiscent of the Chinese policy in the 1950s when they tried to woo and co-opt the traditional ruling class. It implies that the Chinese policy might have had the support of the upper strata of Tibetan society but not the masses who stubbornly continued to cling to their Tibetan ways. Hence the greater attention to the upper strata. The CCP Central Committee's United Front Work Department and State Nationality Affairs Commission held a reception in Lhasa on 9 July 1980 for the 300 upper strata patriots in Tibetan religious circles; on 23 August, a memorial meeting was held for a leading Tibetan aristocrat, Langdun Kunga Wangchuk. Earlier, China released 376 Tibetan prisoners and removed all 'labels' from more than 6,000 others who took part in the 1959 rebellion. About 80 per cent of the Tibetans arrested in 1959 had now been rehabilitated. A notice was also issued to restore the original status of those in Tibet, who were wrongly designated as capitalists in 1975. In May 1981 the government allocated Reminbao 3,146,500 to repay former manorial lords, herd owners and monasteries who did not take part in the 1959 rebellion but whose property was mistakenly confiscated. In June 1980, it was reported that 52 patriotic Tibetan figures, who are former feudal lords, serf owners or agents of feudal lords 'were commended for their patriotism and commitment to socialism'.

Through these measures the Chinese made it clear that the new policy had the orchestrated support of the upper strata, but the common masses, as usual, were not consulted. This was an indirect rejection of the Dalai Lama's demand that the Tibetan people's wishes be determined as to whether they were content with their lot or not. Tibet is a strange country where the old 'feudal' leader can still win a popular mandate but where 'revolutionaries' can lose such a popular mandate, given the chance.

The cryptic slogan, 'Unity, Prosperity and New Civilization' was the Chinese response to the Tibetan demand that Tibet be allowed to retain its own culture. The slogan was first enunciated on 3 June 1980, but it was not until a year later that the slogan was explained. 'What we mean by unity,' declared Yin Fatang in a speech, 'is to be united under the great community of our motherland. Secondly, we must rally around the Party Central Committee. Third, we must do a good job in uniting all the fraternal nationalities in Tibet.' Defining the 'new culture' and a 'highly civilized Tibet' Ying Fatang said it would be necessary to stress the 'spiritual civilization', which included, aside from science and culture, 'the communist ideology, beliefs, ideals, morality and discipline, revolutionary viewpoints and principles and relationship between people'. It did not mean the resurrection of the old Buddhist civilization. Yin argued that the function of literature and art was to propagate among the people ideas of 'patriotism, the superiority of socialism over the feudal and serf systems'.

It should be noted that China published most of the progress reports during the three-member Tibetan delegation's one-month stay in Beijing. Whatever the Chinese leaders might have told the Tibetan delegates, their message was clear. As far as Beijing was concerned its main concern was economic. The general aim of the six-point programme was that Tibet would initially improve its backward economy in the next two or three years, surpass its highest level for the past 30 years in five or six years, and achieve a greater affluence in 10 years.

Chinese reports also claimed that the lives of urban dwellers had improved as a result of the reduction in and exemption of household electricity charges, rent, remission of industrial and commercial taxes, and of road tolls on vehicles used by collective businesses and others. Also city dwellers had been allowed to engage in independent trades as well as factories given greater autonomy.

The lives of peasants and herdsmen had also improved, Beijing claimed. All loans to peasants, herdsmen and craftsmen were declared interest-free with effect from 1 October 1980. They received 23.7 million Reminbao in profits as a result of tax exemption and an increase in prices of agriculture, animal husbandry and manufactured products. By January 1982, animal products increased by 13.8 per cent and the nomads' income rose by 200 Reminbao, per capita. The total output value of handicrafts increased in 1980 by more than six million Reminbao, 21 per cent above the previous year. Plots for private use increased to 24,000 hectares, accounting for 10.3 per cent of the total arable land. The average per capita income from family occupations reached 32 Reminbao.

As we can see, China's new economic policy is not geared towards any long-term economic development in Tibet; it is to render some immediate emergency relief to a poverty-stricken people in the form of making available a few consumer items. The main emphasis is to 'resolutely make a sufficient retreat in capital construction', and shift the industrial focus to light, cottage industries and hydroelectric power industries suited to the needs of the Tibetan people. It remains to be seen whether China will do some genuine economic development in Tibet that is people-oriented and eco-friendly, based on the locally available resources and native manpower.

Since economic conditions have considerably improved and also since state restrictions on religious observances have been somewhat eased, one might think the Tibetans in Deng's Tibet should be relatively happy and content. But this is not the case and this comes as a surprise to the Chinese. In 1987, massive pro-independence demonstrations erupted in Lhasa, in which several Tibetans lost their lives. During the period 1987-92, Tibet (mostly Lhasa) witnessed 140 pro-independence demonstrations, thereby shattering the illusion that Tibetans were reconciled to Chinese rule after the 1959 revolt.

To be sure Tibetan attitudes do not seem uniform. There seems to be a rural-urban divide as well as a generational gap. If we take my aunt as fairly representative of the older generation in the rural areas, most of the Tibetans seem to be more or less resigned to their fate and appreciative of the little crumbs from Deng's economic reforms and the relative religious freedom. They want to die in their beloved villages in peace. But the urban people, especially the youth, are discontented and restive. In 1987, it was largely the young monks and nuns who spearheaded the Lhasa demonstrations. Similarly, the semi-educated and unemployed youth in urban areas might become the future Khampa warriors of Tibet who would revolt against the Chinese rule in Tibet.

In fact I would argue that the majority of Tibetans in Tibet nurse a deep resentment both against Chinese officials who rule with force but without the Tibetan mandate, and against Chinese immigrants who, with state backing, compete for the limited resources in Tibet, not to mention the Chinese People's Liberation Army (PLA) that intimidates them and renders them into voiceless subjects.

If the Tibetans have not revolted more, it is not because they did not wish to – most of them do cherish freedom. But the sheer force and organizational clutches make any scope for revolt almost impossible, except when the party and the army relax their grip over Tibetan society.

The PLA strength in the Tibet Autonomous Region (TAR) is estimated to be from 180,000 to 300,000. Their main function is to suppress any signs of Tibetan nationalistic resistance and to defend 'China's Tibet' from possible external intervention. The PLA was used extensively and ruthlessly to suppress the Tibetan revolts in the 1950s and the late 1980s. If the PLA functions at the regional level as the ultimate coercive instrument of Chinese domination, the People's Militia serves the local 'defence' needs, using the Tibetan 'progressives' to suppress the common Tibetans. The third arm of domination is the so-called Public Security System or the nationwide intelligence surveillance network that spies on every village, monastery, town or city.

The security machinery operates from a hierarchy of organizations created by the Party. The Party penetrates almost every nook and corner of the region, pervading almost every sphere of Tibetan life. The existing system was replaced by Party organizations such as mutual aid teams, co-operatives, communes, neighbourhood village and town committees, Communist Youth League, Women's Association, Democratic Management Committees in monasteries, etc. The indoctrination and surveillance of the workers are enforced through these Party-led organizations.

The Maoists' basic goal has been to destroy the traditional Tibetan society, which they believed was bound up with traditional authority, the old social order and Tibetan cultural identity. They did so by fragmenting the Tibetan society into manageable units for the purposes of labour indoctrination and surveillance. In this way a civil society, where freedom, individuality and privacy prevailed, disappeared altogether in the pre-1979 Tibet; in its place the Party penetrated and pervaded the society as the almighty social god. This Maoist version of totalitarianism violates the very spirit and structure of Tibetan society. Whenever the Party loosens or relaxes its iron grip over the Tibetan society, Tibetans tend to revolt, even though the economic conditions may be better than before.

The pattern of Tibetan revolts following every period of leniency in Chinese policy shows that the Tibetan people, as a whole, are not reconciled to Chinese rule which they perceive to be illegitimate and oppressive. Consider the 'honeymoon' period preceding the 1958-59 revolt in Lhasa. Knowing that they did not have any popular support for the armed 'liberation', the PLA generals pursued a most cautious and liberal policy in the 1950s. They co-opted most of the members of the ruling class with offers of money and posts in the new set-up and granted considerable economic and medical assistance to the masses who were, otherwise, left untouched. Yet in 1959 the Tibetans revolted. Similar was the case with the pro-independence demonstrations in 1987-88.

Following Deng Xiaoping's economic reforms and liberalization, Beijing pursued a particularly lenient policy in Tibet, as we have seen. Tibetans were exempt from taxes and unpaid labour. They were also free from meeting compulsory state purchase quotas and their products could be sold at negotiated prices. Beijing increased Central funds to the TAR (Tibet Autonomous Region) in order to improve living standards and develop the local economy. Restrictions on religious practices were removed. And Tibetan participation in the local administration was enlarged. Yet Tibetans in Lhasa and other towns revolted in 1987.

The chaotic conditions during the Cultural Revolution provided an opportunity for the Tibetans to strike at the Chinese positions of power in Tibet. What this suggests is that whenever Tibetans find an opportune moment, they are ready to strike at the roots of Chinese rule. During this period, the Chinese in Tibet, as everywhere in China, split into two warring factions: the Red Guards and the Revolutionary Rebels. Since the latter were anti-authoritarian and therefore indirectly against the Han power-holders, most Tibetans tended to join the Rebels and revolted against the Chinese regime. Such incidents occurred in Yangpachen, Lhatse and Lhasa.

It is quite clear that neither economic benefits nor limited religious freedom is enough for conflict resolution in Tibet. Whenever Tibetan society regains its breathing space, a revolt or protest tends to occur. This means there are still unresolved basic issues in Tibet. Some of the issues may include the question of the legitimacy of Chinese domination, and the sovereignty of Tibetan civil society and cultural identity. These are difficult for the Han chauvinists and Maoist fundamentalists to comprehend, given their orientation of Han supremacy and Marxist economic determinism.

Why do the Tibetans rebel? It has more to do with ethnicity than economics, as the pattern of Tibetan revolts indicates. The simple fact is that the ordinary Tibetans may not know the latest political vocabulary to describe the Chinese domination such as Han hegemony, neo-colonialism or neo-imperialism, but they draw from the experience of their everyday life and naturally realize that they are under a non-Tibetan rule, and that the alien ruling group does not enjoy the legitimacy of their mandate to rule over them. We know that any rule entails some degree of domination. But according to the logic of ethnicity, a regime is legitimate if the ruling class and the ruled share the same culture, language, tradition and historical memories. This logic makes the Chinese rule in Tibet illegitimate, as far as the simple folks are concerned.

The Tibetan sense of legitimacy and legitimate rule seems to be heavily bound with the Tibetan Buddhist culture which has shaped Tibetan identity, society and history for the last 1000 years. For in the absence of a plebiscite, self-determination or referendum, a commonly shared culture reflects the social consensus on fundamental values and issues of a society and polity. Because it engenders social consensus, culture in its political expression can roughly represent the general will.

In the post-1950 Sino-Tibetan conflicts, the Dalai Lama has increasingly figured as a pan-Tibetan figure, symbolizing Tibetan cultural values and popular aspirations. He appears as the rallying point for ethnic mobilization and opposition.

When the PLA 'liberated' Tibet in 1950, the first reaction of the Lhasa government was not so much how to defend the territorial integrity of Tibet but how to protect the sacred person of the Dalai Lama who symbolized Tibetan culture. Similarly, the first and foremost goal of the 1959 revolt was how to protect the Dalai Lama and safely bring him to India. During the 1980s the picture of the Dalai Lama became a symbol of Tibetan resistance. At several public meetings in Lhasa during the early 1980s, some Tibetans shouted 'Long live His Holiness the Dalai Lama!' and in the same breath, 'Tibet is Independent!'

The importance of the symbolic role of religion and religion-induced culture in the pro-independence demonstrations of the late 1980s cannot be overemphasized. Most of the protests were initiated, led and largely organized by Tibetan monks and nuns. They chose religious sites and auspicious dates that corresponded to religious festivals to hold their major demonstrations in Lhasa. We can see how interconnected are what appears to the uninitiated as disparate happenings in the Tibetan political arena. Because the Tibetans are deeply religious, they perceive the Dalai Lama as the symbol of their religion, their culture and civilization, if not political sovereignty; and it is psychologically this Tibetan sense of cultural sovereignty that resists and opposes Chinese rule in Tibet.

Although the Tibetans both in and outside Tibet popularly perceive the Dalai Lama as their legitimate ruler, this does not mean the restoration of the *ancien regime*. This is evident both from the Dalai Lama's constitutional pronouncements and the Tibetan people's political aspirations. The Dalai Lama's constitution-making projects in exile might reflect the direction in which the politicized sections of the Tibetan population in Tibet seem to be moving. Ronald Schwartz, after several field researches in Tibet, observes: 'Tibetans now associate their struggle for independence with demands for democracy and human rights.'

Such democratic sentiments among the Tibetans may be understood in the post-1959 context of relatively modern conditions in which Tibetans in Tibet and outside find themselves. Inside Tibet, the Communists have widely propagated certain elements of egalitarian ideology such as equality and freedom as their new canon, but they have hardly practised equality and freedom in the minority areas. Maoism in practice has become a twisted justification for Han hegemony and Han supremacy.

This contradiction between the declared freedom and equality on the one hand, and lack of freedom and inequality on the other, constitutes the political and ideological basis of the Tibetan intelligentsia's contention against Chinese domination in Tibet. It is in this sense that democracy, in the broad sense of the term, could be one of the determining forces behind the popular protest against Chinese rule in Tibet.

And in exile, due primarily to the positive influence of a functioning Indian democracy, democratic sentiments among the Tibetan refugees have spread widely, despite the personality cult around the Dalai Lama and his family.

Finally, there has been, since 1951, a wide gulf between the realistic aspirations of the elite and the popular aspirations for independence. These aspirations may be illustrated by the following examples. In early 1952, a popular movement called *mi-man tsogs-du* called for Tibet's independence; in 1980 at several public meetings in Lhasa, Tibetans shouted, 'Tibet is independent' and in the 1987 pro-independence demonstrations, the Tibetan national flag was prominently displayed, as photographed by several Westerners.

We know that such 'dangerous' thoughts are at the moment systematically suppressed by the CCP's reign of terror and the PLA's force. But in the long run, Chinese rule, as it exists in Tibet now, cannot solve the Tibetan problem. In particular, with the globalization of Chinese economy and the emerging democratic waves, the People's Republic of China is unlikely to remain an isolated island of Maoist monolith. In such a situation, it may well be only the Dalai Lama who can persuade the nationalistic Tibetan masses to accept realistic solutions to the conflict in Tibet.

NINETEEN

The Xth Panchen Lama: A Microcosm of Tibet's Tragedy

AS A little boy in Sakya, I hardly heard of the Panchen Lama, even though his monastic seat (Tashilhunpo) was only two or three days by foot away from us. Yet in 1995, not only Tibetans everywhere but the entire world was gripped by his reincarnation controversy. Even the nomads and peasants of Tibet were part of this global communications revolution which was beyond the control of the Chinese overlords.

However, the real significance of the Panchen Lama story lies in the fact that his enigmatic and tragic life-history under the Chinese Communists is, in many ways, the microcosm of the Tibetan people's tragedy in Tibet. This is particularly true of the high lamas and former aristocrats with potential for leadership, but who are caught up in a dilemma. Can they remain mute witnesses to the sufferings of an innocent and helpless people under a ruthless foreign domination? Do the upper classes not feel a moral and ethnic responsibility towards their fellow Tibetans? But if they do and try to act, wouldn't they risk losing everything, including their lives? The Panchen Lama confronted all these critical questions, and acted with tremendous courage and wisdom that few could marshal under the circumstances. In his life-history and reincarnation controversy is reflected the tragic fate of Tibet in all its phases and colours. Here was a man who transcended his immediate family, sect and region to which he belonged. He spoke and acted for the sake of all Tibetans in Tibet even at the risk to his own personal safety.

Unlike the present Dalai Lama who has become a well-known media personality, the life and work of the Xth Panchen Lama is little known to the outside world. A Tibetan scholar living in China, Jampel Gyatso, wrote the Panchen Lama's biography in 1989 but the Chinese authorities banned it on the ground that it was too critical of China's treatment of the Lama. So we are left with very sketchy information on this heroic character in modern Tibetan history.

The origins of the Panchen Lama institution were closely associated with the founding of a well-organized and disciplined sect in Tibetan Buddhism, Gelukpa, inspired by Tsongkhapa (1357-1419). It was Tsongkhapa's third follower, Gedun Drub who, among other things, built the Tashilhunpo Monastery in 1445 which in the seventeenth century became the seat of the Panchen Lamas. But prior to that, neither the Panchen Lama nor Tashilhunpo was a distinct political entity. They were only part of the expanding Gelukpa order. It was only when the institution of Dalai Lamas became well-established and acquired papal and political dimensions by the seventeenth century, did Tashilhunpo acquire a separate entity and political importance.

When the succession problem within the Gelukpa order was more or less resolved with Sonam Gyatso (1543-88) as the IIIrd Dalai Lama, Tashilhunpo was entrusted to a series of senior lamas who came to be regarded later as the predecessors of the Panchen Lamas. The formalization and institutionalization of the Panchen Lama owes its origin to the Vth Dalai Lama who declared that his tutor, Chokyi Gyaltsen (1570-1662) would reincarnate as the IInd Panchen Lama, and so the line continues up to this day. Before the Vth Dalai Lama's recognition, Tashilhunpo was headed by senior abbots, and not by the reincarnation system. They were simply called *Panchen*, a hybrid abbreviated title of *Pandita Chenpo*, meaning the 'Great Scholar'. At that time Tashilhunpo was given three estates as its source of income.

Then in 1728, the then Panchen Lama was given considerable political power. During the Dzungar invasion (during which the then Tibetan authorities requested the Qing emperor to intervene on their behalf) the VIIth Dalai Lama and his family sided with the Dzungar forces. Partly to punish the Dalai Lama and partly to have a counter-balancing force within the Gelukpa hierarchy, the Qing emperor arranged that the Panchen should be made a ruler of Tsang (Western Tibet). A special administrative office called *Chizong* (spyi-rzdon) was established next to Tashilhunpo, administering sixteen districts in Western Tibet from Shigatse. This was the beginning of the Chinese policy of divide and rule during the Gelukpa period of Tibetan history, which continues even to this day.

When the XIIIth Dalai Lama began to consolidate his power and set in motion a certain degree of centralization, the IXth Panchen Lama and Tashilhunpo were one of the first targets of the Tibetan government in Lhasa, as Tashilhunpo had been growing since 1728 as an autonomous local power centre due to Chinese and British encouragement. The XIIIth Dalai Lama's nationalistic government sought to curtail the Panchen Lama's growing influence, by confiscating several of his estates and by reducing the political privileges of his court. This created tensions between Lhasa and Shigatse, and the IXth Panchen Lama and his entourage escaped to China in 1921. Both the British and the Chinese officials tried to intervene and mediate in this Dalai-Panchen dispute, but not with much success; for at the heart of the dispute was a feudal power struggle. The Panchen Lama wanted a return to the earlier system (1728-1920?) in which Tashilhunpo functioned autonomously from Lhasa. Besides, he wanted the right to maintain an armed force of his own. It was only after the XIIIth Dalai Lama's death that the IXth Panchen Lama was to return to Tibet. Unfortunately, he died en route in Jyekundo on 1 December 1937.

In the Gelukpa hagiologies the relations between the Dalai and Panchen Lamas are depicted as the 'sun' and the 'moon', the 'father' and the 'son'. This idealistic state of affairs might have prevailed when the two parties were not involved in a political contest in Tibet, especially during the period 1445-1728. At such times there was a sort of symbiotic relationship between the Dalai and Panchen Lamas. The senior incumbent tended to recognize the junior, giving sanctity and legitimacy to the 'new' Lama. Thus, the IVth Panchen Lama recognized the Vth Dalai Lama. Subsequently the Vth Dalai Lama recognized the Vth Panchen Lama. Later, the Vth Panchen Lama recognized the VIIIth Dalai Lama who, in turn, recognized the VIIth Panchen Lama. The current Dalai Lama's recognition of XIth Panchen Lama may be said to be in keeping with this spiritually fraternalistic tradition, as both belong to the same sect.

But politics soured the 'father' and 'son' relationship. High lamas, sometimes knowingly, sometimes under manipulation by their ambitious entourage, got entangled in the mundane world of power struggle. In this they were often encouraged by dominant neighbouring powers to promote their own national interest in Central Asia. Because high lamas wield enormous influence among their followers, external powers find it expedient to pursue their interest in Tibet through such holy men of influence. High lamas may be men of great influence but often they acted as instruments of the great powers and tended to toe the line so long as their political 'patrons' did not interfere in their religious sphere. However, the Xth Panchen Lama, Choekyi Gyaltsen, made a heroic departure in 1959 from this self-serving path and emerged as the hero of the Tibetan people under Chinese domination.

He was born on 3 February 1938 in Karang Bidho village in Amdo (Qinghai) and his parents named him Gonpo Tseten. After the IXth Panchen Lama's death, the Tashilhunpo Monastery organized searches for the reincarnation, finally short-listing two candidates, one in Amdo and the other in Kham. The former was preferred and declared as the Xth Panchen Lama with the name Lobsang Trinley Lhundrup Choekyi Gyaltsen.

However, considerable complications preceded his formal recognition. The pro-China section of the previous Panchen Lama's court recognized the Amdo child on their own in 1941. But a reincarnation of the Panchen Lama's stature would not be readily and widely accepted unless his authenticity was publicly confirmed by a Dalai Lama. With the then Dalai Lama still a minor, the Tibetan government insisted on the performance of all the traditional tests before the official confirmation. This delayed the Xth Panchen Lama's formal recognition by Lhasa. At the time of the signing of the 17-Point Agreement in 1951, the Chinese delegates insisted that the Tibetan government accept and recognize the 'Chinese candidate' (Gonpo Tseten) as the true reincarnation of IXth Panchen Lama.

Almost from the time of his identification as the probable candidate, the Xth Panchen Lama was caught up in the politics of China's renewed political ambitions towards Tibet. The Kuomintang government tried to use the Panchen Lama card to gain a foothold in Tibet, and when the Communists came to power in 1949, they immediately stepped in and used the child Panchen for their political ends. He was only eleven when the Commander of the Chinese People's Liberation Army division in Lanzhou sent a telegram in the Panchen Lama's name to Mao Zedong, requesting the latter to 'liberate' Tibet. In 1951, the Communists brought the little Panchen Lama to Beijing to put pressure on the Tibetan delegates to sign the Chinese-dictated 17-Point Agreement.

After the Agreement was signed, in which the status of the Dalai and the Panchen Lamas was defined, the young Xth Panchen Lama arrived in Lhasa on 28 April 1952, en route to Tashilhunpo, escorted by Chinese soldiers. During his brief stay in Lhasa, the Panchen Lama had two meetings with the present Dalai Lama, who had formally recognized him in 1951 at the request of the Tashilhunpo Monastery. It is interesting to note the Dalai Lama's impression of the young Panchen Lama, considering the fact that the latter was then depicted as the Chinese candidate. The Dalai Lama writes in his memoirs, *My Land And My People* (1962), that the Panchen Lama 'showed a genuine respect for my position, as the customs of Buddhism require towards a senior monk. He was correct and pleasant in his manners – a true Tibetan, and I had a firm impression of unforced goodwill. I felt sure that left to himself he would have whole-heartedly supported Tibet against the inroads of China' (p. 113). This impression proved to be prophetic in the light of the post-1959 developments in which the Xth Panchen Lama played a heroic role.

Given the fact that his predecessor revolted against the XIIIth Dalai Lama's government and sought China's support, that he was born in Qinghai under Chinese influence and that the Communists supported his candidature, the young Xth Panchen Lama was popularly perceived as being 'pro-Chinese' throughout the 1950s. And there is little doubt that the Communist regime tried to use him as a rival to the Dalai Lama, a counterforce to Tibetan nationalism and, indeed, as the Tibetan spokesman for Chinese policies in Tibet. These roles were well-publicized by the Chinese Communists in the 1950s, and the Tibetans of that generation still remember him as pro-Chinese.

But few Tibetans knew what the young Panchen Lama was doing in the 1950s at Tashilhunpo. He was quietly undergoing his rigorous spiritual training that would transform a mere boy into an incarnate lama, befitting the high status of a Panchen Lama. Gyenak Rinpoche imparted to him all the special teachings of Tashilhunpo in particular and the Gelukpa tradition in general. In the field of tantric theory and practice he was personally tutored by a well-known meditation master, Kachen Ang Nyima. And when Kachen Ang Nyima passed away, the Panchen Lama turned to Kachen Nyulchu Rinpoche from whom he received extensive teachings in Vajrayana and Mahayana Buddhism.

While receiving his spiritual training, the young Panchen did not neglect his social responsibility towards the community he headed. He realized that the antiquated style of administration and ceremonial functioning was inadequate to cope with the challenges of the twentieth century. He believed the old system would not be able to ensure the survival of Tibet in modern times. Thus, in 1956 the Panchen Lama opened a special school called *Chensel Labdra* in Shigatse for 300 students from his domain. The curriculum was revolutionary for a school set up by a high lama; it included Tibetan, Hindi, Chinese, photography, driving, horseback riding, shooting, etc. After the 1959 revolt, this school was suspected of instigating the rebellion and of planning to retreat to India. This was one of the serious charges levelled against the Panchen Lama by the Communists in 1964, as we shall see later.

However, the Chinese had from the beginning a special place for the Panchen Lama in their scheme. He was to be an opponent of or an alternative to the office of the Dalai Lama, as and when the situation arose. Thus, almost immediately after the Dalai Lama's escape in 1959, the Chinese appointed the Panchen Lama as the acting Chairman of the 'Preparatory Committee for Tibet Autonomous Region' (which was to replace the Tibetan government at Lhasa), an office previously held by the Dalai Lama. In 1960, the Chinese appointed the Panchen Lama as a vice-chairman of the National People's Congress, hoping to use him as their puppet spokesman and advocate for Communist policies in Tibet. But the lonely young Lama stuck to his conscience and ethnicity.

In the early 1960s, the Panchen Lama resumed the religious responsibilities of the absentee Dalai Lama in Tibet. Two China-educated Tibetans who escaped to India during the chaotic Cultural Revolution still remember his sermons in 1960 and 1961 at Shugtri Lingka in Lhasa. Tsering Dorje Gashi recalls one such sermon which attracted nearly 10,000 Tibetans in Lhasa. The economic development of Tibet was uppermost in the Panchen Lama's mind, recalls Gashi. So long as the Tibetans did not stand on their own feet, the Chinese would remain in Tibet 'to help them'. Therefore, what had happened was essentially a Tibetan responsibility. He also stressed that Tibet's cultural heritage would not be allowed to die; it should be given every chance for further development. But, the Lama argued, it was right and correct to adapt our culture to modern conditions. Next he turned to the freedom of worship as promised by Mao and guaranteed by the Chinese Constitution. He encouraged the people to worship freely and without fear, and follow their traditions and customs as before.

After his discourse, the Panchen Lama, writes Gashi, looked in every direction with a sigh of regret and sadness. Then slowly the Lama said, 'His Holiness the Dalai Lama was abducted from his country to a foreign land. During this period it is in every Tibetan's interest that His Holiness comes to no harm. I have complete faith that he works with a heavy responsibility. I pray that His Holiness will live long.'

After listening to this moving sermon, Gashi says he wept helplessly, like most Tibetans present there.

The Chinese authorities became critical of the Panchen Lama's sympathetic attitude towards the Dalai Lama and of preaching Buddhism in Lhasa. In 1962 the Chinese Communist Party boss in Tibet, Zhang Jinwu, asked the Panchen Lama to openly denounce the Dalai Lama as 'a reactionary' and a 'traitor', but the young Lama refused. Instead, in his religious sermons in Lhasa, he continued to urge the Tibetans to pray for the long life and success of the Dalai Lama. Furthermore, the Panchen Lama sent a 70,000-character petition (in Chinese) dated 18 May 1962 to the Chinese government. In that long petition he condemned, in no uncertain terms, the indiscriminate armed suppression of Tibetans in 1959 which had drastically reduced the Tibetan population and 'incarcerated' able-bodied and educated men in all the Tibetan areas of Qinghai, Gansu, Sichuan and Yunnan. He criticized the Communist policy on religion which had brought Tibetan Buddhism 'on the verge of extinction' and appealed to the Chinese authorities to improve the pitiable economic condition of the Tibetan people.

Mao Zedong was so shocked to read the critical petition that he at once condemned the Panchen Lama as 'our class enemy'. The Lama had dared to criticize the Communist Party policy in Tibet and had called for its correction. This was unacceptable to the Maoist fundamentalists. It was clear that the Panchen Lama was not playing the role his Communist masters had designed for him. Instead, he was gradually taking the place of the Dalai Lama in a real sense, as the spiritual and temporal leader of the Tibetan people after 1959. This was completely contrary to the Chinese expectations, and in 1964 the Panchen Lama was purged.

In April 1964 the Chinese Communist boss Zhang Guohua in Lhasa was called to Beijing to discuss the situation in Tibet with Mao Zedong and other top leaders. Zhang reported that most Tibetans were 'ready for socialism' but the Panchen Lama was 'blocking the road'. It was clear that the decision to purge the Panchen Lama was made by the highest echelon of the Communist Party leadership in Beijing.

Zhang Guohua came back to Lhasa at the end of July 1964, and by September the purge had begun. At a Tibet Autonomous Region Preparatory Committee (PCTAR) meeting held from 18 September to 4 November 1964, Zhang Guohua and other local officials openly criticized the Panchen Lama's 'anti-party, anti-socialism and anti-people' activities. He was blamed for all the failures of the PCTAR, accused as a 'reactionary enemy of the state' who secretly supported the 'Dalai bandit'. From then on, he was subjected to a series of humiliating *thamzing*, lasting seventeen days during which he was accused of ten crimes. Of these, the more serious ones were that he had attempted to restore serfdom, planned to launch a guerilla war against the state, criticized China in the 70,000-character petition and had openly declared his support for the Dalai Lama. Towards the end of 1964 the Panchen Lama, after being accused and condemned, was deported to Beijing's Qin Cheng prison. His tutor,

Ngulchu Rinpoche, and his steward, Tana Tsethong were imprisoned in Gormo.

In 1967, the Panchen Lama was subjected to severe *thamzing* at the Central Institute of Minority Nationalities in Beijing. For thirteen years he suffered mentally and physically which only his prison inmates knew of. In a 20-page wall poster dated 3 March 1979 China's well-known dissident Wei Jingsheng stated that life in the Qin Cheng prison was so unbearable that the Panchen Lama at one time attempted suicide. The Lama refused to take food, saying he did not want to go on living under the terrible prison conditions. Wei quoted him as having told the prison authorities, 'You can take my body to the Central Committee.'

The Panchen Lama languished in prison for thirteen or fourteen years, but no one knew his whereabouts, or even whether he was dead or alive. The outside world came to know about his re-emergence on 26 February 1978 when the Communist official news agency released a report that he had attended the fifth National Committee of the Chinese People's Political Consultative Conference in Beijing. In 1980 he was reinstated as the vice-chairman of the National People's Congress.

Soon after his release from prison and rehabilitation, the Panchen Lama requested the Chinese authorities for permission to visit his beloved homeland. Permission was granted only in June 1982. On reaching Lhasa, he told Tibetans: 'Tibet is my home and I have a special regard for this land. Although I have not lived here for the last eighteen years, my heart has always been beating with those of the people of Tibet. I have always missed Tibet and its people, and have been thinking about the welfare of Tibetans.'

Even years of torture and humiliation did not dampen his spirit as the conscience-keeper of the subjugated Tibetan people. He began again to speak for them and criticize Chinese policies and practices in Tibet. Perhaps the most scathing criticism of the Chinese policies in Tibet was made by the Panchen

Lama on 28 March 1987 at the TAR Standing Committee meeting in Beijing during the National People's Congress. It was a repeat of the 70,000-character petition but in person. He spoke with the same courage and conviction that characterized the post-1959 Panchen Lama, challenging the military might and ideological pretensions of the People's Republic of China. No Chinese or national minority leader had ever dared to speak so openly inside Communist China since 1949.

The Panchen Lama began his speech with a description of the various ways in which the Hans look down upon Tibetan people and their culture. He referred to a story, 'Pasang And Her Relatives' recently published in a Chinese journal to 'ridicule the Tibetans', despite serious Tibetan objections. Instead, the anti-Tibetan story was filmed and awarded the first prize. He also criticized the lack of educational opportunities for the Tibetans, and pointed out how most of the scholarships abroad were given to the Han students.

Next he turned to China's language policies. He observed vast educational disparities between the Tibetan and Han students, primarily due to Chinese language barriers. The average Tibetan student, he said, 'can never hope to compete with the Chinese as far as the Chinese language is concerned'. He charged that the Han officials in Tibet 'are trying to neglect the Tibetan language completely' in order to suit their purpose: Han supremacy and Han expansionism. He argued that the expense of keeping one Chinese in Tibet was equal to that of four in China. 'Why should Tibet spend its money to feed them? Instead, we should think carefully how best the money can be used for the development of Tibet. Tibet has suffered greatly because of the policy of sending a large number of useless people' (*The Panchen Lama Speaks*, p. 6).

The Lama condemned, as he had in his 70,000-character protest, the Chinese indiscriminate armed suppression of the 1959 rebellion which almost decimated the Tibetan population in certain areas. Drawing examples from his hometown

(Amdo), the Panchen Lama stated that about 10 to 15 per cent of the population had been imprisoned, and 300 to 400 of them had died in prison. In Kham he 'noticed a great deal of devastation caused by large-scale and indiscriminate deforestation. I saw huge landslides caused by this'. Finally, he criticized the leftists and their behaviour in Tibet. 'What are we gaining from the leftist practices in Tibet?' he asked and continued: 'Those with leftist ideology are suppressing everything. When Comrade Hu Yaobang was disgraced recently, the leftist officials exploded fire crackers and drank in celebration. They commented that the stalwart supporter of the Tibetan people had been defeated.'

After being 'rehabilitated' in 1977, the Panchen Lama was made to stay in Beijing. His residence was a simple, one-storey building near the Chinese Academy of Social Sciences. On most days, small crowds of Tibetan and Mongolian devotees would be waiting patiently outside the metal gate. Visitors were usually ushered into his small study. The Panchen Lama sat behind a wooden table on which stood an old, black Panasonic transistor radio. For special visitors, the Lama used to serve his favourite dish: boiled leg of mutton from Amdo. The walls of the dining room were adorned with *thankas* of the complete lineage of the Panchen Lamas. Tall bookshelves were stacked with Tibetan Buddhist scriptures.

The Panchen Lama visited Lhasa six or seven times after 1977, and toured various parts of Tibet, including Kham and Amdo. His last visit was in January 1989 when he arrived at his traditional monastic seat, Tashilhunpo, in Shigatse. After fifteen days, he declared in a public meeting in Shigatse that the Communist rule in Tibet had brought more destruction than benefit to the Tibetan people. On 28 January 1989 the Xth Panchen Lama, aged 51, died at Tashilhunpo Monastery, where his previous incarnations had lived and died.

As religion says, death is not the end but the beginning of another life. So it was with the Panchen Lama. However, in his case, it was also the beginning of a dispute between the Dalai Lama and Beijing. At the heart of the dispute was the political question of who has the power and authority to recognize the XIth Panchen Lama – the Dalai Lama or the Chinese government? The Dalai Lama's claim was based on religious convention and age-old practice, whereas the Communists based their claim on the legacy of the Qing imperial power. In practice both were involved in the final recognition of a Panchen Lama, but the Dalai Lama more so than the Manchu emperor. The Manchu emperor's rubber stamp added more prestige and power but the Dalai Lama's recognition (*ngos-'zin*) sanctified and legitimized the reincarnation in the eyes of the Buddhist world.

What made the Xth Panchen Lama's reincarnation such a controversial issue between Beijing and Dharamsala was its political implications to both parties at a time when politics takes precedence over piety. The issue is of great political significance to Beijing. China's claim to rule Tibet largely rests on the imperial tradition of conferring titles on high lamas and on the imperial custom of sending *ambans* to be present at the recognition and enthronement ceremonies of high reincarnate lamas. This traditional patron-priest relationship, as the Tibetans perceive it, has now been interpreted by the Communist authorities as China's right to 'appoint' high lamas to their posts.

The Communists claim that the presentation of a golden urn by the Manchu Emperor Qianlong in 1792 (the so-called lots drawing system) marked the height of Manchu influence in Tibet. This was so mainly for two reasons. Tibet during this period was invaded four times by the Gorkhas of Nepal, and each time the Lhasa government requested Emperor Qianlong to send Manchu troops to repulse the Gorkha forces. Secondly, Qianlong was perhaps the most expansionist of Manchu emperors, and this affected Tibet too. That is why Communist China takes the golden urn presentation in 1792 as the historic basis of its claim to 'confirm' the reincarnations of the Dalai and Panchen lamas.

Beijing makes out as if the whole 'system of drawing lots' was instituted by the Manchu court. This is not true, either historically or culturally. *Tagdril* is an ancient Tibetan (Bonpo?) tradition long predating the Manchu empire. This ancient Tibetan method involves encasting the names of candidates in dough balls of equal size and weight. The balls are put into a container which is then rotated until one of them pops out. The name of the candidate inscribed on the ejected ball is declared the successful candidate.

With the subsequent spread of Buddhism, certain other Buddhist elements were added, such as saying prayers before the Buddha and other deities and shaking the urn in a clockwise rotation. Emperor Qianlong merely presented a golden urn which would hopefully replace the ordinary container.

Tibetan lamas have seldom used the emperor's urn since then; they mostly continue to adhere to their traditional practices. There have been six Dalai Lamas since Emperor Qianlong presented the urn in the eighteenth century; it was used in confirming only three of them. But the 'golden urn' was seldom used to select Panchen Lama reincarnations. That is why Chadrel Rinpoche and Ngagchen Rinpoche resisted the Communist pressure to use the lottery system.

Nor is the idea of reincarnation a Chinese creation; it is uniquely a Tibetan religio-political institution going back to the twelfth century. Its main secular function was to institutionalize the charisma of some individual lamas with extraordinary achievement. The idea is based on the Buddhist (or Indic) concept of rebirth, which all sentient beings undergo after death. However, *Bodhisattvas*, whose reincarnations most of the High Lamas claim, are superior beings who are on the threshold of enlightenment but who have deliberately postponed it in order to be present in the world and help the suffering sentient beings to become enlightened. As such, Tibetans believe that such High Lamas have a certain degree of freedom over death and rebirth, especially when and where to be reborn. It is this mysterious jigsaw puzzle that lamas try to solve after the death of every high lama – through dreams and visions, oracles and divinations, mysterious signs and close observations.

Soon after the Panchen Lama's death in 1989, Beijing appointed Chadrel Rinpoche, Acting Abbot of Tashilhunpo, as the chairman of the Search Committee. The Chinese officials agreed with Chadrel Rinpoche in 1989 on the official procedure for finding the Panchen Lama's reincarnation. It included using the following steps: (1) mystical signs to identify the child candidate; (2) tests with objects to identify the most likely candidate; (3) oracles and divination to 'reconfirm' the final candidate; (4) the golden urn (lottery system), drawn by a government official, to single out the candidate from the short list; and (5) approval of the final decision by the Central government.

As we can see, before the Dalai Lama's pre-emptive action announcing Gedun Choekyi Nyima as the reincarnation of the XIth Panchan Lama on 14 May 1995, the Chinese authorities gave considerable freedom and power to the Search Committee. And Beijing would most probably have approved the same candidate had it not been for the breakdown in the Beijing-Dalai Lama negotiations and the Dalai Lama's subsequent pre-emptive, and unilateral action, which China perceived as an indirect challenge to its sovereignty. Once this happened, as it did after 4 May 1995, Beijing took direct political action on the Panchen reincarnation issue and completely ignored the duly constituted Search Committee. In fact, Chadrel Rinpoche was detained on 17 May 1995, three days after the Dalai Lama's announcement, of collusion with the latter. Between May and August 1995, 48 Tibetans were arrested on suspicion of helping Chadrel Rinpoche send messages about the child (Gedun Choekyi Nyima) to the Dalai Lama in India. At the same time Chinese authorities appointed pro-Chinese Communist 'lamas' such as Sengchen Lobsang Gyaltsen as the head of Tashilhunpo and as the head of the Gelukpa sect in order to facilitate the staging of the Chinese candidate with some semblance of 'traditional procedures' and to back up the Chinese direct political action in the religious domain.

With the same purpose in mind, Beijing issued instructions to 300 senior lamas in Central Tibet, ordering them to arrive at the Chinese capital by the morning of 5 November 1995. They were told to condemn Chadrel Rinpoche and to support the Chinese decision to use the 'golden urn' method to select their own Panchen Lama.

But this Chinese-imposed method was opposed by almost all the monks and lamas of Tashilhunpo in a special meeting convened by the Chinese authorities on 4 June 1995. In that meeting, a highly respected lama, Ngagchen Rinpoche, recalled how Chadrel Rinpoche, Chung-la and he had visited Lhamoi Lhatso near Lhasa to see visions of the reincarnation. 'Based on this,' Ngagchen declared, 'the reincarnation is the real one. Especially, when we arrived in Nagchu, we experienced many supernatural events. Everywhere there was snow and also suddenly there was brilliant sunshine. When we met the reincarnation he immediately said, "I am Panchen." When we asked him, "do you want to go to the monastery?" he said "Yes, I would like to go."'

In conclusion, Ngagchen Rinpoche said, '...it was clear that the boy was the real Lama, so we asked the Central Government not to hold a lottery because we had already found the reincarnation. All we needed to do was to ask Gong-sa-Choe (His Holiness the Dalai Lama) to recognize him. We asked the Central government this several times.' (Tibet Information Network, London: 1995, pp. 9-10.)

Yet China went ahead with its political action, bypassing the duly constituted Search Committee's recommendation and thereby deeply hurting the religious sentiments of the Tibetan people. On 29 November 1995, the Chinese central authorities announced the name of the boy they had selected as the XIth Panchen Lama. This was a politically motivated action, seeking as it does, to 'invalidate' the Dalai Lama's earlier announced candidate, whom the Search Committee and Tashilhunpo Monastery believed to be the real reincarnation. Chinese authorities correctly suspected that their political action would be opposed by Tibetans inside Tibet unless they enforced the whole 'procedure' with military force. Thus, since July 1995, a de facto martial law has been imposed on Shigatse and Tashilhunpo. Shigatse was closed to tourists, and troops patrolled the streets. The Chinese acclamation rituals at Jokhang (Lhasa) and the enthronement ceremony at Tashilhunpo were conducted with tight security measures, backed by heavy armed police forces around the two places. This was no way to announce such a happy tiding as the Panchen Lama's reincarnation to the Tibetan people, if the Chinese candidate, Gyaltsen Norbu, was not a mere political rival claimant. But Gyaltsen Norbu as the XIth Panchen Lama, no matter how much China might promote him, is suspect in Tibetan and Buddhist eyes, without the Dalai Lama's sanctification and legitimation. Of course, as we have seen, China sought the Dalai's legitimation stamp but Dharamsala bargained for a pound of political flesh from the Chinese. This having failed, the whole matter, which began as a religious issue, became a political struggle between the Dalai Lama and Beijing. The authentic reincarnation of the XIth Panchen Lama is a victim of this political game.

It is clear from both official Chinese sources and the evidences of the Tibetan government in exile that Chadrel Rinpoche tried his best for over six years to get what he believed to be the authentic reincarnation of the Panchen Lama (Gedun Choekyi Nyima) endorsed by both the Chinese government in Beijing and the Dalai Lama in exile. But he tragically failed. As far as Beijing was concerned, it was not bothered about which boy the Tashilhunpo lamas chose but it insisted that the final choice must be officially approved and publicly proclaimed first by the Chinese government, and not the Dalai Lama or the

Tibetan government in exile. So China would have 'approved' Gedun Choekyi Nyima had it not been for the fact that the Dalai Lama in exile pre-empted the Chinese initiative.

Beijing realizes the serious political implications of the Dalai Lama's action which, as its officials have stated, 'negates Chinese sovereignty over Tibet', and begins a 'splitist' process. For Communist China's claim over Tibet rests on the argument that the Qing emperors had 'appointed' high lamas to their charismatic institutions through which, according to the Communists, China had always indirectly ruled Tibet. This is certainly a distorted interpretation of the complex trajectory of Sino-Tibetan relations but that is how the Maoist rulers view the complex matter. It shows how paranoid the Communist rulers are about their takeover of Tibet even after 46 years of occupation. It stems from their increasing ideological guilt that they may have committed an act of imperialism in Tibet.

Therefore, to Beijing the question is not whether the Dalai Lama's or its own candidate is the true reincarnation of the Panchen Lama. Rather the critical question is, who but the Dalai Lama has the ultimate authority to 'appoint' the Panchen Lama, the second highest-ranking lama in the Tibetan Buddhist hierarchy, with a large following not only in Tibet but also in Central Asia and the Cis-Himalayas? In spite of knowing this, China denounced the Dalai Lama's choice and announced its own candidate, Gyaltsen Norbu. High lamas began as saviours of mankind and advisers to Chinese emperors; now they are reduced to being the unfortunate objects of political manipulation. This is particularly true of the previous and present Panchen Lamas.

While China forcibly stage-managed traditional procedures in the search for the Panchen reincarnation, in an obvious bid to give the process a religious garb and to gain credibility which the Communist atheists lacked, the Dalai Lama more or less dispensed with traditional procedures and took the whole issue in his hand. The Tashilhunpo Monastery in exile in Mysore (India) requested the Dalai Lama's permission three times to start searching for the reincarnation of their lama but the Dalai Lama kept dilly-dallying. Meanwhile the monks from Tashilhunpo Monastery in Mysore were brought to Delhi to back up the Dalai Lama's decision after China announced its counter-candidate.

The Dalai Lama followed his own plan and dispensed with much of the traditional conventions and practices customarily associated with the Panchen Lama reincarnation search process. Such a departure, he might have felt, was in keeping with his unconventional spiritualism. But an equally important consideration was to use the Panchen reincarnation issue as part of his political dialogue with China.

The Dalai Lama says he received over 30 names of potential candidates from 18 different places, both in Tibet and India. His divination in 1991 revealed that the reincarnation had been born in Tibet, but one performed in August of the same year indicated that the popularly believed reincarnation was not true. However, his divinations in 1993 and 1994 indicated that the time for the search was not ripe. The Nechung and Gatong oracles in early 1994 also prophesied that the Panchen's reincarnation would soon be found in Tibet. With the oracles' hints, the Dalai Lama speeded up the process. A divination performed on 3 December 1994 suggested that the search process should begin, and in January 1995 the divination revealed that Gedun Choekyi Nyima, whose father is Konchong Phunstog and whose mother is Dechen Choedon of Lhari village in Nagchu, Tibet, was an 'extremely' good candidate. This was verified and confirmed by two more divinations performed in January 1995 at Dharamsala. Regarding the auspicious date of the announcement of the reincarnation, the final divination performed on 13 May 1995 declared 15 May 1995 as being the most auspicious.

In other words, the Dalai Lama chose the divination method to select the Panchen Lama reincarnation, a method which enabled him to take personal control over the whole process. Whether the Dalai Lama's divination was the right method or not, the whereabouts of the six-year-old Gedun Choekyi Nyima, who disappeared from public view under 'official protection' is not known to this day. In any case, China is likely to make sure that the child is kept from public view forever because if he is accessible to the public there would be a spontaneous mass recognition and veneration which would embarrass the Chinese authorities.

It is surprising that His Holiness the Dalai Lama acted in the way he did which ultimately served neither the Buddhist purpose nor the Tibetan cause. As we shall show, he had sufficient information and indication from China that his unilateral action on the Panchen Lama issue would be opposed by Beijing on political grounds. On 21 March 1991, the Dalai Lama's representative in New Delhi conveyed the Lama's message to the Chinese embassy that he would like to send a religious delegation to observe prophetic visions in Lhamoi Lhatso, near Lhasa which will guide the search for the Panchen Lama's reincarnation. China rejected this proposal three months later, saying there was no need for 'outside interference'.

While the Chinese government rejected the Dalai Lama's formal role in the search process at the governmental level, the concerned Chinese authorities, it appears, nodded their approval to the Tashilhunpo Monastery search party to seek the Dalai Lama's co-operation at the purely religious level, as was done in the Karmapa case. Thus, the acting abbot of Tashilhunpo Monastery and head of the Chinese official search party, Chadrel Rinpoche sent through Gyalo Thondup (while the latter was in Beijing) a letter dated 17 July 1993 to the Dalai Lama. In that letter Chadrel Rinpoche reported the progress so far made in the search, namely, that he and his colleagues had made two visits to Lhamoi Lhatso and Rinpung Chamring Yung Tso, and that their visions in the two lakes indicated that the search should be conducted in the east of Tashilhunpo among children born in the years of the Snake, Horse and Sheep, according to the Tibetan calendar.

But the Dalai Lama took the official line. It was not the Lama but his 'government in exile' which delivered a reply (dated 5 August 1993) to the Chinese embassy in New Delhi. The letter suggested that a delegation headed by Chadrel Rinpoche should come to Dharamsala to discuss matters relating to the search for the Panchen's reincarnation. Although there was no written reply to this letter, Beijing informally sent an individual (Yeshi Wangchuk?) in October 1994 to Dharamsala. What this unnamed Chinese individual 'with close ties to the Government in Beijing' discussed in his two meetings with the Dalai Lama was never revealed. Dharamsala disclosed only what the Dalai Lama told the Chinese individual, that the Lama was still waiting for a reply from Chadrel Rinpoche and that the search for the Panchen's reincarnation must be conducted through 'strict traditional religious procedures'. In January 1995, the Dalai Lama's office in Dharmsala sent two letters to the 'Chinese individual' who visited them in October 1994, reminding him of the closed-door discussions they had had in Dharamsala and requesting him to urge the Chinese authorities for an early response. On 14 May 1995, after waiting for four months for a Chinese reply, the Dalai Lama announced Gedun Choekyi Nyima as the reincarnation of the Panchen Lama.

Whether the Dalai Lama's decision was a wise one or not will be debated by future historians. But the tragedy is that neither the Dalai Lama nor his sycophantic advisers anticipated the Chinese reaction which would practically nullify the Dalai Lama's recognition of a little boy in Chinese captivity. It did not cross their mind that Beijing might not only oppose the Dalai Lama's decision but would take steps to arrange for the disappearance of the boy, thereby rendering the Dalai Lama's recognition of the true reincarnation of the XIth Panchen Lama practically meaningless. As I said earlier, the Dalai Lama's decision served neither the Tibetan cause nor that of religion.

Of course His Holiness the Dalai Lama has the right, as validated by tradition and history, to declare his recognition of the Panchen Lama. But this reincarnated boy is, unfortunately, not in a free society. This little boy is in Chinese hands, who will do what serves the Chinese national and political interests, and not act in a religious spirit at this stage when the Dalai Lama's preemptive action is perceived as a challenge to Chinese sovereignty. It does not require an extraordinary foresight on the Dalai Lama's part to have known what to expect from his dealings with the Chinese officials on the Panchen issue for four years (1991-94).

Tibetan critics point out that there were two possible options before the Dalai Lama then. The identified boy as the reincarnation of the Panchen Lama should have been smuggled out of Tibet at an early stage. Such smuggling is not impossible; several monasteries in exile have done so since the early 1980s. This, the critics argue, would have served the Dalai Lama's political purpose equally well. The Dalai Lama and his successor could have educated, trained and brought up the boy for the next twenty years or so, during his minority. Only someone of the stature of a Panchen Lama could unite and lead the Tibetans.

If this option was not palatable to the Dalai Lama, he should have worked harder to reach a consensus with the Chinese authorities on the formal question of who should announce the recognition first. This might have entailed the sacrifice of some of the Dalai Lama's traditional prerogatives but it would have served the larger Tibetan interest. Had Gedun Choekyi Nyima, as identified by the senior lamas of Tashilhunpo and given religious recognition by the Dalai Lama, been formally endorsed by the Chinese government, he might have played, when grown up, a critical role in Sino-Tibetan politics, like his predecessor. His ethnic background and deep lamaistic training at Tashilhunpo would have made sure he became the true successor to the Xth Panchen Lama, as the most influential Tibetan leader in Chinese-occupied Tibet. This would have been a great service to the powerless and voiceless Tibetan masses in Tibet. This was evidently one of the main reasons why Chadrel Rinpoche and his colleagues in the Search Committee tried so hard to get their duly discovered Panchen Lama endorsed both by the Chinese government in Beijing and the Dalai Lama in Dharamsala. But they failed, and in their failure lies yet another Tibetan tragedy whose consequences the innocent Tibetan people will have to suffer in the years to come.

Who is the winner in this political game played on the religious terrain? The Dalai Lama pre-empted Beijing's announcement but his recognized, reincarnated boy 'disappeared' into nothingness. So, as usual, the Dalai Lama captured the international media headlines but with no concrete results for the Tibetan people. Beijing could and did announce its own counter-candidate for the XIth Panchen Lama on 29 November 1995, but a Panchen Lama reincarnate without the Dalai Lama's recognition – which virtually legitimizes and sanctifies the incarnate boy – remains doubtful in the eyes of the Mahayana Buddhist world, as amply demonstrated by protests in Tibet. Gedun Choekyi Nyima was probably the authentic reincarnation according to supernatural signs and close observations of Chadrel Rinpoche and Ngagchen Rinpoche but their candidate has become a victim of the Dalai-Beijing confrontation.

We have devoted more space on the Panchen Lama reincarnation controversy than on the extraordinary character of the man called Choekyi Gyaltsen, the Xth Panchen Lama who defied the Chinese rule in Tibet for over thirty years, fighting for the Tibetan people's rights within the 'enemy lines'. Despite the widespread suspicion of Chinese Communist influence in his early upbringing, the Xth Panchen Lama remained a practising Buddhist throughout his turbulent life. There is no evidence of his having dabbled in 'Buddhist Marxist dialogues' which would have actually enhanced his standing before the Maoist power elites. During his long house-arrest in Beijing, he lost his celibate status to a Chinese woman. (It was rumoured that the Chinese police had been behind this.) And when he returned to Tibet in the late 1970s, he was reluctant to ascend the Panchen Lama's throne but his entourage forced him to do so. Even then he refused to wear the monk's robes again; in public he was seen wearing a yellow brocade *chuba* (the layman's dress).

Above all, he respected his gurus at Tashilhunpo and none of them fell out of favour just because of their political differences with him or his brother. Nor was there any trace of the Gelukpa chauvinism in him. For example, he stated on 24 January 1989, when Beijing asked him to recognize all *tulkus* (reincarnate lamas) in Tibet that he could not and would not recognize them applying the Gelukpa method. He explained, 'since the Central Government has asked me to confirm all the tulkus, I now have to invite Buddha Sakyamuni himself and seek his help'. Buddha Sakyamuni is accepted by all the schools of Tibetan Buddhism. At the same time he retained a profound respect for the institution and the lineage of Dalai Lama, and refused to denounce the XIVth Dalai Lama as a 'reactionary' and a 'traitor' even at the risk to his life in the 1960s.

In politics and administration Choekyi Gyaltsen proved himself to be a most non-feudal High Lama. He did not appoint any of the members of his family to any 'official' or informal posts in Tashilhunpo or in Lhasa, even though he had the power to do so. In a meeting in 1987, he narrated how his aged father from Amdo was not allowed to enter the TAR territory in 1979 when the old man had come for some personal work in Tibet, and how he had to wait in the rain (*The Panchen Lama Speaks*, p. 14).

The Panchen Lama spent his last years in persuading the Chinese authorities to allow the Tibetans to take over trade and commerce in the region. Towards this goal he established the Tibet Ganggyen Development Corporation in 1987. This reflected the Panchen Lama's vision of a future Tibet where the Tibetans would develop and catch up with the modern world through their own initiatives, thereby gradually making the Chinese presence in Tibet redundant. The development corporation was probably his biggest private initiative; yet none of its leading managers, including Gyara Tsering Samdup – whom the Chinese police arrested after the Panchen reincarnation controversy – were the Panchen Lama's relatives or close friends.

After his honest and selfless service for the welfare of the Tibetan people, both in Tibet and within China, which cost him thirteen years of tortuous imprisonment, the Xth Panchen Lama ended his life as a true *blama*. Buddhist believers should see his death as the demonstration of his mystic power, not as a Chinese communist treachery. Four days before his death on 24 January 1989, in a meeting attended by Buddhist leaders from all over China and Tibet, he discussed his next reincarnation. He proposed that after his death 'three infants should be sought who were the potential reincarnations of the living Buddha'. On 9 January 1989, the 51-year-old Panchen Lama arrived in his traditional monastic town of Shigatse, and after consecrating the renovated *stupas* of his predecessors, he died peacefully in his sleep in his traditional monastic seat of Tashilhunpo on 28 January 1989. There was indeed an element of the true Mahayana Buddhist mysticism in his triumphant ending of a tragic yet heroic life.

The Xth Panchen Lama did not have the good fortune of publishing ghost-written books in his name or the constant Western mass media exposure which make instant heroes in our credulous and media-oriented age. But in real life he proved himself to be the tragic hero of the Tibetan drama, and I dedicate this chapter to the memory of Choekyi Gyaltsen, the Xth Panchen Lama, who devoted his life for the cause of Tibetan people under Chinese domination.

TWENTY

Tibet's Future in Post-Deng China

THAT OUR Aunt was able to visit us in India and had noticed considerable improvement in living conditions and relaxation of restrictions on religious practices in Sakya, were primarily due to two factors: Deng Xiaoping's liberalization policy since 1978 and the Dalai Lama's dialogue with Chinese Communist leaders (1979-1990).

When I came back from the United States in early 1983, the Tibetan refugee community in India was in a state of excitement. There were rumours that the Dalai Lama's elder brother Gyalo Thondup was negotiating with top Chinese leaders in Beijing and that soon we would be able to return to Tibet. There was also a lot of controversy about *rangtsen* (independence) and *rang-kyong-jong* (autonomy) among the better informed circles in exile. But what exactly went on between Beijing and Dharamsala in those critical years hardly anyone knew; the Tibetan public was kept in complete darkness. Many feared that the Dalai Lama and his brother were trying to decide the fate of the Tibetan people both in and outside Tibet.

Beijing-Dharamsala Dialogue, 1979-90

Since the matter is rather important, affecting as it does not only the future status of Tibet but also the fate of the Tibetan people, I have researched on the Sino-Tibetan dialogue and want to share with the reader some of my findings as well as discuss future prospects in post-Deng China upon which the future of

Tibet largely depends.

Perhaps the most significant development since 1959 was the dialogue that Deng Xiaoping initiated with the Dalai Lama in December 1978. The primary Chinese motive was – and still is – to persuade the 'self-exiled Tibetan leader to return to the motherland'. For in exile the Dalai Lama not only creates frequent embarrassment to the People's Republic of China (PRC) through his excellent rapport with the Western mass media but what is more important, China fears that the Dalai Lama could be used for anti-Chinese purposes by hostile powers. If, however, the Lama could be persuaded to end his exile, he would automatically cease to be a source of embarrassment and potential danger to China. In addition, China hoped that he could be used at home to legitimize Chinese rule in Tibet.

The Dalai Lama has come to the conclusion that he does not have any alternative but to negotiate for a greater degree of autonomy from China. This realization came about more acutely with the U.S. abandonment of the Tibetan cause in the early 1970s when the Sino-American rapprochement began. Since then, Western moral support for the Dalai Lama's peace initiatives has considerably increased, culminating in the award of the Nobel Peace Prize to the Dalai Lama in 1989.

Given the preceding political changes, it took two equally pragmatic leaders to break the ice in 1978: Deng Xiaoping and the Dalai Lama. The credit, however, must go to Deng. It was part of his reform, introduced since 1978, which included not only the four modernizations but also the bold initiatives to resolve some of the outstanding national problems such as Taiwan and Tibet. Hence, it seems hardly fortuitous that Deng Xiaoping, who was held responsible during the Cultural Revolution for the most unrevolutionary policy in pre-1959 Tibet, once again took steps to contact the Dalai Lama.

On the other hand, the Dalai Lama too had scaled down his demands on the Tibetan question by the late 1970s in shifting the essence of his struggle from claims for independence to concerns about economic welfare. On 10 March 1978 he declared, 'If the six million Tibetans in Tibet are really happy and prosperous as never before, there is no reason for us to argue otherwise.' A year later he explained, 'the main reason why we are in exile is the welfare of the six million Tibetans'. In 1980 he was more explicit: '...the core of the Tibetan issue is the welfare and ultimate happiness of the six million Tibetans in Tibet'. In so doing the Dalai Lama met the basic Chinese precondition for negotiation: the question of Tibetan independence would not be raised.

This was precisely the first of the three points that Deng Xiaoping conveyed to Gyalo Thondup on 3 December 1978. He stated: 'The basic question is whether Tibet is a part of China or not. This should be kept as the criteria for testing the truth.... So long as it is not accepted that Tibet is an integral part of China, there is nothing else to talk about.' The Tibetan side interpreted this as the agenda for all negotiations except those aiming for total independence. Deng's second point was that the Dalai Lama may send delegations to Tibet to investigate the actual conditions there. Third, he accepted the Tibetan suggestion that 50 Tibetan teachers from India be permitted to teach in various parts of Tibet.

After having made the necessary economic concessions which might have met the Dalai Lama's basic demand made in 1978 and 1979, Hu Yaobang specified the Party line on the Lama's personal status upon his return to China. On 28 July 1981, Hu conveyed to Gyalo Thondup China's 'five-point proposal to the Dalai Lama', which is, he emphasized, 'our sincere and serious decision'. First, China now had entered a new era of political stability, economic prosperity and friendly relations among all the nationalities. These trends will not change for a long time to come. Since the Dalai Lama and his entourage 'are intelligent' they should believe in what the new era promises. If they don't, they can wait and see. Second, the Dalai Lama and those appointed by him to represent him at talks must be 'sincere'; they must not 'bargain like businessmen'. On China's part there will be no punishment of those Tibetans who took part in the 1959 rebellion. Third, '... we sincerely welcome back the Dalai Lama and his entourage' to permanently settle down in China; for, once returned, the Dalai Lama can promote national unity, improve relations among nationalities and accelerate the progress of the four modernizations. If and when he returns to China – and this was the fourth point – his political and economic privileges will be as those of pre-1959. He will be appointed as vice-president of the National People's Congress as well as vice-chairman of the Chinese People's Political Consultative Committee. Hu emphasized that neither the Dalai Lama nor his entourage need worry about their living conditions or employment as China would guarantee their privileges. Fifth, the Dalai Lama could decide when he wanted to return, and say whatever he wanted to say. China would organize a grand reception and hold a press conference.

The Dalai Lama's reaction to the Chinese five-point proposal was brief: 'Instead of addressing the real issues facing the six million Tibetan people, China has attempted to reduce the question of Tibet to a discussion of my own personal status.' He therefore put forward before the U.S. Congressional Human Rights Caucus on 21 September 1987, his five-point counterproposal: (1) transformation of the whole of Tibet (Inner and Outer) into a zone of peace; (2) abandonment of China's population transfer policy which threatens the very existence of the Tibetans as a people; (3) respect for the Tibetan people's fundamental human rights and democratic freedoms; (4) restoration and protection of Tibet's natural environment and the abandonment of China's use of Tibet for the production of nuclear weapons and dumping of nuclear waste; (5) commencement of earnest negotiations on the future status of Tibet and of relations between Tibetan and Chinese peoples.

The Dalai Lama's first demand calls for some explanation because it touches Chinese security concerns. He argues that his concept of a peace zone is 'in keeping with Tibet's historical role as a peaceful and neutral Buddhist nation and buffer state separating the continent's great powers'. It would be also in keeping with King Birendra's proposal to proclaim Nepal a peace zone and with China's declared support for such a plan. However, the establishment of a peace zone in Inner Asia would require the withdrawal of Chinese troops and military installations from Tibet, which would enable India also to withdraw its troops and military installations from the Himalayan regions bordering Tibet. 'This would be achieved under an international agreement which would satisfy China's legitimate security needs and build trust among the Tibetan, Indian, Chinese and other peoples of the region.'

A year later, the Dalai Lama outlined at Strasbourg the 'Framework for Sino-Tibetan Negotiations' in which he made major political concessions to China. The PRC, he said, could remain responsible for Tibet's foreign policy and defence. But Tibet should have its own Foreign Affairs Bureau dealing with commerce, education, culture, religion, tourism, science, sports and other non-political activities. With regard to defence, China could have the right to maintain a restricted number of military installations in Tibet until such time as demilitarization and neutralization could be achieved through a regional peace conference and international agreement.

As far as the Dalai Lama is concerned, his Strasbourg Statement represents a compromise solution to the controversial Tibetan question. While eschewing persistent Tibetan claims to independence, it calls for a greater degree of domestic autonomy, which does not conflict with Chinese sovereignty or security concerns. However, he is quite explicit about the kind of political system he wishes to establish in Tibet, implying complete domestic autonomy. The Dalai Lama demands that 'the whole of Tibet, known as Cholka-sum (U-tsang, Kham and Amdo) should become a self-governing democratic political entity founded on law by agreement of the people ... in association with the People's Republic of China.' He specifies 'a self-governing democratic political entity' as one comprising a pop-ularly elected chief executive, a bicameral legislative branch, and an independent judicial system.

China did not issue a written reply to, or rebuttal of, the Tibetan leader's plan until February 1990, although the Chinese Embassy at New Delhi had earlier informed the Dalai Lama's representative, Tashi Wangdi, that neither the Five-Point Peace Plan nor the Strasbourg Statement could be the basis for negoti-ation. The main Chinese objection was the underlying assump-tion by the Dalai Lama that Tibet had historically been an independent state prior to the Communist takeover in 1950. This assertion is repeated three times in the 'Five-Point Peace Plan' and again three times in the Strasbourg Statement. The Dalai Lama's position as reflected in both the statements is that though Tibet was an independent nation prior to 1950, he now recognizes the reality of the Communist takeover which has made Tibet an integral part of China, and on that basis he would be willing to negotiate the future status of Tibet in association with China.

But that is not enough for Beijing whose leaders want not only the implicit recognition by Tibetans of the contemporary reality that Tibet is a part of China; it also wants the Dalai Lama's public acknowledgement that what China did in 1950 was a historically valid and ideologically justified action and that Tibet has always been part of China. China thus faces a dilemma in Tibet for although almost the whole world recog-nizes Tibet as part of China since 1950, many contend that Tibet was independent prior to the Communist takeover which makes the Communists feel guilty of an act of imperialism. This ideological accusation is unacceptable to Communists whose revolution was based more on anti-imperialism than anything else. That is why the Chinese leaders are paranoid about the slightest suggestion that Tibet in the past was independent. The Dalai Lama's references to Tibet's past independence are seen as 'a necessary part of his continuing plan of separation'.

We now turn to the two exploratory talks held in Beijing between the CCP Central Committee functionaries and the Dalai Lama's delegates in 1982 and 1984. These talks covered more concrete and specific issues which could become the agenda for future Sino-Tibetan negotiations if both parties show a serious interest in reaching a compromise on the Tibetan question.

The three-member Tibetan delegation in 1982 made three demands. Juchen Thubten Namgyal stated that the PRC had given a nine-point proposal to Taiwan and that China should grant even more to Tibet because of Tibet's unique historical status and special characteristics which warrant a separate treatment. The Chinese replied that Tibet had been liberated in 1950 and was now well on its way to socialism, whereas Taiwan is yet to be liberated and that 'Tibetans should not turn back the wheel of history.'

Having received a reply couched in Marxist-Leninist terms, the Tibetan side decided to argue in the Communists' own jargon. They referred to the Resolution of the First All-China Congress of Soviets on the Question of National Minorities (November 1931) to the effect that the Chinese Communist Party 'categorically and unconditionally recognizes the right of national minorities to self-determination. This means that in districts like Mongolia, Tibet, Xinjiang, Yunnan, Guizhou, and others, where the majority of the population belongs to non-Chinese nationalities, the toiling masses of these nationalities shall have [the] right to determine for themselves whether they wish to leave the Chinese Soviet Republic and create their own independent state, or whether they wish to join the Union of Soviet Republics, or form an autonomous area inside the Chinese Soviet Republic.' Juchen Thubten Namgyal urged that the PRC should respect the Tibetan people's right to national self-determination. The Chinese reply was brief and frank: 'We (CCP) were a child at that time but now we have grown up.'

The Tibetan delegates rounded off the discussions with a

realistic proposition that Beijing should consider the reincorporation of Kham and Amdo (Inner Tibet) into the Tibet Autonomous Region (Outer Tibet) – that is to say the reunification of the entire Tibetan-speaking people on the Tibetan plateau into one administrative unit, whose status would be subsequently negotiated between Beijing and the Dalai Lama. The Chinese reply was that this was administratively impossible since the territory covered by Inner and Outer Tibet is so vast. However, there appeared to be no consensus among the Chinese leaders. Hu Yaobang told Gyalo Thondup in 1981, 'this is a new idea which needs to be considered'. Ulan Fu also supported the Tibetan demand when he recalled that the late Zhou Enlai assured the Tibetan delegates to the 17-Point Agreement in 1951 that the question of reunification of Inner and Outer Tibet 'would be separately looked into'.

On 24 October 1984, the same Tibetan delegation conveyed their views on various subjects to Jiang Ping, deputy director of the CCP Central Committee, United Front Work Department in Beijing. The Tibetan delegates complained that the recently arrested Tibetan dissidents must be released so as to create the proper atmosphere for the negotiations. They suggested that more fact-finding Tibetan delegations should be allowed to visit Tibet. They declared that the Dalai Lama did not accept the Chinese five-point proposal and reiterated some of the basic Tibetan demands, such as the reunification of Inner and Outer Tibet, high degree of autonomy in association with China, and withdrawal of Chinese troops, thereby paving the way to making Tibet a zone of peace, etc.

On 28 October 1984, Jiang Ping conveyed to the Tibetan delegates the Chinese official view on what they considered to be the central issues. The Central Committee welcomed the Dalai Lama's return either to settle permanently or as a visit to China. It acknowledged that Sino-Tibetan dialogue over the years had promoted mutual understanding. Although there were differences of opinion on certain issues, such differences would not be an obstacle to further visits and exchange of views. With regard to the Dalai Lama's status upon his return, Jiang reiterated Hu Yaobang's five-point proposal and in a subsequent interview with a Japanese reporter, Hu stated that the Dalai Lama's status as a religious figure, as a member of nobility and as a popular historical character of Tibet would be guaranteed; and if he proved himself to be a Chinese patriot, the Dalai Lama would enjoy equal or similar status as the Panchen Lama. Next, Jiang Ping went to great lengths to elaborate and 'prove' that Tibet had been an integral part of China since the thirteenth century AD and that the Tibetan exiles must accept that premise as the unalterable condition for Sino-Tibetan dialogue. Finally, Jiang Ping indirectly reminded the Tibetan delegates that they should concentrate on the question of 'Tibetan happiness' as the Dalai Lama indicated before.

On 23 September 1988, the Chinese Embassy in India delivered a formal message to the Dalai Lama's representative in New Delhi:

'We welcome the Dalai Lama to have talks with the Central Government at any time. The talks may be held in Beijing, Hong Kong or any of our embassies or consulates abroad. If the Dalai Lama finds it inconvenient to conduct talks at these places, he may choose any place he wishes. But there is one condition, that is no foreigners should be involved. We are ready to designate one official with a certain rank to have direct dialogue with the Dalai Lama.

'There are two points which need to be clarified: (1) We have never recognized 'the Kashag Government' which has all along indulged in the activities of the independence of Tibet. We will not receive any delegation or fact-finding group designated by the 'Kashag [Tibetan cabinet] Government'. (2) The 'new proposal' put forward by the Dalai Lama in Strasbourg cannot be considered as the basis for talks with the Central Government because it has not at all relinquished the concept of the 'independence of Tibet'. If the Dalai Lama is sincere in improving relations with the Central Government and really concerned for the happiness of the Tibetan people, for the economic development and prosperity of the Tibetan nationality, he should truly give up the 'idea of independence'. The Dalai Lama should place himself in the great family of the unified motherland and join the Central Government, the People's Government of Tibet and the Tibetan people in discussing the major policies concerning Tibet.'

To demonstrate that the Tibetans meant official bilateral talks, a deputy minister of the Tibetan government, Ala Jigme Lhundup, delivered, on 25 October 1988, the Tibetan reply to the Chinese message of 23 September. The 'Tibetan Government in exile' suggested that they were willing to hold the first round of talks with the Chinese government in Geneva in January 1989. 'Deputy Minister' Ala could not meet the Chinese ambassador at New Delhi and so delivered the message to Councillor Zhao Xingsong. Zhao asked Ala whether the Dalai Lama would participate in the talks, to which Ala replied negatively. However, the 'Tibetan government had earlier announced the formation of a six-member negotiating team' of which Ala was a member. The Chinese councillor also inquired if a Dutch lawyer was a member of the team. The Tibetan minister replied that he was 'one of the three aides assisting the team and not one of the negotiators'.

Zhao's questions are pertinent because the Tibetan refusal to conform to them violated the procedural conditions laid down by China in its message of 23 September 1988. This was precisely what vice-minister of State Nationalities Affairs Commission, Chen Xin, stated in November 1988. He said the Dalai Lama was 'insincere' towards the proposed talks in Geneva because the Lama was not going to attend the talks personally. 'We have never recognized the government-in-exile headed by the Dalai Lama. That is why we will only hold talks with the Dalai Lama himself and will not hold talks with a so-called "government" delegation sent by the Dalai Lama.' Chen also pointed out that the inclusion of a foreigner in the Tibetan delegation 'contravenes the principle adhered to by the Central People's Government'.

Four months later at the second session of the Seventh National People's Congress, Ngapoi Ngawang Jigme, a former leading Tibetan aristocrat and official, and subsequently vice-chairman of the National People's Congress Standing Committee, repeated Chen Xin's statement.

On 12 April 1989, the Bureau of His Holiness The Dalai Lama (New Delhi) issued public clarifications on the three objections raised by China. The statement said, ...the delay in the commencement of the negotiation has been on account of the Chinese intransigence on three points: (1) independence cannot be the basis for the negotiations; (2) the negotiating team must represent His Holiness the Dalai Lama; and (3) there should be no foreign participation in the negotiation. It explained the Dalai Lama's position as follows:

'We have conveyed to the Chinese government on num-erous occasions through their embassy in New Delhi that (1) the framework for negotiations proposed by His Holiness the Dalai Lama refers specifically to the positive notion of association with the People's Republic of China; (2) the Tibetan negotiating team has been appointed by His Holiness the Dalai Lama and it is within His right to appoint whosoever He considers compe-tent to represent Him; and (3) there is no foreign participation in the negotiating team. There are both Tibetan and non-Tibetan advisers to the team. It is quite natural for the team to seek advice from qualified persons regardless of their nationalities.'

It is not very clear whether the Chinese authorities had accepted the Tibetan clarifications, because the Dalai Lama cut off contacts with China after the imposition of martial law in Lhasa on 7 March 1989; the contacts have not yet been resumed. However, just before the Chinese students' pro-democracy demonstration was crushed, Beijing sent a message to the Dalai Lama through its embassy in New Delhi. The message said that although the Chinese government disagreed with the Dalai

Lama's Strasbourg proposal as a basis for negotiation, 'at the same time they still insist they want [a] dialogue'. Being a seasoned politician, the Dalai Lama preferred to join the global wave of condemnation rather than profit from the opportunity offered by Beijing.

It would be misleading to suggest that there was some sort of consensus among the Chinese leaders with regard to the Tibetan question; a considerable divergence of opinion is discernible on the issue, reflecting perhaps a hardliner-pragmatic divide. For example, according to the former CCP general secretary Zhao Ziyang and writer Sha Zhou, there was no question of a dialogue with the Dalai Lama; the Lama should have returned to China and the condition for his return was that he should stop working for the independence of Tibet. On the other hand, for Deng Xiaoping and Hu Yaobang the Tibetan question must be resolved through negotiation with the Tibetan leader. Ngapoi Ngawang Jigme also hinted that the Dalai Lama's Strasbourg Statement was a more acceptable proposition than the previous one at Washington because at Strasbourg the Dalai Lama said that he was 'willing to talk to the Central Government of China and allow the Central Government to take care of Tibet's diplomatic and defence issues'. It should be noted that most Chinese leaders had not made such a differentiation.

However, in view of the ongoing dialogue between China and the Dalai Lama, the top Tibetan cadres had to wait for the Centre's 'line' on the alleged Dalai involvement in the Lhasa disturbances. Thus, when *Renmin Ribao* (3 October 1987) charged that the Lhasa incidents were 'instigated and plotted by the Dalai clique' and that the Lama 'has openly advocated the independence of Tibet in the USA and in other nations', the Tibetan cadres in positions of power at Lhasa immediately convened public meetings to condemn the Dalai Lama and the demonstrators.

We may, therefore, infer that the top local cadres in Lhasa, both Tibetan and Han, evidently used the alleged Dalai involvement in the pro-independence demonstrations to argue against the centre's pragmatic policy of reconciliation with the Dalai Lama to defend their class interest. This further strengthened the position of hardliners (operative since mid-1986) within the central leadership in Beijing and complicated the two-line policy debate which probably continued up to 1989. This largely explains the long delay in China's response to the Strasbourg Statement and the eventual emergence of a hardline policy by February 1990. This policy indicates that the hardliners, both in Lhasa and Beijing, had successfully used the alleged Dalai Lama's hand in the pro-independence demonstrations of 1987 and 1988 to prove their point that the Lama had violated Deng Xiaoping's condition for dialogue: that of no discussion of Tibetan independence. If the Dalai Lama was in any way behind the pro-independence demonstration in Lhasa at all, his intention might not have been independence per se but to increase pressure on China to make it concede some of his political demands. But this intention might have been deliberately misinterpreted by the hardliners as a demand for independence on the part of the Dalai Lama which indirectly compelled Beijing to adopt a hardline policy.

In its essential features, the Dalai Lama's concept of 'associate status' resembles Beijing's one country two systems formula designed for Taiwan, Hong Kong and Macau. Both concepts surrender sovereignty to the PRC but retain a large measure of domestic autonomy including the right to establish or continue capitalist democracy. In fact a Tibetan delegate, Lodo Gyari, to the 1982 exploratory talks demanded the 'one country two systems' formula as promised to Taiwan, but the Chinese side rejected this on the ground that the case of Tibet was different; China's relations with Tibet were determined by the 17-Point Agreement signed between Beijing and Lhasa in 1951. But the Tibetans asserted that they were compelled to repudiate the agreement because it was signed 'under duress' and because the Chinese authorities in Tibet betrayed 'every clause of the agreement'.

As we have seen, the Dalai Lama's representatives in China had been quite flexible on a number of issues and perhaps understandably so because they lacked any bargaining power; but they had been most persistent on the question of reunification of Inner and Outer Tibet. First raised by Gyalo Thondup to Hu Yaobang in 1981, it was repeated by the Tibetan delegates both during the 1982 and 1984 talks in Beijing. The Dalai Lama made the same demand in his Strasbourg and Washington statements and the Tibetans were likely to continue to press the issue, because common language, religion, culture and race bound the people in Inner and Outer Tibet as one identifiable ethnic group. Moreover, the Dharamsala power elites, including the Dalai Lama, were from Kham and Amdo who would try their best to ensure that whatever benefits they could get from China also extended to their homeland.

The Chinese authorities had considered certain issues such as the Tibetan demands for more domestic autonomy and reunification as being within the scope of further discussion, even though initially they had rejected such demands. Nevertheless, they have refused to even touch certain other issues such as independence, national self-determination, buffer state, peace zone, etc., viewing the raising of such issues as a clear violation of Deng Xiaoping's cardinal preconditions for a dialogue. They have also refused to reply to the Dalai Lama's five-point demands such as the cessation of Han population transfer to Tibet, nuclear activities on the Tibetan plateau, respect for human rights and democratic freedom, etc.

However, the Dalai Lama's proposals of 1987 and 1988 were well received by the international community. The Nobel Peace Prize in 1989 had indicated Western if not world public opinion. The Norwegian Nobel Committee chairman had stated, while awarding the prize: 'It would be difficult to cite any historical example of a minority's struggle to secure its rights, in which a more conciliatory attitude to the adversary has been adopted than in the case of Dalai Lama.' Between 1987 and 1991 the U.S.

Congress passed six resolutions on Tibet; the European
Parliament two resolutions in 1987 and 1989; the Council of
Europe in 1988; the West German Bundestag in 1987; and the
Italian Parliament in 1989. International conventions and hear-
ings on Tibet were held in Bonn in April 1989, in New Delhi in
August 1989, in Tokyo in May 1990, and in London in July 1990.

The Dalai Lama's proposals received wide support because
they represented the most realistic means by which to establish
Tibet's separate identity and restore the fundamental rights of
the Tibetan people while accommodating China's vital
interests. The solution he sought was close to what Chinese dissidents called a 'Federal Constitution with confederal characteristics', even though he never uses terms like 'federation' or
'confederation'. He prefers the term 'union' or 'association'
which, he says, 'can only come about voluntarily, when there is
satisfactory benefit to all parties concerned' and cites the
example of the European Community as the closest to his vision
of China-Tibet relations. However, on the whole, most of the
Dalai Lama's demands made in 1988 have been more or less met
by the overseas Chinese drafted Federal Constitution for China,
which we shall discuss later.

The Dalai Lama's 1988 proposal, even though it is a carefully drafted document, raises a couple of questions. He
implicitly proposes that a regional peace conference on demilitarization and neutralization of Tibet should be held *after* the
establishment of a 'genuine union or association'. If past
experience is any indication, then this sequential procedure
might not work. It has to be an international package in which
Sino-Tibetan negotiations on the status of Tibet and the neutralization of Inner Asia by regional powers proceed side by side.
(This is where one sees a constructive role for the UN with its
wide mandate in conflict resolution in Tibet.) For as I shall try to
show later, in a larger sense, Tibet in the modern era has become
a tragic victim of intense Sino-Indian strategic rivalry in Inner
Asia and the Cis-Himalayas; and unless this rivalry is resolved

through a mutually agreed neutralization of Tibet, no lasting solution to the Tibetan question can be found. Otherwise strategic imperatives of China and India will transform Tibet into an active arena of power games that plagued Inner Asia in the late nineteenth and early twentieth century.

My second comment concerns the role of the modern educated class in the making of a future Tibet, which the Dalai Lama ignores. The Dalai Lama's strategy is that the people of Tibet or their representatives 'will prepare Tibet's new constitution on the basis of various drafts prepared in exile' under his supervision. He knows that his charismatic influence among the Tibetans would ensure the acceptance of his drafts. The only 'critical' role in this exercise is given to the so-called 'leaders of Cholka-sum'. The Dalai Lama writes, 'I shall constitute a small committee of leaders from Cholka-sum. ... This committee, in consultation with the officials of various departments throughout Tibet, will summon an emergency meeting of the deputies representing administrative divisions no smaller than a district.'

The Chinese Communists, as a matter of policy and ideology, have strictly prohibited the emergence of alternative leaders who might compete with the Party monopoly of power. And it is unfortunate but equally true that the Dalai Lama in exile has tended to discourage the emergence of alternative leaders, unless officially approved by him. However, both in exile and inside Tibet, one observes the emergence of a modern educated class that is independent of Communist or lamaist domination. Inside Tibet the colonial administration and propaganda apparatus have brought about an educated, bilingual class that is becoming increasingly critical of Chinese domination. In exile too, thanks to Indian and Western patronage of modern education among the refugees, there is a growing number of free thinking young Tibetans. It is tragic that the Dalai Lama sees no role for such modern educated Tibetans in his vision of a future Tibet in association with China.

While the Chinese Communist leaders have more or less rejected the Dalai Lama's reasonable proposals, some leading Chinese dissidents abroad and Chinese intellectuals from Hong Kong and Taiwan have, as stated before, responded positively to the proposals. We know that such dissidents might not come to power in Beijing in the near future. However, I believe their *new thinking* on the Tibetan question might become a significant pointer to the future shape of things in China-Tibet relations. This means that the same dissidents who drafted the constitution might not come to power in China. Nor does it imply that their draft constitution might be accepted *in toto* in post-Deng China. But the *ideas* contained in the draft constitution of the 'Federal Republic of China' and Tibet's place in it might fall on fertile ground in the context of future democratic developments in China.

The biggest illusion that the last generation of Maoist elites entertain is that they can control the political and social consequences of their economic reforms. They delude themselves into thinking that their desirable economic changes would have no 'undesirable' social and political consequences in China. A study of the Marxist theory might help the orthodox Communists to understand what is in store for them. Marx said, 'The changes in the economic foundation lead sooner or later to the transformation of the whole immense superstructure.' In other words, economic changes will necessarily bring social change. And such 'undesirable' changes cannot, in the long run, be localized in 'Special Economic Zones' or insulated from the larger Chinese society.

As they grant more and more freedom to enterprises and as they increase the number of Special Economic Zones, the Maoist elites will realize, impelled by economic necessity, the importance of creating and expanding the socio-political conditions that are conducive to the development of freedom and multi-party democracy. Their intention may not be to grant freedom to their subjects; their primary aim is to promote speedy industrial development but that, in turn, necessitates certain favourable conditions for democratic evolution. In this way, democracy in China might come almost by default.

In any case, the status quo cannot be maintained for long. Economic reforms, introduced with such enthusiasm by Dengist power elites, generate their own dynamics of social change beyond the control of even 'smart' Maoists. The result might well be a slow but systematic undermining of the ideological legitimacy of the CCP's claim to power monopoly. Such an evolutionary revolution seems much more certain than any intra-elite conflict or counter-elite revolt in China.

The assumption underlying the preceding hypothesis is this: the economic reforms which Deng initiated are bound to breed a new class of Chinese who will have ideas other than what the party propagates on various issues. Their careers and lifestyles might be bound up with the future of freedom and democracy in China. Thus, they may be more amenable to democratic ideas than the Communist Party dictatorship and its decaying ideology and guided more by economic rationality than the Han glory in such emotional issues as Tibet. A deprogrammed and democratized generation of Chinese might come to realize that China's continued occupation of Tibet results not in Han glory but the reverse; not in economic benefits either to the Tibetans or the Hans but a waste of scarce resources. This is neither impossible nor improbable. The Chinese dissidents' stand on various issues affecting China, particularly their stand on China-Tibet relations, reflects a new thinking of a post-Communist critical generation that is in the making. That is why I am more interested in what the overseas Chinese dissidents have to say on the future of Tibet.

Dalai and Dissidents' Future Visions

On 31 January 1994, a group of Chinese intellectuals from the PRC, Taiwan and Hong Kong released a 'proposed draft' of a

'Constitution of Federal Republic of China'. They described it as 'a federal system with confederal characteristics'. The confederal characteristics refer to the special Autonomous Statehood given to Inner Mongolia, Taiwan, Tibet, Xinjiang, Ningxia and Guangxi (Article 28). The Autonomous Provinces and Cities, which fall within China proper are 'more closely tied to the federal Republic, in a relationship similar to that found in a normal federal republic'. It is this ethnic sensitivity that characterizes this draft constitution.

Article 30 declares that each Autonomous State makes its own constitution. Each Autonomous Province, Autonomous Municipality or Special Region makes its own Basic Law. And any power that is not constitutionally vested in the federal government is exercised by the individual Autonomous States, Autonomous Provinces, Autonomous Municipalities, Special Regions and the entire citizenry (Article 29).

Besides the power to make its own Constitution, each Autonomous State has the right to sign non-military agreements with foreign countries, and the right to make its own decisions about joining international organizations and setting up representative offices in foreign countries (Article 33). Article 39 is exclusively devoted to Tibet:

The Autonomous State of Tibet is a national nature conservation area, where the testing of nuclear, chemical and biological weapons and the storage of nuclear wastes are prohibited.

The Autonomous State of Tibet is financially independent and not required to pay federal tax. The Autonomous State of Tibet has the right to set up its state court of final appeal.

The position of the Autonomous State of Tibet will be reviewed 25 years after this Constitution is promulgated. The review will be in the form of a referendum by the citizens of the state and not subject to Article 36 of this Constitution.

The draft Constitution for a Federal China marks a serious new thinking among the emancipated Chinese intellectuals on the larger question of the power equations between the Han and the minorities in China, which is likely to gain increasing acceptance among the Han public, and which the non-Han social groups would welcome. The Chinese dissidents, living as they do in free societies, have the courage to question the Maoist concept of a unitary state which has degenerated into Han hegemony. They are also far-sighted enough to recognize the hidden forces of history and society, namely the ethnicity that sharply differentiates the Tibetans, Turks or Mongols from the Hans, who through the tyranny of their majority, have dominated the minority ethnic groups since 1949, and reduced the latter to minorities in their own homelands.

The proposed Chinese federation envisages a finely tuned hierarchy of political entities for different regional and ethnic groups, taking into account the politico-economic factors, and their historical identities in pre-modern Asian history. In this sense, the authors of the federal constitution may be right in their declaration in the Preamble: 'The basic principle used in dividing the Federal Republic into its component elements is: Respect for the status quo and respect for history.' In other words, Chinese dissidents see an urgent need not only to deconstruct the post-1949 Communist history in the PRC but also to decentralize the centre-periphery power relations. For what the Communists had done in the name of 'liberation' and 'revolution', 'ideology' and 'progress' has resulted in Han expansionism and Han hegemony in non-Han territories, where non-Han ethnic groups enjoyed complete autonomy or even independence for centuries.

In particular, the draft federal constitution makes special provisions for Tibet, as warranted by her history and culture. In so doing, the constitution meets most of the Dalai Lama's basic demands made in 1988, including the right of Tibet to make its own Constitution (Article 30), to sign non-military agreements with foreign states, as well as the right to join international organizations and set up representative offices in foreign countries (Article 33). Besides, Tibet, Taiwan and Hong Kong are given the right to restrict external population movement into their respective states/regions (Article 10). And Article 39 makes Tibet virtually a nuclear-free zone. But by far the most significant concession given to the Tibetan people is that they can, in the form of a referendum, decide, after staying in the proposed federation for 25 years, whether to secede from or remain within the Chinese federation (Article 39).

The draft constitution raises a few questions which must be discussed in order to find a lasting solution to the conflict in Tibet that is satisfactory to all parties concerned. The pioneering authors do not specify what areas are covered in their usage of the term 'Tibet'. Do they mean only the Tibet Autonomous Region (TAR) as created by the Communists since 1951? Or do they include Kham and Amdo as well within the TAR, as claimed by the Dalai Lama? If they accept only the Communist definition of 'Tibet', they exclude nearly two-thirds of the Tibetan population from what they envisage as the Autonomous State of Tibet. Even according to the 1982 census, out of a total Tibetan population of 38,85,500 in the PRC, 9,45,000 Tibetans are in Sichuan; 7,50,500 in Qinghai; 3,05,000 in Gansu; and 95,000 in Yunnan.

If this is so, then would it be fair and just to exclude the majority of the Tibetans from the Autonomous State of Tibet? Though these people are called Khampas and Amdowas for purposes of internal differentiation within Tibetan society, they have many fundamental ethnic, linguistic and cultural features in common with the rest of Tibet. We know there are Tibetan culture areas in the Cis-Himalayas and elsewhere, but the point of departure is that the Khampas and Amdowas have, since 1949 increasingly identified with Lhasa as the epicentre of their culture and loyalty. They were the first to revolt against the Chinese takeover. Therefore, from the perspective of conflict resolution in Tibet the Khampas' and Amdowas' problems have to be addressed, and tackled within the framework of the Autonomous State of Tibet.

Another set of questions raised by the draft constitution are the terms and conditions under which a referendum in Tibet would be held 25 years after the proposed constitution comes into effect. On the surface, the idea of a referendum appears to be a courageous step to determine the consent and consensus of the governed. However, a closer scrutiny reveals a couple of lacunae. Article 39 gives the right to vote in the referendum to the 'citizens' in the state and not primarily to the Tibetan population, who by virtue of their different cultural identity and historical status, need the referendum the most. The unstated calculation is that after 25 years the present Dalai Lama would have passed away and the continuing Han population transfer to Tibetan areas would have created an unprecedented demographic transformation in Tibet that would maintain the status quo even in the eventuality of a referendum.

If the Dalai Lama's figures are correct, at present there are six million Tibetans and seven million Chinese in Tibet. With the increasing population transfer, the Chinese majority in Tibet will be even greater. This makes the proposed referendum a meaningless exercise, not a case of democratic self-determination, but only a constitutional formality. It would simply empower the majority ethnic group (the Hans) to vote for the status quo and deny the sons of the soil their right to self-determination.

The simple fact is that in most traditional societies, modern democratic concepts like election, self-determination or even referendum tend to run along cultural and ethnic lines, and are not based on ideology. The general will, in such culture-saturated cases, resides in a shared culture which represents the collective conscience of a particular ethnic group; and the social contract is made possible by a high degree of social consensus engendered by a collectively shared culture.

Finally, the validity of Clause (1) of Article 31, which empowers the federal government alone to declare war, presumably in any part of the federation, is debatable. This is particularly so in the case of Tibet which, according to Article 39, is 'a national nature conservation area, where the testing of nuclear, chemical and biological weapons and the storage of nuclear wastes are prohibited'. This is exactly what the Dalai Lama, in his 1987 address to the U.S. Congressional Human Rights Caucus meant when he called for the transformation of 'the whole of Tibet, including the eastern provinces of Kham and Amdo' into 'a zone of *ahimsa*', a Sanskrit term used to mean a state of peace and non-violence. This sentiment was again echoed in his 1988 address to the European Parliament when he called for the 'conversion of Tibet into a zone of peace, a sanctuary in which humanity and nature can live together in harmony'.

If there is such a consensus between the Dalai Lama and the Chinese intellectuals who framed the draft constitution of a 'federal China', the monopolistic power to make war should not rest only with the federal government, which most probably would be dominated by the Hans. The proposed Autonomous State of Tibet must have a say in this vital issue which perhaps concerns the Tibetans more than other ethnic groups, Tibet being one of the most strategic regions in Asia. The answer may well be, as I shall argue, complete neutralization of Tibet by the regional powers concerned, including China, and possibly endorsed by the United Nations.

Tibet's geography has exercised considerable influence on the evolution of her peculiar polity and unique culture. Her relative isolation from countries around her, surrounded on all sides by mountainous ranges but with sufficient culture contacts with neighbouring civilizations, ensured an independent cultural development upto 1950. However, her geostrategic location tended to periodically invite foreign interference in her antiquated political system in pre-modern times and more frequently in our times, leading to the current Communist takeover.

During the Tang dynasty (AD 618-756) the Tibetan empire in Central Asia had posed a security threat to China. But it was not so much the matrimonial alliances with the Tibetan King Songtsen Gampo that brought peace to Inner Asia. Introduced in the eighth century, Buddhism, gradually but systematically, transformed a warrior nation into a peaceful community. Tibet then ceased to be a security threat to the Chinese empire.

However, the various Mongol tribes continued to pose a security threat to China throughout the medieval period. It is in this context that the Chinese imperial court began to see a new role for Buddhist Tibet. The high lamas of Tibet, through their enormous spiritual influence among the Mongols, were perceived as peace-makers and peace-keepers in China's relation with Buddhist Central Asia. Therefore, most of the Chinese emperors made it a point to cultivate the friendship of the charismatic lamas of Tibet. This remained the policy so long as Central Asia continued to be a major source of threat to the Chinese security system.

But with the establishment of the British empire in South Asia, China's threat perceptions underwent a major change. In an era dominated by Western colonial and imperial powers, the Mongol warriors of Central Asia ceased to be a danger to Chinese national security. Increasingly, Chinese security became preoccupied with what Chinese radicals called Western imperialism, and more specifically in relation to Tibet, with the expanding British power in India, and its active interest in Inner Asia.

British interest in Tibet began in the 1770s, primarily as a trade outlet and as a gateway to further trade in north-west China. But soon they discovered that trade prospects in Inner Asia were poor in view of the difficult terrain and lack of communication. This, however, did not rule out British strategic and political interest in Tibet because as the colonial officials repeatedly emphasized, British India shared over 2000 miles of border with Tibet and not directly with China proper.

By the 1870s, British interest in Tibet was more strategic than commercial. With the commencement of the 'Great Game' in

Central Asia, British activities in Tibet fell just short of colonization, giving rise to Chinese suspicion and insecurity. British agents, disguised as explorers, adventurers or missionaries, deepened Chinese suspicions about Tibet. In particular, the 1904 Younghusband Expedition sensitized the Chinese government and the public to the strategic importance of Tibet as never before. Thus, by the turn of this century the traditional Chinese image of Tibet as a deeply spiritual realm was transformed into one of a high security region. In this transformation, which had fatal consequences for Tibet, the British colonial officials, though unintentionally, played no small role. It is strategic concerns and defence that now dominate the current Chinese thinking on Tibet.

We know that both Jawaharlal Nehru and Indira Gandhi had dismissed ideas of a buffer zone and balance of power as outmoded imperialist scheming. But given the favourable opportunities and in the absence of Chinese military might in Inner Asia, Nehru would have pursued a modified policy towards Tibet, as an autonomous buffer state, like the British did. This was in fact the substance of Nehru's Tibet policy from 1947 to 1954. The 1962 Sino-Indian war, the Nathula border clashes in 1967 and the near-conflict situation in Sumdo-rong Chu Valley in 1987 inevitably questioned the fundamental assumptions of Nehru's post-1954 policy of *Hindi-Chini-Bhai-Bhai*, driving the Indian political elite to rediscover the British policy towards Tibet.

There has been an enormous arms build-up on both sides of the once tranquil Himalayas. The Indian Ministry of Defence sources estimated the PLA strength in Tibet alone to be 130,000 to 180,000. The Chinese sources estimated in mid-1980s that India deployed 10 Mountain Divisions, 32 Infantry Brigades and 10 Mountain Artilleries along the Himalayas. This mutual arms build-up was preceded, as in Tibet, or simultaneously accompanied by extensive strategic road-building on both sides of the Himalayas. Such drastic transformation of a traditional peace region into one of the most dangerous conflict zones in the world has taken place because the autonomous state that had historically functioned as a buffer between the two Asian giants disappeared after 1950.

The crux of the rivalry between the PRC and India is that both consider Tibet to be strategically important to their national security. If India dominates Tibet (as the British rulers did up to 1947), the Chinese feel insecure and threatened. Conversely, if China dominates Tibet (as the PRC has been doing since 1950), the Indians feel their whole northern security system is open to external danger. This can only be resolved through the neutralization of the contested country – Tibet – so that mutual tensions may be reduced, as Britain and Russia did in their bilateral treaty in 1907. Such a treaty on the neutraliza-tion of Tibet should now be signed by China and India, as the two great Asian powers with equal interest in Tibet.

If the pattern of Central Asian geopolitics suggests a Sino-Indian agreement to neutralize Tibet, what does Sino-Tibetan history have to say? What is the actual historical status of China in Tibet as it evolved over the ages? Have the Communist mas-ters overstepped the limits of Chinese role in Tibet? And what sort of structure does history suggest in the near future for Tibet? We have raised more questions than we can answer. Our intention is to make some tentative generalizations, based on my reading of Sino-Tibetan history.

A survey of the periods of Tibetan history which have a bearing on Sino-Tibetan relations, allows us to draw some tentative conclusions. During the Kingless Period (842-1247) lasting for 405 years and the Hegemonic Struggle Period (1350-1642) lasting 92 years, China displayed a political indifference to the happenings in Tibet. There was no Chinese intervention, nor were even tributary relations conducted regularly. This is surprising in view of the current Chinese claim that Tibet has always been an integral part of China. During these two periods Tibet was not dependent on China.

However, Sino-Tibetan relations were more regular during

the two periods of Lama rule – the Sakya, 1249-1358 and the Gelukpa, 1642-1911. This tends to support the Tibetan historians' claim that Sino-Tibetan relations were essentially between a lay patron and the priests, or more specifically, between the Sakya Lamas and Mongol emperors, between the Dalai Lamas and Manchu emperors.

In short, in her recorded history, Tibet was independent for 281 years (600-842 and 1911-50); neither dependent on nor independent from China for 497 years (842-1247 and 1350-1642); and dependent on Mongol and Manchu empires for 378 years (1249-1358 and 1642-1911). Thus, we may say that the history of Sino-Tibetan relations is ambiguous. But even during her dependency periods, Tibet enjoyed a high degree of genuine, domestic autonomy that most fair-minded historians of any persuasion would not deny. Of course a complex historical phenomenon like the Tibet-China relationship cannot be reduced to a matter of arithmetic. But one hopes that these numbers will help to persuade readers of the argument set out here.

What did this emperor-lama relationship imply? The core of this relationship demanded a *symbolic* act, periodically, of subordination by the Lama or his envoy to the Son of Heaven (emperor) as the military protector of a non-coercive regime which the Lama in question headed in Tibet. And the tributary relationship, through which this periodical symbolic act of subordination was maintained, was characterized by ceremonialism, not by political domination. Such superordinate-subordinate relations were not confined to Tibet alone, though the priest-patron relationship was peculiarly Sino-Tibetan; symbolic unequal relations were the ideological basis of Confucian foreign relations. They did not recognize the modern Western concept of legal equality between sovereign states.

However, this symbolic acceptance of a superordinate-subordinate ceremonial relationship did not, on the whole, entail: (1) Chinese interference in Tibetan domestic affairs; (2) Chinese army presence in Tibet (except when requested for by

lama rulers); (3) Han colonization of any part of Tibetan territory; and (4) integration of Tibet into China, either politically,
economically, or culturally. In short, pre-1950 Tibet enjoyed
complete and genuine autonomy.

In the name of ideology and Marxist mission in Tibet (which
has degenerated into Han expansionism and Han hegemony),
Chinese Communists have distorted the pattern of Sino-Tibetan
history. It is now time for the Communists to respect the verdict
of history and restructure the centre-periphery power relations
on a democratic and durable basis. The Communist justification
or rationale in the post-Communist era has become invalid.

While the Chinese imperial court at Beijing and the Tibetan
ruling class at Lhasa maintained formal relations, there was no
people-to-people contact except near Sino-Tibetan border areas
such as in parts of Amdo and Kham. This means that throughout Tibetan history, Tibetan cultural identity and civil society,
which are fundamentally different from those of Hans (or any
other ethnic groups in Central Asia), remained sovereign, independent of any external influence or intervention for nearly
1000 years. It is this informal but effective sovereignty of
Tibetan cultural identity and civil society that constitutes the
psychological core of Tibetan opposition to the Communist
takeover and subsequent integration with China. Therefore, we
observe a close correlation between popular folk aspirations for
Tibetan independence and the cultural sovereignty that ordinary Tibetans psychologically feel in and outside Tibet.
Independence (free from Chinese influence or interference) has
been what they used to enjoy, despite the domination and
exploitation by the Tibetan governing class.

But the cultural and civil sovereignty that common Tibetans
feel, as warranted by their unique culture and way of life, has
been tempered by the patterns of political history, dominated
by the power elites of China and Tibet. That is why since 1950
the Dalai Lama and the Tibetan ruling class, on the whole, have
compromised on the question of Tibetan independence, while

negotiating with the Chinese overlords. The Dalai Lama's Strasbourg Statement, in which he surrendered Tibet's defence and foreign policy to the PRC but demanded genuine and complete autonomy was a reasonable solution which is basically backed by the Chinese dissidents' federal constitution. It is a realistic compromise between the high expectations of the Tibetan masses for complete independence and the Han imperial power that completely denies it.

Our attempt to seek clues to conflict resolution in Tibet from the history of pre-modern Sino-Tibetan relations, does not lead to much fresh discovery. Our findings tend to be largely congruent with future political structures for Tibet as proposed by the Dalai Lama in 1988, and endorsed and elaborated by the federal Constitution of China in 1994. However, our assessment is an objective reflection of the regional geopolitics which dictates the conditions for such an outcome. Without the neutralization of Tibet as a precondition, neither an autonomous democratic Tibet in association with China nor an 'Autonomous State of Tibet' can last long. For the geostrategic location of Tibet (equally important both to China and India) invites, willy-nilly, external interference in one context or another, thus engendering suspicion, tension and an arms race in Inner Asia and the Cis-Himalayas. In other words, without the neutralization of Tibet, the dialectics of her geopolitics might propel her to either Chinese or Indian domination. Tibet thus finds herself in her current predicament: a victim of the Sino-Indian strategic rivalry in Inner Asia.

In short, while the sovereignty of Tibetan cultural identity and civil society *vis-a-vis* the Hans is clear, the history of Sino-Tibetan relations is ambiguous. This ambiguity springs from Tibet's uncertain political status between independence and dependency. But even such a limited sovereignty cannot be achieved without understanding the dialectics of regional geopolitics. These indicate the actual underlying conditions within which Tibet's future structures of peace will have to operate.

One of the major obstacles to ethnic conflict resolution is the rigid orthodoxy of state sovereignty that still resists creative flexibility. The beleaguered monoethnic state nervously quibbles over arcane legal implications of ethnic demands to its jealously-guarded sovereignty. It still insists on antiquated diplomatic protocols, all of which freeze any potentially creative solutions into counterproductive orthodoxies or even worse – merciless repression of non-dominant ethnic groups. The state behaves and acts in ways that feed on its obsession with 'sovereignty' while society, which ought to be the basis of state sovereignty, burns and tears itself apart.

It does not seem to me that even in the post-cold-war era the nation state is entirely obsolete, as the current advocates of globalization would have us believe. But what is clear is that the monoethnic states should not be too obsessed with the 19th century idea of sovereignty if they sincerely desire to resolve ethnic conflicts within their territorial boundaries. For ethnic conflicts are often belated multi-dimensional democratic struggles launched by isolated groups who were previously cut off from the mainstream of historical developments but who are now resurging in an age of multi-party democracy and economic globalization. They demand autonomy within ethnic perimeters as the most effective means of achieving their group rights.

Tibet Between Nuclear India and Nuclear China

Tibet looms large in Sino-Indian relations and politics, even after 45 years of Chinese occupation because of its intimate connection with the strategic interests of both parties. It is a manifestation of continuing Sino-Indian strategic rivalry in inner Asia and the Himalayas. The crux of the Sino-Indian strategic rivalry is this: if the Chinese power elite consider Tibet to be strategically important to China, the Indian counterpart think it is equally vital to Indian national security. Tibet thus presents itself even today as a strategic dilemma for both parties. If India dominates Tibet (as the British *raj* had done until 1947), the Chinese feel insecure and threatened. Conversely, if China occupies Tibet (as it has since 1950), India feels that its whole northern security system, stretching over 2,000 miles, is open to external danger. Such a strategic zero-sum game over Tibet may be resolved through neutralization of the contested territory, as Britain and Russia did in their treaty of 1907, which ensured peace for 43 years.

What makes this historical lesson to neutralize Tibet (or more specifically Outer Tibet) is the nuclearization of India. Since most of China's nuclear facilities are located in Inner Tibet (Amdo and Kham), well within the reach of India's nuclear facilities, the need to transform Outer Tibet into a nuclear-free and buffer zone in order to increase peace-friendly strategic space for both and prevent nuclear accidents or war – has become more urgent than ever before. This will enlarge Nepal's nuclear-free zone proposal which China used to support. The neutralization of Outer Tibet will have a peace-inducing effect on the whole of Asia in general and on Sino-Indian relations in particular. It might also have its demonstration-effect on other contested territories and conflict zones in Asia.

As we have observed, India has conceded to the Chinese creation of buffer states along the cis-Himalayas which during the British *raj* constituted the inner rampart of India's defense system. Now it is time (and the nuclearization of South Asia makes it more urgent) for the Chinese to create a buffer zone out of their territory which had historically functioned as an autonomous buffer state. These two buffer lines from Chinese and Indian sides will increase the overall strategic peace-friendly space that might minimize the chances of a nuclear arms race or even conflict between China and India.

Fortunately, I see some favourable global tendencies which might encourage the neutralization of Tibet. Firstly, the end of the Cold War has meant a considerable reduction of international tension, which might in turn lead to the reduction of mutual suspicion and tension between India and China in the long run. Secondly, the current globalization tends to lay more stress on economic gains and less on national glory. Both of these factors make sense when we remember that Tibet's modern fate has been as a victim of Sino-Indian strategic rivalry whose uncompromising logic has reduced the Tibet issue into a zero-sum game. This has been a costly game for both China and India. For example, up to 1947, seventy-five Indian policemen were enough to guard the Indo-Tibetan border, now India has to deploy seven to eight divisions in the Himalayas. Up to 1911 the Chinese military presence in Lhasa was limited to 250-300 soldiers; now China has to deploy 150,000 soldiers in Tibet. If, therefore, the Dalai Lama's middle way conflict resolution is accepted, followed or preceded by the neutralization of Tibet, then both the Chinese and Indian 'defence' budgets will be drastically reduced.

The nuclearization of the Tibetan Plateau and of India will have a profound effect on the Tibet issue. Tibet is theoretically transformed into a nuclear launching pad, and there is therefore an urgent need to make Outer Tibet, at least, a nuclear-free zone so as to enlarge Nepal's idea of also becoming nuclear free, a concept which China supports. Otherwise the danger of a nuclear strike, targeted or accidental, is not remote.

Beijing's main concern is whether or not India decides to increase the number of its weapons and deploy along the Sino-Indian border, which seems likely, given the present Government's (1999) perceptions of threat. If they do, then China might decide to do so more openly and actively. As John Ackerly has documented, China's 'Los Alamos' is Inner Tibet and India is well within its nuclear reach.

Seen from such a perspective a nuclear arms race is likely to be more between India and China, and less between India and Pakistan because the latter, due to its limited resources, cannot keep up the nuclear race. Its informal allies such as China might find it too costly to continue to aid Pakistan in a nuclear arms race with India. China might as well confront and concentrate

on India rather directly than through an expensive proxy
nuclear race. If such a reading is correct, then nuclear dangers
involving the Tibetan Plateau, the Himalayan region and South
Asia are real. The nuclearization of the Tibetan Plateau and
South Asia is sure to increase tensions along the Sino-Indian
borders; it might trigger a nuclear arms race and the possibilities of a nuclear conflict cannot be ruled out, given the
pending, emotive, contentious issues between the two sides.

Faced with such grave dangers to regional peace, the
responsible task of an area specialist with interest in strategic
studies is not to instigate war. Rather, it is to research and present relatively objective or realistic structures of peace that
minimize the chances of regional conflict. Nuclear China is a
well-recognized fact now, and that is why Beijing perceives
India's nuclear tests as a challenge to its nuclear monopoly in
Asia. But India's recent nuclear explosions are a new reality
which, though not on the same scale as China's capability at
present, have to be recognized and taken into account when we
propose any enduring peace plan on Tibet.

What, unfortunately, makes our projections of nuclear arms
races and nuclear dangers into such a serious issue, is the sheer
proximity of Chinese and Indian nuclear sites. Such proximities
have inherent nuclear dangers. When nuclear weapons were
placed in the former Soviet Union and the USA, long distances
way from each other, nuclear crisis could be managed. But when
Russian nuclear missiles were moved to Cuba, at once a serious
nuclear crisis in the USA started. At present Chinese nuclear
sites in Inner Tibet are roughly 2,000 km from New Delhi. And
if India decides to deploy its nuclear weapons along the
Himalayan border, we face a dangerous eyeball-to-eyeball
situation. This will give no peace of mind either to the Chinese
or the Indians, and much less to the Tibetans who inhabit the
plateau. Therefore, there is an urgent need to increase the buffer
or strategic space between the two nuclear states. I would not
suggest, even though it would be ideal, making the entire

Tibetan Plateau and the cis-Himalayas a nuclear-free zone because almost all the Chinese nuclear facilities are located in Inner Tibet close to the traditional Sino-Tibetan border. Therefore Beijing is unlikely to entertain such sweeping proposals. However, it is realistic that Outer Tibet (or the TAR) should be transformed into a nuclear-free zone to enlarge Nepal's concept of a nuclear-free zone. Another reason why I suggest Outer Tibet (or the TAR) is that the resumed Sino-Tibetan dialogue is increasingly narrowing down to Outer Tibet as a realistic subject of negotiation rather than the entire Tibetan Plateau.

Finally, the neutralization and denuclearization of Outer Tibet that immediately borders India would have an overall peace-producing effect on both sides of the Himalayas because it removes, almost automatically, one major cause of Sino-Indian strategic rivalry in Inner Asia and cis-Himalayas.

It will also bring peace dividends to both the parties – a reduction in defence expenditure. India's defence expenditure on the Himalayas is fifty to sixty million rupees per day. China's defence expenditure on Tibet may be even more. The Chinese have to burn three to four litres of petrol in order to bring one litre of oil to Outer Tibet. It costs China four times more to feed and clothe a soldier in Tibet than in China proper. And the cost of the nuclear arms race between China and India is beyond our simple calculation. It benefits neither the Chinese nor Indian peasants who constitute over 80 per cent of their respective populations. Nor does it benefit the average Tibetan nomad or peasant. In short, neutralization and transformation of the TAR into an autonomous, nuclear-free zone would increase the chances of peace and stability in Asia and also, cut down Chinese and Indian defence budgets, which could be rightly directed toward economic developments. I believe this is in the interests of all the parties involved – Chinese, Indians and Tibetans – and is a small concession that a great power like China can well afford to make for the Tibetan people, whose struggle has enjoyed worldwide support.

Glossary of Tibetan and Chinese Words used in the book

(There are various systems for transliterating Tibetan words: the following glossary is intended as a guide only.)

Amban	Imperial envoy from the Manchu dynasty to the Dalai Lama and usually resident in Lhasa during the period 1727-1913.
barched	misfortune
Bardo	period between death and rebirth
Blama	Transliteration of lama in Tibetan
Bodshung	government of Tibet
Bon	pre-Buddhist shamanist religion of Tibet
cham	dance performed by lamas
chang	beer
chang-ku	inscription placed on dead man's effigy
chapé	scriptures
chema	*tsampa* and butter offering to dieties
chitsog ringlung	classless society
chomé	votive butter lamp
chos-rgyal	dharma-rajya
zhou	district
chorten	pagoda
chuba	layman's robe
dayuan	Chinese silver dollar
Dharma	The Way, according to Buddhist religion
dogpa	ritual against evil by clapping hands
donnye	legal commissioner
drapa	monk

dré	measure of weight
duchung	non-tax payer
dukchu	Communist repentance meeting (literally, 'tears of sorrow')
ganpo	village headman
garpa	collection of nomad groups
Gelukpa	Yellow Hat sect
geshé	doctor of divinity
gonkhang	tantric temple
gyalpo	king
gyalche chidru	a special tax (lit., 'grains of patriotism')
Han	Chinese
jinlap	holy pill
kang	measure of land (135 acres)
karma	law of cause and effect
Khache	Tibetan Muslim
khadar	ceremonial scarf
Khatsar	Tibetan with Nepalese citizenship
khel	measure of weight (271 lbs) also measure of area (2 1/4 acres)
khushi	freedom
Kunchok-Sum	Buddhist Trinity (Buddha, Dharma, Sangha)
kusang	incense-offering ritual
-la	suffix of respect
lama	Tibetan Buddhist priest
lhakhang	temple where Buddhas and Bodhisattvas are housed
lhamo	Tibetan opera
lhoshang	comrade
lobjong	political education
Losar	New Year festival
lungta	luck ritual
lungten	prophecy
lusgyur	bodily transformation
magdog	ritual to prevent war
magmi-lamka	military roads
mantra	sacred text

mi-man tsogs-du	name of a popular movement
ngapa	lay tantrist
ngos-'zin	formal recognition of a reincarnate lama by a senior lama
Om mani padme hun	(literally) hail to the jewel in the lotus – the most popular Tibetan prayer
pak	dough made of tsampa, with chang or tea
patuk	head-dress
pho-wa	service for the dead
phurpa	lama's sceptre
pompola	overlord
pon	nomad leader
rangtsen	independence
rang-kyong-jong	Autonomy
re	yes
Rinpoche	high incarnate lama
rnyinpa-bzhi	Transliteration of 'four ancients'
Rogre Tsogchung	Mutual Aid Team
sang	unit of money
Sangha	religious community (as opposed to the laity)
shabdag	drinking contest
shibso	container for tsampa
shi-sha	meat of naturally dead sheep or goat
sho-gang	coin
shugno	pleading
sog	life-force
sonam	luck
song-du	ribbon worn round neck, carrying blessings
sutra	text spoken by Buddha
tagdril (brtag-sgril/ zan-sgril)	Translated by the Chinese 'lottery drawing' or 'lots drawing system.' It is actually an ancient Tibetan method of divination in which *tsampa* or balls of dough of equal size are carefully enclosed in with names of different candidates. These balls are then put in a container and shaken until one ball pops out.
tamka	silver coin

tantra	occult writing
thamzing	Communist accusation meeting
thanka	Buddhist painted scroll
Thonpe Dronchung	Communist production campaign
thukpa	soup of bone-broth and flour
tisri	imperial chaplain (high Lama)
tulkus	reincarnate lamas
tola	measure of weight
torma	sacrificial object made of tsampa and butter
tralpa	tax-paying family
tsampa	dried barley
tsedrung	monk official
tsethar	rescued life
tsewang	blessing to bestow longer life
tsongpa	seller
uchen	printed script
ume	written script
umtse	chantmaster or chantmistress
Yar-thonpa	A 'progressive' who 'leaps forward before the masses'.
Zodpa	Governor

Tibetan Calendar

Date	Name of Year	Date	Name of Year
1944	Wood Monkey	1973	Water Bull
1945	Wood Bird	1974	Wood Tiger
1946	Fire Dog	1975	Wood Hare
1947	Fire Boar	1976	Fire Dragon
1948	Earth Mouse	1977	Fire Serpent
1949	Earth Bull	1978	Earth Horse
1950	Iron Tiger	1979	Earth Sheep
1951	Iron Hare	1980	Iron Monkey
1952	Water Dragon	1981	Iron Bird
1953	Water Snake	1982	Water Dog
1954	Wood Horse	1983	Water Pig
1955	Wood Sheep	1984	Wood Mouse
1956	Fire Monkey	1985	Wood Bull
1957	Fire Bird	1986	Fire Tiger
1958	Earth Dog	1987	Fire Hare
1959	Earth Boar	1988	Earth Dragon
1960	Iron Mouse	1989	Earth Snake
1961	Iron Bull	1990	Iron Horse
1962	Water Tiger	1991	Iron Sheep
1963	Water Hare	1992	Water Monkey
1964	Wood Dragon	1993	Water Bird
1965	Wood Snake	1994	Wood Dog
1966	Fire Horse	1995	Wood Pig
1967	Fire Sheep	1996	Fire Mouse
1968	Earth Monkey	1997	Fire Bull
1969	Earth Bird	1998	Earth Tiger
1970	Iron Dog	1999	Earth Hare
1971	Iron Boar	2000	Iron Dragon
1972	Water Mouse		

Chronology of Events

1949
1 October – The Chinese communists takeover Beijing and establish People's Republic of China.

1950
7 October – The Chinese People's Liberation Army invades Tibet.
11 November – Tibetan Government seeks UN help to stop the invasion.

1951
23 May – The Tibetan delegates coerced to sign the 17-Point Agreement (Agreement on Measures for the Peaceful Liberation of Tibet) at Beijing.

1954
29 April – India and China sign the Panch Shila or Sino-Indian agreement on Trade and Communications between India and the Tibet Region of China which was 'basically a trade agreement over Tibet without the Tibetans having a say in it'.

1954-55
September - May – The Dalai and Panchen Lamas visit China.

1956
25 April – China sets up Preparatory Committee for Tibet Autonomous Region in Lhasa.

1956-57
November - March – The Dalai and the Panchen Lamas visit India on the occasion of the 2500th birth anniversary of the Buddha.

1957
10 August – China postpones 'reform' in Tibet for six years.

1958

16 June – Voluntary National Defence Army (dan-lans bstan-srun dmag-sgar), also commonly known as *Chushi Gangdruk* (chu-bzhi sgan-drug) was formed under the leadership of Andruk Gompo Tashi in Lhoka. This marked, in a sense, the culmination of Khampa revolts that began in 1956-57 in Kham and Amdo.

1959

10 March – Tibetan uprising in Lhasa.
17 March – The Dalai Lama flees Lhasa.
29 March – The Dalai Lama reaches India.
21 March – The UN General Assembly Resolution 1353 (XIV) passed on Tibet.

1960

24 October – The Dalai Lama and his entourage move to Dharamsala and set up their 'exile government' there.
2 September – Representatives of the Tibetan people and Lamas from various sects meet in Dharamsala as the Tibetan Constituent Assembly. This day is celebrated every year by Tibetan exiles as Democracy Day.

1961

10 October – The Tibetan Constitution is promulgated by the Dalai Lama.
20 December – The UN General Assembly passes Resolution 1723 (XVI) on Tibet. Tibet's right to self-determination figures for the first time in it.

1962

18 October - 21 November – The Sino-Indian conflict.

1964

September – China begins anti-Panchen Lama campaign in Tibet.

1965

9 September – China establishes 'Tibet Autonomous Region' (TAR).
18 December – The UN General Assembly passes resolution 2079(XX) on Tibet.

1966-69

May 1966 - January 1969 – The period of the Proletarian Cultural Revolution, during which the Red Guards destroyed nearly 95 per cent of Tibet's monasteries and temples.

1976

27-28 July – Mao dies.

1978

25 February – Beijing rehabilitates the Panchen Lama. Deng Xiaoping returns to power.

1979

16 January – Radio Beijing broadcast urges Tibetan exiles to return.

August - November – The Dalai Lama's first (in a series of five) fact-finding delegation tours Tibet.

1980

30 April – A Buddhist delegation from the Soviet Union to India declares in New Delhi that Russia is willing to support the Tibetan cause if the Tibetans so desire.

1983

12 September – Beijing decides on population transfer to Tibet as a policy.

1987

21 September – The Dalai Lama addresses the US Congressional Human Rights Caucus, outlining his Five-Point Peace Plan for Tibet, which in part, is a reply to the Chinese five-point plan for the Dalai Lama's return to China.

22 September – The US Congress passes H. Con. Res. 191 welcoming the Dalai Lama's peace initiative.

27 September – Pro-independence demonstrations in Lhasa.

14 October – The European Parliament at Strasbourg passes resolution on Tibet.

15 October – The West German Bundestag at Bonn passes resolution on Tibet.

22 December – US Public Law 100-204. 'Foreign Relations Authorization Act fiscal years 1988 and 1989' is passed, condemning human rights violations in Tibet and sanctioning assistance to Tibetan refugees.

1988

15 June – The Dalai Lama makes his 'Strasbourg Statement' before the European Parliament, conceding defence and foreign affairs to China but demanding genuine and complete autonomy for Tibet.

16 September – The US Congress passes S. Con. Res. 129, supporting the Dalai Lama's peace initiative as outlined in his Strasbourg Statement.

1989

28 January – The Panchen Lama passes away in Shigatse.

7 March – Beijing imposes martial law in Tibet.

15 March – The US Congress passes S. Res. 82, condemning the Chinese use of force against peaceful protesters in Tibet.

15 March – The European Parliament passes its second resolution on Tibet.

12 April – The Italian Parliament passes resolution on Tibet.

20-21 April – The Bonn International and Non-Partisan Hearing on Tibet and Human Rights, Bonn.

15 April - 9 June – Demonstrations are held in Tiananmen Square, Beijing.

16 May – The US Congress passes H. Con. Res. 63, condemning the lethal use of force against Tibetan protestors.

12-14 August – International convention on Tibet and Peace in South Asia, New Delhi.

10 December – The Dalai Lama is awarded the Nobel Peace Prize.

1990

16 February – The US Public Law 101-246 (H.R. 3792) is passed, sanctioning scholarships to Tibetan refugee students.

5 April – The US Congress passes S.J. Res. 275, supporting National Day in Support of Freedom and Human Rights in China and Tibet.

24-25 May – The International Convention on Asian Peace is held in Tokyo.

6-8 July – The International Consultation on Tibet is held in London.

5 November – The US Public Law 101-513 grants $5,000,000 to Tibetan refugees in South Asia.

29 November – The US Public Law 101-649 sanctions 1,000 immigrant visas for Tibetan refugees residing in India and Nepal.

6 December – Australian Parliament passes resolution on Tibet, Canberra.

1991

25 March – Voice of America starts a Tibetan language service.

16 April – President George Bush receives the Dalai Lama at the White House.

18 April – The US Public Law passes resolution 102-138 (H.R. 1415) on Foreign Relations Authorization Act for fiscal years 1992 and 1993, which declares that 'Tibet including these areas incorporated into the Chinese provinces of Sichaung, Yunnan, Gansu and Qinghai, is an occupied country under the established principles of international law.'

6 June – The Australian Parliament (Canberra) passes resolution on Tibet.

6-7 September – The Liberal International Congress at Luzern passes resolution on Tibet.

28 October – The above mentioned law [102-138 (1415)] is enacted by the Senate and House of Representatives of the US Congress.

1992

6 October – The US Public Law 102-391 (H.R. 5368) is passed granting $1,500,000 to Tibetan refugees (Dharamsala).

19 November – The European Parliament in Strasbourg passes resolution on Tibet.

20 November – The verdict of the Permanent Tribunal of People's Session on Tibet concludes that the Tibetan people have, from 1950, been continuously deprived of their right to self-determination.

1993

6-10 January – The Conference of International Lawyers, London resolution on Self-Determination and Independence for Tibet is passed.

8 December – British Parliamentary Hearing on Tibet is held.

1994

25 January – Radio Free Asia begins its Tibetan broadcast.

7 February – The Dalai Lama, in interview with a Japanese newspaper *Mainichi Shimbun*, says he favours federation with China.

28 April – The Dalai Lama meets President Clinton and Vice-President Gore in the White House.

2 September – The National Democratic Party of Tibet is launched in Dharamsala, India.

1995

14 May – The Dalai Lama announces his selection of the 11th Panchen Lama, Gedun Chokyi Nyima.

4-15 September – Five Tibetan women gatecrash the 4th United Nations World Conference on Women held in Beijing.

29 November – Beijing announces its selection of the 11th Panchen Lama, Gyaltsen Norbu.

1996

January – A bomb is detonated in Nagchu.

18 January – A bomb is detonated outside Sengchen Lobsang Gyaltsen's house, a pro-Communist lama who supports the Chinese selection of the Panchen Lama.

18 March – A bomb explodes outside Tibet Communist Party Headquarters.

9 May – 'Strike Hard Campaign' is launched to crack down on criminals and 'splittists'.

14 May – 'Patriotic Education Campaign' is launched with view to the eradication of the Dalai Lama's and Tibetan Buddhist influences, which are believed to be the cause of Tibetan nationalism. On the same day Voice of Tibet Radio is launched.

25 December – A large explosive goes off in Lhasa near the city metropolitan office.

1997

19 February – Deng Xiaoping dies.

17-22 April – *Xinhua* releases four major articles criticizing the Dalai Lama.

23-27 March – The Dalai Lama visits Taiwan.

7 May – Chadrel Rinpoche, the former Panchen Lama's tutor, is sentenced to six years imprisonment.

25 May – The Dalai Lama tells Tibetan exiles in New York that his reincarnation will 'definitely' be born outside Tibet.

1 July – Hong Kong reverts to Chinese sovereignty.

1 August – 'US Secretary of State, Madelaine Albright announces the decision to appoint a special coordinator for Tibet.

15 October – *Xinhua* calls Chang Thang the 'last and largest oil belt on the continents', like the Persian Gulf.

1998

10 March - 15 May – Members of Tibetan Youth Congress (TYC) fast-unto-death in New Delhi.

27 April – One of the TYC volunteers, Thubten Ngodub, immolates himself and dies later.

25 June - 3 July – US President Bill Clinton visits China.

27 July – President Clinton, during the news conference said, 'I urge President Jiang to resume a dialogue with the Dalai Lama in return for the recognition of Tibet as a part of China, and the recognition of the unique cultural and religious heritage of that region.' President Jiang Zemin replied, among other things '. . . But still I have a question; that is, during my visit to the United States last year, and also during my previous visits to other European countries, I found that, although education, science and technology have developed to a very high level, and people are enjoying modern civilization, still quite a number of them believe in Lamaism. This is the question that I am still studying and still looking into.'

25 August – Hu Jintao is given special charge of Tibetan affairs in Beijing.

28 October – The Government of India welcomes the reported prospects of negotiations between the Dalai Lama and the Chinese government.

10 November – President Clinton meets the Dalai Lama and China bitterly criticizes the meeting.

Transformation of a Warrior Nation to a Peaceful Community: A Historical Perspective

The following is an abridged version of a seminar paper ('Btsan, Blama-dponpo and Sprul-sku') presented at the University of Wisconsin, Madison (7-8 November 1980), which traces the transformation of a warrior nation into a peaceful Buddhist community. Although written for an academic occasion, I hope it will serve as a historical background to this book.

Apart from the Dunhuang documents discovered at the beginning of this century, there has been little objective data on the ancient history of Tibet. This makes our evaluation of Tibetan kingship, which precedes the Buddhist era in Tibet, somewhat problematic. The problem is compounded by the Buddhisization of ancient Tibetan history that went on during the Buddhist renaissance in Tibet, AD 978-1419. Indeed our conventional view of Tibetan kings including the myth of Choegyal or Dharmaraja (Chos-rgyal) has come down to us from what I might call lamaist hagiography that flourished during that period.

1. The Warrior Kings (AD 634-842)

It may seem ironic but it is true that a Buddhist renaissance took place during what Tibetan historians call Sil-bui dus, a veritable dark age that began with the fall of the Chos-rgyal or the religious kings in the 830s and ended with the rise of the Sa-Skya lamas (Blamas) in the 1230s. This period witnessed not only a renewal but a rebirth of Buddhism in Tibet. The four major sects of Tibetan Buddhism as we know them today took shape during this period; most of the great lama scholars wrote their monumental works during this period; and of course, most of the translation of Sanskrit works into Tibetan that fuelled the renaissance was done during this period.

Under the impact of such an intellectual revolution, a new conception of history emerged – the Choe-jung (Chos-'byun). And although the old concept of history (Rgyal-rabs) continued to survive, it was Chos-'byun that dominated the quasi-historical work. What is Chos-'byun? Usually rendered as a history of religion, it means how Chos or *dharma* came into being in Tibet. Most of the authors of this genre were lama scholars whose pious but partisan preoccupation was not history per se, religious or otherwise, but the progress of Chos. From then on, history could not be a record of what men and women did, but what anyone did for or against Chos. While recording what they called Bstan-pa snga-dar (AD 232-842), meaning the spread of Buddhism under the royal patronage, they established an invidious contrast between the pro- and anti-Buddhist forces. The former, the Srong-Btsan Sgampo were glorified and the latter, the Lang Dharma were vilified. In short, the ancient Tibetan history was largely rewritten in terms of Buddhist logic during the Buddhist renaissance. The myth of Chos-rgyal is an intellectual legacy of this period.

That such a myth should have developed is not surprising when we recall the early vicissitudes of Buddhism in Central Tibet – the mixed reception at the court; then its disappearance from the centre and diffusion in the peripheries as a result of pro-Bon, anti-Buddhist forces, and finally its triumphant resurgence after AD 982 all over Tibet. For any adherent to write about the persecution of one's belief system is hard enough; and to an author of any Chos-'byun work, it seems not only human but a duty to exaggerate the royal patronage of and the Bon opposition to Buddhism.

But, so far, there is no evidence to prove that any of the Tibetan kings ever called himself or was called by his contemporaries Chos-rgyal. We search in vain for the term in any of the ancient historical records available today, in the Dunhuang documents or in the ancient edicts and treaty documents that Hugh Richardson has published over the years. Nor has Erik Haarh found the term in his lengthy study, *The Yar-Lun Dynasty Kings* (1969). The myth of Chos-rgyal then appears to be a post-Glang Darma phenomenon. It was an honorific title conferred posthumously on those Tibetan kings who were believed to have patronized Buddhism by the authors of Chos-'byun works and by other lama scholars in gratitude. The surprising fact is that not only has this myth survived in Tibetan literature to this day but that it has also found its way into the Western scholarship on Tibet as well. But neither the concept of Tibetan kingship nor the magnitude of the Buddhist revolution in Inner Asia can be fully understood without questioning this myth first.

Sarat Chandra Das in his *Tibetan-English Dictionary* gives two meanings for the term btsan. First, that it is 'a species of demon, inhabiting a given locality'. Guiseppe Tucci adds that it is one of the most powerful deities in the hierarchy of the indigenous religion. Its second meaning, probably metaphorically deriving from the first, is 'puissant, mighty, powerful, strong, violent', and Das adds the following historical note: 'It is said that while Tibet was under early monarchy the laws were enforced with (the) greatest severity and rigour, and because the kings administered them so well they were called Tsan (Btsanpo).'

It is the second meaning that the *Tibetan-Chinese Dictionary* gives to btsan. It is, therefore, interesting to note that after the so-called liberation of Tibet when the Chinese communists had to create a new political language for their ideology, they coined the Tibetan equivalent of 'imperialism' as deriving from Btsan: Btsan-rgyal ring-lugs, literally the ideology of a forceful/powerful nation. Similarly the XIVth Dalai Lama in his memoirs, *Ngos-Kyi Yul Dang Ngos-Kyi Mimang* (1963) uses Btsan-'Zul to mean the Chinese invasion.

Our discussion of btsan should not be construed as an abstraction without material basis. In what follows, we shall briefly describe (i) contemporary images of the Tibetan people, (ii) the organization of society, (iii) general law and military discipline and (iv) Tibet's expansion into the neighbouring countries from the 7th to 8th centuries. All of these point the direction of Btsan, not Chos-rgyal.

(i) *The warriors.* The portrait of Tibetan people that emerges from contemporary Chinese records during the btsan period is one of warriors. The Song Annals depict them as always wearing swords and arrows. The latter disappeared but the sword-wearing tradition, especially among the Khampas continued until April 1959. The Sui annals, while recording a tribute mission, registered Tibet as a 'women's nation' (Nuer guo), being ruled by a queen and an assistant queen. 'Men were engaged in military activities.' How widespread and how long such a matriarchal society lasted is not known. But what is interesting is the military motivation and military criteria apparent in such a social structure. A similar pattern is apparent in the even earlier Chinese descriptions of Tibet; the young were held in high esteem, the old were not. 'Those who are strong are made leaders' we read again, 'and the weak were forced to be subjects.' A Song historian, Lui Shen, describes what might be termed 'warrior ethic':

> Those who died in the battlefield were honoured; those who died a natural death in bed were contemptuously treated as if no purpose was served; and those who were defeated or ran away from the battlefield were put to shame by tying a fox's tail on their heads, suggesting that they were as cunning and cowardly as the fox.

In other words, physical prowess was the criterion for leadership as well as social prestige. This warrior ethic and warrior spirit pervades the whole of Gesar epic which Tibetans believe actually happened in history and which Shakabpa locates in the 11th-12th centuries. This warrior spirit survived the Buddhist revolution to a considerable degree, especially among the Khampas. Historically too it was mostly the people of what we today broadly call Kham who did most of the fighting against China in the 7th and 8th centuries. As late as 1666 the Chinese described certain tribes in Kham as people who 'delight in wars and conflicts, not hesitant to die'.

(ii) *Militarization of society.* Both the Tibetan and Chinese sources confirm that the entire country was organized on a war footing. The Chinese sources, in particular, note the severity of military discipline maintained in the Tibetan army. A contemporary Chinese historian has devoted a whole chapter to an analysis of the military organization. It may be summarized as follows: (a) the entire country was organized into four major and four minor regiments (ru); (b) each regiment was broken down into groups of one hundred and one thousand soldiers; (c) effective control was exercised through the army unit of one hundred soldiers with each regiment commanded by a general, assistant general and a military police chief; (d) the military chiefs were also head of civil administration; and (e) the four regiments had a total of 462,400 soldiers. All this indicates a very complex military organization and an effective chain of command operative during the btsan period.

(iii) *Law allegiance and sacrifice.* The well-known traditional Chinese ethnocentric bias is nowhere more apparent than in their comments on the ancient Tibetan legal practices. A word is now in order about the Chinese sources as compiled and translated by Phuntsog Tashi Takla, which we have used in this paper. In 1965, *A History of China* by Lin Hanwen was published in Beijing. He devoted one chapter to the ancient Tibetan legal practices describing the most brutal punishments that the btsans allegedly used to inflict upon the deviant or the recalcitrant, such as gouging out eyeballs, cutting off noses, limbs, etc. Published on the eve of the Cultural Revolution in China (1966-1969), these grotesque details were publicized at home and abroad in various forms of propaganda on contemporary Tibet. Two points may be briefly mentioned here. First, there is little doubt that the whole control system was strict and punishments were very severe. But to say or imply that such brutal punishments continued till the Communist 'liberation' is to deny the whole process of Buddhist revolution in Tibet. Secondly, the Tibetan sources maintain that Srong-btsan sgampo introduced a series of laws which were strict but benign. Whatever the sources, there is little doubt that the laws were severe during the btsan period.

The distinguishing features of the btsan legal system were (a) the threat or actual use of force and (b) magic in the form of swearing-in ceremonies. Indeed, the threat or actual use of force was always present in the exercise of authority. The conclusion of a treaty with China or of a swearing-in allegiance ceremony was always marked by animal sacrifice. Sometimes swearing-in was done by dipping fingers in the blood of the sacrificed animals. The idea was to warn that if a promise was not kept, the violator would meet the same fate as the animal. The sky and the earth, which the pre-Buddhist Tibetans worshipped were called upon to witness such solemn ceremonies. 'Whoever changes his mind and turns a traitor, may the earth and the sky witness that he may be punished like this animal.'

(iv) *Tibet's expansion into neighbouring countries.* From AD 635 onwards the Tibetan warriors extended their 'warrior-like activities in all directions with remarkable vigour'. In particular, they were a 'constant source of trouble' to the Tang dynasty. The Chinese have kept precise records of the Tibetan military activities in or around southwest China from which several facts emerge. Between AD 634 and 849, nineteen instances of major conflicts occurred between China and Tibet, of which almost 90 per cent were cases of Tibetan aggression against China. The average deployment of Tibetan troops in each incident was more than a million soldiers. Of these conflicts, eight occurred during the reign of one of the most religious kings, Khrisrong lde-btsan (740-798). These facts question the conventional assumptions about the so-called Chos-rgyal.

A contemporary Chinese publication lists names of twenty-seven places in the present-day Gansu, Sichuan, Qinghai and Yunnan provinces invaded by Tibetans. Most of the battles were fought, for almost 120 years, against Tang China, in the region of Koko Nor and Chinese Turkistan, described as the 'pools of Chinese blood' and the 'field of Chinese graves'. The two most important Tibetan campaigns were when Srong-btsan sgam-po's huge army marched into China demanding Princess Wenchen Gungchu in marriage from the Tang Emperor Taizong in AD 640; and in AD 763, an equally large army captured the Chinese capital (Xian) and installed for a while a Tibetan puppet as Emperor of China.

After the Sino-Tibetan treaty of AD 783 Tibetan military attention was diverted to the Arabs in the West. According to E. Bretschneider, the Tibetans were continually engaged in military operations against the Arabs between AD 785 and 805. Crossing the river Oxus, they penetrated as far as the Farghana and Samarkand. Today a lake in the north of the river stands as a monument to their expedition, aptly called Al-Tubban (little Tibetan lake). The extent of Tibetan threat to West Asia perhaps may be gauged by the fact that the Caliph of Baghdad, Harun Al-Rashid had to ally himself with the Chinese against the Tibetans. As Professor Luciana Petech notes, 'The very fact that nothing less than the coalition of the two most powerful empires of early Middle Ages was necessary for checking the expansion of the Tibetan state, is a magnificent witness of the political capacities and military valour of those sturdy mountaineers.'

2. The Buddhist Revolution

Perhaps the most significant political development in Tibet since the fall of the btsans is the fact that central power as such had withered away and authority had gradually shifted from lay to lama (blama) rulers, from kings to priests, culminating in the Sakya Pandita's accession to power in 1249. From then on it would be impossible for any non-priest, no matter how powerful, to rule, or even reign in Tibet without some religious sanction and active support provided by one sect or the other. The period in-between the first and second wave of Lama rule bears testimony to this. Within a period of 292 years, there were three major struggles for power among lay rulers. But neither Phagmo Drupa (Phag-mo-gru-pa) (1350-1450), Ring-pung-pa (Rin-spungs-pa) (1450-1550) or the Tsangpa kings (Gtsang-pa) (1550-1642) could exercise effective authority without allying with the most popular sects of the Gelukpa (Dge-lugs-pa) and Kargyudpa (Bka-rgyud-pa).

This shows, on the one hand, the reluctance on the part of the nobility and the landed gentry to accept the lamas' monopoly of power and authority and, on the other, the utter futility of such an attempt, particularly the one made by Chang-chub Gyaltsen (Byang-chub rgyal-mtsan) to restore the btsan glory. Lamas had come to stay at the apex of authority and power in Tibet for good.

The commencement of the Sakya Lamas' rule marked not only a sectarian victory; it was the consummation of the Buddhist revolution that really began in earnest after the anti-Buddhist king Lang Dharma's death in AD 842. From 1247 on, all legitimacy and mandate to rule had to come from Buddhism. In practice, this meant the political pre-eminence of lamas in both state and society. This in turn tended to create a fundamental structural contradiction in lamaist polity: while Buddhism provided adequate legitimacy, a proof of which is the unprecedented social harmony, it denigrated the use of force as a matter of policy. In this respect the effect of the myth of Choe-gyal was actually felt by the lama rulers. In other words, the lamas had the popular mandate to rule once the population had converted to Buddhism, but they possessed little power to enforce their rule.

This change in the concept of authority presupposes a considerable degree of social change in order for the political change to be acceptable to people at large. This indeed happened during the 405-year period of general disintegration brought about by the fall of btsans and the subsequent Buddhist renaissance in Tibet. The reasons for the btsans' downfall and Buddhism's success are complex, the answers to which must await further research. What seems evident from limited research is that Buddhism prospered not during the rule of Choe-gyals, as conventionally believed, but after their fall. If the Choe-gyals patronized and promoted Buddhism to the extent the Tibetans believe, then surely Lang Dharma could not have shaken its foundations to the extent that they believed he did.

It should be reiterated here that the royal patronage of Buddhism seems highly exaggerated. Only 13 temples were built during the btsan period and all of them were sponsored by royalty. We know of hardly any private individuals building temples during this period. This makes one wonder if the so-called royal patronage was actually designed to control the spread of Buddhism as happened in China during the same period. Only after the disintegration of the power at the centre did the mushrooming of monasteries and temples begin in Tibet, i.e., during the Kingless Age (Silbu' dus). Buddhism was rescued from confinement of the courts to the society at large only after the end of the btsan period. Lang Dharma's contribution, undoubtedly unintended, was to release Buddhist energy from the centre where it was confined, to the peripheries where it could freely flourish and eventually engulf the whole of Tibet. His intention might have been anti-Buddhist but his actions promoted Buddhism.

There can then be little doubt that the Bonpo-Buddhist conflict which wrecked the unity of the Tibetan elite was one of the main causes of the downfall of the btsan rulers. In AD 869 civil war broke out in Kham which gradually spread to the rest of Tibet. Soon Tibet split into four main principalities centred around Ngari (Mnga-ris) in the extreme west, Tsang (Gtsang) in the south-west, Lhasa in central and Lhokha in southern Tibet. Of these, Ngari, which soon extended into Ladakh, became one of the most powerful principalities and this proved crucially important to the Buddhist renaissance. When the persecution of Buddhists began in central Tibet, some lama scholars escaped to western and eastern Tibet. Typical of such migration seemed to be one by the three monks of Gom-drawa Monastery, who escaped to western Tibet and then to eastern Kham, and another by the so-called 'Ten Men of dbus and gtsang' who travelled to Kham to receive ordination there. A similar migration pattern was followed by Bonpos once Buddhism became entrenched in central Tibet; they found sanctuary mostly in the peripheries of Buddhist Tibet such as Dolpo or Amdo.

Ngari, in particular, became the principal agent of the Buddhist renaissance. As Gos Lotsaba Zhon-nu Pal wrote in his well-known Chos-'byun, the 'service rendered to the Doctrine by three kings of upper Ngari find no parallel in other countries'. If one looks at a map of Tibet, it becomes clear why Ngari became a fertile place for Buddhist revival. It is far away from Lhasa, and therefore historically it enjoyed a greater degree of autonomy. This is true also of Kham. Secondly, Ngari is adjacent to Kashmir, which, before the Muslim arrival in the 12th century, used to be a great centre of Buddhist learning.

How Buddhism spread from the peripheries to the centre is still not quite clear. In general, it seems that after the destruction of the political basis of Bon at Lhasa, the new religion might have become an ideological weapon. In central Tibet, many rival petty principalities emerged, some of which were ruled by lamas or laymen closely allied with the former. A whole new class of what Shakabpa calls 'priest chieftains' emerged, whose worldliness surprised the great Indian pandit, Atisha, during his visit to western and central Tibet in 1042. There seemed to have been keen rivalry and competition among the well-to-do about inviting gurus from India and Nepal. The patronage of Buddhism had become a matter of social prestige and means of political rivalry. It was no longer the royal prerogative and monopoly. That seemed to have been the way in which Buddhism was transformed from a courtly interest into a social force. This social transformation was a prerequisite for the rise of lamas to power.

In 1195, Chingghis Khan's forces reached the eastern border areas, and in 1207, they entered Tibet proper. Through some adroit diplomatic moves, including a gesture of voluntary submission to the Khan's overlordship, the Tibetans were spared a large-scale invasion or permanent occupation of their country. But thirty-two years later, when the Tibetans failed to pay tribute as agreed upon, Chingghis Khan's second son Godan Khan invaded Tibet with 300,000 soldiers. In 1247, Godan selected the most eminent lama of the day, Sakya Pandita, the virtual ruler of the thirteen 'districts' of Tibet (Khhri-khor bcu-gsum); and the Mongols opted for indirect domination of Tibet. It seems Tibet, to rephrase Owen Lattimore, brought diminishing returns to pre-industrial imperialism because of its geography and difficulties of communication. Godan's choice of the Sakya Pandita was deliberate, and it reflected the Mongol's recognition of the new realities in Tibet. The man with influence was no longer the btsan with force at his disposal, but the lama was, with his religious knowledge and a certain charismatic power. He had the potential to enjoy the popular mandate to rule.

Tibetan religious texts, especially the Saskya bka-bum, describe the critical transfer of power in a characteristic religious idiom: the Mongol chief (disciple) 'offered' (in a religious sense) Tibet to his guru, the Sakya Pandita. Although such an explanation appears rather naïve and simplistic in our sceptical age, the claim is not without some historical basis. For a proper understanding of such political 'irrationalities' we need to transcend the immediate situation and empathetically participate in the historical situation itself. According to Mongol annals, Chingghis Khan was in central Tibet when he was forty-five years old – probably around 1207. At that time he expressed his desire to invite the Sakya Pandita to Mongolia to spread the Buddhist teachings there. 'But still I have not yet finished some political affairs of the kingdom. From here I depend (spiritually) upon you, and you will from there protect me,' so the Khan wrote to the Lama.

Although there were other contemporary lamas equally famous in their own way, Godan Khan selected the 62-year-old Sakya Pandita because he was believed to be the most learned Buddhist scholar of the age as well as a 'Buddha who came to this earth'. In other words, the Sakya Lama enjoyed a universal reputation in Tibet, and this was important both politically and spiritually for the Mongol warrior. Dealing with such matters, one is never quite sure where religious devotion ends, and political manipulation begins. How else can one understand the Khan's insistence that the 62-year-old Sakya Pandita must come to Mongolia to preach there, and yet make him the titular or spiritual ruler of Tibet *in absentia*? The Khan's letters to and dialogues with the Lama are filled with magnificent ambiguities. However, he made one thing clear, though with surprising subtlety. 'I will rule the world of men,' the Khan told the Pandita, 'and if you reign (in) the religious domain, the Buddha's teachings will spread beyond the seas.' Kublai Khan was even more explicit with 'Phags-pa who succeeded the Pandita as the royal chaplain-cum-ruler of Tibet. After the Lama gave the Khan Hevajra initiations which formally symbolized the beginning of a guru-disciple relationship, there follows an

interesting dialogue between the two which must be read in its
entirety to get the full meaning and the spirit of lamaist politics. The
Khan thanks the Lama for the blessings. The Lama hints that he could
not give more teachings because the Khan might not be able to keep
the necessary religious commitment. 'What vows do I have to keep?'
the Khan asks. And the Lama replies:

'After (you) have received the initiations from the Lama, (you
must allow) the Lama to sit before and above (you); (you) must prostrate (before the Lama), listen to whatever (the Lama) says, and never
do anything that would hurt (the Lama's) feelings.'

The Khan replies:

'When receiving religious teachings and on other ordinary occasions, the Lama should be seated in the centre; but when members of
the royalty, sons-in-law, leaders and people gather, the king should be
seated in the centre since he has to dominate the kingdom. With
regard to Tibetan affairs, whatever the Lama says will be carried out.
Without the Lama's consent, the king will not issue edicts.'

Kublai Khan delineated three sets of very delicate relationships:
(i) the Khan-Lama relations; (ii) the Khan-Lama-Tibet relations; and
(iii) the Lama-Buddhist-world relations. The Lama was the Khan's
guru and the Khan would behave accordingly on religious occasions.
But in the political sphere, the Khan would not be subordinated to the
Lama. However, since the Lama was a Tibetan, the Khan would make
no major decision on Tibetan affairs without consulting the Lama. The
Lama was not only the king's teacher; he was also the declared head
of the Buddhist world. In recognizing the universal significance and
influence of the Lama, the Khan probably saw the potential political
benefits he could derive. Finally, it was implied that Tibet would be
ruled with the consent of the Lama. As it evolved in due course with
the Mongol conquest of China, the Yuan emperors would let the Sakya
lamas rule Tibet but not from Lhasa or Sakya; they would rule Tibet
indirectly from Beijing, while living there in opulent captivity or on
religious duty.

Without the authority of the lama, Tibet could not be legitimately
ruled by the Mongol Yuan emperors. It was this kind of mediation by
eminent lamas which made the indirect colonial domination bearable
to the native populace. The Manchu Dynasty sought to achieve similar
objectives through the good office of the Dalai Lama since the 18th

century. The Chinese Communists were merely following such imperial footsteps when they used the Dalai Lama and the Panchen Lama
in the fifties as agents of 'liberation'.

3. The Dalai Lama Rule, 1642-1950

The rise of the Dalai Lamas, which radically altered the concept of
kingship has to be traced, like the Sakya Lamas, to the ascendance of
yet a new sect in Tibetan Buddhism, namely the Gelukpa (Dge-
lugspa), founded by Tsongkhapa (1357-1419). Tsongkhapa's message
had a revolutionary appeal to the public who had helplessly watched
the decline in the moral standards of the Sangha. His plea to a stricter
observance of religious discipline (Vinaya), which implicitly criticized
the existing state of religious practice, brought the new sect increasingly in conflict with the older orders who were for the status quo. In
particular, it clashed with the dominant sect, Kargyudpa (Bka-rgyud-
pa) whose head, Lama Karmapa had been the most influential lama
since the fall of Sakya. The Gelukpa-Kargyudpa conflict lasted for
over a century. It commenced in 1537 with the Kargyudpa monks'
attack on a Gelukpa monastery near Lhasa and ended symbolically in
1648 with the forcible conversion of several Bka-rgyud monasteries to
the Dge-lugspa order. Each side was supported by a rival regional
ruler: Kargyudpa by Ring-pung, the ruler of western Tibet, and
Gelukpa by the declining Gongma, the ruler of central Tibet.
However, it was evident from the century-long conflict that as long as
there was no external power to tilt the balance of domestic forces one
way or the other, the intrasectarian struggle would remain indecisive,
and probably the old sect would continue to maintain its dominant
position. It was, therefore, clear to the Gelukpa order that without outside help they could not challenge the *de facto* established church.

A comment is now in order on the political basis of the Kargyudpa
sect – how and why it came to be purely domestic-oriented after 1256.
It was not the founder of the sect, Dusum Khenpa (1110-1190) whose
reincarnation the followers sought. It was the charismatic figure of his
successor Karma Pakshi (1206-1283) that they wished to preserve and
perpetuate. Like the Sakya Lamas, Karma Pakshi claimed that his
family had descended from the ancient Tibetan royalty, and like the
Sakya Pandita, though less successfully, he made his sect politically

significant through his connection with Kublai Khan. It was, therefore, his spiritual charisma and political influence that probably prompted the Kargyudpa order to search for his reincarnation. His successor, Karmapa Rang-'byung rdo-rje (1284-1339), the IIIrd Karmapa, became the first reincarnate lama in Tibetan history. Two and a half centuries later the Kargyudpa's rival sect, Gelukpa would do exactly the same.

Karma Pakshi's charismatic reputation attracted the attention of Kublai Khan who invited him to his camp in 1251. The Khan was probably looking for a successor to the Sakya Pandita who had passed away the same year. But by the time the Karmapa reached the Mongol court in 1254, the Pandita's nephew Phagspa had already been appointed to the coveted post a year earlier. The Khan, however, received the Karmapa well, and asked him to remain permanently at his court 'but Karma Pakshi declined, foreseeing the potential for trouble in the factional interests at the court'. The Karmapa was not willing to play second fiddle to Phagpa, who was much younger, in his early 20s. He would seek his fortune – or misfortune, as it turned out to be – elsewhere.

On his way back home when he reached Amdo in 1256, Karma Pakshi heard the news that Kublai Khan had been subjugated by his elder brother, Mongke Khan. Apparently, the two brothers were at that time racing to conquer China, with the elder being already in control over a large part of China proper and the younger one pressing in from the southwest. 'At this point,' so the Tibetan version goes, 'Mongke Khan invited him (Karma Pakshi) to return to China to teach *dharma*.' The invitation was, of course, readily accepted and Karmapa remained at Mongke's court until the Lama sensed a palace intrigue brewing at the imminent death of Mongke Khan. However, before Karmapa could safely reach Tibet, Kublai Khan who had killed Mongke's successors caught the traitorous lama. He was subjected to various indignities and tortures such as burning, poisoning and being thrown off a cliff.

After this bad luck with the Mongols, the Kargyudpa sect would concentrate at home, building an indigenous following, and a Tibetan rather than foreign base of power. Hence, after the foreign-backed Sakya's fall and before the rise of another such lama regime, Kargyudpa became the ruling party as well as the reigning orthodoxy. This de facto established church could not be easily challenged by the

Gelukpa, even with some domestic political backing. External support was needed. So in 1577, Sonam Gyatso, the high priest of the new˘sect, visited Altan Khan, the chief of the Ordos Mongols. Again, as in the conversion of Kublai Khan by the Sakya Pandita, the Tibetan texts speak in a similar vein – Sonam Gyatso converted Altan Khan to the Dge-lugspa order. The sectarian distinction is important here. If Altan's ambition was political conquest, the Lama's avowed aim was to fight against his rival sect, the Bka'-rgyud and settle sectarian scores.

As a symbol of mutual respect and agreement, the warrior king and the Lama exchanged honorary titles: the latter was called 'Dalai' (meaning Ocean of Wisdom) and the former, Chos-rgyal. Once again the vital link between the Mongol warriors and Tibetan lamas was revived. For the latter, the Mongol sword was a necessary instrument for seizing state power at Lhasa; for the former, prominent lamas would serve as de facto agents of legitimization of Mongol conquest and domination. This time, however, although the Dalai Lama was in power, Gushri Khan would not conquer China as Kublai did. Their cultural cousins, the Manchus would. Even then, as we shall see, Manchu-Tibetan connection pre-dates the Manchu conquest of China. It was closer than we might think.

The importance the new sect attached to its Mongol connection might be gauged by the fact that the reincarnation of Sonam Gyatso was discovered in the great-grandson of Altan Khan. He was proclaimed as the IIIrd Dalai Lama and escorted to Lhasa by an armed body of Mongol horsemen in 1601. However, it was not until twenty years later that the Gelukpa, with the help of more Mongol troops, could capture Lhasa, which gives us an idea of the protracted nature of the sectarian struggle. When the new sect was more or less in parity with the old, their champion, Altan Khan died and their hopes of a nationwide victory receded. Then suddenly Altan's former rival, Gushri Khan came to help the Gelukpa, defeated the Tsangpa king who had been fighting for the Kargyudpa order and put the Vth Dalai Lama in power in Lhasa in 1642.

After the Gelukpa victory a triangular power structure that existed during the Sakya period emerged. At its apex was the supreme pontiff, the Vth Dalai Lama; on either side were Gushri Khan as the self-appointed Bod-gyal (King of Tibet) but 'content to act as a commander-in-chief, ready to protect the new regime' from any challenge, and Bde-Srid, a Tibetan, who functioned more like a chief minister. But while the Sakya Lama had to remain a virtual captive at the Yuan court in Beijing, the Dalai Lama was able to live in Lhasa and directly rule Tibet from there. Moreover, after Gushri's death (1654), not only all authority but even executive power fell into the capable hands of the Vth Dalai Lama.

Over the centuries, notions of kingship have changed. But the basic pattern of institutions formed under the early kings continued. Both Bon and Buddhist notions regarding kingship continued to co-exist. One common thread is the belief that the ruler is a possessor of magical powers. Thus, even the eminent lamas who attracted the attention of the Mongol chiefs and Chinese emperors, claimed extra-ordinary powers such as performing miracles, predicting the future, curing the incurable, etc. How different is such a belief from the pre-Buddhist belief that the btsan the ruler can magically transform himself into a fierce demon called btsan?

As Buddhism began to rapidly replace Bon, Buddhist ideas naturally dominated the concept of kingship. Thus with the Dalai Lama the idea reaches its full maturation. He is no longer an attribute or aspect of the Buddha but the Buddha himself in human form.

By embracing Buddhism, the last Tibetan kings lost the mandate to rule, as sanctioned by their native religion Bon. As we have seen, it took more than four hundred years for the subsequent Tibetan rulers to get a new mythical sanction from Buddhism. In course of time, the pacifist nature of Buddhism killed the Tibetan martial character. Thus, by AD 840, the Tibetan king had neither the mandate nor the power with which the earlier kings ruled and expanded their kingdom.

During the course of about three hundred years (from the seventh to the ninth century AD), the ideological or mythical basis of royal authority has gradually undergone a change – from Bonpo notions to Buddhist concepts as Buddhism progressed in Tibet; from power (btsan) to compassion (snying-rje) as the ideological basis of their rule. If the earlier Bon kings traced their origin to the sky, the latter-day Buddhist rulers traced theirs to their Mecca, India. If the earlier rulers considered themselves as the embodiment of power and force, the latter-day rulers saw themselves as the manifestation of compassion.

However, it would be naïve to assume that such a conceptual

transformation was either complete or absolute. Conflicting Bon and Buddhist notions continued to compound the concept of kingship. Bonpo notions were used by even Buddhist priest rulers in the 12th and 16th centuries, as we have seen. But the basic trend is unmistakable: from violence to non-violence as a way of life.

During the btsan rule kings enjoyed near-absolute power. Although basically lacking in legitimacy, Buddhism caught the Tibetan imagination quite easily. Its primary source of legitimacy was the theogonic origin of the btsan kings, and therefore a kind of divine right. If we treat the king as a manifestation of btsan, then the actuality of power and notions of authority roughly correspond to each other. Both smack of power and force.

By 1207 Tibet's military power had dissipated, as symbolized by the Tibetan surrender to Chingghis Khan in that year. The primary source of power during the Sakya rule was the Yuan Dynasty but authority as such remained in Tibetan hands. In this respect the Mongol conquerors and, subsequently, the Chinese emperors realized the legitimizing value of lamas. The Sakya Lamas marked a historic transition from royal authority based on force and Tibetan independence, to lamaist authority that rested on external military support, and so progressively lost Tibetans their independence. Without the Yuan dynastic support, the Sakya rule could not have withstood challenges from other sects. Hence the Sakya regime fell almost simultaneously with the Yuan dynasty in China. And, without the lamas' legitimization, Tibetans would not have readily accepted the Chinese indirect political domination of their country.

The Dalai Lamas' rule represented a further development of the Sakya ideas and institutions. Their primary source of power was initially the Mongols and subsequently the Manchu (or Qing) emperors. What made the Dalai Lamas' rule different from that of the previous lama rulers was the dramatic institutionalization of charisma (bsod-nams dbang-thang or byin-rlabs) by means of reincarnation. This novel institution proved efficacious for domestic purposes as a primary means of legitimation. This is attested by the remarkable social stability in Tibet since 1642 despite the virtual absence of the use of force at home.

Buddhist Tibet was probably one of the greatest tributes to Buddhism in this sense; it successfully transformed a warrior nation into a pacifist community. But the pacifying transformation led to the development of an apolitical state, which, in turn led to military dependency on external powers.

While essentializing the contours of Tibetan historical development from warrior kings to lama rulers, I do not suggest that violence had completely disappeared from Tibetan social life. Inter-sectarian struggles between the Gelukpa and Kargyudpa sects as well as intra-monastic strifes within the Gelukpa order are clear testimonies to this residue of violence. But what I am suggesting is that the transformation from warrior kings, whose way of life seemed to have been warfare, to lama rulers is quite remarkable. At least force as the basis of polity and policy disappeared from Tibetan social life after AD 842 and this brought about a great attitudinal transformation in Tibetan life and mind. The lama rulers tried to model Tibetan government on the basic principles of Buddhism, which were more conducive to a peaceful way of life. This again does not mean that lama rulers were free from human weaknesses or that their government was perfect. But the change from people 'who delighted in killing' others, to people who avoided killing even the fleas on their bodies is remarkable by any standards.

Index